CHILDREN IN THE MUSLIM MIDDLE EAST

Children in the Delta village of Shanawan, Egypt
PHOTO BY HEATHER LOGAN TAYLOR

CHILDREN
IN THE MUSLIM
MIDDLE EAST

EDITED BY ELIZABETH WARNOCK FERNEA

UNIVERSITY OF TEXAS PRESS

AUSTIN

LIBRARY OF CONGRESS
CATALOGING-IN-PUBLICATION DATA

Children in the Muslim Middle East / edited by Elizabeth Warnock
Fernea. — 1st ed.
    p.   cm.
Includes bibliographical references (p.   ).
ISBN 0-292-71133-6
ISBN 0-292-72490-x (pbk.)
    1. Children—Middle East—Social conditions.   2. Child rearing—
Religious aspects—Islam.   3. Parenting—Religious aspects—Islam.
4. Islamic education—Middle East.   I. Fernea, Elizabeth Warnock.
HQ792.M628C45   1995
305.23'0956—dc20   94-46181

CONTENTS

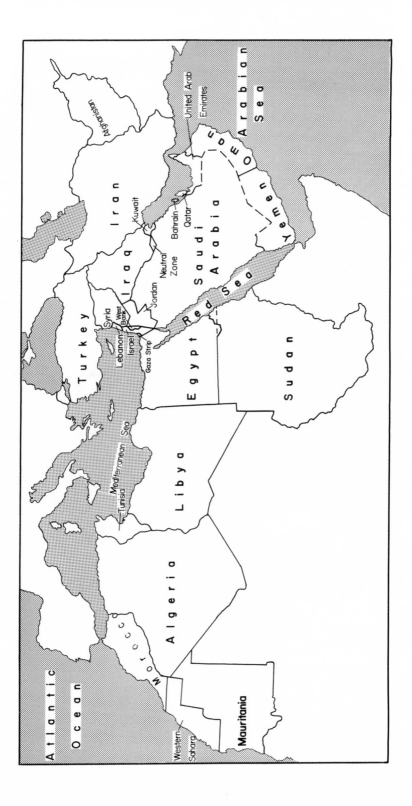

Moroccan boys listening to a tape recorder
PHOTO BY DOROTHY ANDRAKE

PREFACE

The Middle East has been undergoing vast social, political and economic change for the past fifty years, a phenomenon which has been noted in western books, films, and media reports. Yet in all of the materials available today, very little attention has been paid to the situation of children. Perhaps this is a reflection of western priorities: the same observation could be made, until recently, about children in the West.

Those who seek to understand what is happening in the Middle East today, and to speculate about the area's future, would do well to look carefully at the youth, for they are the next generation in the process of becoming adults.

The book that follows contains forty-one works about children, presented in many genres—scholarly articles (in social science, history, and literature), poetry, speeches, proverbs, interviews, short stories, folk tales, lullabies. More than thirty Middle Eastern writers and scholars are represented; some of the works are collaborative efforts between Middle Eastern and western scholars. They have been collected to give both a sense of children's lives today and a sense of attitudes toward children and their problems by leaders, writers, parents, teachers, and social scientists. Fifteen countries are represented in the collection: Kuwait, Morocco, Egypt, Jordan, Turkey, Saudi Arabia, Yemen, Iran, Lebanon, Syria, Afghanistan, Tunisia, Sudan, Iraq, and the Occupied Territories. (And there are absences: Algeria, Israel, Libya, for example.)

The book has been divided into sections, which are rather arbitrary and sometimes overlapping. For example, one could argue that work is part of the traditional growing up process. Yet for some children, this is not the case today. The divisions, hopefully, will be useful for the reader.

The diversity of voice, tone, and genre is purposeful. A passionate call to

Arab leaders to consider seriously the problems of children is juxtaposed with works such as the life stories of working children in Cairo, the songs of Sudanese children, a historical account of adoption in Islam, an analysis of Iraqi children's reactions to the Arab equivalent of *Sesame Street,* and poems about the children of the Intifada. These texts and many more will, I hope, provide an overview of the changing situation of children in the Muslim Middle East today.

E.W.F.

ACKNOWLEDGMENTS

This book began with a summer Fulbright-Hays grant to the Middle East which I received in 1988. The stated purpose of the grant was to conduct a brief preliminary survey for a larger project on the state of children in several countries: Egypt, Kuwait, Jordan, Morocco, and Turkey. In each country, I was fortunate to meet scholars, both men and women, who were already involved in substantive long-range research about children, and who were eager to share their results. My own plan—to do some research myself—began to seem gratuitous, given so much good work in progress in the area. Thus I proposed a book, to make available to the English-speaking audience the ongoing research in the Muslim Middle East that was relevant to global concerns about children. Frankie Westbrook, then editor at the University of Texas Press, shared my interest, and I have appreciated her support as well as that of Betsy Williams and the present editor, Ali Hussaini.

I am indebted to the Fulbright Commission for making the initial survey possible. I am also indebted to public officials and scholars in many countries who facilitated meetings and future correspondence, especially Dr. Hassan al-Ebraheem, director of the Institute for the Advancement of Arab Children, Kuwait; Dr. Fatima Mernissi, Mohammed Cinq University, Rabat, Morocco; and the staff at the Arab League Commission on the Welfare of the Child, Cairo, Egypt. Particular credit must be given to the translators, Caroline Attieh, Tura Campanella Cook, Sascha B. Cohen, Farha Ghannam, Akilé Gürsoy, Moncef Lahlou and Wafaa Lahlou, Christopher Middleton, Najib Mokhtari, Ahmad Sweity, and Jenny White, who worked to make the materials in Arabic, French, and Turkish accessible to the English-speaking audience.

Thanks to Sascha B. Cohen, Sharon Doerre, Laila Fernea, Persis Karim,

Roberta Micallef, Jennifer O'Connor, and Jenny White for research, editing and copy-editing assistance during the five years of putting the collection together. Thanks also to Cora Boyett and Virginia Howell who cheerfully typed the numerous translated and edited versions of the multidisciplinary materials.

I also wish to once more thank Robert A. Fernea, for his encouragement and his critical judgment which helped immeasurably in the development of the book which follows.

E.W.F.

Girls in their holiday dresses near Irbid, Jordan
PHOTO BY HEATHER LOGAN TAYLOR

Two friends in Morocco
PHOTO BY DOROTHY ANDRAKE

PART I

INTRODUCTION

Wealth and children are the riches of this world.

THE QURAN

Moroccan boys posing for the camera
PHOTO BY DOROTHY ANDRAKE

I

CHILDHOOD IN THE MUSLIM MIDDLE EAST

by Elizabeth Warnock Fernea

The recent interest in social history has resulted in a new appreciation for the processes by which cultures create their own social constructs of reality. Childhood is one such construct, and in the Middle East it is fair to say that, after centuries of relative stability, the construct has been transformed in this century, and continues to change ever more rapidly.

The idea of childhood, the place of the child, the duties of the child: these are basic and important issues in the Middle East and have been since recorded history in the area began, about 3000 B.C. They continue to be important issues today, but for context, we must look first at the cultural ideal of the place of the child, as expressed by people who live in the area, by religious leaders, and by ethnographers and sociologists who are both inside and outside the culture. The cultural ideal, we shall see, is expressed through images in scholarly work and ethnographic observation at different periods of history, images which are necessarily partial and fragmented. The cultural ideal in the past varied according to class and religious affiliation, as well as geographic area and rural or urban residence. Still, some common elements cut across those lines, and it is on these common elements that the first part of this essay is focused.

The second part of the essay concerns the rapid change which began at the end of the eighteenth century, with the European colonial invasion, and continued at a rapid pace through the first half of the twentieth century. My husband and I first began to do research in the area in 1956. By the summer

This is an expanded and updated version of an earlier essay published as a chapter in *Children in Historical and Comparative Perspective,* ed. Joseph M. Hawes and N. Ray Hines (New York: Greenwood Press, an imprint of Greenwood Publishing Group, Inc., Westport, CT, 1991).

of 1988, when I returned on a three-month Fulbright study grant, changes were apparent in all aspects of society, including the realm of childhood and socialization. Children under the age of fifteen today constitute more than 40 percent of the population in the majority of the countries of the Middle East. The needs of this burgeoning segment of the population can no longer be met by their families alone, as was the case in the past. Rather, the nation-states have assumed an unprecedented role in taking care of children, a burden which poorer countries find hard to bear. But it is not merely an economic issue. As Dr. Mohammed Shoufani, of the Ministry of Education office in Marrakech, Morocco, stated in an interview during June 1988,

> Children are the most important and the most complicated people in our society today, pulled as they are between two worlds, that of their illiterate, unambitious, resigned parents and that of their "modern" educated, highly aspiring peers. At a time when old absolutes are crumbling and old values are disregarded, what are young people to do? They are endangered because they are, in terms of values at least, at sea. And the government is left with the responsibility of making this new life more meaningful.

This new, complex contemporary generation of young people is the subject of the book which follows.

Childhood and family patterns of the Middle East are in many ways similar across religious and ethnic lines. But some significant differences also obtain: the ban on divorce in Christian groups, in contrast to Jewish and Muslim groups, means that the world of the child, as well as that of the adult, is not the same. In this essay I have chosen to focus on childhood in the Muslim context, since 90 percent of the area's population is Muslim. Of course the economic and political changes now in progress have affected and continue to affect all people in the area.

THE CULTURAL IDEAL

In the Middle East, the child is seen as the crucial generational link in the family unit, the key to its continuation, the living person that ties the present to the past and to the future. Parents in the area seem to have had, until very recently, few doubts about child-rearing practices, or about the goals of parents, children, and family unit. In the United States, the received wisdom about child-rearing practices in the twentieth century has varied widely between permissive and restrictive norms and has been promulgated by experts outside the family home. In contrast, child rearing and the concept of childhood in the Middle East were until recently based on widely accepted assumptions about the structure of society and the functions of individuals of all ages within that society.

In the predominantly agrarian societies of the past, the primary social unit in the Middle East was the extended family, which might range in size from 20 to 200 persons, related on both sides of the marital connection. Within this kin group, each child received identity, affection, discipline, role models, and economic and social support, ideally from birth to death; in exchange, the family required conformity and loyalty from all members, beginning in early childhood.[1] The crucial test of allegiance came at the time of marriage, when the man or woman either acceded to or rebelled against the wishes of the family in preparing to extend the family unit into another generation, for marriage in the system was not officially perceived as an emotional attachment between individuals (though this might develop later) but as an economic and social contract between two family groups, a contract that was to benefit both.[2] Although marriage was a crucial step in tying individual members to the group, it was the birth of children that conferred full adult status on both the man and the woman. Only after the birth of children were the newly married man and woman considered full members of their particular family unit and adult members of the wider society.

Such attitudes toward marriage and children are found among Jewish and Christian groups, but within Islam, they are intensified. "When a man has children he has fulfilled half of his religion, so let him fear God for the remaining half," states one of the hadith, or sayings of the Prophet Muhammad.[3] Children, then, have always been valued in Middle Eastern traditions, not only for economic and political but also for religious reasons.

The Judaic, Christian, and Muslim family systems are patrilineal; that is, in the reckoning of one's descent, kin-group membership passes to one through the male line on the father's side. A girl is a member of her father's family, but unlike her brother, she cannot pass that membership on to her children. In the Islamic tradition, male and female descendants of the same father inherit from him, and continue to carry his name throughout their lives. A daughter never takes her husband's surname, for example, but retains, like a son, the name of the father. Should divorce or the death of a spouse occur, both men and women have the customary right to return to their father's household, where theory and practice hold that they may expect themselves to be cared for; a woman should always enjoy the protection of a husband or male relative, according to the traditional Islamic view.[4]

The patrilineal system is hierarchically organized with the oldest male ideally holding publicly accepted authority over his descendants. The oldest male, whether father or son, is the primary economic provider for the group, and head of that group and controller of its economic resources, including the labor of its members, as long as he lives, a situation attested to with bitterness or affection by both men and women, depending on personal experience.[5] Without issue, and particularly male issue, the kin group as traditionally constituted clearly cannot continue. Hence great pressure is placed on newly married couples to produce sons, who can carry the name and take over the burdens of work for the family. Daughters are also important, to help mothers and grandmothers, and as potential brides for men within the kin group, but sons are of primary importance. Marriage between paternal cousins or other more distant kinsmen has long been viewed with favor among Arab peoples, but such marriages are far from being the general rule today. A man has custody of his children since they are of his patrilineage. Thus a man who divorces or who is widowed will take his children to his natal home, where his female relatives will care for them. This varies in practice, depending on class, economic circumstances, and personal affection. Sometimes families may be too poor to support a divorced daughter or their son and his children; wealthy families of a divorced wife on the other hand will negotiate with the husband in order to obtain partial custody of the children.

This patrilineal system has existed in broad outline in the Near East for at least five thousand years, having come into existence with the development of agriculture and the forms of property ownership and labor which such a source of subsistence favors.[6] It was in the seventh century A.D. that Islam altered the system somewhat, first by giving women legal status as persons, rather than as property; second by banning infanticide, or the exposure of unwanted children, and especially female children; and third by prescribing that the father's inheritance should be shared by both sons and daughters; according to Islamic law, daughters were to receive half a brother's share.[7] While the child does not have the same legal rights as an adult under Islamic law, he or she theoretically can inherit from both mother and father. Specific instructions about the care of the child, sometimes expanding on tenets expressed in Judaism and Christianity, are found in the hadith, such as, "Cherish your children. Treat children with a view to inculcate self-respect in them. Verily a man teaching his child manners is better for him than giving one bushel of grain in alms."[8] During the Islamic medieval period from 900 to 1200 A.D., several treatises were written on the method of raising a child.[9]

Little of this material from the Middle East found its way into the West until the recent interest in childhood as a historical construct led to research on the subject. Long-held animosity toward Islam as a Christian heresy contributed to the lack of western interest in Muslim child rearing and socialization and other aspects of Muslim life. Only after World War II did western social scientists begin to work on this subject in the Middle East.

The small body of literature available in English on the socialization of children in the area varies in emphasis and in scope of research. Hilma Granqvist lived in the house of a European missionary in Artas, a small Palestinian village; Edwin T. Prothro conducted a longitudinal survey of child-rearing practices in several Lebanese towns; Hamed Ammar undertook in-depth research into the process of coming of age in Silwa, an Upper Egyptian village where he himself had grown up. Judith Williams did an ethnographic study of the Lebanese mountain community of Haouch el-Harimi. Susan Dorsky, in *Women of Amran,* adds some further recent details from Yemen.[10]

From these works, some general patterns emerge, which are confirmed by Robert Fernea and my own ethnographic observations in Iraq (1956–1958), Egypt (1959–1965), and Morocco (1971–1972, 1976). Early indulgence of babies and demand breast-feeding are widely shared throughout the region, plus a great deal of affectionate behavior toward the baby, primarily from the mother but also from the father, older siblings, and other relatives. The Quran endorses this.[11] In Morocco, a baby is carried in a sling on its mother's back; in Egypt, toddlers in the countryside ride astride their mother's shoulder. Physical closeness and indulgence are combined with early toilet training, before the age of one year; either long-term breast-feeding or abrupt weaning may occur, depending on when the next child is born into the family. The arrival of a new sibling usually signals the end of the period of indulgence for the older child.

Banishment from the mother's breast also means the beginning of social-ization into specific gender roles, cultural values, and the division of a child's labor according to sex and age. The Prophet Muhammad is reported to have said, "Be gentle to your children the first seven years and in the following seven be firm,"[12] but in practice, discipline (*adab*) began long before the age of seven. Girls as young as four or five were expected to share responsibility for a younger sibling; small boys at the same age would also be given respon-sibilities. In rural areas, this might mean caring for animals; in urban areas, the boy would be asked to run errands or help in a family business. Such expectations are still common.

Socialization for other important societal norms of behavior began almost as soon as a child was conscious of others. These included respect for food, for religion, for the kin group, hospitality to guests, and, above all, respect for and obedience to the authority of the father. Hospitality to guests was expressed by small children in many ways, such as politely greeting visitors to the house and learning to wait patiently while guests ate first.[13] The small child was taught the names and relationships of members of his or her kin group, and preschoolers could often recite their genealogies on both sides, going back five generations or more.[14] Religion involved a respect for food as well as learning to pray and understand religious duties as Muslims. Boys were ordinarily not taken to the mosque for Friday prayers until the age of puberty. Girls seldom went to the mosque; they more commonly go there today. In fact, children are not required to fast during the holy month of Ramadan, but some often choose to do so, for a few days at least, in imitation of their parents. According to Hamed Ammar, a good child is one who is *mu'addab(a)*, i.e., polite and disciplined, and conforming to the values of the group. A child was said to be without *'aql*, or reason, and the goal of child rearing was to instill and develop the reason which is seen to be necessary for successful adult life in the society. Punishment included spanking or beating, as well as teasing and shaming before peers and before other members of the family.[15] The type of punishment varied from group to group. Some parents argued that corporal punishment was not condoned by the Quran, but most were in full accord with the "spare the rod and spoil the child" approach favored in some western times and places.

Ritual events in the life of the child also played a part in socialization. Primary among these were ceremonies surrounding birth and naming; circumcision, for all boys and for some girls; graduation from Quranic school, particularly for boys; and finally marriage.

Naming ceremonies are remarkably similar across a large part of the area. Granqvist does not record a formal naming ceremony for the child in Artas, the village in Palestine where she worked, but other Palestinian informants testify to the presence of such a ceremony. Westermarck notes it in Morocco, both among the Berber tribes of the mountains and among the Arabs of the towns.[16] Like the Egyptian ceremony, described by Ammar and more recently by el-Guindi, it is called *sebua,* from the Arabic word for the "seventh" day after birth, and is marked by sacrifice of an ox or a sheep and the gathering of the kin group for a feast.[17] Naming ceremonies are not found in Turkey, however, perhaps reflecting the different historical origins of the Turkish people. Between the ages of three and six, all Muslim boys were circumcised. This was an important event in a boy's life, with religious ramifications, as in Judaism and Christianity, though it is not specifically required in the Quran. Circumcision marked the change from babyhood to boyhood, the public noting of the acceptance of male identity, and was accompanied, like the naming ceremony, by feasting, sacrifice, and a family gathering. E. W. Lane notes the elaborate circumcision ceremony for a rich Egyptian merchant's son in the mid-nineteenth century, when the child, wearing white, was paraded through the streets of the neighborhood on a white horse,[18] just as Hamed Ammar describes in Upper Egypt more recently.

The circumcision of girls (clitoridectomy) was not universal and has no religious justification; the Quran does not mention it. According to Ammar, "the circumcision of girls has never had the universality of that of the boys; the religious authority behind it is very weak and could be rejected, and even its practice is not universal throughout the Moslem world at present." The practice occurs mainly along the Nile, among Christian and Muslim groups from Egypt to Somalia and Kenya, but not in North Africa or Turkey and only incidentally in other parts of the Muslim world. When practiced, the ritual is attended only by female relatives, but was perceived as acceptance by the girl of her female identity, and as a necessary preparation for marriage.[19] Girls in North Africa had a different rite of passage, an ear-piercing ceremony, held when the child was four or five years old. Women family members gathered to feast and celebrate the child's assumption of female identity. This was made symbolically clear by the white veil the child wore, like a bridal veil, and the gifts of gold, similar to those given the bride by the female members of her family.[20]

Religious socialization took place not only in the home (for boys and girls) and in the mosque (for boys) but also in the Quranic school, or *kuttab*. A knowledge of the Quran was deemed necessary for a child's religious development, just as knowledge of the Bible or the Torah was deemed necessary for a Christian or Jewish child. Most parents, even the poorest, tried to send their sons and sometimes their daughters to a kuttab for some period of time. Successful completion of the course of study at the kuttab, involving memorization of the entire Quran, was an occasion for family gathering and celebration, which might also include the city neighborhood or, in rural areas, the entire village.[21] Boys traditionally spent more time in Quranic schools than girls, but there were always exceptions. Rich parents often hired Quranic tutors for their daughters at home. Daughters of poor families had a more difficult time.[22]

Socialization of the child took place primarily within the home, and the father and mother were ultimately responsible for their offspring. However, grandparents, aunts, uncles, and cousins were also expected to participate in a child's rearing and usually did so, by acting as disciplinarians if parents were seen to be neglecting the child's progress toward becoming mu'addab(a) or by acting as affectionate supportive figures if parents were seen as being too harsh. This varied according to class. In the homes of the elite, servants and nannies, often poor relatives, helped socialize the children. In both rural and urban areas, neighbors also became involved in the child's socialization, as did the Quranic schoolteachers. Thus many adults were participants in the discipline and development of the child, reinforcing each other and providing alternate role models and sources of support for the child as it grew to maturity.

In this general and idealized picture there is little evidence of the idea of carefree childhood or indeed of childhood as an important stage in itself. According to Ammar, "in adult eyes, the period of childhood is a nuisance, and childhood activities, especially play, are a waste of time." [23] This does not mean that children did not play, but that play was the child's business; for adults the emphasis was on the serious business of preparing children for their roles in the world of adulthood. In this system, then, childhood was not seen as a specific bounded time period, and adolescence, as perceived in western modern thought, scarcely existed. One moved from babyhood through childhood to puberty and adulthood. Adult privileges and social status may be assumed with marriage and childbearing, but adult economic responsibilities might begin at any age past infancy, an attitude not very different from that depicted by Charles Dickens in the novels of Victorian England.

Marriage, which took place after puberty, marked the end of childhood and the assumption of adult responsibility for the beginning of another family group, with its own children to socialize. Marriage was the significant moment when family honor was tested, a concept that might be defined as the reputation of the group for morality, courage, religiosity, and hospitality.

However, honor was defined differently for boys and girls: a boy's honor, *sharaf,* concerned all the above issues, as did that of a girl, but for the girl, honor had a further, crucial meaning. A girl's honor, or *'ard,* was defined as her chastity before marriage and her sexual fidelity after marriage. A man's honor, once lost, could be regained. A girl's honor could not. The woman therefore had a greater burden of honor to protect, and was said to carry the honor of the group with her. Any breath of gossip impugning a girl's sexual behavior was cause for her to be severely punished and ultimately could result in her death. No such restriction was placed on the boys. For a girl, the intention to protect her honor was stated by modest behavior and by the wearing of modest dress. Carried to its extreme in some contexts, it meant the wearing of the veil by girls after the age of puberty and seclusion of women after marriage.

The concept of honor is found in societies around the Mediterranean basin, including Greece, Spain, and Italy, as well as in nomadic Arab societies far from the Mediterranean. So-called honor and shame societies stress the responsibility and the reputation of the group, and the maintenance of a public image, free from dishonor. The moment of testing honor came at the climax of the marriage ceremony, the consummation. A man's honor and that of his family required him to be virile enough to consummate the marriage; a woman's honor and that of her family required that she be a virgin at marriage. To provide evidence of that virginity, a blood-stained sheet, which family members traditionally publicly displayed, was offered as tangible proof that the groom's honor and the bride's honor were intact. Small children were present at weddings from their earliest years, so these tests of honor were made clear through observation and example, and through admonition and discussion of honor by parents, grandparents, siblings, and cousins. Honorable as opposed to shameful behavior was one of the strongest values for which male and particularly female children were socialized. Parental admonitions categorized much of children's behavior as either honorable (good) or dishonorable (bad).[24]

An Islamic family implied the possibility of polygamy, as the Prophet Muhammad states that a man was allowed to take up to four legal wives provided he could provide for them equally. In practice, the number of polygamous households was small, but the possibility that the father might take another wife was always present. Very little evidence exists of the effects of polygamy on children, but occasional memoirs indicate that it was not always an easy lot.[25] Much depended on the stress or lack of stress on the issue in individual households, a matter of great variation.

In sum, the cultural ideal in the past contained several elements: the primacy of the group over its individual members; the importance of children, especially sons, to continue and maintain the group; the values of honor, morality, religiosity, generosity, hospitality, respect for parents (especially the father) and responsibility for their care in old age; strong masculine and feminine identity and the primacy of male over female in terms of authority; the division of labor by sex and age; and the idea of adab to develop a child who was mu'addab(a), who would become an adult who was honorable and conformed to the norms of the group. The group was hierarchical, with adult males at the top. Religious ideology reinforced this ideal. This cultural construct was ideologically based on traditional idealism and religious dogma but also on recognition of the pragmatic fit of this set of expectations and ideals to the economic, political, and social Middle East. The social system it reflects was not based on equality and was not always just, but it fulfilled the needs of the people within the region for many centuries. The family unit remained the basic unit of support and control during the centuries that the Middle East was a loose confederation of large and small groups—families, clans, tribes, religious and ethnic communities—within territories and empires. This began to change at the end of the eighteenth century, with the invasion of the area by western European colonial powers followed by independence, and the development of modern nation-states.

HISTORICAL CHANGE:
COLONIALISM AND AFTER

Napoleon invaded Egypt in 1798, a date that marks the beginning of the colonial period in the Middle East. For a hundred and fifty years, until the end
of the Algerian revolution in 1962, western Europeans ruled the Middle East,
bringing new ideas and technology, but also disrupting existing economic
systems, and attempting to change social patterns. A good deal of recent literature deals with the political and economic effects of the colonial incur-
sion,[26] but less has been written about the effects of western European rule
on people's daily lives.[27] By its very nature, western rule meant a devaluation
of all aspects of the traditional society: language, technology, arts, religion
(Islam was called the "stagnant hand of the past"), and family structure. Rule
by powerful foreigners who were non-Muslims led to self-doubt and some reevaluation among the foreign-educated at the intellectual level of Middle Eastern society,[28] including writings on improving the position of women.[29] Although such works may have influenced some members of the society's elite
to reconsider family patterns, very few such doubts seem to have touched the
rest of the society, if the ethnographic studies cited above are any indication.
Further, though colonial rulers took over, religious affairs and family law
were usually left to the local populations. Indeed, as the colonial presence
became more pervasive and intrusive, the family (and thus the rearing of children) became the last relatively independent refuge of Middle Eastern people
under colonial rule. Fathers, denied a political role in public affairs, turned to
the family to reassert their authority. (This was true not only in the Middle
East but in other parts of the world affected by European colonialism and
imperialism.[30]) Therefore, one could argue that while the western European
presence may have influenced a few people to change or at least reconsider
long-held norms, in general colonialism intensified traditional family patterns, particularly those involving the differentials of gender identity and the
protection of women and the preservation of family honor. For example, the
all-enveloping *djellaba* with hood and half-face veil was not worn in Morocco
until after the French invasion in 1912. The djellaba first appears in illustrated
books in about 1914.[31]

As opposition to the colonial presence grew and movements for self-
determination gained momentum, the family became a center of resistance.
Since the family was seen as the base of society, the survival of the society
depended on the survival of the family group. Within the independence
movement across the area, from Morocco to Sudan, all members of the family
group participated, children as well as parents, men as well as women.[32]

At the same time the family was being touted as the center of the society, however, some groups within that society argued for a need to modernize the family, to change family law so that men and women were more equal, and that children, too, might have legal rights. This meant that when independence came, the family's future was visualized in contradictory terms. When the new independent governments took power between 1948 and 1962, their manifestos included promises of free public education; land reform; political reform; industrialization; revival of devalued language, culture, and arts; and reform of family law. The family would continue to be the basis upon which the new independent states would be constructed, but what kind of family: One which conformed to the ideas of the past, or one which took from both western and eastern traditions and accepted the rule of the state?[33] This is the context within which today's children in the Middle East must be viewed.

NOTES

1. See Halim Barakat, "The Arab Family and the Challenge of Social Transformation," and Safia K. Mohsen, "New Images, Old Reflections: Working Middle-Class Women in Egypt," in Elizabeth Warnock Fernea, ed., *Women and the Family in the Middle East: New Voices of Change,* pp. 27–48, 56–71; see also Andrea Rugh, *The Family in Contemporary Egypt.*

2. Romantic attachments were important, though not always within marriages. See Arabic poetry both classical and modern, and the new ethnographic literature on poetry in everyday life, e.g., Michael Sells, trans., *Desert Tracings: Six Classic Arabian Odes;* S. K. Jayyusi, ed., *Modern Arabic Poetry;* Lila Abu-Lughod, *Veiled Sentiments;* and Roger Joseph and Terri Brint Joseph, *The Rose and the Thorn.*

3. Ghazi Ahmad, *Sayings of Muhammad,* p. 21.

4. In contrast, according to Hindu tradition a bride leaves her natal family and becomes part of her husband's family. Her own natal family has no further legal tie or responsibility to her.

5. See for example the following novels and memoirs: Driss Chraibi, *Heirs to the Past;* Aziz Nesin, *Istanbul Boy;* Najib Mahfuz, "The Mistake" (an excerpt from his novel *Bayna al-Qasrayn*) in Elizabeth Warnock Fernea and Basima Qattan Bezirgan, eds., *Middle Eastern Muslim Women Speak.*

6. See for example Samuel Noah Kramer, *The Sumerians,* and Gerda Lerner, *The Creation of Patriarchy.*

7. Mohammad Marmaduke Pickthall, trans., *The Meaning of the Glorious Koran: An Explanatory Translation,* Sura 4, verse 11.

8. Inamullah Khan, *Maxims of Mohummud,* p. 41.

9. Ahmad ibn Muhammad ibn Miskawayh, *Tahdhib al-Aklaq;* Muhammad ibn Muhammad Abi Hamid al-Ghazzali, *Ayuha al-Walad.*

10. Edwin T. Prothro, *Child Rearing in Lebanon;* Hammed Ammar, *Growing Up in an Egyptian Village;* Hilma Granqvist, *Birth and Childhood among the Arabs* and *Child Problems among the Arabs;* Judith R. Williams, *The Youth of Haouch el Harimi, a Lebanese Village;* and Susan Dorsky, *Women of Amran.*

11. Pickthall, trans., *Meaning of the Glorious Koran,* Sura 2, verse 233.

12. Quoted by a Nubian man in John G. Kennedy, *Struggle for Change in a Nubian Community,* p. 75.

13. On numerous occasions in Egyptian Nubia in 1962 I witnessed two- and three-year-old children sitting quietly while I and my restless American children of the same age were served tea, dates, and popcorn.

14. See Elizabeth Warnock Fernea, *Guests of the Sheik: An Ethnography of an Iraqi Village,* p. 190.

15. Ammar, *Growing Up in an Egyptian Village,* pp. 125–127, 139.

16. E. A. Westermarck, *Ritual and Belief in Morocco,* vol. 2, pp. 386–395.

17. Ammar, *Growing Up in an Egyptian Village,* pp. 91–93; also Fadwa el-Guindi, producer, *Sebua* (ethnographic film, 1987).

18. E. W. Lane, *Manners and Customs of the Modern Egyptians,* pp. 89, 512–513.

19. Ammar, *Growing Up in an Egyptian Village,* pp. 110–121.

20. Elizabeth Warnock Fernea, research in Morocco; also see the film *Some Women of Marrakech* (PBS version of Granada Television, London, ethnographic film, 1982).

21. Ammar, *Growing Up in an Egyptian Village,* pp. 206–210.

22. Umm Kulthum, excerpts from *The Umm Kulthum Nobody Knows,* in Fernea and Bezirgan, eds., *Middle Eastern Muslim Women Speak,* pp. 139–140.

23. Ammar, *Growing Up in an Egyptian Village,* p. 126.

24. See John G. Peristiany, ed., *Honor and Shame: The Values of Mediterranean Society,* particularly Ahmed Abou-Zeid, "Honor and Shame among the Bedouin of Egypt"; Abu-Lughod, *Veiled Sentiments;* Julian Pitt-Rivers, *The Fate of the Schechem; or, The Politics of Sex.* See also Elizabeth Warnock Fernea and Robert Fernea, "A Look behind the Veil," in *Annual Editions Anthropology 80/81.*

25. Halide E. Adivar, excerpts from "Memoirs," in Fernea and Bezirgan, eds., *Middle Eastern Muslim Women Speak,* p. 75.

26. W. Roger Louis, *The British Empire in the Middle East, 1945–1951;* William Cleveland, *Islam against the West: Shahib Arslan and the Campaign for Islamic Nationalism;* Bernard Lewis, *Middle East and the West;* also Vanessa Maher, *Women and Property in Morocco.*

27. Amal Rassam, "The Colonial Mirror: Reflections on the Politics of Sex in Morocco," and Alf Heggoy, "Cultural Disrespect: European and Algerian Views on Women in Colonial and Independent Algeria" (unpublished papers).

28. See John J. Donohue and John L. Esposito, eds., *Islam in Transition: Muslim Perspectives,* especially Sayyid Jamal al-Din al-Afghani, "An Islamic Response to Imperialism" and "Islamic Solidarity"; Shayk Muhammad Abduh, "Islam, Reason and Civilization"; Sir Sayyid Ahmad Khan, "India and English Government" and "Islam: The Religion of Reason and Nature"; Chiragh Ali, "Islam and Change."

29. Qasim Amin, excerpts in Mona Mikhail, *Images of Arab Women;* see also Aziza al-Hibri, *Women in Islam.*

30. Gail Minault, *Women and Political Participation in India and Pakistan.*

31. Kenneth Brown, personal communication.

32. Frantz Fanon, *A Dying Colonialism;* see also "Interviews with Jamilah Buhrayd, Legendary Algerian Hero," in Fernea and Bezirgan, eds., *Middle Eastern Muslim Women Speak,* pp. 263–266; also Carolyn Fluehr-Lobban, "The Woman's Movement

in the Sudan and Its Impact on Sudanese Law and Politics," Ahfad University College Symposium, 1979; Afaf Lutfi al-Sayyid Marsot, "The Revolutionary Gentlewomen in Egypt," in Lois Beck and Nikki Keddie, eds., *Women in the Muslim World;* Richard Antoun, "On the Modesty of Women in Arab Muslim Villages: A Study in the Accommodation of Traditions," *American Anthropologist* 70 (1968): 671–697.

33. Fadela M'rabet, excerpts from "Les Algériennes," in Fernea and Bezirgan, eds., *Middle Eastern Muslim Women Speak,* pp. 319–358; Deniz Kandiyoti, "Sex Roles and Social Change: A Comparative Appraisal of Turkey's Women," *Signs* 3 (1977).

BIBLIOGRAPHY

Abu-Lughod, Lila. *Veiled Sentiments.* Berkeley: UCLA Press, 1986.

Ahmad, Ghazi. *Sayings of Muhammad.* Lahore: S. H. Muhammad Ashraf, 1968.

Ammar, Hamed. *Growing Up in an Egyptian Village.* London: Routledge & Kegan Paul, 1954.

Antoun, Richard. "On the Modesty of Women in Arab Muslim Villages: A Study in the Accommodation of Traditions." *American Anthropologist* 70 (1968): 671–697.

Beck, Lois, and Nikki Keddie, eds. *Women in the Muslim World.* Cambridge: Harvard University Press, 1978.

Chraibi, Driss. *Heirs to the Past,* trans. Len Ortzen. London: Heinemann Educational, 1972.

Cleveland, William. *Islam against the West: Shahib Arslan and the Campaign for Islamic Nationalism.* Austin: University of Texas Press, 1985.

Donohue, John J., and John L. Esposito, eds. *Islam in Transition: Muslim Perspectives.* Oxford: Oxford University Press, 1982.

Dorsky, Susan. *Women of Amran.* Salt Lake City: University of Utah Press, 1986.

el-Guindi, Fadwa, producer. *Sebua.* Los Angeles: Ethnographic Film, 1987.

Fanon, Frantz. *A Dying Colonialism.* New York: Grove Press, 1965.

Fernea, Elizabeth Warnock. *Guests of the Sheik: An Ethnography of an Iraqi Village.* New York: Doubleday & Co., 1965.

———, ed. *Women and the Family in the Middle East: New Voices of Change.* Austin: University of Texas Press, 1985.

Fernea, Elizabeth Warnock, and Basima Qattan Bezirgan, eds. *Middle Eastern Muslim Women Speak.* Austin: University of Texas Press, 1977.

Fernea, Elizabeth Warnock, and Robert Fernea. "A Look behind the Veil." In *Annual Editions Anthropology 80/81.* Guilford, Conn.: Dushkin Publishing Group, 1981.

al-Ghazzali, Muhammad ibn Muhammad Abi Hamid. *Ayyuha al-Walad.* Cairo: Dar al-I'tisam, 1983.

Granqvist, Hilma. *Birth and Childhood among Arabs.* Helsingfors: Stodersom & Co., 1947.

———. *Child Problems among the Arabs.* Helsingfors: Sorderstrom Press, 1947.

Hammam, Mona. "Egypt's Women Workers." *Middle East Report* 82 (November 1979).

al-Hibri, Aziza. *Women in Islam.* London: Pergamon Press, 1982.

Ibn Miskawayh, Ahmad ibn Muhammad. *Tahdhib al-Aklaq,* trans. Constantine K. Zwrayk. Beirut: American University of Beirut, 1968.

Jayyusi, S. K., ed. *Modern Arabic Poetry.* New York: Columbia University Press, 1987.

Joseph, Roger, and Terri Brint Joseph. *The Rose and the Thorn.* Tucson: University of Arizona Press, 1982.

Kandiyoti, Deniz. "Sex Roles and Social Change: A Comparative Appraisal of Turkey's Women." *Signs* 3 (1977).

Kennedy, John G. *Struggle for Change in a Nubian Community.* Palo Alto: Mayfield Publishing Co., 1977.

Khan, Inamullah. *Maxims of Mohummud.* Karachi: Umma Publishing House, 1965.

Kramer, Samuel Noah. *The Sumerians.* Chicago: University of Chicago Press, 1963.

Lane, E. W. *An Account of the Manners and Customs of the Modern Egyptians.* London: J. Murray Press, 1860. Reprint, London: East West Publications, 1978.

Lerner, Gerda. *The Creation of Patriarchy.* Oxford: Oxford University Press, 1986.

Lewis, Bernard. *Middle East and the West.* New York: Harper & Row Publishers, 1964.

Louis, W. Roger. *The British Empire in the Middle East, 1945 – 1951.* New York: Oxford University Press, 1984.

Maher, Vanessa. *Women and Property in Morocco.* London: Cambridge University Press, 1974.

Mikhail, Mona. *Images of Arab Women.* Washington, D.C.: Three Continents Press, 1979.

Minault, Gail. *Women and Political Participation in India and Pakistan.* Columbia, Mo.: South Asia Books, 1982.

Nesin, Aziz. *Istanbul Boy.* Austin: University of Texas Press, 1977.

Peristiany, John G., ed. *Honor and Shame: The Values of Mediterranean Society.* London: Weidenfeld & Nicolson, 1965.

Pickthall, Mohammad Marmaduke, trans. *The Meaning of the Glorious Koran: An Explanatory Translation.* New York: New English Library, 1953.

Pitt-Rivers, Julian. *The Fate of the Schechem; or, The Politics of Sex.* London: Cambridge University Press, 1977.

Prothro, Edwin T. *Child Rearing in Lebanon.* Cambridge: Harvard University Press, 1961.

Rugh, Andrea. *The Family in Contemporary Egypt.* Syracuse: Syracuse University Press, 1984.

———. "Orphanages and Homes for the Aged in Egypt: Contradiction or Affirmation in a Family Oriented Society." *International Journal of Sociology of the Family* 11 (1981).

Sells, Michael, trans. *Desert Tracings: Six Classic Arabian Odes.* Middletown, Conn.: Wesleyan University Press, 1989.

Some Women of Marrakech. Produced and directed by Melissa Llewelyn-Davies. London: Ethnographic Film, 1977. PBS version coproduced by Elizabeth Fernea. Boston, 1982.

Sullivan, Earl. *Women in Egyptian Public Life.* Syracuse: Syracuse University Press, 1986.

Westermarck, E. A. *Ritual and Belief in Morocco.* New York: University Books, 1968.

Williams, Judith R. *The Youth of Haouch el-Harimi, a Lebanese Village.* Cambridge: Harvard University Press, 1968.

CHILDREN IN THE ARAB GULF STATES: SOME IMPORTANT AND URGENT ISSUES

by Hassan al-Ebraheem

During a symposium convened to discuss development priorities for children in the Arabian Gulf States, held in Dubai from March 7 to 9, 1989, statistics were presented which spoke to the realities of child deprivation in the Arab world. These frightful figures caused us to tremble and stirred in the participants feelings of sadness, embarrassment, and shame. What have we educators done in the last thirty years? What has all the media focus on education accomplished? We had grown accustomed to claims of growth, of ever expanding facilities and enrollment, which since the sixties had been equated with progress. Now we are confronted with the shock of figures which are neither merciful nor kind in matters pertaining to our children, tomorrow's future. And what do these figures tell us?

• The number of Arab children under the age of fifteen was estimated at more than 90 million. These children represent between 45 and 50 percent of the total population of the Arab world, a segment which in the industrialized world does not exceed 23 percent. It is no secret that such a high percentage of children has vast political, economic, and social implications which will affect the prospects for stability and development in Arab societies.

• Of these 90 million children half today are threatened in their physical health by the dangers of hunger, poverty, and war.

• Only 16 percent of all Arab children enjoy the opportunity of learning at the kindergarten stage. Also, studies point out that our educational systems will remain incapable for many years to come of accommodating all children of school age. Thus, it is expected, according to studies predicting future trends, that there will be 8 million Arab children without places in the elementary education system. We find that at present about 17 percent of all Egyptian children are outside the elementary education system and 30 percent are outside the secondary education system.

• About 3,500 Arab children die daily from treatable diseases and a fifth of this number die from diseases for which vaccination is available. The infant mortality rate in some Arab countries reaches 160 per thousand, according to 1985 statistics. This is a very high rate in comparison with such countries as Costa Rica and Sri Lanka, where the infant mortality rate does not exceed 12 and 17 per thousand respectively.

• Arab children suffer from severe poverty in many countries where statistics show that the proportion of the population under the poverty level reaches 80 percent.

• The majority of Arab children suffer from unsuitable dwelling conditions. Statistics show that between one half and one third of the inhabitants of some Arab states are still living in houses consisting of a single room. These houses usually lack sanitation facilities and have no access to general services. Even worse is the fact that suitable drinking water is unavailable for 80 percent of the inhabitants of some Arab states.

The above figures provide only a few glimpses of the adverse conditions facing children in the Arab world, conditions which confronted the 1989 symposium participants. They provide some idea of deteriorating conditions which will gravely affect real development in the region.

Since the fifties the Arab world has witnessed the establishment of numerous ministries and councils for planning, and many of their policies have been adopted. Development plans were also set forth with the assistance of various experts and scientists, but unfortunately Arab children were not included in these plans.

Arab states were, of course, not the only countries to apply traditional western models in search of development. For example, Iran's development plans during the fifties and sixties concentrated on industrial development and infrastructure. Dependence on western aid and investment in these plans was at the expense of the just distribution of wealth and of self-reliance. This led not only to the deterioration of economic conditions and a maldistribution of wealth but also probably provided the catalyst for the 1979 Iranian Revolution.

Whatever the difficulties in facing up to societal failures, there is now a sense of candor in the Arab world which will hopefully permit an honest evaluation of problem areas so as to avert national disaster. This awareness of inadequacy now expresses itself in increased attention to the necessity of comprehensive development. Recommendations advanced by several regional conferences and symposia in recent years are now being reviewed and revitalized. A symposium for the heads of kindergartens in the Arab world, held in Khartoum in October 1984, appealed to the Arab states, on the basis of careful study, to give a prominent place to the expansion and establishment of kindergartens in their development plans.

One of the recommendations of a symposium on the education of the Arab child, held in Kuwait in November 1983, was to establish a center responsible for the advancement of child care in the Arab world. Another recommendation focused attention on the importance of establishing an Arab fund for financing children's educational projects in order to raise awareness of the importance of the early childhood years.

A study prepared by Dr. Ismail Sabri Abdullah and colleagues for the Arab League was discussed at the Arab Conference for Children, held by the General Secretariat of the Arab League in conjunction with UNICEF in April 1980. Its recommendations were later adopted by the Arab ministers for social affairs and constituted the general framework for a national strategy for child development. The first recommendation was most important, for it stated that fulfilling the basic needs for the development of the Arab child represents a political and national priority which must be adhered to by planners and policymakers. It further stated that this priority should be reflected in political and other sector programs.

In spite of our certainty about the failure of the traditional concept of development and past attempts to adopt a concept of comprehensive development, Arab regional plans remain deficient and unintegrated. This deficiency was summarized in the keynote speech of His Highness Prince Talal bin Abdulaziz al-Saud, delivered at the Symposium on the Present and the Future of the Gulf Child, held in March 1984 in Bahrain. The prince stated:

> Although some of our development plans embrace the notion of comprehensive planning and contain some human, social and cultural concepts, they certainly lack the elements that guarantee society's active participation in the development process in all its aspects. They neglect some sectors of society like children, women, old people, poor people of the rural areas and the desert, and even of the city. This prevents these plans from realizing the real and integrated demands of society for whose sake they were enacted.

I believe that His Highness's remarks apply to most Arab countries. The success of any plan must be based on society's participation as a whole and there must be a consensus by all sectors of society on its adoption. Without that we remain like one who plows the sea. We must keep in our mind that if we want to plant for one year, we must grow wheat, and if we want to plant for ten years, we must plant trees, and if we want to plant for a hundred years, we must raise men and women who are competent in their minds and bodies.

Awareness of the negligence of children's rights in the Arab world has been noted in institutional approaches to the problem. We can cite as an example of this institutional awareness the Arab League's cooperation with the regional office of UNICEF in 1980 in Tunis. At that time it charged a team of experts, headed by Dr. Abdullah, to conduct a study to determine the strategic elements necessary for the development of the Arab child. The results of that study were adopted as a basic document by the Arab Conference for the Child that same year. The recommendations of this conference were later adopted by the Council of the Arab Ministers of Social Affairs and constituted the framework for a national strategy for child development in the Arab homeland.

The work of this conference received active support from a number of leaders in the Arab Gulf region, and in 1980 the Kuwait Society for the Advancement of Arab Children (KSAAC) was established with the objective of advancing research, publication, and media utilization to spread awareness of issues relating to the Arab child. In 1987 the Arab Council for Children and Development was established as a nongovernmental Arab organization that handles issues of the Arab child on the national level in both their scientific and service aspects. Also, there has been a call to establish regional councils for children in the Arab countries.

Thus, we can claim that the decade of the eighties was the decade of the emergence of awareness of the dangers that threaten the nation's future due to neglect of children's rights. This awareness began to crystallize with the enactment of the Charter of the Rights of the Arab Child, which was prepared by the Arab League and approved by the conference of the Arab Ministers of Social Affairs in December 1984. This official concern was accompanied by acknowledgment at the public level with the establishment of the Arab Council for Children and Development in 1987. That year will enter Arab history as the year in which the Arab states became fully aware of the dangers which threaten their future as a consequence of neglecting the rights of their children.

While it is possible that there was no deliberate neglect of the rights of Arab children in the past, neglect was there. As a result of this neglect, the creative and productive powers of the region's youth have been wasted. None of us can dispute that the death of 3,500 Arab children daily, which is equivalent to more than 1 million children annually, represents a great loss to the

Arab nation. Also, no one disputes that the deprivation of 8 million Arab children of their simplest educational rights—the right to an elementary education—means a great cultural loss for the nation as a whole. This loss is a form of social injustice against huge sectors of the Arab populace. Whether this loss has occurred intentionally or not makes little difference, for the resulting harm is what is at issue.

In the constitutive meeting of the Arab Council for Children and Development in Amman, Jordan, in April 1987, His Highness Prince Hasan Bin Talal of Jordan observed that about half of all Arab children are threatened in their physical health by the danger of hunger, poverty, and war. He was speaking about 40 million children from the Atlantic Ocean to the Arabian Gulf—the threat for some being imminent daily danger, in Lebanon, in the Palestinian camps, in Iraq, and in Sudan. These children pay a high price for the decisions and mistakes of adults, the scheming of external enemies, or for the effects of nature.

At the same meeting, His Highness Prince Talal bin Abdulaziz directed our attention to the fact that the conditions of Arab children are even more depressing because they reveal that only 16 per thousand of all Arab children enjoy the opportunity of education at the kindergarten level. These facts reveal our failure in carrying out our moral obligations toward our children. These obligations are internationally agreed upon and are not disputed. For example, the Edgar Faure Committee has emphasized in its report, which is known as "Learn in Order to Be," that providing care and education which are appropriate for the needs of young children of all ages represents one of the most basic requirements for every educational and cultural policy. In his book, *On Planning for the Protection and Education of Children in the Developing Countries,* Professor Alistaire Heron classifies the basic objectives of preschooling as follows:

1. Preparing the child for elementary school.

2. Physical growth of the child.

3. Caring and assuming responsibility for the child.

4. Cultivation of language.

5. Development of emotional faculties.

6. Development of moral and religious feelings.

Radical economic changes during the past thirty years in the Arab Gulf states have led to unstable social conditions. On the level of social growth, we find that our children are exposed to undeclared wars, wars that are especially destructive of children. Adults have paid scant attention to the impact which these changes have had on children because they are seen as adult values beyond the cognitive level of children. If, for example, we look at the effect of the social instability which colors our contemporary life, we find, in the words of Dr. Khaldoon al-Nakeeb, that our children "live in an age without spirit. . . . [They are] negative to a frightful level, deprived of a will, and suffer from many frightful disease symptoms. But these symptoms are in the process of transition from this generation to future generations through the educational process which is going on at the present." [1]

Dr. al-Nakeeb has further noted that among these symptomatic diseases there is nothing more threatening to the adequate education of children than "the absence of the values of tolerance and democracy from our general life," a state of affairs which will expose these children to religious and sectarian prejudice. There is also the educational danger for children which results from the flattening of culture, decreases in the fund of lexical items, weakness or poverty of common expressions, and triviality of information and general knowledge which is presented to children. According to Dr. al-Nakeeb, all of this expresses in simple terms the fact that we are on the edge of a national crisis because our utilization of human resources does not yield appropriate results. [2]

Connected with the danger of lack of formal education is the linguistic deficiency of the Arab child. As another prominent researcher, M. J. Rada, has observed, there is

an active danger to the minds and emotions of children which we witness daily and with which we live without doing anything to protect them from it. This danger is represented by the splitting of the Arab tongue into two languages, high and colloquial; it confronts the children with an extremely complicated condition, for they either think in the colloquial and express themselves in the high Arab or think in the high Arabic and express themselves in the colloquial; they do not think and express themselves in the high Arabic. This in fact means the impossibility of correct thinking among children due to the discrepancy of linguistic media through which they interpret whatever goes on in their minds. Thus, their image of the world and people is distorted in proportion to the distortion of their own image in the minds of others surrounding them. This splitting of the language will necessarily be followed by a splitting of the ways of understanding. This will entail a difference in the systems of thought and the quality of knowledge which guide the life of the individual and society. If this splitting is destined to continue we can be certain after this of the impossibility of national unity within one state; thus, how can we expect unity on the level of the nation as a whole? [3]

As for methods to be employed in the development of scientific thinking by children, there is a real danger of the spread of mythical thinking which is antagonistic to science and reason. We frequently hear public statements which underestimate the value of scientific thinking and emphasize with disturbing simplicity the shortcomings of scientific knowledge and the failure of science to explain many of what they call "extraordinary phenomena." What attracts one's attention here is that, in validating this view which is antagonistic to scientific thinking, its proponents use scientific terms in a sense different from those generally agreed upon by the scientific community.[4]

In addition to these tangible dangers there are intangible ones which relate to the dark corners of the mind and the emotions. Among these intangible dangers is the distortion of the self-concept and its complete destruction intentionally or unintentionally by some of the educational methods employed. One education expert holds "that the quality of the methods used in the education of the child is like the social atmosphere which either allows room for the development of a positive understanding of the self or impedes the development of this understanding in the way it should take place."[5]

The influence of the social and educational atmosphere on the future capabilities of the child is a clear and established matter. Husni A'yesh, in *A Letter to Fathers and Mothers,* has stated that

> interaction in teaching and learning is considered . . . one of the most important
> contemporary theories of teaching and learning. According to this theory, the
> size, kind, and level of achievement of the child depends upon his conception
> of himself or, more accurately, upon his abilities. This conception is the out-
> come of the child's interactions with others in the family, the school, and so-
> ciety; and if the outcome of these interactions was negative, that is, if it formed
> in the child an idea of himself as being unable to learn mathematics, or lan-
> guage, or science, for example, as a consequence of this idea, he will not learn
> these things. Instead, he might fail to learn them as a response to or as a verifi-
> cation of this idea and a confirmation of the expectations which were formed
> in him.

Who among us forgets what the late Abbas Mahmood Akkad said about Sheikh Muhammad Abdo. Sheikh Abdo, who was the mufti at that time, visited Akkad's school in Aswan while he was in the fourth grade. After Sheikh Abdo entered the classroom and conversed with the teacher, he picked up a composition notebook with Akkad's name on it from the pile of notebooks which lay on the teacher's table. The mufti then whispered in the teacher's ear that this was an excellent boy. Akkad heard this statement and asserted later that he thrived on the mufti's words for the rest of his life.[6]

A principal educational method in this age is television, which over the past twenty-five years has ranked as the primary influence on the cultural life of Arab children. It has become customary for Arab television to devote special programs to children. There are various reasons for this programming, some educational, some cultural, some recreational, and some sociopolitical. While all of this is undoubtedly natural, it should presuppose a great deal of reflection and deliberation about the effects of this instrument upon the life of a child. The UNICEF expert, Dr. Othman Farraj, says:

> no doubt the introduction of television to any home represents a great joy for young and adult, but soon enough the parents discover that it is an incomplete joy because it has stolen what is dearest to them. It has become clear that this magical box is the absolute ruler in the home; it is the one that determines how the child uses his daily time, the child's bedtime, and also the family budget; but what is more important is that it has become the primary education of the child. Neither home nor school has traditional authority any longer in the process of social education since this new guest has replaced both of them.

The ability of television to overpower the minds and imagination of Arab children has increased to unprecedented heights with respect to its cultural influence on the education of children. Figures are the best indicators of this increase. It has been shown in research conducted by the American University in Cairo that the Egyptian child spends an average of thirty-three hours in front of the television every week. This exceeds the time he spends in play, at school, with his parents, or in doing his homework. It was also shown that the average television-viewing family spends six hours daily watching television, and it is expected that this percentage will increase with the rapid spread of VCR sets in homes, clubs, and public cafes. This means that even more family time goes to television at the expense of time allocated for study, rest, work, or production.

UNESCO statistics indicate that the number of television sets in the Arab World has increased from 756,000 in 1965 to about 1.7 million in 1970 and to more than 7 million sets in 1980. The number of television sets is estimated to range at present between 11 million and 13 million. In 1980 there were, on average, 337 television sets for every one thousand inhabitants of the Arab Gulf states, and it is expected that at present the number is more than 500 sets for every thousand inhabitants in the Arab world as a whole and double that number in the Arab Gulf region. The highest rate for the spread of television is in the state of Qatar, where there are 2,040 television sets for every thousand inhabitants, the highest rate in the world. The lowest rate for the spread of television in the Arab world is in the Sudan, where there are only 6 sets for every thousand inhabitants, and in South Yemen, with 18 sets for every thousand citizens.

The time allocated for children's programs represents another indicator of the increase of television's influence upon the intellectual and aesthetic education of future generations. The percentage of these programs in relation to the total hours of transmission varies from 5.6 percent in Egypt to 7 percent in the Emirates, 10 percent in both Bahrain and Oman, 14 percent in Saudi Arabia, 6 percent in Iraq, 10.5 percent in Kuwait, 4 percent in Morocco, and 3 percent in Syria.

In the Arab world today there are more than thirty television stations which transmit annually over 5,000 hours of programming expressly for children. But what impact do these transmissions have upon the children and what is their content? First, it should be noted, as Dr. Farraj has observed, that television has provided

an open window to the minds of our children and youth. They see television series, movies, violence, corruption, blood, rape, crime, exciting scenes, and that sort of dialogue in which the authors make their characters say things that make society unconsciously doubt itself, its values, and its religion. We see that even the local programs such as television series, movies, and plays, including commercials, are not all free from contamination. This is no longer innocent cultural subject matter but has become a continuous media uproar, a kind of collective hysteria which creates an atmosphere of anxiety, tension, and a fertile ground which fosters the growth of violence, crime, and drugs, and which pushes the youth to extremism as a final solution to their suffering, conflicts, and problems.

The results of a study conducted by the Kuwait Ministry of Information on intermediate school children has shown that 67.1 percent of a sample of 1,005 children tended to imitate the characters they admired and adopted their personalities as models of heroism. It is not, therefore, surprising to hear that a judge in the United Arab Emirates asserted in an armed robbery case that this crime was alien and new and that it was an inevitable result of the movies and other series which are shown on television.[7] It is also not surprising to hear about a youth, also in the Emirates, who applied what he saw in a police program by stealing the life savings of his neighbor.[8]

In view of the flood of television influence on the minds and emotions of Arab children, it is time to utilize this instrument of civilization constructively in the field of children's education and to offer objective facts about children and their growth to parents and teachers in a stimulating and simplified scientific way.

Before I finish this discussion on the social education of the child, I must mention an influence which distinguishes the Gulf child from the rest of Arab children. Dependence on foreign nannies in the family has increased among the Arab societies of the Gulf region. Studies in this area point to the negative influence of this practice upon the values, behavior, and language of the child. A study done by the Kuwait Ministry of Social Affairs on Kuwaiti families with children between the ages of two and six which employ foreign nannies has revealed a high rate of illiteracy among them which reached a level of 86.1 percent. Dr. Juhaina al-Eesa has concluded that there is a positive causal relationship between a mother's educational level and her degree of supervision of the nanny. She warns that this supervision decreases among families with lower educational levels and focuses on the negative effects which result when a foreign nanny replaces the mother in the educational process. These effects are reflected in the values, behavior, language, habits, and character of the child.[9] These effects are probably inevitable in the light of the high rate of illiteracy among women of the Gulf societies. Statistics indicate that illiteracy among Gulf women ranges between 45 and 90 percent. Without doubt this excessive dependence upon nannies continues to have a negative impact upon the Arab child in the Gulf.

Let us now move to the place of the Gulf child in the development plans of the Arab Gulf states. Here we find that concentration is still on the traditional concept of development where the main focus of the planners is primarily on economic aspects. The second half of the seventies witnessed the birth of four Gulf five-year development plans as advanced by Iraq, Saudi Arabia, Kuwait, and Oman. Are there any common factors among these plans? According to Professor Saeed Abbood Saleh it is possible to summarize the most important aspects of the development strategy of these plans as follows:

1. The development of new production services in addition to oil by concentrating on petroleum industry products and also on agriculture.

2. The creation of new export outlets for national products and the direction of those products to satisfy local needs.

3. Interest in development projects which relate to basic infrastructure and basic services.

4. Ensuring the influx of laborers and raising their level of productivity.

5. Reliance on modern technology by importing and utilizing foreign technology.

6. The necessity of cooperating and coordinating with other Arab economies and adopting the formula of project sharing.

Prof. Saleh goes on to say that the main objective of all the economic development plans in the Gulf states is to safeguard the oil industries. As for health and education services, they rank second in importance and are frequently deficient. Concern for development plans is restricted in these areas to the construction of school buildings, without furnishing them with needed equipment or teachers, and to the construction of hospitals, without equipping them with sufficient manpower. As for the construction of kindergartens and special libraries and playgrounds for children, there is little, if any, concern and no development plan has touched them.[10]

One may add to this planning failure the lack of concern with the development of women in the Gulf states where statistics indicate that women at the age of fertility constitute about 25 percent of the total population and the percentage of children under the age of five is about 40 percent. Therefore, the total proportion of these two groups in relation to the population as a whole is 65 percent. Accordingly, how is it possible for a society to develop and grow if the majority of its population is excluded from its development plans? Unfortunately, we may find that these statistics are fairly representative of those of the other Arab states.

Recent studies of women and children in the Gulf states indicate that in spite of the spread of health services the fact remains that most doctors and nurses are foreigners. There is a corresponding lack of communication and understanding between doctors and patients. Doctors see that the only way out of this difficulty is heavy reliance on brief prescriptions instead of taking the time to advise the patient of needed protective measures.

Studies also point out the high correlation between female education and child mortality. For each year of primary education received by females the mortality rate of nursing babies of that group decreases far below the mortality rate of nursing babies among illiterate women. This is reflected in figures which show that in many poor countries where women's education is prevalent the mortality rate of nursing babies decreases, while in those rich countries where female education is low the infant mortality rate increases.[11] This is why we find that the infant mortality rate in Kerala, the poorest state of India, is much lower than the infant mortality rate of some of the Gulf Cooperation Council states.

A symposium entitled "On Development: Between Planning and Execution in the Arab World," which was held in Kuwait in October 1989, concluded that the development plans of the Arab states have all fallen short of their original aims since the fifties. The reason for this failure was attributed to almost total emphasis on economic growth while neglecting qualitative human development, which, after all, is the ultimate goal.

Recognition of deficiencies in the traditional development plans was followed by putting forth new concepts of development. Professor Joe F. Dakosta summarized a new conception of development in twelve recommendations. The most important recommendation was that development should be comprehensive, that is, it should take into consideration what lies beyond the economic boundaries; it must include social factors such as nutrition, health, living conditions, services, the perfection of the individual's cultural and spiritual personality, the potential for creativity, quality of life, and human rights. Development, he said, should also be directed toward a legal and just social order.

One of the major reasons accounting for the neglect of children and women in the regional development plans of the Gulf states is the social and political weakness of these communities. Since they do not represent an aggressive power, no urgent need is seen to establish societies and foundations which would recognize their usurped rights.

This is the current situation of Arab children in general and of the Gulf children in particular. In conclusion, let me go back one hundred years and share with you George Auguste Vallin's description of the bedouin child in the Arabian Peninsula. He said:

> At the beginning of my living among the wandering Arabs I was very surprised to see the young, whose ages range between three and twelve years, accompany their elders; they are permitted to converse with them, and they are at times consulted on subjects which surpass their level, and they are listened to. The young live with their families lovingly and harmoniously. I have not seen in the desert those distasteful and familiar scenes (in some Arab countries of the Orient) of an angry father beating his son, and I have not seen the enslavement which the young face, for they are not allowed to sit or speak in the presence of their arrogant parents. I have not seen in the whole world boys who are more sensible and more behaved than the children of the bedouins.[12]

This was the Gulf child one hundred years ago. I wonder what has happened to him now!

NOTES

1. Khaldoon al-Nakeeb, "Social Education in an Age of Anxiety," in *Children and Various Wars in the Arab World,* Third Annual Yearbook of the Kuwait Society for the Advancement of Arab Children (KSAAC), Kuwait, 1985–1986.

2. Ibid.

3. M. J. Rada, "The Child and Linguistic Deficiency in the Arab World," in *Children and Various Wars*.

4. Osama al-Khuli, "Methods of Scientific Thinking among Arab Children," in *Children and Various Wars*.

5. Bader al-Omar, "Valid Methods for Safeguarding the Self among Arab Children," in *Children and Various Wars*.

6. Husni A'yesh, *A Letter to Fathers and Mothers* (n.p.).

7. Hassan al-Ebraheem, "Negative Effects of Public Communication upon the Child," *Social Affairs* 11 (1986), UAE.

8. Ibid.

9. Juhaina al-Eesa.

10. Saeed A. al-Samarra'i, "Development Plans of Arab Gulf Regions and Their Effects upon the Future of the Child," paper presented at a symposium organized by the Women's Federation of Iraq in cooperation with Basra University, January 13 – 15, 1979.

11. See "An Exposition of Services for the Protection of Children in the States of the Gulf Council," *Journal of Cooperation* 1 (1986).

12. George A. Vallin, *Images from the North of the Arabian Peninsula in the Middle of the Nineteenth Century (Gaz'eirat al-'Arab fi Muntassif al-Q'arn al-tasa' 'Ashar),* trans. S. Shiballi (Beirut, 1970), p. 107.

THE CODE OF CHILDREN'S RIGHTS IN ISLAM

by Muhammad Abdelkebir Alaoui M'Daghri
Translated by Moncef Lahlou

Editor's note: On the ninth of Ramadan 1407 (May 8, 1987) in the framework of the religious talks presided over each year at the Royal Palace in Morocco by His Majesty Hassan II, the Minister of Habous and Islamic Affairs Muhammad Abdelkebir Alaoui M'Daghri delivered an important lecture, "The Code of Children's Rights in Islam," based on the following text.

In the name of God, the compassionate and merciful, peace and health be granted to our prophet Muhammad, his family and all his companions. Nothing can lead astray him whom God guides, and no one can guide him whom God leads astray.

The sincerest words being those of God in His holy book and the best conduct being that adopted by the Prophet Muhammad, the worst of things is innovation, because every new practice is an aberration and every aberration leads to Hell.

God the Most High says, "God is the master of the heavens and the earth. He creates what He wishes, He gives daughters to whom He wishes; He gives the sons to whom He wishes, or He gives them in pairs, boys and girls. He makes sterile whom He wishes. He is wise and powerful."

This verse is part of the Sura of the Consultation. The divine words "God is the lord of the heavens and the earth" mean that the kingdom of the heavens and the earth belong exclusively to Him and that He disposes of them with complete liberty and so, He alone enjoys the power of giving or denying what He wishes. The preamble of the verse has as its purpose the preparation of souls and spirits to accept the power of God over all things and to accept what He gives, be this a boy or a girl, be it much or little. This preamble aims to reassure the hearts so that they may be happy with that which the Most High gives.

In the phrase "He gives daughters to whom He wishes" God the Most High uses the word "gives" to make clear that children, whether boys or girls, are purely a gift from God who grants His grace without demanding reciprocation. Man would be ungrateful to refuse or disdain that which God grants him as a simple gift, because gifts are never refused.

In the phrase "He gives daughters to whom He wishes and He gives the sons to whom He wishes" God the Most High cites daughters before sons, be it to please their mothers, since men usually prefer boys to girls, and this is why God insists on pleasing women by naming them first in this verse, or in view of the greater number of women than of men, or because of the weakness of girls and the interest God takes in them in order to motivate them to demonstrate more obedience and submission, or in order to please women and to prevent any inferiority complex. Likewise, to please boys, God names them in the definite form, using the article, "He gives girls to whom He wishes, He gives the sons to whom He wishes"; He then names them first at the end of the following sentence: "He gives girls to whom He wishes, He gives the sons to whom He wishes, or He gives them in pairs, boys and girls," which means that, through His power and His will, God gives to whom He wishes both sons and daughters.

With regard to the phrase "He makes sterile whom He wishes" let it be pointed out that sterility means infertility and the incapacity to produce, and the adjective "sterile" is used equally for women and men, as has been expressed admirably by certain poets.

The last phrase of the verse "He is wise and powerful" explains the fact that God, knowing fully the interests of his servants, gives to each that which he needs, and that, through His power, He evaluates things according to His knowledge, taking into account the interests of His servants and His capacity to act freely in His realm. I will limit my discussion of relevant exegeses of our Quranic verse to a treatment of an important aspect of the Shari'a, specifically the code of children's rights. It should be noted that the Shari'a dedicates to the child a complete and detailed code which covers every stage in life and every phase of its childhood and provides guarantees and so protects these rights under normal circumstances and likewise under unusual conditions, no matter what the circumstances. Islam gives importance to the child before birth and indeed before conception.

When he said, "Choose your wives well because the origin hides another," the messenger of God called on us to choose the mothers of our children from among women outside our families out of concern for conserving our power of procreation. When he says likewise, "Choose as your wives women outside your families in order to avoid any weakness," he encourages exogamous marriage with a view to avoiding the defects which can result from endogamy, an idea expressed in the words of the poet:

Whereas the child whose mother is other than a close cousin may be strong, healthy and sound,
Sickly, weak and defective will be the child issue of the union of closely related parents.

THE CONCERN OF ISLAM FOR THE CHILD

Divine law makes adultery prohibited and illicit so as to avoid the fetus's contracting venereal diseases. To assure the protection of the child in its mother's womb, abortion is prohibited. Imam Muslim reports that, according to Abu Huraira, two women of Hudail were fighting and one was so violent that she aborted. The penance prescribed by the Messenger of God was that of freeing a slave.

The importance given to the fetus by Islamic law manifests itself in other ways: it permits a pregnant woman not to fast during the month of Ramadan in consideration of the fetus and with a concern for protecting it from any harm that might result from the fast. It prohibits subjecting her to any punishment before the birth of her child out of pity for her and with the aim of protecting the fetus. Likewise Islamic law provides the pregnant woman with support and the right to live in the conjugal domicile until delivery so that she is not abandoned as the result of repudiation or death and the child that she carries is not endangered.

For the child, once born, the law contains precise and detailed provisions which show the importance it gives to the child, even to the point of calling for the whispering of the call to prayer in the newborn's right ear and the appropriate formula in his left ear. On the seventh day one puts a mashed date in the child's mouth and one slaughters a sheep called "Aqiqa," just as the newborn's hair is cut the same day and is given the same name, "Aqiqa."

The right of choosing a name for the child belongs to its parents, but in the case of disagreement this right belongs to the father, since it is he who sacrifices the sheep and he is responsible for the support of the child. It is the legal obligation of the father toward his child to choose an agreeable name. The Prophet says on this subject, "If you send someone, see to it that he bears an agreeable name and has a pleasant face." It is reported that the Prophet had asked that a camel be milked, and when one man wanted to do it, he asked him, "What is your name?" "Musa," he answered. "Stay where you are." There came another man, to whom he said, "What is your name?" "Jamra," he answered. "Stay where you are." To the third man who volunteered to milk the camel the Prophet said, "What is your name?" "Aish." "You can milk her."

It is also reported, according to Nafia after Abdallah ben Omar, that Omar ibn al-Khattab had a daughter named Assia whom the Prophet gave the name Jamila. Thus we see that Islamic law is concerned even with the name to be chosen for the child. Along with the name there is the question of filiation. Of course the ties of filiation of the child may or may not be well established. He whose relationship to his father is not established is called a "bastard." The child whose father and mother are both unknown has not been deprived of the attention of Islamic law, which provides for him the same treatment as the one whose ties of filiation are established and which guarantees him a noble and decent life. It stipulates that the bastard belongs to whoever takes him in, with this person to support him if he can; otherwise support falls to the public treasury. It is reported that a man who had found a bastard came to see Omar ibn al-Khattab, who said, "Keep it. You will be its guardian and you will take care of its support."

The man to whom the bastard belongs must not establish any family tie or adopt it, as adoption is prohibited by Islamic law. He can however provide guardianship, which extends to the person as well as to property. He may keep the child either until he decides to give up the child, in which case he or she will be placed in an orphanage at public expense, or until he no longer fulfills the necessary requirements, as is the case where he apostatizes and is not able to exercise guardianship, or where his behavior or morals lead to fears for the future of the child. Under these circumstances the child must be removed and placed in good hands. A bastard found in Muslim territories, even if by a Christian, is considered a Muslim. If it is found in infidel territory, it is considered a Muslim if it is found by a Muslim, and a non-Muslim if found by a non-Muslim.

Islamic law has shown great concern for this matter because a Muslim upbringing involves many obligations. He who takes in a bastard must provide him with an education or teach him a craft so as to allow his integration as a useful member of society.

Just as both parents are sometimes unknown, there are cases where only the father is unknown. Likewise both parents of a child born illegitimately may be known. The last two cases have not been neglected by Islamic law, which has given them great attention. The rights of the child of which only the mother is known are the responsibility of the mother, who must provide for care and education. They inherit from each other. Maternal uncles can exercise guardianship over the child's person as well as over his or her property. If there is no maternal uncle, guardianship will be exercised by the qadi. In no case does Islamic law lose sight of children's rights.

ALL RIGHTS AND ALL SAFEGUARDS

A child whose mother and father are known, but who is illegitimate, is not related to his or her father, who is not obligated for support or anything else, but rather to his or her mother, who must provide for care, maintenance, and guardianship. Thus Islamic law provides for and accords all rights and safeguards equally to children of known filiation and unknown filiation, as it does to the child of which only the mother is known or whose mother and father are known but who is born illegitimately. Nevertheless, in practice, despite the promulgation of precise legislation, well established and in accordance with the principles of Islamic law concerning personal status and the child— the subject of our talk—we observe that between the stringency of the positive law and the tolerance of divine law there is a gap which might mean the loss of rights for a good number of children. It is completely natural that there should be this gap between the divine law and the positive law, which represents only a part or a glimmer of the former, which is a great lantern whose light radiates in all directions in all situations. Several examples may be given: First the law stipulates that the validity of the marriage ceremony is dependent on the presence of two *adul* to witness the exchange of vows. If the ceremony is not carried out in front of the adul, the bonds of marriage are not established. The law does provide for exceptional cases where the bonds of marriage may be established by means of witnesses; these cases however remain limited to marriage ceremonies carried out before the publication of the Moudawana, i.e. before 1957, and to those carried out in localities far from the centers in which the adul practice. But except for these two cases, the marriage cannot be recognized. In addition, the law provides that in the case where the marriage is established by witnesses, the qadi must justify the circumstances which led him to give his approval and to dispense with the certificate. We know that our ancestors were satisfied for the validation of a legal marriage with the collective recitation of the Fatiha and the organization of a marriage ceremony, and that this practice continues in certain areas, especially in the country. But nowadays if the adul establish a marriage through witnesses, the qadi will refuse to ratify it by reason of the fact that it has occurred after the date of the publication of the Moudawana, in localities where the adul practice, or where nothing prevents the establishment of the certificate by the adul. Consequently the woman will not be able to establish her marriage, and the problem becomes thornier if the partners deny each other after having brought forth children. The law is categorical and the woman cannot establish the marriage bonds without a certificate. Even worse, the court will not approve the marriage so long as the requirements for special cases are not met.

On the other hand, Islamic law treats this case with tolerance. Indeed in our Malikite rite, the validation of a marriage is not entirely dependent on a marriage certificate but it is enough to organize a wedding ceremony on the day of the consummation. Abu el-Walid Baji says in his work entitled "Al-Muntaqa" that the opinion of the Malikites in this regard is confirmed by Bokhari, who reports, according to Anas ibn-Malik, that the Prophet organized three nights of ceremonies between Khaibar and Medina to celebrate the consummation of his marriage to Safia, daughter of Huyain ibn Akhtab. After having been present and eaten at the ceremonies, some said that she would be among the Mothers of the Believers, others claimed that she would be among his servants. But when the Prophet appeared and she had gotten on his horse behind him with a veil covering her face, the people were convinced that she numbered among the Mothers of the Believers. Abu el-Walid Baji said, "If the Prophet had had the marriage established in the presence of the adul, the people would not have had any doubts as to whether she counted among the Mothers of the Faithful or among the servants." All this proves that the Prophet got married without a prior marriage ceremony. Such is the procedure adopted in the Malikite rite, and as proof, the Moudawana of civil status, which stipulates the preceding, specifies at the end of each of its chapters that "All cases that cannot be resolved by applying the present code shall be resolved in reference to predominant opinion and to the jurisprudence of the Malikite rite." Our Moudawana is therefore sound and without defect. It must nevertheless be subject to a sound and serious application taking into account the general principles of divine law and all opinions approved by Muslim law parallel to all applicable texts. Then there is another example, that of marriage contracted without a guardian (wali). The Moudawana of civil status stipulates that the validity of a marriage is contingent on the participation of the guardian in conformance with the words of the Prophet: "Any marriage contracted without the participation of the guardian and the presence of an adul is considered null." Consequently the adul must never write a certificate in the absence of a guardian, so that, even when we resort to the establishment of a marriage by means of witnesses, we cannot do so if we learn that the marriage was contracted without a guardian.

A woman who is already a mother will find it impossible to establish her marriage or to establish the rights of her children, even though Malikite law contains two opinions attributed to the Imam Malik on this subject: the first, reported by al-Ashab, according to which the validity of a marriage is contingent on the participation of a guardian, it otherwise being considered null; the other, reported by Ibn Qasim, according to which the participation of a guardian, which is simply a complementary condition, has the character of a rule drawn from the sunna and not that of a legal obligation. One should note that Malikite law is very broad and offers many possibilities for the resolution of problems. One must in no case neglect the mother who demands her children's rights. Even if we admit that the validity of a marriage is contingent on the participation of a guardian and we ignore the account of Ibn Qasim, the worst case would consist of considering the marriage void either for reasons of form or for the absence of a dowry. In all cases the marriage is annulled and the children are considered their father's. This counts among the important principles provided by Islamic law for guaranteeing children's rights. If we allow the relatedness of the children to their father, we will have guaranteed all of the child's rights.

PROCREATION AND ISLAM

Nevertheless, this woman will never be able to establish her marriage because no one will accept a marriage in the absence of a guardian. And so her rights will be lost even in the absence of errors or omissions in the law because, as I have already said, the Moudawana, which is sound, is based on clear, precise texts and goes back to predominant opinion and the jurisprudence of the Malikite rite. But if these texts are badly applied, the rights of children are in danger of being lost. The two examples that we have given are equally applicable to the other cases of invalidated marriages such as marriages contracted during the waiting period required for women, marriages prohibited because of relatedness through marriage, marriages annulled for nonobservance of the rules of dowry, as well as the case where a man gives as a dowry prohibited goods, such as wine, pork, etc. In the worst case the marriage is invalidated and the child is related to his father. This succinct analysis shows that Islamic law takes care of the child in the most difficult cases and at the times when he or she has the greatest need for help and support, and demonstrates the tolerance and the flexibility of this law.

Just as these rights may be lost for the reasons discussed above, they may also be lost for artificial reasons. Indeed we observe the appearance of a new type of child which results from artificial insemination and is known as the test-tube baby. We should concern ourselves with this kind of child and seek in Islamic law provisions which can be applied so that we are not surprised by cases of difficult resolution where we would not be able to find solutions in time for children born as a result of such procedures. Nevertheless this form of insemination may be considered part of procreation, since creation in its strictest sense proceeds from the will of God the Most High who uniquely has the power to give life to matter and to bring it forth from nothingness. As for procreation, it consists solely of treating matter in such a way as to release from it the object of the real creation. While Islamic scholars know of this system of procreation and have dedicated a good number of studies to it on a theoretical level, they have not pursued the practical application to such a degree as to obtain the results achieved by the West. Abderrahman ibn Khaldun raised the question of artificial insemination and of procreation in his prolegomena, in which he stated in relation to chemistry: "If we accept that the alchemist can transform iron into gold, we must also accept that a wise man can procreate a human life from seed as long as he knows its essence, its stages of development, and its composition in the smallest and most precise detail. Alas, how can one attain such a level of knowledge?" This quotation is enough in order to show that the wise men of Islam have concerned themselves with this question.

Thanks to science, in Great Britain in 1977 a fertilized egg was produced in a test tube from an ovum taken from a woman and fertilized by the sperm of a man and then reimplanted in the mother's uterus. Thus a so-called test-tube baby was born. Then a five-month fetus was taken from its mother's uterus, kept in a test flask, then implanted in the uterus of another woman (surrogate mother), who bore the child. This type of operation is one of the innovations in artificial insemination. Since becoming aware of this new technique, the ulema of Islamic law have begun to reflect seriously on the position of the law on this question. In the wake of the opinions issued, the question was submitted to the Academy of Islamic Law in Mecca, which has made a number of decisions on the matter. To sum up, artificial insemination is practiced in two forms:

1. Intrauterine fertilization, which comprises two cases: that in which the ovum is fertilized by the sperm of a woman's legal husband, and that in which the woman's ovum is fertilized by the sperm of someone else. It goes forth from the opinions issued and the decisions made that in the first case, the child is legitimate because the operation carried out inside the uterus related to two spouses; in the second case, the child is illegitimate, is not related to the father, and has no legal claim. He is only related to the mother who bore him.

2. Extrauterine fertilization, which takes place in a test tube or an artificial container where the fertilized egg multiplies and develops up to a given

level during a given time span and then is reimplanted in the original uterus or in the uterus of a different woman (surrogate woman). This type of insemination comprises five cases:

   a. After development the fertilized egg is implanted in the mother's own uterus. In this case the ulema have decided that the child is legitimate and its filiation is also legitimate.

   b. Taken from two spouses, the fertilized egg is implanted in the uterus of a second wife. In this case the ulema have decided that the child is legitimate and related to the father in view of the absence of a third person.

   c. Taken from two spouses, the fertilized egg is implanted in the uterus of a different woman, who is married to another man (surrogate mother). In this case the ulema have decided that the child is illegitimate and not related to the father.

   d. Taken from two unmarried people, the fertilized egg is implanted in the wife's uterus. In this case the child is illegitimate.

   e. Taken from two people (a donor and a woman) not married to one another, the fertilized egg is implanted in the uterus of a third person (surrogate mother) or of a woman who hires out her uterus. In this case filiation is illegitimate.

This is a summary of the opinions issued and the decisions made by the ulema in order deal with the problem. Nevertheless this effort remains insufficient in more than one regard. First of all it deals with the situations and their subcases case by case and applies to each case a special rule. Now if the cases are disparate and their subcases are unlimited, we cannot examine separately all the cases in order to apply to each the corresponding rule. It would have been more appropriate to establish a general rule covering all cases no matter the degree of disparity. It is therefore necessary to determine the principles and to fix the rules applicable to all these cases instead of instituting a special rule for each case. Then, once a marriage has been established, the child will not be disavowed by his or her father.

The only case where the ties between a father and child are broken and the former is not related to the latter is when a husband accuses his wife. But if the husband does not make a complaint against his wife, he recognizes his child, and the marriage ties are maintained, it is difficult for the child to be taken from him and for their relationship not to be recognized. In addition, these decisions, which establish the illegitimacy of the filiation, are silent on the situation of the couple itself. To say that the filiation is illegitimate is to recognize that there has been an illegal act. However, couldn't this act as adultery mean the invalidation of the marriage and the separation of the spouses? This is mandatory. If we accept that insemination falls within the framework of adultery, the marriage between the spouses must be dissolved and the wife must observe a period of abstinence (*istibra*). The decisions made by the ulema are silent on all this as if artificial insemination, while bringing in an outside element, did not necessitate the separation of the spouses, oblige the wife to observe a period of abstinence, or carry with it the consequences of adultery. If these opinions and decisions opt for the upholding and continuation of the marriage, why do they not opt for the keeping of the child within the framework of this marriage?

In fact this question is very complicated; but the conclusion we wish to draw from an examination of these decisions and recommendations comes down to the fact that the question needs more study and reflection. I shall give an example in order to convince us of the need for continued study of the subject and the insufficient scope of the above-mentioned decisions. This example concerns one of the most important matters in Islamic law. It is the rule concerning the presumption of legitimate parenthood inspired by the words of the Prophet: "A child is considered legitimate through the relationship which unites its mother with her husband, and one born of adultery is to be deprived thereof." This means that if the ties of marriage are maintained from consummation until the expiration of a minimum duration of pregnancy of six months, the child must be presumed to be of legitimate parenthood no matter what the circumstances, even if the father refuses to recognize it. If the father refuses to recognize it, the wife by virtue of this rule need only produce the marriage certificate and establish the passing of the minimum period between consummation and birth for the child to be considered his father's in accordance with the words of the Prophet: "A child is considered legitimate . . . ". Malikite law has dealt with a case of a similar type which produced a decision in this sense. It deals with a husband who accuses his wife of adultery but recognizes his relationship to the child. This paradox is strange since the husband accuses his wife but recognizes the child. Imam Malik issued three opinions on this subject:

1. The husband must be punished and the child is recognized as his without the oath of accusation.

2. He pronounces the oath of accusation and the child is not recognized as his.

3. The child is recognized as his but he must pronounce the oath of accusation in order to avoid punishment.

According to opinions 1 and 3, the child is recognized as the father's, but according to opinion 2, the relationship is not repudiated and the child is not taken from his father until after his pronouncement of an accusation. Although this last case is in a juridical sense more complicated than that of artificial insemination, the rule applied to it is also highly favorable to the child. According to two opinions by Malik, the child must be recognized as the father's and, according to the third, the relationship is not repudiated until the oath of accusation has been pronounced.

ISLAMIC LAW IS FLEXIBLE AND TOLERANT

We would hasten to say that the child born of artificial insemination is illegitimate. We might take the precaution of conditioning the application of the rule of "the presumption of legitimate parenthood" to artificial insemination on the sine qua non that insemination cannot be authorized except in case of necessity. If this is the case, we would have to take a look at another chapter of Islamic law, that of the justification of means. This justification derives from the fact that a means prohibited by the law which allows the realization of a certain utility or which answers a given need becomes authorized. It is obvious that Islam, which does not approve the principle that the end justifies the means, does not authorize theft to meet the needs of one's family, nor games of chance to aid charitable purposes, nor deceit to help in the sale of merchandise. But if this prohibited means covers a given need or permits the realization of a certain utility, the need or utility must be given due weight and the means recognized as permissible. In this case, the need to have children being well established, one resorts to artificial insemination. And so this legitimate need must in fairness be given due weight. Still, the authorization of artificial insemination or any other procedure of this type must be conditioned on a pressing need.

It is clear from this overview that Islamic law is flexible and tolerant and that our ulema must allow our community to profit from the law's tolerance, not out of concern for making licit what is prohibited or by forbidding what is authorized but by the application of well-established legal principles, the pronouncement of just and equitable decisions, and the consideration of the risks that result from any judgment, since it is a question of the fate of innocent children who place their hopes in the tolerance of Islamic law and who should rightly benefit from it. If Islamic law has such tolerance for the child in these particularly critical cases, how will it treat him or her in normal situations? Since this law shows mercy toward the child in the most difficult circumstances, trying to show that it is so is like proving the existence of day.

Of course another aspect of the verse still needs to be examined, that of its relation to the invisible world, which is so vast and which constitutes another problem, another subject whose development would require another talk. It is enough then for us to note that the question of the invisible counts among those on which the ulema of Islamic law must take a clear, well-defined position, because numerous questions which used to belong to the realm of the invisible have come into man's reach thanks to the evolution of modern science. Under these circumstances we are obliged to distinguish that which belongs to the invisible world and that which does not by referring to the Quran and the Tradition of the Prophet and not only to the opinions of our ancestors. No one doubts the opinions expressed by the ulema were often influenced by their times, their situations, and their circumstances, as well as by the level of the science of their age. This reference to the Quran and the Tradition offers us considerable possibilities in distinguishing what belongs to this realm and what does not, so as to ensure that our religious presuppositions are not in contradiction with science and so that minds and spirits are not troubled by new discoveries.

Father and son near Amman, Jordan
PHOTO BY STAFFAN JANSON

PART II

GROWING UP

Angels don't enter a house where there is no child.

TURKISH PROVERB

The economic, political, and social changes that have taken place in the Middle East over the last half-century have left their mark on children and the family. The general patterns described in the introduction to this volume are here supported by case studies and articles from different countries. The Turkish poem by Bedir Rahmi Eyuboglu celebrates an old ideal, "To my son Mehmet, I present our fruits," but Andrea Rugh's account of the rise of orphanages suggests that the old ideal is not always realized. Adoption is being reconsidered as an option for those children victimized by war, poverty, death, and family disunity, and its historic background within Islam is outlined by Amira Sonbol. Child-rearing practices are changing in an Egyptian village, according to Judy Brink, who attributes this to a multitude of factors, including the recent education of women who are prospective mothers. In poorer quarters of Jordan, older child-rearing patterns can be seen, particularly in extended family households, where the mother-in-law has authority, according to Seteney Shami and Lucine Taminian. The lullabies from Kuwait, translated by Farha Ghannam, express the close relationship that continues between mothers and children, and the two excerpts from religious handbooks demonstrate modern adaptations of older religious indoctrination. Susan and Douglas Davis, however, point to a new stage of child development receiving recognition in Morocco—adolescence. Tradition and change, then, are both part of children's experience in growing up in the Middle East at the end of the twentieth century.

Teenagers in a new suburb of Casablanca, Morocco
PHOTO BY HEATHER LOGAN TAYLOR

Teenagers in the village of Shanawan, Egypt
PHOTO BY HEATHER LOGAN TAYLOR

ADOPTION IN ISLAMIC SOCIETY: A HISTORICAL SURVEY

by Amira al-Azhary Sonbol

Laws concerning adoption and the handling of orphans in Islamic society are based on principles established by the Prophet Muhammad. These principles were, in certain ways, a reaction to what had existed in pre-Islamic Arabia. At the same time they were needed by the members of the new *umma,* or community, that the Prophet was creating. These laws were further consolidated during the time of the Caliph Umar and were later to grow and change in response to historical conditions. Today's laws pertaining to orphans and adoption are the accumulation of the laws and practices of Islamic society since the Prophet's time. Generally, they are tied to issues of inheritance and property. But some discrepancy also is found between the laws themselves and actual social practice. This seems consistent with the needs of different classes within society; propertied classes were naturally interested in formalizing laws that assured their control of property, while poorer people to whom property meant little adopted orphans on an informal basis. Unfortunately, whereas the laws are recorded, informal transactions are not.

The purpose of this chapter is to discuss the system of child adoption in Islamic society. The method used is to compare actual practices regarding orphaned children to pertinent laws during different periods of Islamic history: the Jahiliya period, the early Islamic period, and the Quran's treatment of adoption; the medieval period and the interpretation of prophetic traditions by theologians of the time; and finally the modern period, with a description of how Islamic society handles the issue today. The subject of adoption specifically and of orphans in general has not been well studied; therefore this essay will be raising questions concerning the significance of such micro-level issues in understanding historical transformations.

THE HISTORICAL BACKGROUND

The Jahiliya Period

Social institutions like marriage, divorce, inheritance, and adoption had a more loosely defined structure before the coming of Islam than after, and therefore a wide divergence existed between different areas of Arabia during the Jahiliya, or pre-Islamic, period.[1] Still, generally speaking, bedouin society was tribally based, with clans associating for economic and defense purposes, sharing the responsibilities of the tribe, its good and bad fortune. The larger the clan the more important it was within the tribe, and the larger the tribe, the stronger it was. The size of the clan was dependent on socioeconomic and demographic conditions; adopting into the clan increased its size. As Marshall Hodgson pointed out, even though tribes "defined themselves in terms of a real or fictive common descent . . . newcomers might be adopted into them. No man who had sufficient kin could want for protection and status."[2]

Before Islam, then, adoption into a tribe took place for socioeconomic reasons just as did the practice of infanticide of both male and female children. If infanticide was practiced on female more than male children, it may have been caused by the "father's intense disappointment and fear of disgrace which might be brought on him by the birth of a daughter."[3] More likely, however, male children were needed to strengthen the protective ability of the tribe; and since the blood price was considered to be the basis of law, a tribe's protection of its members depended to a large extent on the tribe's ability to exact such a price.

Perhaps because tribal grounds were the property of the tribe as a whole, and there was no private ownership of land, the issue of inheritance did not cause problems when it came to adoption.[4] Thus, during the period of the Jahiliya, adoption was quite widespread and took place in various forms: one man adopted another's son, who took the adopted father's name in preference to his natural parent's name, even though the natural parent was usually known to him. Freedmen often took the names of their previous owners, and if they then became their *mawali,* they took the title of mawla or brother of the previous owner.[5] Slaves were usually captives or purchased children with no family of their own and it was customary for them to become part of the clan.

However, if widespread adoption was the norm, the actual pattern of adoption is less clear—whether clans adopted indiscriminately or class consciousness was involved in such adoptions. In the most widely used example of adoption before Islam, the case of Zayd b. Haritha, the adopted son of the Prophet, Zayd was originally from the Quda'a, close to Quraysh and equal in prestige. Being adopted by a Qurayshite may have been due to his parentage and the fact that his *nasab,* or lineage, was known. It may be that, like today, children of unknown origin were received into clans only with apprehension, and those adopted, particularly by the aristocracy, were of known heritage.

Bedouins had long supplemented their herding activity through trading and raiding, becoming involved in commercial activity between Southern Arabia and the Mediterranean.[6] The tribe of Quraysh in particular, situated near the north-south trade routes, sporting the famous water well of Zamzam and the religious sanctuary, or Haram, of the Ka'ba, became an important trade center by the sixth century. They consolidated their position through alliances with the tribes surrounding Mecca, and through military power they created a prominent position for themselves. They also made out of the pilgrimage an activity involving the rest of Arabia. Arabia was undergoing a process of deep structural change toward the end of the sixth century, and the Quraysh tribe was playing a central role, creating a framework of personal moral responsibility and political allegiance with itself at the center.[7]

The Coming of Islam

By the time the Prophet appeared, in the early seventh century, Mecca was already an important center; merchant capital was the established system of exchange, and the tribal system was breaking down. Whether Islam can be seen as a reaction to the breakdown of the earlier security provided by a tribe, or whether it represented a logical step toward the establishment of a new order already being brought into existence through the Meccan elite, is not clear. The regulations that were set by Islam regarding family laws can be interpreted variously as complete departures from what came before, as answers to immediate needs of the community, as answers to tribal needs due to the dislocations caused by merchant capital, or as a cohesive system necessitated by the evolution of a new historical bloc that was seeing the final stages of its metamorphosis.

Whenever a new order is set up, certain traditions become acceptable as law and are included in the official, legal categories that the new order sets out for itself. The Prophet's treatment of marriage is consistent with the type of organization he was building: a new allegiance built on religious belief in which Islam was to play the paramount role in cementing society together. Whether that meant he was building a state, or umma, is questionable. But in the new system, informal adoption declined, for the Quran forbade formal adoption.

The family laws instituted by the Quran can be seen as stressing the nuclear family, and this may be taken as an indication that the Prophet intended to deemphasize larger groupings like tribes and clans. This in itself would discourage adoption. Research on the microlevel, however, leads to different findings. It is less clear whether the laws and regulations set up were specifically directed toward bringing about a new order, or whether the new order evolved through the unfolding of the historical process. The latter seems more likely, as the emergence of an umma was already in the making, and was brought into its final shape after Muhammad. Viewing the Prophet as building a state is more the result of conceptualizing the past according to modern concepts than it is of reality. Quranic laws pertaining to the family were focused around the questions of property and distribution of wealth rather than toward undermining clan structures and strengthening an umma. The connections between the issues of inheritance, family structure, and property illustrate this central interest. Furthermore, when Quranic laws regarding the family are compared to later legal and social practices, it can be seen that most legal practices regarding social institutions are the work of generations following the Prophet.

When it comes to the specific subject of adoption, the laws of adoption presented by Islam appear as a clear-cut departure from what existed before, yet social practices in regard to adoption continued to reflect pre-Islamic customs. Before Islam, an adopted son took the name of the adopting parent, but after Islam this was forbidden and the son used the name of his physical parent when it was known, as in the case of Zayd b. Haritha, who was called Zayd b. Muhammad until the revelation of Surat al-Ahzab:4, after which he was called by his real name, Zayd b. Haritha.[8] Still, orphans of unknown lineage were claimed. Ziyad b. Abih, the Ummayyad Governor of Basra, was claimed as an illegitimate brother by Mucawiya b. Abi Sufyan, who manipulated the relationship to their mutual benefit. Others remained famous with the names of their adopted fathers, for example al-Miqdad b. al-Aswad, whose real father was 'Amru b. Tha'laba al-Barhani.[9]

In Islamic *fiqh* (jurisprudence), inheritance is explained as "the transfer of property from one person to another,"[10] while the tie by *nasab* (lineage) is considered to be one of God's great gifts to his *'ibad* (worshipers).[11] The Quran established rules to assure the sanctity of the family and the purity of the *'asab*, and hence the nasab. To assure nasab, on which inheritance depended, blood relations were emphasized: "Those related through the womb are worthier one of the other."[12] This went beyond emphasizing the nuclear family, since the degrees of relationship centered around the 'asab, or the main "nerve," were the basis for nasab (relationship by blood), and that included uncles, aunts, and cousins of varying degrees, all of whom could have rights to inherit. Thus, though Malik b. Anas began his account of degrees of nasab and right to inherit with the statement that "a brother from [the same] father and mother is closer [in nasab] than a brother from the father alone," he finishes with "the paternal cousin is more worthy than the father's uncle, the brother of the grandfather whether to the father or mother." [13] Islam also stresses the importance of holding on to blood relations: "The loss of nasab and its confusion leads to great personal and social immorality . . . it leads to economic and financial dislocation." [14]

To assure nasab, a moral code was prescribed for Muslims. Built on a strict separation of the two sexes, it was meant to eliminate mixing that could lead to sin and hence to a confusion of nasab. The child was regarded as belonging to the father, except in particular cases: "The newborn belongs to the father, whether [the mother] was free or a slave." [15] Among the controls set up to assure parentage was the 'ida (a three-month period of waiting after divorce) to ascertain whether pregnancy occurred. Strict moral codes controlling sexual relations were also prescribed.

> Say to the believing men that they should lower their gaze and guard their mod-
> esty, that will make for greater purity for them. And God is well-acquainted
> with all that they do. And say to the believing women that they should lower
> their gaze and guard their modesty, that they should not display their beauty
> and ornaments except what (must ordinarily) appear thereof.[16]

Even though, as these verses demonstrate, the Quran deals with both males and females equally on the matter of modesty, it is women who carry the culpability of immorality among the *fugaha'*. Thus the prescribed dress code covering "enticing" parts of the human body and advocating lowering the voice while speaking applies to women but not to men. The basic belief behind this is that women are the source of evil; according to a prophetic hadith, "Women are the tentacles of Satan (Shaytan)." [17] Besides, even though the Quran does not differentiate between virgins and nonvirgins when it comes to preference in marriage, the Prophet's wives having been mostly of the latter, later fiqh has made much out of the issue: "Islam called for a preference to marry virgins in most cases, especially when the young man has not been married before and has no smaller children in need of his protection." [18]

Family arrangements based on Quranic rules forbid any kind of sexual association outside formalized, legally sanctioned marriage. In his list of *kaba'ir* (great sins), Imam al-Dhahabi (b. 1274) placed *qat'sillat al-arham* (ending relations in relatives) as the ninth and *zina* as the tenth. Quoting the Quran, Surat al-Nur: "[As to] the [male] fornicator and the [female] fornicator, whip each a hundred strokes and do not feel pity for them if you believe in God and the day of judgement and let there be witnesses to their agony from among the believers." [19] Prophetic hadiths are more graphic regarding the sin of zina. According to one tradition, as the Prophet ascended on the day of

Isra', he saw screaming women hanging by their breasts or by their legs. When he questioned Gibril, the latter informed him that they were "the women who committed *zina,* killed their children, and gave their husbands heirs other than their own." [20] In such a system it was natural that orphans or children of unknown origins would be considered less than desirable.

That is how we can explain inheritance laws in Islam which fragment property, allowing the dispersion of wealth through inheritance. Shares of inheritance are prescribed by the Quran, including specific allotments to each member of the family. There is no means of assuring that wealth remains accumulated in one hand after death, since no individual can control the inheritance of more than one third of his property. New laws regarding inheritance offered a revamped approach toward communal property. Even though immediate family members became the principal heirs, the way property was divided after death meant that most family members could inherit certain portions assigned by the Quran. Wealth thus did not accumulate in the same hands from one period to the other, and ultimately was constantly redistributed from one generation to the next. Thus wider sectors of society enjoyed this wealth rather than the immediate family, as had been the case before Islam, in merchant Mecca, when Muhammad himself was left a destitute orphan.

In fact, even though the Quran *forbids* adoption, it calls upon Muslims to leave part of their wealth to those who are dependent on them such as *mawali,* slaves, and "adopted" children. The one third of an estate left to the prerogative of an individual was most probably allowed by Islamic law for that purpose. Other laws in Islam demanded that the rich support the poor, and this included the payment of *zakat* and the support of poor relatives. All these injunctions had the impact of distributing wealth to wider sectors of society.

Another interesting technique of assuring parentage which has a close connection with property issues is the system of *mula'ana.* Mula'ana occurs when a husband suspects his wife of adultery but cannot produce the required four witnesses. In such cases, the husband then takes the matter to a judge of the court and swears to his allegation. If the wife confesses to adultery, she is punished accordingly, but if she professes her innocence and takes an oath in front of the judge and witnesses but the husband refuses to believe her, then the judge declares the marriage at an end. Whether she can be remarried to him or not has been dealt with differently by different schools.[21] When it comes to a child that the wife may be carrying at the time of *li'an,* he cannot inherit from the father since he is not recognized as his son, and among Shafis, if a girl is born, it is legal for the "father" to marry her since she is a daughter of mula'ana. However, the general public refuse such marriages since the child may have been raised by him.[22] The child of mula'ana inherits from the mother and she inherits from him.[23] "A woman has the right to three inheritances: that of her freed slave, her *laqit* (foundling), and her son on whom she was mula'anat." [24] This tradition equates the son of mula'ana to a slave and a laqit. Although the tradition gives the woman the right to inherit the laqit, this is not supported elsewhere.

Mula'ana, which continues as a basis for divorce until today and is proved by the Quran, Sunna, qiyas, and ijma,[25] is similar to pre-Islamic matrilineal traditions, when the wife stayed with her own clan, and the children were considered hers rather than the father's. The subject of mula'ana is not well known and is among the various questions raised by this study that are deserving of special focus.

The Shari'a (Islamic law) has specific injunctions about adoption. Official adoption by which adults become the acknowledged parents of a child and a child their acknowledged heir is not recognized by Islamic law. One Quranic verse seems to be central to Islamic society's approach to the question of adoption:

God has not made for any man two hearts in his body: nor has He made your wives whom ye divorce by zihar your mothers: nor has He made your adopted sons your sons. . . . Attribute them to their fathers: that is juster in the sight of God. But if ye know not their fathers, they are your brothers in faith, or your mawlas. But there is no blame on you if ye make a mistake therein.[26]

Even though this verse, the only one in the Quran to deal directly with the subject of adoption, does not actually forbid adoption, prophetic tradition has strengthened that belief, making adoption a sin equal to *kufr*, apostasy. Thus the Prophet is supposed to have said, "Do not wish for other than your fathers, whosoever wishes for other than his father, it is kufr." Another version of this tradition reads: "He who claims another father and he knows his real father, it is kufr." [27] A stronger hadith explaining this verse reads: "He who claims other than his father while knowing that he is not his father, then paradise is forbidden him." [28] Still other hadiths emphasize blood relationship as the only basis for paternity.

Another verse not dealing directly with adoption but still significant because of the particular situation it was meant to address, i.e. Muhammad's marriage to Zaynab b. Jahsh, reads:

And if you say to he who has received the grace of God and your favor: cleave to your wife and fear God, but you hide in your heart that which God had initiated, and you fear the people when fearing God is more fitting. Then when Zaid was through [with the marriage], we joined her in marriage to you so that [in future] the believers may not be embarrassed [*harag*] to marry the wives of their adopted sons once the latter have dissolved their marriage. And God's command was fulfilled.[29]

The affair of Zaynab b. Jahsh is a controversial one. She was married to Zayd b. Haritha, Muhammad's adopted son. The verse was revealed at the time the Prophet was establishing rules defining categories of family members permitted or forbidden in marriage to an individual member of the family. Had adoption been recognized, then Zayd's wife would have been forbidden to Muhammad. Not recognizing adoption, therefore, opened the way to such a marriage. Whether this was one way of establishing rules for the Muslim community by setting a precedent through the person of the Prophet, as is the general interpretation given by Muslims to this incident, or whether the matter of adoption was an issue "due entirely to self-interest," [30] as the critics of Muhammad assume, continues to be an issue of controversy; the *aya* (verse) itself has confirmed the directive that adopted sons are not full sons since, according to marriage laws, father and son could never marry the same woman, even if at different times.

The word *laqit* is used in modern vocabulary to describe a child who has not reached *bulugh,* or majority, who is found in the street, and does not know his nasab. It is generally assumed by modern society that such a child was born illegitimately and therefore carries a stigma of immorality for the illicit act committed by his parents. The word *laqit* is hardly used in early Islam, and its usage during the medieval period is limited. Originally *luqta* defined "that which is picked up," something that is of value which should be returned to its owner if the owner is known, or enjoyed by he who found it if its owner is not known.[31] During the modern period the term *laqit,* denoting a child of unknown origins, has gained notoriety because of the different social context, and the laqit continues to be discussed as property in books of fiqh, usually under the title "awlad al-zina" or "kitab al-luqta," as it has since the medieval period.

In the past, the nature of the lost item determined how its founder was to deal with it. A prophetic tradition is often quoted in this case:

A bedouin came to the Prophet and asked him what is to be done with whatever he finds. He [the Prophet] answered: get to know it for one year, learn all its characteristics, and if no one comes and asks you about it, then you can slaughter it. He [the bedouin] asked: what about a lost sheep? The Prophet answered: it is for you, your brother, and the wolf. He asked: what about a lost camel? The Prophet answered with anger: What do you want with it, it has its shoes, its drink, it regurgitates water and eats trees.[32]

The essence of this is that a sheep is helpless, while a camel can take care of itself and find its own way home. This is how the hadith is interpreted, therefore: "His saying 'it is for you, your brother, and the wolf,' is a permission that it can be legitimately appropriated and is the same as if the Prophet had said: it is weak since it cannot survive alone and is exposed to destruction. Thus it needs a protector who can then enjoy the luqta." [33] There are differences in opinion regarding when a luqta becomes the right of its finder; one year is usually taken to be the proper period. For that one year the luqta is no more than a *wadi'a* (deposit) with the person who found it. So what is of importance here is establishing who has the right to that property. The central question in regard to the laqit remains: who has the primary right to the laqit? A usual answer gives the primary right to he who found the laqit as long as "he is fair, honest, and rational." In this case the laqit benefits from being raised and educated by he who has found him. [34] This interpretation, like most other shari'a regulations regarding the luqata', dates from the time of Umar rather than from the time of the Prophet or directly from the Quran.

The Shari'a's treatment of slaves, sons of mula'ana, and particularly orphans, all of whom would be helpless without a protector, throws light on the laqit's position. Thus the laqit's inheritance is studied in books of fiqh in sections dealing with freed slaves, the central question being who inherits both. In this context it is agreed that the allegiance of the slave is to he who has freed him, i.e. bought him and then freed him. The same is applied to the laqit, a tradition of Caliph Umar being a basis: "He [the laqit] is free, his expenses are our [the state's] responsibility, and his allegiance is to you [the finder]." [35] But when it comes to the question of inheritance, Umar determined that since there was no proof that the laqit was a slave, he cannot be treated as someone's property, therefore what he owns cannot automatically become that of his guardian. If any money is found on the laqit, therefore, it is to be used for his support; if none is found, then the state treasury supports him from the money set for the needs of Muslims. If the treasury is unable to support him then it is the duty of Muslims who learn of his condition to provide for him and help keep him alive. If there is someone to support the orphan, then the treasury need not be resorted to except if the judge orders it.

As for the inheritance of a laqit, if he dies and does not leave an heir, then his wealth goes to the treasury, and any indemnity paid if he is killed also goes to the treasury; his guardian has no right to his wealth. Those who declare relationships to a laqit have to prove a blood relationship and cannot inherit them or be inherited by them unless such proof is convincing to a court of law. [36] In several cases pertaining to such matters, the Egyptian courts have come up with similar decisions: "Since proving paternity means gaining inheritance—under dispute." There is general recognition and acceptance that the two go together.[37] If more than one person declares such a relationship, then specialists should be brought in to determine whom the laqit resembles most, and thereby the relationship is settled. It is interesting that the tradition usually referred to in this context is a prophetic tradition having to do with the determination of paternity of Zayd b. Haritha and his son Usama. In this tradition, Muhammad is said to have covered the head of both Zayd and Usama and pointed to the similarity in their feet to prove that paternity. According to Bukhari, if such physical resemblance does not determine parentage, then it can be decided by luck, which the more legalistic Hanafi sect refuses to acknowledge.[38]

The connection between rights of usage and children is further illustrated by the general handling of orphans in the Shari'a. The handling of orphans in the Quran and by the Prophet were in answer to two particular issues, the early life of the Prophet and the large numbers of orphaned Muslim children following the Battle of Uhud, when casualties were great. The Prophet seemed to have faced two questions in terms of the battle orphans: on the one hand many of the orphans were quite poor, and on the other those who survived Uhud had to be rewarded. When it came to poor orphans his own life provided the example for their treatment; hence generosity to orphans is strongly advocated by the Quran and orphans are dealt with as a community responsibility. What is stressed is the individual's obligations toward those who are poor, in need, or orphans. The treatment of orphans by medieval theologians is proof of this; the ayas chosen and the way they are interpreted emphasize the moral issues and the expectations from an individual in fulfillment of God's wishes. "As to the orphan, do not oppress. And as for the beggar, do not repulse." [39] The word tanhar, translated here as "oppress," is further described as "do not cheat him of his wealth and do not treat him with disdain." [40] The treatment of orphans is part of the category of charities. In one source the heading of the chapter dealing with orphans reads: "Chapter on the treatment of orphans, girls, others who are helpless, the poor, and the bankrupt: Giving them charity, feeling compassion for them, treating them with humbleness, and assisting them." [41] Significantly, under the title "Concerning forbidding a person's claim of relationship to other than his father and gaining control over other than his mawali," the concern is with adults claiming what is not theirs rather than with orphans who may be given affiliations other than their blood relationship.

Charity toward orphans is usually placed together with the beggar and the wayfarer: "al-miskin, ibn al-sabil, and the orphan." Various hadiths stress the responsibility of he who wishes to do God's will to provide for those who are needy.[42] The orphans are dealt with under the heading "Kitab al-Zakat," and charity toward them was considered an important sadaqa. Orphans are also itemized under "Kitab al-Adab," which deals with social relations, including treatment of parents, husbands, wives, children, and neighbors. According to Bukhari, the Prophet admonished believers to support orphans whether related to them or not. Orphans related to them might include a mother whose husband had died and who was left to raise her child alone, or even a father whose wife had died. The category also included orphans whose parents were not related to the individual, or whose parents were unknown. In this case the rewards were all in heaven: "I and the kafil [supporter, who spends on and raises] of an orphan will be together in heaven like this: and the Prophet crossed his two fingers." [43]

Thus the Quran admonishes Muslims not to mistreat or cheat orphans, but to treat them with fairness, kindness, and generosity. More specific verses involving orphans are usually tied to matters of wealth and property and often, like the following, admonish believers not to rob orphans:

> Let those who would fear leaving their own helpless family behind: let them fear God, and speak words of appropriate comfort. Those who unjustly devour the property of orphans, they do but eat a fire into their own bodies, and will soon be enduring a blazing fire.[44]

> Do not come near the orphan's money except with kindness until he attains the age of full strength; and honor your obligations, for obligations will be enquired about [by God].[45]

These warnings follow others involving infanticide,[46] adultery,[47] taking of human life,[48] cheating in the marketplace (weighing and measuring),[49] idle curiosity,[50] and vanity,[51] all actions that are described as being evil and hateful to God.[52] Thus, treatment of orphans is placed as a primary moral obligation for Muslims.

One form of reward to those who fought at Uhud allowed them to take over the responsibility of wealthy orphans and control their wealth. At the same time, however, the rights of those orphans had to be assured and this was to be done through principles that allowed for a compromise between the two. "They ask thee concerning orphans. Say: The best thing to do is what is for their good; and if you mix their affairs with yours, they are your brethren; but God knows the man who means mischief from the man who means good." [53] Thus guardians had the right to invest their wards' money; in fact that was best for the orphan. Another verse alludes to a strict separation of the affairs of ward and guardian, so there would not be an advantage to the latter in their relationship. "To orphans restore their property and do not exchange the good with the worthless, and do not devour their wealth." [54] Prophetic traditions pick up on whether the guardian should invest the property of his ward, making out of it a duty: "Beware! Whoever is the guardian of an orphan who has property, should trade with it, and should not leave it [undeveloped], so that the zakat should consume it." [55]

Even though the verses pertaining to orphans apply equally to males and females, special treatment is given to the latter. Particular stress is laid on the rights of the girls to their wealth, perhaps in fear of their vulnerability in the hands of guardians who may wish to keep them from marrying and thereby never relinquish their property. Yet the Quran also allows guardians to enjoy such property when the ward is living under the guardian's roof and to claim a portion even after her marriage.

> If you fear that you will not deal justly with the orphans, marry [from among them] women of your choice, two, or three, or four. But if you fear that you will not deal justly [between them], then only one, or [a captive] that your right hands possess. That will be more suitable lest you oppress. And give the women their dower as a free gift, but if it pleases them to remit any part of it to you, take it with joy and enjoy it. Do not turn over your money to the incompetent [or foolish], but feed and clothe them from it and speak to them words of kindness and justice.[56]

This verse carries a clear message to benefit from the wealth of an orphan by marrying her, by accepting a portion of her property when given freely, and by keeping it all in cases when the orphan is considered incapable of handling such property. But such advantages were to be used within limits and were to be looked at as a form of compensation: "Make trial of orphans until they reach the age of marriage; if then ye find sound judgement in them, release their money to them; but consume it not wastefully, nor in haste against their growing up." [57] Accordingly, guardians seem to be permitted to use their wards' wealth as long as they are careful how they use it. "If the guardian is well-off, let him claim no remuneration, but if he is poor, let him have for himself what is just and reasonable. When ye release their money to them, take witnesses in their presence: but all-sufficient is God in taking account."

Traditions lay stress upon the right of the poor guardian to enjoy part of the wealth of his ward. In one tradition transmitted through 'Aisha, "If the guardian is well-off, let him claim no remuneration, but if he is poor, let him have for himself what is just and reasonable." [58] Others have differed, indicating that a guardian takes from the money of the ward when he is in need. But there is general agreement that the guardian has the right to take a portion of the ward's wealth as long as it is with *ma'ruf,* or what is acceptable.[59]

In explaining the basis upon which the guardian was given the right to dispose of the property of his ward, Muslim scholars evidence a communal approach to property that seems at the heart of Islam's approach to the issue. Since all wealth is seen as ultimately belonging to God, it is God who sets out the rules for distributing and spending that wealth. Thus any property held by an individual is to be spent for the good of society, and that individual will be judged accordingly.

> Property has not only its rights but also its responsibilities. The owner may not do just what he likes absolutely: his right is limited by the good of the community of which he is a member, and if he is incapable of understanding it, his control should be removed. . . . Ultimately all property belongs to the community and is intended for the support of the community. It is held in trust by a particular individual. If he is incapable, he is put aside but gently and with kindness.[60]

But such explanations do not deny the close connection between dealing with orphans and the question of property by which the orphan is looked at as a financial asset, bringing benefits to the guardian to whom he or she is assigned. These benefits are not to be understood in terms of strict property ownership, i.e. ownership that is alienable, but as property in the sense of the "right of usage," which seems to be the Islamic outlook toward the issue of property, i.e. property that belongs to the community at large but is given to the individual (by God) for his own temporary use which he should apply for the good of the community at large. As long as an individual is acting as guardian, he is entitled to enjoy the benefits that come with that role. Whether this outlook toward property applied to children alone as belonging to the community at large or applied to society's approach to property is not clear. The topic is worthy of further study.

THE LAQIT IN THE MEDIEVAL PERIOD

Notwithstanding the fact that both the courts and society have accepted the general indictment of adoption as being *haram* (forbidden), this has never stopped the wide practice of adoption, which took place and continues to take place in various forms. As indicated earlier, adoption did not end with the coming of Islam. Legally speaking, an adopted individual was defined by the courts as "a person of known parentage or unknown parentage [who] is adopted and permitted to declare his son even though he is not truly his son, is haram and unacceptable in the Islamic Shari'a, and thus no legal decision applicable (to sons) would apply to him."[61] This leads to the presumption that adopted sons enjoyed equal privileges with natural sons before the coming of Islam, particularly that they had equal rights to inherit. However, in researching this essay I found no evidence that this was the case, nor that inheritance was that significant a legal issue during the Jahiliya.

As indicated earlier, during the time of the Caliph Umar there was a need to formulate laws for the treatment of luqata', to determine who has the right to them, who supports and inherits them, as well as what religious affiliation should be given to them in case this was not known. Large numbers of luqata' must have existed in various areas of the growing Muslim territories for such regulations to become necessary. During the medieval and modern periods that continued to be the case, and Shari'a courts had to deal with luqata' and formulate laws as to their position in society. During the medieval period when few orphanages existed, most children were adopted into families and raised by them. Very often, because of the inability to beget children and the social stigma of not having children was quite widespread, women adopted children and claimed them as their own. "When a woman, having used up all her resources . . . is [still] not lucky enough to become a mother, or to keep alive the children to whom she gave birth, then adoption makes up for the privations that nature has imposed."[62]

Taking in orphans was quite widespread, particularly since for many there was hardly anywhere else to go. Treatment of orphan children was similar among Muslims and non-Muslims in Islamic society. Of course in the case of non-Muslims the children were most often of known nasab, and thus the luqata' usually were considered Muslims since that was the religion of the majority. S. D. Goitein has shown how among Egyptian Jews husbands quite often ran away, leaving their children to live with their mothers. These children were known as aytam al-ahya', or "orphans whose parents are still alive." The death of the father also meant orphans, and such children and their mothers were regarded as "needy and miserable," a description applied not only to poor families. Among the Jewish community, as elsewhere, orphan girls were the "poorest of the poor" and it was of great religious merit to marry an orphan girl. Protection of orphans by the community seems to have been basic in the Jewish community, as it was in society at large. If the child's mother or her family could not take care of him, he could be taken in by another family under the supervision of the court.[63]

Orphanages were a modern phenomenon; there were no orphanages in the medieval period except for "the so-called orphanages erected by Muslim rulers in a later period [which] were often nothing but training schools for future soldiers."[64] Goitein was referring to the practice of recruiting children and raising them in the household of the rulers to become soldiers and officials of the future. This was practiced by the Mamluks and the Ottomans. One can actually talk of Mamluk practice as a form of adoption, since the relationship between the young male recruits and their Mamluk masters was quite close, the Mamluks being raised within the household and thus forming close, siblinglike relations with other Mamluks. In fact the continuation of the Mamluk system depended on the existence of this type of household affiliation and loyalty.

> The *lafz* used for different levels of relationship [between Mamluks] were usually military terms; the relationship between those immigrants and the master who gave them a home took the shape of adoption for which military terms were used; it is settled according to the same systems used by Mongol tribes in regards to cases of normal adoption: the blood of the adopted and the adopting parents are mixed with milk, or an oath is sworn that a new relationship was being set up, or a simple kissing and answer takes place. After this all that is entailed in normal adoption takes place, including the right to inherit and other rights of legal children; the children carry the name of the new family and the name given to them by their new fathers. That was the case between Tamerlane and Jenghis Khan. . . . this was similar to the relationship between the Mamluks of Egypt and their masters.[65]

THE MODERN PERIOD

The treatment of orphans and the question of adoption have undergone important changes in the modern period. Yet the basis of the law regarding adoption remains very much what it had been before, for adoption continues to be regarded as haram. What has changed is that a new order is in place, an order which reflects the rise of nation-state structures, centralized governments, social systematization and categorization modeled after the West, and the government's assumption of social functions and responsibilities. This is part of a new hegemony built on nationalism, positivism, and reform. The new formal order does not mean the end of informal adoption practices, but that new structures and regulations have been established.

Orphanages were and continue to be one of the most effective showpieces of the modern state. In the Islamic world today, orphanages are of three general types: those opened and run by the state, those run by religious foundations (which is the usual case among minorities), and those run and supported by individuals or as a communal activity. In all three the modern state enjoys supervisory and often decision-making responsibilities.

In Egypt, orphans are normally categorized according to age, nasab, and how they are found. Thus if a lost child is old enough to know his name, he is categorized as a lost child and not as an orphan, even though he is sent to an orphanage. Such a child cannot be adopted since the parents are presumed to be in search of that child. Even after all possible hope of finding the parents is gone, these children are still kept in orphanages. Given the widespread abandonment of children in Egypt's cities due to urbanization, poverty, and homelessness, the majority of children found in orphanages are of this type, a situation perhaps not surprising. Frequent articles in Egyptian newspapers discuss the large numbers of abandoned children in Cairo and give estimates in the tens of thousands. Many of these children form a beggar population or become a security hazard, and often end up in "state reformatories until they [reach] age eighteen." [66]

Interestingly, orphanages often act as social relief for poor families. Such children left in orphanages may know who their parents are, but often the parents are in prison, or have a job or family situation that makes it impossible for them to take care of the child. In the latter case, the family usually consists of a mother who has no one to take care of her child, or who remarried and was not allowed by her second husband to keep the child with her. In such cases, even though it may not be officially allowed, the mother visits her child regularly, and the orphanage staff simply pretends not to notice.

The other two types of orphans are allowed to be "adopted." These include those that are lost or abandoned very young and therefore do not know their names, and those who are newborn foundlings abandoned at the doors of mosques, churches, police stations, hospitals, or even in the streets. These foundlings are considered illegitimate children abandoned soon after birth because their presence could not be hidden from the family or neighbors, and such an illegitimacy would give the mother the status of a *zaniya*. Although zina is practically speaking no longer treated as a crime as it was in the past, the social disgrace to the individual and the family, as well as the unwed mother's fear for her life from disgruntled fathers, brothers, and male cousins, forces the mother to abandon her child. Besides, illegitimate children themselves are regarded as a real stigma, almost a threat, a source of evil.

Despite the new rules and regulations various informal forms of adoption take place. A common example is when someone finds a grown child, informs the police, and then takes the child to live in his home, or as is often the case with newly born abandoned children, someone takes the child home and raises it within the family without informing the authorities. Often orphans and abandoned children are taken in by their neighbors or by the individuals for which their father or mother worked. Quite often no police record is kept for such children. Such incidents are quite common, particularly in the more populous quarters of cities.

In the countryside this is much less the case, for any pregnancy becomes known more quickly. A pregnant woman may go to the city to bear her child;

then the child may be abandoned if the woman cannot find a man who will give her *satr* (hide dishonor). However, even in the countryside there are ways of handling this type of situation. In a short story in Alifa Rifaat's *A View from a Minaret,* a peasant mother sends the father off to work in an Arab country. After the farewells, she turns to her teenage pregnant daughter and orders her to pack her things so as to travel to her aunt in the city where she is to stay until it is time for her confinement. As she speaks, the mother begins to wind sheets of cloth around her naked body to give it fullness. When the daughter complains that she does not want to leave, the mother concludes, "Isn't it better for your father when he returns to find that he has a son rather than an illegitimate grandson?" So society has developed its own mechanisms to deal with such issues.

In a very popular film based on a novel by Ihsan 'Abdal-Kudoos, *Al-Khat-taya,* a woman has to give up her son, the result of an illegitimate affair with a man who is killed in an accident before he could marry her. After her marriage to another, she manages to adopt the son as though he is a laqit, and she keeps this fact a secret from everyone. But the father, who is quite traditional, never accepts the boy, always considers him a stranger, and is jealous of the mother's affection for him. The story develops very dramatically, showing the ways in which society views the laqit, the contradictions involved in the rational outlook toward his lack of responsibility for his parents' sin and the emotional feelings that cannot differentiate between the laqit and the act that conceived him. Only at the very end, in a scene of high drama, the sin is punished by rejection before all is forgiven and the young man can go on with his life. The frequency and popularity of such films and novels demonstrate how common informal adoption is in Egyptian society despite the official belief that it is haram.

As for legal adoption, the question of inheritance invariably plays an important role. Children whose parents are unknown are allowed out for "adoption" but they retain the name given to them by the police when they are found. Essentially this is the method followed: when a child is found a police record is opened. A name and parentage, names for father, mother, grandparents, place of birth, time of birth, are all made up, usually by the policemen filing the report. The child is registered in the orphanage accordingly. A family name is given to a laqit for functional purposes having to do with statistics of births and deaths, but also for identifying purposes, and to safeguard the child in a society that regards illegitimate children as carrying the evil of their parents.[67]

However, giving the child a name does not give him or her the right to an affiliation with an individual of the same name or to demand a portion of his inheritance. Since numerous court decisions have repeated the official stand on this matter, we must assume that such acts on the part of luqata' are common. In one case the Egyptian court of appeals declared that the existence of a birth certificate was no proof in itself and that "registering the laqit in orphanage records under a certain name and surname does not mean that he is of known nasab." [68]

If a child is "adopted" the new parents have to accept the status as guardians only, and that is achieved through a court order. The child retains his own name so there is no confusion with the adopting parents' heirs or concern that the "adopted" may lay future claim on property or other rights that do not belong to him or her.

Changing the name of the child is a complicated matter. In Egypt, for example, first the permission of the Ministry of Social Affairs must be obtained. In fact it is punishable by law if a person tampers in any way with the name of an "adopted" child without reference to the ministry. Even if approval is granted, or if the child has not been "adopted" through the auspices of an orphanage, the father has to go to court and swear that the child is his physical child and that he is recognizing him, thereby legitimizing him. The same procedure cannot be done by a woman because declaring a laqit a long-lost illegitimate child would have severe social implications for the woman. A zaniya is considered a fallen woman and has no civil rights.

Outwardly it appears that Orthodox Christian Copts have a different system that allows for complete adoption. On closer scrutiny, however, inheritance laws based on the Shari'a continue to set the limits to the relationship. Illegitimate children can be legitimized through the marriage of the parents, or can be recognized by declaration of paternity by the father, which allows the child to gain full rights like children born to married parents. Also a child of unknown parentage can be recognized by declaration as long as proof exists of testimony by the woman who delivered the baby. A mother can thus prove paternity of her child in case of rape or by proving that the father "used authority or deception through promises of marriage." [69]

In the church, adoption is possible for men and women, whether they are married or not, but there are conditions which include a minimum age of forty, that he or she have no children or legitimate offspring at the time of adoption, and that he or she be of good repute. Another interesting divergence from Muslim patterns is that the adoptee need not be a minor; the requirement is that he be at least fifteen years younger than the parent.[70] If the parents of the person being adopted are still alive, then their agreement has to be obtained first. The child can be given the name of the adopting parent, which would be added to his original name.[71] This is contrary to Islamic law, which makes the act of extending the parents' name to the child a sin and forbidden by law.[72] Notwithstanding the differences, the issue of inheritance is the same as for Muslims, since the law does not allow the adopted to inherit from his adoptive parents except through a *wasiya,* or will. Similarly a will is needed for the parent to inherit from his adopted child.[73]

The subject of many cases before the courts is proving paternity, which involves various steps but is basically simple. The person must prove that another is his son or daughter or the son or daughter must prove that another is father or mother. This can be accomplished through a simple declaration of paternity on the basis that there is no reason to make such a declaration if it is not true. For example, in a court decision regarding proof of nasab the Naqd court had the following to say: "It is established in Naqd cases, that nasab is proven by declaration, that being a simple [*mugarad*] declaration of nasab involving a confession of paternity of the boy as a true paternity, that he was begotten of his semen [*ma'uh*]. Such an admission cannot be denied and cannot be revoked under any conditions"[74] whether he is telling a lie or the truth.[75] The most important condition of such a declaration is that the child be of unknown parentage.[76] If there is no declaration of paternity, then items that constitute proof of paternity include a marriage certificate or proof of cohabitation of parents.[77] Even though there is no indication that this was the original intent of the law, the easiness with which the law permits a declaration bestowing legitimacy on a child allows for the extension of social and physical protection for that child. More important, in a society where families live closely together, the "adoptee" can live with the family without any fear of sexual molestation by close "relatives" in the case of a female child, or fear for the female members of society in case the adoptee is a male child. In short, legal protection is extended to both the family and the adoptee once the relationship is clearly defined in accordance to Islamic laws that forbid sexual relations between relatives of the first degree.

Some modern theologians and lawyers consider the treatment of orphans as part of the issue of *kifaya,* or sufficiency for members of the Muslim community as guaranteed by the Quran and Sunna. By *kifaya* is meant "the needs that Islam required for the umma to ensure for each of its citizens."[78] Such connections seem to be the result of socialist ideas rather than actual demands of the Quran. The particular ayas pointed to in this case, Taha 118 and 119, do not use the word *kifaya* and yet they speak to Adam about the world: "It is due you that, in it, you do not go hungry, nor naked, nor thirsty, nor suffer from the sun's heat."[79]

In an interesting argument by socialists, *furud al-kifaya* are taken to permit revolutionary action against the rich: "Concentrating property in the hands of a few in any society—particularly if this society was backward—must multiply the extent of the problem of poverty and make it more complicated. The poor will necessarily be burdened with the severity of poverty and social injustice . . . which would lead to serious and dangerous results."[80] An intriguing quote backs this up: "I am surprised that he who finds no food in his home, can desist from brandishing his sword and attacking the [rich] people."[81] In short, legal interpretations have changed with changing conditions and new ideologies have influenced Islamic concepts and, as interpreted by Muslims, these ideologies have in turn been influenced by Islam.

CONCLUSION

Adoption, like other social institutions, is tied to the social relations of any period. Before Islam, during the Jahiliya period, adoption filled an important function and was thus categorized as officially acceptable and thereby legal. The practice of adoption did not cease after Islam, but the "adopted" individual was forbidden the name of the father who adopted him. Whether this also meant losing legal rights and duties that were attached to a son during the Jahiliya period is not clear and constitutes one of the many questions posed by this study. Other questions that require further research include the different treatment of foster (*rida'a*) children and adopted children in Islam. For although adoption is *not* sanctioned by Islam, fostering *is,* and while foster children are forbidden to marry those with whom they were fostered, adopted children can marry into the family that adopts them. Notwithstanding this difference, both foster children and adopted children have no right of inheritance except as *sadaqa,* or gift. This was encouraged by the Quran particularly when *mawali,* or friends, or wards, were left destitute: "And those sworn to you leave them their share."[82]

Last but not least is the question of mula'ana, the roots of the concept and what it suggests about historical continuity and change. The concept is clearly related to adoption, but has other ramifications in the definition of identity, social acceptance, and responsibility for the other in Islamic society.

NOTES

1. Gertrude Stern, *Marriage in Early Islam* (London: Royal Asiatic Society, 1939), p. 43, discusses the looseness of systems of marriage and divorce in pre-Islamic Arabia. Even though published in 1939, this source continues to be important considering the research involved in this study and the lack of more recent sources on the subject.

2. Marshall Hodgson, *The Venture of Islam: The Classical Age* (Chicago: University of Chicago Press, 1974), p. 154.

3. Avner Giladi, "Some Observations on Infanticide in Medieval Muslim Society," *International Journal of Middle East Studies* 22, 2 (May 1990): 187.

4. Hodgson, *Venture of Islam,* p. 149.

5. Yusuf Ali, *The Holy Quran* (Brentwood, Md.: Amana Corp., 1983), ft. 3672, p. 1103.

6. Hodgson, *Venture of Islam,* p. 151.

7. Mahmood Ibrahim bases the rise of Mecca on the existence of the haram. Since there was no agricultural surplus for exchange, the haram provided a basis for exchange. Mahmood Ibrahim, *Merchant Capital and Islam* (Austin: University of Texas Press, 1990).

8. Ahmad b. Hajar al-Asqalani, *Fath al-Bari bi Sharh Sahih al-Bukhari,* vol. 8 (Cairo: Dar al-Rayan l'il-Turath, 1986), p. 377.

9. Ibid., p. 56.

10. Sheikh Muhammad Mohi el-din al-Aguz, *Al-Mirath al-Adil fi'l-Islam* (Beirut: Mu'asasat al-Ma'arif, 1986), p. 10.

11. Ahmad Nasr al-Gindi, *Mabadi' al-Qada' fi'l-Ahwal al'Shakhsiya,* 3d ed. (Cairo, 1968), p. 270.

12. "Wa ula al-Arham ba'dahum awla bi-ba'd." Surat al-Ma'un 107 : 2 – 3.

13. Imam Malik ab. Anas, *Al-Muwwata'* (al-Muhammadiya, Morocco: Manshurat dar al-Afaq al-Jadida, 1990), p. 76.

14. 'Abdal-Hamid Mahmud Tahmaz, *Al-Ansab wa'l-Awlad* (Damascus: Dar al-Qalam, 1987), p. 16.

15. Al-Asqalani, *Fath al-Bari,* vol. 12, p. 33: "Al-walid li-sahib al-firash hurat kanat aw umma."

16. Quran 14 : 30 – 31.

17. Imam Abu Hamid al-Ghazali, *Adab al-Nikah wa kasr al-Shahwatayn* (Susa, Tunisia: Manshurat Dar al-Ma'arif, 1990), p. 112.

18. Tariq Ismail Kakhia, *Al-Zawaj al-Islami* (Hims, Syria: Mu'asasat al-Zu'bi), p. 59.

19. Imam al-Hafiz Shams al-Din al-Dhahabi, *Al-Kaba'ir* (Alexandria: Maktabat Hamidu, 1987), pp. 42 – 45.

20. Ibn Qiyyam al-Gawziya (H. 691 – 751), *Akhbar al-Nisa'* (Beirut: Manshurat Dar Maktabat al-Hayah, 1988), p. 168.

21. Al-Asqalani, *Fath al-Bari,* vol. 9, p. 369.

22. Ibid., vol. 9, p. 371.

23. Ibid., vol. 12, pp. 32 – 35, and vol. 9, pp. 370 – 371.

24. Ibid., vol. 12, p. 32.

25. Al-Sayyiol Sabiq, *Fiqh al-Sunna* (Beirut: Dar al-Kitab al-'Arabi, 1987), vol. 2, p. 283.

26. Surat al-Ahzab 33 : 4.

27. Al-Asqalani, *Fath al-Bari,* vol. 112, p. 56.

28. Abi Zakariya al-Nawawi al-Dimashqi, *Riyad al-Salihin* (Cairo: Dar al-Turath al-'Arabi, 1983), p. 456. The Imam al-Dimashqi lived in the thirteenth century.

29. Surat al-Ahzab 33 : 37.

30. Robert Roberts, *The Social Laws of the Quran* (London: Curzon Press, 1990) first pub. 1927, p. 51.

31. Al-Asqalani *Fath al-Bari,* vol. 5, pp. 94 – 95.

32. Ibid., p. 96.

33. Ibid., p. 99.

34. Sabiq, *Fiqh al-Sunna,* vol. 3, p. 229.

35. Ibid.

36. Al-Gindi, *Mabadi' al-Qada',* p. 29.

37. Ibid. Reference is to case S11/383, Naqd Court 2/28, 5-5-60.

38. Sabiq, *Fiqh al-Sunna,* pp. 229–230.

39. Surat al-Duha 93 : 9 – 10.

40. Shaykh Hasanein Muhammad Makhluf, *Kalimat al-Quran: Al-Tafsir ws'l-Bayan* (Cairo: Dar al-Ma'arif, 1956), p. 426. Makhluf was the mufti of Egypt during the early fifties.

41. Al-Dimashqi, *Riyad al-Salihin,* p. 98.

42. Al-Asqalani, *Fath al-Bari,* vol. 3, p. 384.

43. Ibid., vol. 10, pp. 450–451.

44. Surat al-Nisa' 4 : 9 – 10.

45. Surat al-Isra' 17 : 34.

46. Ibid.

47. Ibid., 17 : 32.

48. Ibid., 17 : 33.

49. Ibid.

50. Ibid., 17 : 36.

51. Ibid.

52. Ibid., 17 : 37.

53. Surat al-Baqara 2 : 220.

54. Surat al-Nisa' 4 : 2.

55. Maulana Muhammad Ali, *A Manual of Hadith* (London: Curzon Press, 1983), p. 218.

56. Surat al-Nisa' 4 : 3.

57. Ibid., 4 : 6.

58. Ibid., "Wa min kana ghaniyan fliyasta'fi, wa man kan faqiran fliya'kul bi'l-ma'ruf."

59. It is interesting that these issues are not of exclusive interest to the Muslim community, but that in fact they are a cause of great debate among the medieval Jewish community. See S. D. Goitein, *A Mediterranean Society,* vol. 1 (Berkeley: University of California Press, 1971).

60. Ali, *Holy Quran,* p. 179, fts. 510 and 511.

61. Al-Gindi, *Mabadi' al-Qada',* p. 287.

62. Chabrol, "Essai sur les moeurs des habitants modernes de l'Egypte," *Descripton de l'Egypte, etat moderne,* vol. 2 (Paris: L'Imprimérie Royal, 1822), p. 387.

63. S. D. Goitein, *A Mediterranean Society,* vol. 3: The Family (Berkeley: University of California Press, 1978), pp. 302–311.

64. Ibid., p. 304.

65. Sobhi Wahida, *Fi Usul al-Mas'ala al-Misriya* (Cairo: 1950), pp. 88–89.

66. Judith Tucker, *Women in Nineteenth Century Egypt* (Cairo: American University in Cairo Press, 1985), p. 156.

67. Ibid., p. 176. Reference "Personal matters" register 27 p. 592, *ta'n.* This decision was based on Law 23, item 10, for 1912.

68. Ibid., p. 176, referring to a case of *ta'n* register 27 p. 398 for 4-2-1976.

69. 'Abdal-Salam Muqalad, *Ahkam al-Talaq wa'l-Ta'a l'l-Aqbat al-Urthoduqs* (Alexandria: Dar al-Matbu'at al-Gami'iya, 1991), pp. 24–29.

70. Ibid., p. 30.

71. Ibid., p. 31.

72. Mu'awad 'Abdal-Tawab, *Al-Mustahdath fi Qada' al-Ahwal al-Shakhsiya* (Alexandria: Mansha'at al-Ma'arif, 1991), p. 178.

73. Muqalad, *Ahkam al-Talaq,* p. 31.

74. Al-Gindi, *Mabadi' Al-Qada',* p. 37. Case: Naqd 2/43, file 27, p. 594.

75. Ibid., p. 281.

76. Ibid., p. 17.

77. Ibid., p. 25.

78. 'Abd al-Sami' al-Misri, *'Adalat Tawzi' al-Thawra fi'l-Islam* (Cairo: Maktabat Wahba, 1986), p. 7.

79. Surat Taha 20 : 118, 119.

80. Al-Misri, *'Adalat Tawzi' al-Tharwa fi'l-Islam,* p. 68.

81. Ibid., p. 74.

82. "Wa-lathin 'aqadt imanika fa atuhum nbahum."

CHILDREN OF AMMAN:
CHILDHOOD AND CHILD CARE
IN SQUATTER AREAS
OF AMMAN, JORDAN

by Seteney Shami and Lucine Taminian

The experience of childhood is as yet understudied in the Middle East. By focusing upon the social environment of children in a squatter area of Amman, this essay addresses some of the aspects that determine the quality of life for children, particularly the impact of the household and kin-group on the one hand, and the residential community on the other.

Within the household, the position and role of women and their ability to make decisions concerning their childbearing and child-rearing behavior varies in accordance with the household structure and composition. This in turn depends upon the stage of the household in the developmental cycle. The household structure also determines the amount of help upon which a child-bearing woman can depend. The kin-group and community are also a resource in that reciprocal relations between households provide help and information concerning reproduction and child care. Besides this, the community sets the general expectations for behavior, especially as it affects childbearing and child rearing. However, these expectations are articulated differently in individual households. Although differences in income and education do affect child care and may explain some variations, in this community, household and kin-group structure plays the determining role.

THE SETTING OF THE STUDY

The Wadi is a squatter slum area in the heart of Amman. Its inhabitants are mainly Palestinian refugees who, for a variety of reasons, were unable or unwilling to live in refugee camps. The area was first settled after 1948, but more than half the families moved in after 1967. A 1980 survey of the area shows a community composed of 284 households, with the average size of a household being 6.58 and a density of 3.54 persons per room. The average income for the household was 90 Jordan dinars per month, earned by one or possibly two members of the household. (At the time of the research (1985), 1 Jordan dinar equaled approximately 3 U.S. dollars. Since then the dinar has been devalued to equal about 1.4 U.S. dollars.) Work was mostly in small-scale workshops, the construction industry, and low-level government employment (Urban Development Department 1980). Services such as water, electricity, and sewage were extended only gradually into the community after 1969 and the area is still largely dependent upon services provided in the camp by the United Nations Relief and Works Agency, such as schools and clinics. (The UNRWA was created to deal with the Palestinian refugee problem. It administers refugee camps and distributes aid as well as providing primary health care, schooling, and technical training for registered refugees.)

Socially the Wadi is a stable community with a small amount of in- and out-migration (Urban Development Department 1980). The most important networks are based on kinship and extend to the adjacent neighborhoods, into the refugee camp, and beyond. In addition, the Wadi and its inhabitants, similar to squatter areas elsewhere in the world, are fully integrated economically and politically into the urban dynamics of the city (Lomnitz 1977, Perlman 1976, Velez-Ibanez 1983). The network of relationships within the Wadi are thus determined by kinship and secondarily by physical proximity. To a certain extent, the Wadi during the daytime is an extension of the domestic sphere of the courtyard. It is a world of women and children while men spend their days at work and then sit in coffeehouses or shops owned by their friends up on the main street. On Fridays and holidays, men and children stroll in the alleys while women are restricted to their houses.

Physically the Wadi is subdivided into two major parts by the road which bisects it roughly from southeast to northwest. The heavy traffic on the road deters easy communication between the two parts and prevents children from going back and forth. Another defining feature of the settlement is the wide ditch (the seil) that runs through it carrying wastewater from the refugee camp up the hill. Winter rains cause the seil to flood, sometimes forcing the people living alongside it to evacuate their houses for some days. In particularly bad winters, children have been drowned in the seil.

Communal areas consist of a rocky area or a few trees by the seil providing a space for women to sit together over their embroidery. A communal clothesline by the side of the road serves the nearby households. The steep sides of the Wadi and the seil are a favorite playground where the children find wooden boxes, rusty tins, and wires to create toys. The seil is also where wastewater is thrown out, rubbish is burnt, and a few households keep goats and sheep during the daytime.

During our eighteen months of fieldwork in the Wadi we came to know twenty-one households intimately. Of these households, at the beginning of the study, ten were single-family households (SFH: father-mother-children), two were extended-family households (EFH: father-mother-children-parent or sibling(s) of father), seven were multiple-family households (MFH: two or more simple or extended families), and two were what we came to call multiple-household dwellings (MHD) (see Shami and Taminian 1990).

HOUSEHOLDS AND MUTUAL AID UNITS

The authority to make decisions in the household is first of all divided between men and women. The recognized head of the household is the father as long as he is still working and in good health. The working sons, especially those who are married, also have a measure of authority in the household. However, the domain of male authority is that which determines the general contours of the life of the household: the income, the place of residence, the relationship with other heads of households within the kinship group. Within these constraints the women make the intricate decisions: how the income is spent, the living conditions, and the daily interaction with kinsfolk. Thus while men may set the general policy of the family for marriage and childbearing, it is the women who will make such expectations succeed or fail. A father may express the desire to have his son marry his brother's daughter, but it is the mother who will either arrange the marriage or, instead, arrange for the son to marry *her* brother's daughter. As for child care, it is women who decide upon nutrition and general care and treatment for illness. Men's role in child care is restricted to major emergencies and to a few hours in the evening when the children are already fed and are expected to look clean and be obedient.

The authority within the women's domain usually falls to the oldest woman, the mother or the mother-in-law, unless she is too old or inactive; however, other women in the household also have some share in this authority. The older unmarried daughters eventually share in their mother's authority vis-à-vis the other children, even vis-à-vis the father/husband (see Shami 1985). The other contender for authority is the daughter-in-law.

A daughter-in-law gains status and thus authority in the family, and among her husband's kin in general, through the financial resources she controls, the number of her children, and the quality of her relationship with her husband. A woman's financial resources consist of her portion of the bride-price, mostly in the form of gold jewelry or money presented to her by her own family, and especially her brothers, on special occasions, and the spending money given to her by her husband. However, such resources do not always guarantee status. In some cases, especially in MFH, there is pressure on the daughter-in-law to sell her gold to help the family through some crisis or another. In such cases, if her own family do not come to her support, the young wife may find herself quite powerless. Others, with the help of their families, may use their resources to help the husband buy or rent a separate dwelling and thus gain independence from their in-laws.

Most men in the Wadi turn over their entire wages, except for a small amount of "cigarette money," to their wives or to their mothers. This money is an indication of a woman's authority in the household and the measure of her control over it. It also means that it is up to the woman to make the money last the month and to provide for the food, the necessities, and the emergencies.

Running a large household on a small amount of money is a time-consuming and difficult matter. Women in different households have to rely upon each other for help in housework, shopping, and child care; for aid in financial emergencies; and for information on where the cheapest vegetables or the cheapest doctors are to be found. Households that reciprocate daily in such matters may be said to form "mutual aid units." Such units are generally based on kinship, yet they are formed selectively. That is, not all households related by kinship will form one unit. Rather, from all the possible combinations, one or two units will emerge. The prevalent pattern is that units tend to be formed between sisters-in-law, between husband's sister and brother's wife. These mutual aid units are formed and maintained by women, irrespective of the quality of the relationship between the male heads of these households.

Reciprocity within the units flows from women to women and children to children. In addition there are adult-child relations as in child care and in the services that children perform for women, such as shopping and running errands and carrying messages. Thus children play as important a role in the maintenance and perpetuation of these units as the women.

CHILDBEARING

Children are seen as necessary in consolidating a marriage as well as in ensuring the continuity of a family. The general expectations concerning child-bearing are conveyed by the kin group of the husband and of the wife, as well as by the community at large. A woman fulfills these expectations by having four to five children, at least two being males, at a fairly rapid pace. Having thus proven her ability in bearing children through her fertility and general good health, a woman gains security and status in her husband's household.

Factors encouraging continued childbearing vary according to the woman's status in the household. In a single-family household a woman has enough independence to make her own decisions for she can withstand pressure from kin and community. However, in a multifamily household or an extended-family household she has to deal with direct pressure and competition from other members of the household. If her decision-making powers are limited, then she may seek to gain authority within the household by having a large number of children and, at the same time, urge her husband to set up an independent household.

CHILD REARING

In an EFH or MFH, the mother-in-law plays a major role in child care, and especially during the first few years of her daughter-in-law's presence in the household. Since the mother-in-law runs the household and controls the financial resources, she decides on what the children will be fed and how they will be treated for illness and whether a doctor is necessary or not. Much of the conflict between mother- and daughter-in-law stems from the attempts of the latter to make her own decisions concerning her children.

The larger the household the less control a mother has over her children. Even a woman who has authority in the household cannot, and does not, control the behavior of all the members of the household. Thus the older children, the aunts, and the uncles all feed, play with, and discipline the younger members of the household. All members of the household express their opinions on child health and the treatment of illness and all are listened to.

A mother cannot set rules for her children that run contrary to the rhythm of life in the household. Some of the younger women, and especially those with a high level of education (beyond secondary school), do express their dissatisfaction with the behavior of the children in their household and criticize their mother-in-law's lack of discipline. However, they do little to enforce their own ideas. This is true also of daughters-in-law who work outside the household and, by having their own income, are to some measure independent and have authority within the household. However, they cannot afford to be too critical since their living in the same house means that they depend completely on their in-laws for child care.

CASE STUDY: UM FARID AL-SAADI

For two and a half years after her marriage, Um Farid lived with her mother-in-law, a paternal aunt of hers. During that time her mother-in-law was in full charge of running the house. She let Um Farid do the "unimportant" tasks of cleaning and washing. Um Farid did not mind this because she felt that it was her mother-in-law's house in the first place. Um Farid did not want to challenge her authority by interfering or doing the important tasks.

Um Farid believed that her mother-in-law was far more knowledgeable than she in matters concerning child care. So when her first baby was born she let her mother-in-law make all the decisions concerning his health and feeding. Her mother-in-law decided that Um Farid should only breast-feed Farid and give him no supplementary food. Um Farid stopped breast-feeding Farid when she got pregnant again. He was three months old and Um Farid wanted to give him baby milk formula. But her mother-in-law insisted that Farid should have only solid food. When he was sick her mother-in-law treated him by massaging him with olive oil. When he was teething she rubbed his gums with her fingers to make the teeth come out faster, and this caused an infection, but he was not taken to the doctor till his mouth became inflamed. Um Farid never doubted the wisdom of her mother-in-law's knowledge, yet she mentions that Farid was more often sick than any of her later babies, one of whom was born shortly before her mother-in-law's death and two after her death.

Um Farid's mother-in-law's death was sudden and Um Farid found herself in a very difficult situation: she had to run the house, take care of her children, and take care of the visitors who came from outside the country for the funeral and stayed with her for weeks. All of a sudden Um Farid found herself in a position of decision making, a position she had never had before. She believed that she could not run her house nor take care of her children by herself. Her husband was not sympathetic; he always reminded her of his mother's efficiency in running the house.

It was at this time that Um Farid sought the help of her neighbors, and Karima, who was ten at the time, began to help Um Farid with shopping and taking care of the children. Once Um Farid got the help she needed she began to calm down and regain confidence. She rearranged the furniture completely, got rid of her mother-in-law's clothes and bed, and thus gained control of her house. Um Farid's new independence caused great changes in her relationship with her husband's kin group. However, in terms of children she continued to follow her mother-in-law's practices in general. Although she does take the children to the doctor more often, she only does so when they are seriously ill. As the number of Um Farid's children increased, she came to rely more and more upon Karima in all aspects including child care.

YOUNG GIRLS AS CHILD-REARERS

Young girls play a major role in child rearing. This may start at an extremely young age with a four-year-old girl being told to carry her baby sibling and sit with him in the sun. This task is not confined only to little girls, but is part of the role preschool children of both sexes play in these households. Little boys and girls run errands, are sent to borrow money from relatives, and are called in from playing in the street to hold the baby and give it its bottle. Children may also perform these services for neighbors and relatives who live close by.

Once the child enters school his or her tasks decrease somewhat, except for the eldest girl, who will start playing an active role in housework around the age of eight. She will also be left alone in charge of all her brothers and sisters when the mother has to go out. However, the significant role of a girl in child rearing begins at the age of fourteen or so, especially if she leaves school around this age. Thus the extent to which a young girl incorporates housework and child rearing into her life depends on many factors such as her age, her birth order among her siblings, and whether she has left school.

During adolescence, the young girl's chores and errands are transformed into active responsibilities. The eldest daughter assumes these tasks first, unless she is still at school while a younger sister has left school. These tasks include baking bread, preparing certain meals, and the almost daily chore of washing clothes. The mother may gradually hand over these tasks to her daughter completely but often retains control of cooking the main meal, which requires her special touch.

A child born at this time to the mother often becomes this young girl's charge. This is especially true if the mother experiences some kind of crisis at, or soon after, the arrival of the newly born. Elder children are regarded as more valuable than the newly born, whose survival is, after all, still a matter of doubt. A mother's crisis is often the reason to start bottle-feeding the baby and leaving its care to the elder sister.

But even without a crisis, the mother's busy life and daily absences from home (for shopping etc.) are reason enough for the child to be gradually "adopted" by the older sister. A situation may even develop where each one of the adolescent daughters in the household is in charge of a younger sibling. While the eldest sister will eventually be in charge of supervising the meals, baths, and studies of all her younger siblings, her role in child rearing is the total bonding with one infant. The child grows up to call its elder sister "mother," sometimes "my young mother" as opposed to "my old mother." The "young mother" is responsible for feeding, bathing, clothing the child, and even for taking it to the doctor when sick. In addition, the child sleeps next to its young mother at night. The child is later subjected to much teasing and questioning about whom he loves more: his young mother or his old mother. At the same time, the child experiences a great deal more love and care than his old mother alone can afford to give him.

CONCLUSION

The children of the Wadi lead active lives. Since the alleys are too narrow for cars, children are granted a great deal of mobility and even infants crawl in and out of courtyards as they will. Thus children move constantly back and forth between their house and other households in the community. This movement is not random but structured by kinship and mutual-aid relationships maintained by the mother. Children eat, sleep, and play freely in these mutual-aid households and are often given money to go out and buy what they wish from the several small shops scattered throughout the Wadi. Moreover, children accompany their mothers everywhere. Tiny babies are taken to weddings where they are handed from one person to another the whole evening. Whenever a mother leaves the house—whether to do shopping, to go visiting, or to see the doctor—she takes at least one of her children with her as a sign that she is a married woman going on a necessary errand. Unmarried girls will take their younger siblings for much the same reason of chaperoning. Little boys often are conscious of this role and carry it out very seriously.

In this way, the children of the Wadi grow up in a rich and varied environment of social relations. They are full members of the intertwined social units within which they fulfill certain functions. In terms of communications, children are the prime carriers of messages and gossip and have the advantage of providing the adults with the possibility of denial if necessary. They also cement reciprocal obligations since they are the object of requests for help and, when a little older, the providers of help. With these activities, children establish their own relations with other children and with adults outside their immediate family. They also play an important economic role in the home by peddling homemade goods, investigating the best prices in the vegetable market, and enabling the mother to maximize scarce resources (Shami and Taminian 1990).

In addition, children are obviously the means for the reproduction of these social units. Children secure the continuity of marriage and family ties. Through children, mothers obtain security in their youth and status in their prime. Through children, fathers obtain status in their youth and security when elderly. Children are both objects and actors in the complex, and often competitive, relationships embodied in kinship and community. Equally, they are sources of amusement, affection, and pride. Just as the children of the Wadi often hold center stage in the lives of their families, so the centrality of children should be recognized in the ethnographic text.

ACKNOWLEDGMENTS

This study was made possible by a grant from the International Development Research Center of Canada. The anthropological study conducted in 1984–1985 was one component of the Amman Follow-up Health and Population Assessment project, codirected by Dr. Leila Bisharat and Dr. Seteney Shami and conducted under the auspices of the Urban Development Department—Municipality of Amman.

REFERENCES

Laslett, Peter. 1972–1978. *Household and Family in Past Time.* London: Cambridge University Press.

Lomnitz, L. 1977. *Networks and Marginality: Life in a Mexican Shantytown.* New York: Academic Press.

Perlman, J. 1976. *The Myth of Marginality: Urban Poverty and Politics in Rio de Janeiro.* Berkeley: University of California Press.

Shami, Seteney. 1985. "Maternal Practices in Child Care in an Urban Area." A paper presented to the Workshop on Girls in the Middle East and North Africa, UNICEF, Amman (March).

Shami, Seteney, and Lucine Taminian. 1990. "Women's Participation in the Jordanian Labor Force: A Comparison of Urban and Rural Patterns." In S. Shami et al., *Women in Arab Society: Work Patterns and Gender Relations in Egypt, Jordan, and Sudan* (London: Berg/Unesco), pp. 1–86.

Urban Development Department. 1980. *Summary Table of Comprehensive Social-Physical Survey.* Amman.

Velez-Ibanez, Carlos. 1983. *Rituals of Marginality: Politics, Process, and Cultural Change in Urban Central Mexico.* Berkeley: University of California Press.

KUWAITI LULLABIES

Translated and introduced by Farha Ghannam

Lullabies are considered a very basic part of the child socialization process. They are designed to teach children societal norms, values, and traditions. The songs and lullabies that follow were collected in Kuwait and included in a book entitled *Children's Songs in Kuwait* written by Ibrahim al-Farhan (1984). The songs are divided into lullabies that the mother sings to put her baby to bed; songs to transmit to the child some social norms and values, or to teach the child certain actions and skills like standing, walking, talking; and songs that the children (male or female) themselves perform in their games.

LULLABIES

The mother sings these songs to put her child to sleep. She expresses her love and emotion toward her baby and wishes him or her a nice sleep. She does not hesitate to pray and ask God to protect her child.

LU LAH

Lu lah, Lu lah
Sleep nicely on a mattress and carpet
Sleep like deer in the wild
Sleep like your mother did when she was a baby
Sleep. You have a God who never sleeps
By the honor of Moses, Jesus, and the Prophet [Muhammad], peace be
   upon him.

While singing, the mother often expresses fears of her children's possible misbehavior in the future. She complains to her young children that after investing a long time and effort raising the child's brothers, they may not take good care of her in her old age. Still, despite her fears, the mother expresses her deep love for her baby.

I HAVE RAISED YOU, MY CHILDREN

I have raised you my children when you were many and small,
And I fed you the tree's fruit.
Now you have married and burnt my heart with fire:
Seven sons who cannot provide my supper,
The oldest son kicked me out and closed the door behind me,
Yet I love you, the fruit of my valley, and your love is my daily food,
The food of my heart.
I love you, my darling, and hope that anyone who hates you will die.
I hope he will be sick and drink enough saber [1] to send him to his death.
I hope death will come to him unawares.
I love you, sight of my eye, I love and adore you.
My heart is medicine [sa'ut] [2] that will heal you.

The mother also sings to her baby to teach certain actions or skills like standing, walking, talking, and clapping. The mother plays on the rhythm of these songs, to teach the child how to dance. The mother sings to encourage her baby to try his or her first steps. However, the mother starts worrying if her child does not start walking at the right age. She tries to treat this in different ways. One of the traditional cures is to take the baby to neighboring houses and to collect different kinds of food like rice and dates. It is believed that when the child eats this food, he or she will walk. This is the kind of song the mother sings at that time.

GIVE THE CRIPPLE

Give the cripple dinner
So he will come to you walking, walking.

Lullabies are sung to both male and female children. However, daughters have specific lullabies. The mother expresses her emotions and her pride in having female children. She sings about the advantages of having more than one daughter. The latter will not only help in preparing the food, such as grinding the wheat, but she will also help the neighbors and will assist her mother when the family has guests.

DAUGHTER AND DAUGHTER

A daughter and another daughter
Are better than an unemployed son
One daughter grinds wheat with a handmill,
And another daughter helps the neighbors,
And still another daughter says,
Mother, today we have guests.

Lullabies also express some of the community's socioeconomic relations and document part of its history. The following song, for example, not only shows the importance of pearl diving in the community's economy but also reflects part of its social practices and relations, such as having more than one wife, and the conflict that may result between the two wives.

DANCE, DANCER!

Dance, dancer!
Your father went diving,
He'll bring your mother pearls
And your stepmother only a rattle toy.

SONGS OF CHILDREN

Children have their own songs that they perform during their own games and in celebrating certain occasions. These songs may be performed individually and/or collectively. Some songs are exclusively for one gender while others could be performed by both male and female children. Some document part of the past and present the socioeconomic structure of the community, as the following song shows.

MOTHER, STAND UP
AND HAVE A LOOK

Mother stand up!
Have a look there!
See, the sea is rough.
See my father's sail
White as a sheet of paper,
And see the sail of Abu-Ghabour[3]
Black as smoke.

Other songs may describe the division of labor and the activities that are assigned to different gender and age groups. In the following song, the eldest girl of the group performs the mother role and the rest of the girls act as daughters.

MOTHERS AND DAUGHTERS

The mother sings and the daughters answer with *hayya*.[4]

Come on my young daughters
   Hayya
My helper
   Hayya
With the handmill,
   Hayya
That dog your father
   Hayya
Is barking at me
   Hayya
I cried for your aunt [mother's sister]
   Hayya
She did not answer.
   Hayya
I cried for your aunt [father's sister]
   Hayya
She came walking arrogantly,
   Hayya
Wearing a fancy green dress
   Hayya
Oh, bring my horse,
   Hayya
Saddle and bridle it,
   Hayya
Sit in the saddle
   Hayya
And go to Ena'za[5]
   Hayya
To buy a duck
   Hayya
And divide it between the tribes.
   Hayya
I have my own tribe
   Hayya

I count to ten
Hayya
And the one who can *not* count to ten
Hayya
Shall have grief in her heart.
Hayya

Other songs describe other aspects of group life such as the importance of rain. Some record travel to other areas as part of the group's economic need.

MY STEPMOTHER

[The group sings a question and the stepmother answers.]
My stepmother, where is my father?
He went to Basra,
My stepmother, where is my father?
He went to Basra,
What is he going to bring to me?
Decorated paper,
What is he going to bring to me?
Decorated paper,
Where shall I put it?
In my box,
Where shall I put it?
In my box,
[The two parts join in the singing at this point.]
The box has no key,
And the key is with the blacksmith.
The blacksmith wants money,
And the money is with the bride.
And the bride wants children,
And the children want milk.
And the milk is in the cow,
And the cow needs grass.
And the grass needs rain,
And the rain is with God.
There is no God but Allah,
So, fall, rain, fall.
Our house is new,
And our gutter is made of iron.

Part of this song and other songs are performed in different ways in other Arab countries like Jordan and the West Bank.

Children's songs also document certain negative aspects of the relation-ships between the children. Resolving quarrels, which most of the time do end peacefully, often depends upon the skill of one group of children to per-form or sing certain songs, such as the following:

> Night covers the mountains
> We are lions and we are pounding the earth
> If anyone steps on you, step on him, cousin [6]
> Let's defeat their team!

Children's songs also document important occasions in the life of the group: drought, eclipse of the moon, and religious occasions (fasting, feasts, pilgrimage). On some of these occasions, children's songs are essential parts of the rituals performed. For example, during a moon eclipse, folk beliefs state that a big whale swallows the moon. A group of people carrying the Quran walks through the town. The group prays and asks God to liberate the moon from the belly of the whale.

> [The leader sings and the group answers with a refrain.]
>> There is no God but Allah;
>>> There is no God but Allah.
>> Muhammad is God's messenger;
>>> There is no God but Allah.
>> We circulate carrying the Quran;
>>> There is no God but Allah.
>> We seek our Lord's satisfaction;
>>> There is no God but Allah.
>> Our Lord, our Lord,
>>> There is no God but Allah.
>> The one who hears our prayer,
>>> There is no God but Allah.
>> Muhammad is beautiful. He is beautiful!
>>> There is no God but Allah.
>> He was born on a Monday morning
>>> There is no God but Allah.
>> Muhammad is on his carpet
>>> There is no God but Allah.
>> Oh whale, give us back our moon!
>>> There is no God but Allah.

During Ramadan (the fasting month for the Muslims) children also have songs. They feel impatient waiting for the evening prayers that signal the breaking of the fasting day. Some sing to hurry up the Muezzin.[7] When they hear him praying, they run to their houses to enjoy the food that their mothers have prepared. And they sing:

THE MUEZZIN

> Muezzin, hurry up and call the prayer.
> Muezzin, hurry up and call the prayer.
> The fasters are hungry, hungry, hungry,
> Those who are not fasting are full, full, full.
> Call the prayer, oh, Issa!
> They've prepared the food.
> The plates are ready.
> Call the prayer, then, oh, Ismael!

NOTES

1. Saber is a very bitter substance.
2. Sa'ut is a medicine that is sniffed.
3. Abu-Ghabour is derived from dust.
4. *Hayya* means in Arabic "up," "come on," "let's go," "now then."
5. Ena'za is a city in Saudi Arabia.
6. The father's brother's son.
7. The Muezzin is the announcer of the hour of prayer.

CHANGING CHILD-REARING PATTERNS IN AN EGYPTIAN VILLAGE

by Judy H. Brink

For sixteen months during 1983 and 1984 and three months during the summer of 1990 I was a participant observer in a village in Giza that is an hour's drive from the city of Cairo. In this village agricultural land is devoted primarily to cash crops such as dates and citrus. Families depend primarily on the wage labor of men in factories, government employment, and in the booming construction industry. Women no longer work regularly in the fields and most women are either housewives dependent on their husbands' incomes or are employed in traditional village jobs such as seamstress, shopkeeper, or food vender. A very small minority of women are educated and work in modern jobs as secretaries and teachers. I was primarily engaged in observing the effect of education and employment on women's status, but since women are usually in the company of their children, I was constantly observing the interaction of women and their children and I became aware of two distinct styles of child rearing in the village.

Most women in the village live in extended families and expect to maintain intimate ties with their children after they are adults. They expect that their sons will continue to live with them after they marry and that their daughters will marry men who live nearby. Their main concern in training children is to instill in them loyalty to the family and more specifically loyalty to themselves. Family expectations for children are not related to their children's success in school. Most women want their daughters to make a good marriage at an early age and regard education as unnecessary and even dangerous for girls. They train their daughters for their future role by teaching them household skills and ensuring that they have virtuous reputations. They aspire for their sons to have a well-paying job near the village so that they can afford to marry and bring a daughter-in-law and grandchildren into the family. A high school education is considered desirable for boys, but not necessary, as men can make high wages without an education. These women are not concerned with their children's success in school. They raise their children in such a way that insures their children are loyal family members.

The educated women in the village were not typical village women. All of them had a high school or college education and most were born in urban areas and had moved to the village and married village men. Most of the women were employed full-time as teachers in the village's primary school or as secretaries in nearby factories. These women are unusual in that they are the only women in the village who can establish nuclear families at the beginning of their marriages (Brink 1985). They also are unusual in that most of them work full-time at government jobs that provide them with such benefits as health insurance and old-age pensions. Most of these women were not raised in extended families and do not expect that their children will live with them after they marry; therefore they are not primarily concerned with training their children to be loyal to the family. Their major concern is that their children excel in school. They are very ambitious for both their sons and daughters and want their children to go to college and become professionals. They train their children to be more independent at an early age and to be ego-oriented rather than family-oriented. As one mother put it, "It is not good enough for my daughter to get forty-eight or forty-nine out of fifty on an exam; she must get fifty out of fifty."

Most women in the village, who have little or no formal education, have an infant-rearing technique which Levine (1977) terms indulgent. Characteristics of this form of infant rearing are: carrying the child, attending to crying immediately, and nursing on demand. Levine suggests that the indulgent treatment of infants is adaptive and the only way to ensure survival of an infant in a dangerous environment. (In the case of rural Egypt I consider the main dangers to infants disease, especially summer diarrhea, and burning from kerosene stoves that are on the ground and within reach of a crawling or toddling baby.) In large extended families adults and children, who are consistently loving and nurturing, surround infants and engage them in almost constant social interaction. These infants do not have toys to play with and do not form attachments to blankets or dolls as do American infants. They learn to play with people, not inanimate objects.

Weaning ends this wonderful world of indulgence. A new infant typically occupies the mother and weaned children are turned over to child caretakers. As soon as children can walk they join groups of children who play in the street and children no longer spend all their time with the mother. The nurturing style of mothers to children at this stage is similar to what Whiting and Edwards (1988: 142) call "inconsistent nurturance" among mothers in North India. As in India the uneducated mothers "respond intermittently to their children's demands for comfort, care and attention and often only after delays and persistent crying by their infants or children." This type of nurturing reinforces seeking behavior and "encourage[s] an active, insistent, almost aggressive style of dependency" (Whiting and Edwards 1988: 142).

Kuczynski (1984:1063) characterizes the child-rearing style described above as a short-term disciplinary style in which the mother uses power to gain compliance. This type of discipline promotes dependence of children and produces negative verbal reactions such as whining, crying, or tantrums. Although this type of discipline requires less effort and thought, since the child does not internalize norms and simply is forced to comply, this means that the same battles must be fought repeatedly. A typical example of this pattern is a child demanding money from his or her mother to purchase candy. The mother typically responds "No" and the child persists in the request by whining or crying. The mother then reacts by ignoring the request until the child becomes extremely upset. She then either gives the child the money or hits the child to stop the whining or crying. Most mothers are inconsistent, sometimes hitting the child and sometimes giving in, and so the child never knows if demands are going to be met or if he will be punished. Still, since some of the time whining and crying are successful, this encourages the child to continue this strategy.

A typical reaction after the child is punished is to show aggression toward the mother, both physical and verbal. I have seen children hit their mothers, threaten to and actually throw rocks at their mothers. Typically mothers react to the aggression with amusement. The result of this type of discipline style is that mothers are unable to discipline their children effectively and they must rely on the father or an older son to discipline children. The threat of "I will tell your father" is the most effective disciplinary technique these mothers wield. The role of father as disciplinarian is very strongly ingrained in most village families and children fear their father's anger, therefore these threats are usually sufficient to insure good behavior. Egyptian fathers are effective as disciplinarians because, while they are loving and affectionate with infants and very young children, they assume a more stern and authoritative relationship with older children. A man's power and authority in the home are unquestioned by both his wife and children.

I observed a very different style of child rearing when I visited the small number of educated women in the village. Table 1's statistics describe some of the similarities and differences between these two groups of women that I will refer to as educated and uneducated women.

Educated mothers are not quite as indulgent with infants as uneducated mothers. They nurse their children for a shorter time, are less likely to sleep with their children, and are more likely to use cribs, swings, and strollers

TABLE I

Statistical Analysis of Educated and Uneducated Women

Trait	Uneducated	Educated
Number of children wanted	3	2.3
Use birth control	45%	67%
Age at marriage	14.5	21.1
Age at time of interview	33	30
Menopausal or sterilized	10%	1%
Number of living children	4.25	2.7
	range 0 – 10	range 1 – 4
Number of children died or miscarried	1.1	0.3
Total pregnancies	5.35	3
Years married	17	11
Effectively discipline children	26%	71%
Years of breast-feeding	1.9	1.1
Husbands high school or above	28%	93%
Believe girls should be educated	57%	100%
Tolerate aggression from children	67%	0%
Sample size	65	16

rather than carry the infant. There is contradictory evidence about the effect that carrying has on the development of infants. Some research has found that children who are constantly carried score lower on the Bayley Mental and Motor Scale presumably because they do not use their limbs as much as children who are not held (Monroe and Monroe 1984, Sigman et al. 1988). Other researchers, on the other hand, claim that the kinesthetic stimulation (that is, the constant rocking and jiggling that carried children experience) can be associated with more advanced cognitive and motor development in young infants (Yarrow et al. 1977: 551).

Another difference between the educated and uneducated mothers is that uneducated mothers are more likely to use child caretakers. There seems to be agreement in the literature that the use of child caretakers has a profound effect on both the infants and the children who are caring for them. Research indicates that children who have young caretakers perform lower on cognitive tests and that children who act as caretakers become more nurturing and more loyal to the family, have reduced sibling rivalry, and are not as achievement oriented (Werner 1979: 311 – 313, Whiting and Edwards 1988). Given the goals of uneducated mothers, these would all be qualities that uneducated women want to encourage in their children. It seems that using child caretakers is functional for uneducated women.

The most striking result of having older children take care of younger children, at least to an American observer, is the lack of sibling rivalry among these children. Since they are in charge of infants who are very vulnerable, older children, because of rigorous training, do not show jealousy or aggression toward their younger siblings. Even the youngest children will undergo this training as they will likely be called upon to take care of their cousins. The older child becomes more prosocial, cooperative, and responsible by tending children and identifies with the mother as her helpmate instead of identifying with the infant and feeling jealousy. A very common strategy to quiet a disturbed young child is for the mother to pretend to punish the child tender to soothe the feelings of the upset child. For example, if a child falls and cries, his mother may hit the older brother or sister who was tending the child and say angrily, "Why did you let him fall?" This is not real punishment but a sort of game played by the mother and the older child to placate the younger child. In the same way a mother or child tender will pretend to punish a wall, floor, or any object that hurts or frustrates the child, thus assuring the younger children of their mother's love and support. The older child, far from being angry at being made the scapegoat, enjoys the feeling of "being in on the joke" and cooperating with the mother.

There is a danger, however, in this type of behavior. When children are crying and an adult or older child caretaker wants to know why the child is crying, he or she does not say, "What's wrong? Why are you crying?" but, "Who hit you?" The correct response of the adult or child tender then is to hit whoever frustrated the child, be it another child or an inanimate object. Thus children learn very early to relieve any frustration by hitting, therefore the high degree of physical aggression against mothers. The problem comes when children are old enough to hit effectively but are not yet socialized to be nurturing child tenders. Children start being child tenders when they are six or seven. Four-year-olds often want to tend infants but they are not strong enough to carry an infant, often drop the infant, or overstimulate infants who then cry. This exasperates the child who may react by hitting the infant. I knew of one case in which a four-year-old boy hit his younger sister over the head with a stick that resulted in her death. Children of four and five have to be supervised very strictly around infants, as they want to help but are not yet fully socialized to be nurturing and responsible.

As educated mothers do not expect that their children will live with them when they are adults and family loyalty is less important to them than achievement, it seems that the use of child caretakers is less functional for educated women; and in fact none of them regularly used children as babysitters. Educated mothers use a variety of child tenders. Some mothers leave their children with their mother-in-law, some take their children to work with them or leave them in a day-care center at work, and some women leave their children on the weekends. They do not encourage their older children to care for younger children as do uneducated women. They prefer their older children to spend their time quietly playing or studying. Unlike uneducated mothers, educated mothers provide toys for their children. This is significant because the manipulation of toys has been found to be associated with greater psychomotor development (Yarrow et al. 1977: 558–559). It seems that the child-rearing style of educated mothers is also functional given the goals and aspirations that these mothers have for their children.

Another difference between the two groups is that educated mothers do not allow their children to play with other village children, as they feel that these children are a bad influence. This means that children are more often in the company of their mothers and confined within the house. Educated mothers are not "inconsistent nurturers." Their child-rearing style can be characterized as highly verbal, using positive reinforcement to gain children's compliance. According to Kuczynski (1984), this kind of discipline encourages children to internalize norms and values that promote independence. Research has shown that this verbal style of child rearing is associated with cognitive development, as children whose mothers are highly verbal scored higher on the Bayley Mental Scale (Sigman et al. 1988).

At this point I think an anecdote can best characterize the differences between the two mothering styles. An uneducated mother who notices that her toddler has a runny nose would be most likely to grab the child and without saying anything attempt to wipe the child's nose. This usually results in a struggle and the mother either uses physical force to overcome the child's resistance or gives in and lets the child remain dirty. In either case no effort will be made on the mother's part to teach the child to wipe his or her own nose. Educated women in the same situation will say something like "Look at how dirty your face is! Why can't you stay clean? Go over to the table and get a tissue and wipe your nose." The mother will then verbally coach her child until he or she has completed the task.

One of the most striking differences between the two groups of women is that educated women will not tolerate either physical or verbal aggression from their children and will punish children who demonstrate even mild verbal aggression. It was extraordinary how compliant the children of educated women were, especially since they are kept inside all the time and have no opportunity to run and play. Fathers are not symbols of authority in these families, as women are capable of effectively disciplining their children themselves. It is interesting to note that Minturn and Lambert (1964) also found that women who contribute economically to the family were not likely to tolerate aggression of children toward the mother.

These women have a more egalitarian relationship with their husbands than do other women in the village. Most of the educated women met their husbands at their place of work and moved to the village when they married. An authoritarian relationship between husband and wife did not develop because the spouses are close together in age and because they often continue at home the egalitarian relationship that they established at work. The more egalitarian relationship of these couples is demonstrated in several ways, but the most important in this context is that husbands do not believe they have the right to chastise, physically or verbally, their wives as if they were children. In these families husbands and wives are a parenting team who keep a common budget and make financial decisions and decisions about the children jointly. In the uneducated women's families, however, wives and children are both in a subservient position to the father/husband and both are physically and verbally punished by the father/husband (Brink 1985).

McClelland (1976: 352) has found that children with less authoritarian fathers have greater ability to achieve. The more egalitarian relationship between educated spouses means that both parents share in disciplining their children and that the father can be less authoritative. This may help their children to be high achievers in school, a primary goal for these parents.

CONCLUSION

It seems that the child-rearing style of educated women trains their children to think for themselves and not to rely on family members. The expectation is that older children will not do major household chores or child tending but instead concentrate on their studies. These educated couples live in nuclear families and expect that their children will not live with them as adults. They expect that their children, both male and female, will be professionals and that their future success will depend on their level of education. I believe that the pattern of child-rearing traits that educated women use—weaning children early, sleeping in a separate bed, holding infants less, encouraging children to manipulate toys, using a verbal form of discipline that encourages children to internalize norms, allowing the father to be less authoritarian, and encouraging children to be ego-oriented and to concentrate on studies—produces children who have the cognitive and emotional characteristics to fulfill their parents' expectations for achievement.

The child-rearing style of uneducated women that is characterized by a long period of breast feeding, sleeping with the infant and child, constant holding of infants, social interaction instead of playing with toys, a short-term discipline technique that encourages children to be dependent, a more authoritarian father, and training of older children to be nurturing and responsible child tenders produces children who have the cognitive and emotional characteristics to fulfill their parents' expectations that are primarily family oriented.

Uneducated women raise their children to be dependent on the mother and protective and nurturing toward younger siblings in order to produce children whose primary loyalty is to their family. Educated women train their children to be self-motivated achievers. This pattern of encouragement of achievement by educated parents who live in nuclear families was documented in several other developing countries as well (Werner 1979, Clignet 1967, Lloyd 1973).

It is clear to me that these differing child-rearing styles were to some extent a conscious effort on the part of mothers to mold their children. Certainly educated and uneducated mothers were aware of the differences in their child-care styles. Educated mothers tried to minimize their children's exposure to child tenders who used the uneducated style of child rearing even to the point of sending their children to their mothers in the city. They thought it was preferable not to be able to see their children during weekdays than to have their children cared for by their mothers-in-law. It was also clear from comments made by uneducated women that they disapproved of the way educated women were raising their children, especially for not letting them play outside with the neighbor children.

REFERENCES

Brink, Judy H. 1985. *The Effect of Education and Employment on Rural Egyptian Women*. Ph.D. dissertation, University of Pittsburgh; Cambridge, Mass.: University Microfilms.

Clignet, Remi. 1967. "Environmental Change, Types of Descent, and Child Rearing Practices." In H. Miner, ed., *The City in Modern Africa* (New York: Praeger), pp. 257–296.

Kuczynski, Leon. 1984. "Socialization Goals and Mother-Child Interaction: Strategies for Long Term and Short Term Compliance." *Developmental Psychology* 20(6): 1061–1073.

Levine, Robert. 1977. "Child Rearing as Cultural Adaption." In P. Herbert Leiderman, Steven R. Tulkin, and Ann Rosenfeld, eds., *Culture and Infancy Variations in Human Experience* (New York: Academic Press), pp. 15–27.

Lloyd, Barbara B. 1973. "Yoruba Mothers' Reports of Child-rearing: Some Theoretical and Methodological Considerations." In P. Mayer, ed., *Socialization: The Approach from Social Anthropology* (London: Tavistock), pp. 75–107.

McClelland, David C. 1976. *The Achieving Society*. New York: John Wiley and Sons.

Minturn, Leigh, and William W. Lambert. 1964. *Mothers of Six Cultures: Antecedents of Child Rearing*. New York: John Wiley and Sons.

Monroe, Ruth H., and Robert L. Monroe. 1984. "Infant Experience and Childhood Cognition: A Longitudinal Study among the Logoli of Kenya." *Ethos* 12(4): 291–305.

Sigman, Marion, et al. 1988. "Home Interaction and the Development of Embu Toddlers in Kenya." *Child Development* 59: 1251–1261.

Werner, E. E. 1979. *Cross Cultural Child Development: A View from the Planet Earth.* Monterey, Calif.: Brooks Cole.

Whiting, Beatrice, and Carolyn Edwards. 1988. *Children of Different Worlds.* Cambridge: Harvard University Press.

Yarrow, Leon, et al. 1977. "Mother-Infant Interaction and Development in Infancy." In P. Herbert Leiderman, Steven R. Tulkin, and Ann Rosenfeld, eds., *Culture and Infancy Variations in Human Experience* (New York: Academic Press), pp. 539–564.

LOVE CONQUERS ALL?
CHANGING IMAGES OF GENDER
AND RELATIONSHIP IN MOROCCO

by Susan Schaefer Davis and Douglas A. Davis

In the cities and towns of today's Morocco, as in much of the developing world, relations between the sexes appear to be in rapid transition. But from what, and to what? The lives of most Moroccan youth are different in many ways from those of their parents and grandparents. Although the older generations continue to be respected by the young and to have a strong influence on their socialization, things are changing. Two important changes are, first, the influence of peers, primarily through large amounts of time spent together at school, and, second, the exposure of the young to a broader range of experiences and cultural influences than their elders. The area of changing gender relations allows us to examine both kinds of influence and to assess the types and degree of change.

In Zawiya—an Arabic-speaking town of 12,000 where we have been observing and questioning adolescents in recent years—young people are accommodating to imported images of gender and love, and seeking to reconcile these with their still-strong sense of themselves as Moroccans and Muslims. These young people have had access to a greater range of experience, and to different representations of relationships, than have their uneducated and monolingual parents. Today's youth of both sexes attend school and often socialize together. Most women are unveiled, and many young women work outside the household. Young people watch daily TV and occasional motion pictures, flirt with each other en route to school, plan liaisons at the edge of town at night, and travel to the cities of Morocco. Increased contact with the other sex and the pervasiveness of imported Egyptian, European, and American images of romantic and sexual relationships in popular music, magazines, and television programs have led young people to expect more choice in marriage partners, more chance to establish relationships with whom they will, more freedom to fall in love.

On the other hand, the socialization of males and females is still remarkably distinct by western standards, and expectations regarding gender relations after marriage are hard to characterize simply as either western or Arab, foreign or traditional. Most households display a strong division of labor by sex: girls typically have a number of daily chores not expected of boys; they start to perform these chores at a younger age and continue for more years than do their brothers. Many more girls attend school than in the past, but almost twice as many boys reach high school, and it is they who are typically relied upon to help support the family by wage labor. Girls are expected to marry, whether educated and working or not. Once a young woman is married, the use of her earning power often becomes a matter for dispute between her marital and birth families. The formal education and the informal influence of modern media are themselves inconsistent in suggesting what these Moroccan youth may expect of future marriage and employment, offering images both of assertively self-promoting and of devotedly caring spouses. Furthermore, the sexes have rather different media preferences, suggesting different models for gender relations. The result is a sharp sexual double standard, and often contradictory male expectations of girlfriend, wife, and mother.

Here we explore both continuity and changes in the gender socialization of the young people of Zawiya. Drawing on our ethnographic observations of a neighborhood in the early eighties, our participation in several families over a period of more than twenty years, and interviews conducted by Susan Schaefer Davis in Zawiya and in Morocco's capital, Rabat, during the past several years, we will construct a picture of changing gender relations in both the semirural and the contemporary urban setting. Finally, we will speculate about future relations between the sexes in Morocco.

THE TOWN

Zawiya is semirural, with ready access to a number of urban amenities such as rail transportation and bureaucratic services. Although some of the most valuable citrus and grain-growing land in Morocco lies at the edge of town, more of the population works in commerce or trades than in agriculture. Zawiya is two kilometers from the provincial capital, a market town of about 50,000, which it now serves as a low-rent suburb. This mix of urban and rural, of marginal wage labor and agriculture, is like that of many towns in northern Morocco. Indeed, by the late eighties, Morocco as a whole was roughly half urban and half rural,[1] so the population studied was not atypical in that sense.

The observations on which we report here come in part from a cross-cultural study of adolescence,[2] in which roughly 150 children and young adults in Zawiya formed the Moroccan sample. These young people belonged to fifty families with modest incomes living in one well-established neighborhood. The general picture of local adolescence gleaned from this study is reported in our book *Adolescence in a Moroccan Town: Making Social Sense* (Davis and Davis 1989). Broadly speaking, several sorts of data shape our present portrayal of changing gender roles. We describe in detail the *influences on* young people suggested by their socialization in the family, their heterosexual friendships, and their experience with the educational system. We also characterize the *feelings of* young people concerning choice of a spouse, the desire to be like parents, and appropriate behavior for females and for males. Finally, Susan's recent interviews with young-adult couples in Zawiya and in Rabat allow us to specify some of the postadolescent possibilities facing young Moroccans.

EDUCATION, GENDER, AND CHANGE

There have been great apparent changes in Moroccan gender relations in the last twenty years. In the past one saw few females on the street, and those one did see typically wore the traditional ankle-length *djellaba*, covered their heads, and veiled their faces. They were usually accompanied by other women or by their children, and they interacted with male shopkeepers and officials with apparent reticence. Urban women seldom dined in restaurants, and almost never did so alone or with female companions. Few women went to the beach, and those who did still wore the djellaba as they supervised the bathing of young children.

Today, the crowds strolling on Rabat's main avenue in the early evening seem to be almost half female, mostly quite young, and most often in western-style clothing. One is hard put to find a veiled woman, and conservatively dressed women with covered heads and arms are often in the company of female friends or family members wearing short skirts or jeans and blouses. Some are walking with young men, or in mixed groups, and a few couples hold hands. At the beach, young people in swimsuits participate in lively mixed-sex volleyball games.

A major source of the increased contact between the sexes has been mass public education, which brings unrelated young men and women together outside the supervision of family. After forty-four years of colonial rule, the French protectorate left behind in 1956 an estimated forty university graduates, all of them male, and only six girls who had graduated from secondary school (Fernea 1989: xix). Morocco rapidly created a public educational system after independence, with most rural classes initially composed mainly of males. Female attendance has increased steadily, however, until now most urban children of both sexes attend primary school. By 1982, 80 percent of urban females between 10 and 14 were literate, compared to 10 percent of urban females over age 40 (Ministere du Plan 1989: 49). In urban areas, primary students were 46 percent female and 54 percent male in the early eighties (Wagner and Spratt 1989: 33).

There is a similar trend in smaller towns. For example, in our Zawiya sample of fifty families, only two of the parental generation (both females) had completed primary school. Yet of 146 youths between ages 9 and 21, 92 percent had attended school at some time and 55 percent were currently enrolled in 1982. Among those of primary school age, 63 percent of the girls and 82 percent of the boys were attending (Davis and Davis 1989: 61–62). It appears that since 1973, parents have at least begun schooling for children of both sexes.

Education increases contact between the sexes in many ways. Most of Morocco's schools are not sex-segregated, and the classroom offers daily opportunity for observation and conversation. Students meet and talk walking to and from school, where they are beyond the scrutiny of both parents and teachers. As schoolgirls have become common, it is more acceptable for all girls to be seen in public. Rather than speculating about the destination of a girl in the street, people assume she is en route to school. Thus there is less social pressure on all families to keep daughters respectably secluded and girls, with freer access to the public domain, have more opportunity to interact with boys. While obvious boy-girl conversations or dating are still disapproved in Zawiya, they are no longer uncommon.[3]

The rapid increase in female participation in schooling in the last generation is associated with a similar interest in white-collar careers, despite the fact that these are at variance with traditional roles for women. From teachers of the opposite sex, both male and female students are likely to learn for the first time ways of relating to an authoritative older person who is not a family member. Females who successfully train for jobs in teaching have substantial autonomy. The role of female teacher is especially important to young women. Many girls look to teaching as a respected, visible female profession, and the possibility of teaching jobs encourages parents to send girls to school, in the hope they will later help support the family. For the few women who actually become teachers, posting to a remote rural or urban school often requires living away from home, and leads to professional and social contact with males.

THE MEDIA

The Moroccan airwaves are now filled with a wide range of images. We asked adolescents about their familiarity with sources of information that might be associated with changed gender roles. These included listening to radio or recorded music, watching television, reading books, attending films, and traveling beyond Zawiya. We asked about specific preferences for Arab or for western programs and music. The range of radio programming is wide in Morocco. Tangier's Medi-Un, for example, is a favorite with the young men of Zawiya. A typical weekend morning's broadcast schedule may include al-Warda al-Jaza'iria or another Middle Eastern Arabic romantic singer, Dolly Parton or another American country-western or rock singer, and a European classical selection. Commentators and news briefs alternate between French and Arabic. More traditional stations broadcast both colloquial Arabic and Berber music. On television, Egyptian romances share the evening schedule with *Dallas,* police dramas, and European musical variety shows. Theaters in the nearby town feature last year's American hits, spaghetti westerns, Hindi romances, and karate films.

While education makes for more contact between males and females, the media play an important role in shaping the expected results of this contact. Marriages in Morocco were traditionally arranged by parents, based more on familial than individual compatibility, and with economic support more important than emotional. Today, after meeting potential spouses in school, young people have more of an idea of what they want in a spouse. This inclination is fed by romantic magazines and especially television programs, many from Egypt. A recurrent theme is the love match opposed by parents, who prefer a rich older man for their daughter; the love match usually triumphs.[4] In terms of media preferences, significantly more girls than boys preferred Arabic entertainment on radio, cassettes, and television. For radio, 83 percent of the girls said they preferred Arabic programs compared to 35 percent of the boys; for cassettes 85 percent of girls and 56 percent of boys preferred Arabic music.

With respect to television, 44 percent of girls and 12 percent of boys said they preferred Arabic programs. While these boys on the average were more educated than girls (and thus more comfortable with non-Arabic languages), these differences seem to us to be due more to gender-specific tastes than to language competence. For example, a young woman described an Arabic television show she had just seen:

> Someone wanted to marry his daughter to a rich man like him, and she talked to him but she did not accept him. She said, "I prefer a modest man," because

she knew someone else she loved in her heart. But she does not love the one her father wanted to marry her to out of greed, because he's rich and can help him if he has a problem. She thought about it and took the ring off and said, "I won't marry him." Her father said, "Why? You must marry him." And she said, "I want to marry the man I love to be happy."

Western programs imported from the United States and France devote a higher proportion of their time to "modern" relationships, and present more extreme violations of traditional sex norms: couples embrace, rather than simply exchanging flirtatious glances, and premarital sexual relations are often implied. Males thus become familiar with more explicit portrayals of sexual behavior than do females. Yet regardless of language or country of origin, much of what adolescents see and listen to deals with romance and couples; regardless of sex, about half of those interviewed said they like both Arab and western programs. Both sexes want to see what is going on all over the world, and the visual character of television makes language differences less important. A majority of both sexes also said they read for pleasure. Reading materials included newspapers, poetry, books rented from teachers, and magazines. Particularly for the girls, the latter were often of the *photo-roman* type: a romantic story in a format like a comic, illustrated with photos and text.

One might conclude that girls' preference for Arabic programming reflects more traditional gender roles; yet the Moroccan Arabic, Egyptian, Lebanese, and Berber songs enjoyed by these teenage girls typically have themes of love and modern interactions of unmarried couples. Although males may spend more time watching couples in western-style relationships, girls probably watch more intently. As one young Zawiya woman said, "Girls today learn a lot from films. They learn how to lead their lives. They show the problems of marriage and divorce and everything in those films. TV explains a lot. TV has made girls aware—boys too, but mainly girls."

The two sexes in Zawiya have a very different exposure to motion pictures. Of girls interviewed in 1982, 80 percent had *never* been to a commercial movie theater, while 40 percent of boys reported going occasionally and another 40 percent said they went weekly or more often. Like television, movies in the nearby town's three theaters offer exposure to a range of cultures. In addition to Egyptian, French, and American films, Italian westerns, Hindi fantasies, and Oriental karate films are popular. Among these, the most important influence on gender relations may be the soft-core European films shown at one of the theaters, portraying interpersonal behavior that is banned on television. The young men who watch these films develop physical expectations—or at least fantasies—that go well beyond traditional Moroccan mores. Males' fantasies of the way western couples behave are shaped by these media images; and what they see of the European and American tourists who crowd the cities and beaches of Morocco during the summer does not disabuse them of the idea that easy sex and casual commitments are the western norm.

Travel is another increasingly important source of exposure to new ideas. These are a quite well-traveled group of young people. Of roughly 100 youths who supplied us with information about travel, 69 percent of girls and 57 percent of boys said they visited large cities, and another quarter of the girls and a third of the boys reported visiting smaller towns or villages. Thus girls as well as boys seem typically to be exposed to the more varied gender roles of the city.

GENDER CONTINUITIES AND CHANGES

Despite the appearance of great change in gender relations, the socialization of males and of females in Zawiya is still remarkably different. Although the content of much of modern Zawiya life has changed, there has been relatively little change in the *degree* of gender-differentiation in the household. Socialization for the two sexes varies greatly in terms of helping in the home, in level of education reached, and in exposure to influences such as music and films. In addition to these influences acting upon them, we have data on how adolescents feel about gender roles, including more or less conscious preferences for each gender role, and whether they reported wanting to be similar to or different from their parents when they have families. Occasional claims to the contrary notwithstanding, young people's feelings about gender roles show evidence of real continuity with the parents' generation.

Perhaps the most striking gender disparity in socialization today is in division of labor in the Zawiya household.[5] Girls, whether in school or not, are expected to carry a full load of chores, including housekeeping, fetching water, running errands, washing clothing, cooking, and caring for siblings. Boys may run a few errands or fetch water, but do much less than their sisters. The only exception is in households without daughters, in which boys do help with cooking and housekeeping. While such families are rare, they illustrate that there is a degree of flexibility in gender roles. Associated with this division of labor is the greater freedom of boys: they have fewer tasks, so their time is more their own, and they spend it unsupervised. Parents determine and enforce these gender roles, seemingly based on their own experience, from a time when girls were more restricted in their movements and did not attend school.

Although girls typically do not complete as many years of school as boys, their career aspirations are quite similar. Of the 102 youths we asked, "What do you hope for in the future?" 47 percent of males and 37 percent of females said they wanted to be teachers, and 20 percent and 16 percent respectively wanted other professional jobs like doctor and engineer. Nonprofessional jobs (such as sales, police) were mentioned by 27 percent of males and 9 percent of females. More females (21 percent) stated general goals such as a good family life or material comfort; this was a rare response for males (2 percent). What is most striking about these interview results is that over half of each sex desired modern professional careers requiring a high level of education, despite the extremely low likelihood that these young people will complete high school. Based on our educational histories from 1982 and subsequent inquiries, the proportion of Zawiya students progressing all the way from primary school through the high school baccalaureate is *under 2 percent*. In the course of the last generation education first emerged as the great hope of Morocco's poor and then came to be seen by many as an additional, poignant evidence of the hopelessness of their situation.

MALE-FEMALE RELATIONS

While most of the about 100 Zawiya youth we asked, "Who should choose the spouse?" answered, "The parents" (64 percent of females and 55 percent of males), about 25 percent of each sex wanted to take part in the decision.[6] The number saying they wanted to be involved increased significantly as youth increased in age and in level of education (Davis 1984).

We got a more specific idea of Zawiya youth's goals for marriage when we asked them to describe the ideal spouse. Most responses of both sexes included general characteristics that could be judged by parents who arrange a marriage, such as that a woman should be beautiful "in body and mind," and that a man should hold a good job. However, 16 percent of males and 33 percent of females gave answers that included the quality of their relationship. This implies both that they should have spent some time together before deciding on marriage and that they desire some emotional rapport. This is obvious in responses like "I have to like her—to agree with her" and "He should be good; he should have a good personality, and we should respect each other and be honest with each other, not insulting each other" (Davis and Davis 1989: 125).

Douglas's conversations with teenage males and young men in Zawiya in 1982 revealed several strikingly contradictory attitudes toward sexual relationships with women. These males fantasized about both romance and sex; they courted girls they met in school and on walks to town; and they tried to involve the girls in sexual intimacy. Yet most young men continued to express a strong preference for marrying a virgin, or at least a woman whose sexual experience had been confined to himself. None questioned the assumption that their own sisters must remain chaste. The images of the wife given in interviews about the ideal spouse often stressed the ideal of beauty, and of forty-four males asked to list the qualities of their ideal wife only a couple mentioned similarity of interests or employment.

Susan asked fifteen young women whom she knew especially well whether they wanted to be like their parents or different when they grew up. While nine of the fifteen said they wanted to be different and only six the same, their answers did not focus on gender roles. Instead, most said they wanted to teach their children better manners, discipline them more, be more open with them, or to have fewer children (two or four, rather than the local average of six). Asked about the ideal parents, a fourteen-year-old girl's response was typical in that it stressed traditional gender roles: "The mother should take care of her children and husband, clean the house, and not fight with the neighbors unless provoked. The father should take care of the children by being a good worker, buying clothes, and also take care of his wife."

Eleven girls and three boys were asked direct questions concerning gender ambivalence. All three males and half of the females said it was better to be a male·in Morocco. Some reasons for the preference of the male role are clear from their responses. For example, Susan asked a young woman in secondary school, "Did it ever happen that you said to yourself, 'If only God had made me a boy, not a girl'?":

> Yes, I do, I say it. But only when I am alone and all that. For example, when I am alone at night, I say, "Look now I am alone. If I were a boy I would be outdoors. I wouldn't be alone, I would be outside with boys having fun. At the movies, taking a walk, and doing anything and coming back and all that." Not like a girl; as soon as it gets dark, she has to get back home and that's it. . . . It is also that the girl does a lot of housework. The boy gets up, has breakfast and leaves. He comes back at lunchtime, has lunch and leaves. He does not care about anything. That is not the case for the girl. She has to do the laundry, sweep the floor, and cook. She gets exhausted by work. (Davis and Davis 1989: 139)

And when a young man of eighteen who left school after four years was asked, "Have you ever said to yourself, 'I wish God had created me a girl'?":

No never. [But] there are girls I hear in the market say, "We wish we were born guys"; and there are a lot of guys who say, "We wish we were girls." A lot of my friends say so.

Why do they think it's better to be female?

Each has his own character. There are those who envy good things. For example, a girl who is very lucky, and who gets married to some rich man who can take care of her abroad. Then they say, "We wish we were girls." Or again, when one sees a girl here in Morocco with her own riches and who has a lot of money, he says, "I wish I were a girl." . . . It's as though they were jealous. (Davis and Davis 1989: 140)

In Morocco today, the household head has a difficult time making ends meet, and some young men may find it enviable that females are not expected to face such problems.[7]

HINTS OF THE FUTURE

Although there are readily apparent changes in gender roles in Morocco today, most relating to less seclusion and restriction of females, these semirural youths are still trying to adhere to most of the traditional gender roles reinforced by such practices as the household division of labor. Among more educated urban couples in which the wife works outside the household, however, we already find striking changes. With an increase in education and jobs for women, we can expect such changes to multiply, and this is one clue to the future of gender relations.

It seems females rather than males are more inclined to desire and pursue different gender roles. The reason for this is clear: with change, females have more to gain, and males more to lose. A more active economic role appears rewarding to most young women, at least in principle. For women employed outside the home, having a husband who will help with some of the "female" labor of cooking, housekeeping, and child care and who will share decisions is highly desirable. Even those who have household help must still coordinate and supervise all these activities.[8] Men, on the other hand, do not want to lose their leisure time, nor their clear role as chief of the household.[9] This disjunction between female and male goals in marriage is probably a strong contributing factor to what seems to be a rising divorce rate. Since many women can now support themselves (though not well; two incomes are often necessary for a middle-class urban life-style), they often choose to escape what they feel are oppressive marriages in which males impose much control and offer little support.[10]

Susan's current research on women's relationships with their friends, family, and husbands around the time of marriage provides a picture of changing gender relations as women enter adulthood. These data include interviews with women in both Zawiya and Rabat, with both career women and house-wives, and with a few husbands in each setting. While the urban career women are different in a number of regards from the women of Zawiya, they do suggest possibilities for the future of Moroccan society.

When asked how their lives had changed after marriage, many women in both settings said they had less freedom and more responsibility. The lack of freedom was often indicated by the husband's control of her activities. A Za-wiya woman who had not been to school was very clear about this:

> My life before marriage was better. There are problems in marriage: "You did this wrong. This is not great. You didn't take good care of the baby." When one was not married, one was quiet—one was quiet. You were just with your family; you did as you pleased. With the husband, you are responsible. When he says, "You must do this," you have to do it. No way. If he says, "Don't go there," you don't go.

A Rabat career woman, with a postgraduate education including training abroad, was one of the few who described a very different relationship with her husband:

> I wanted my husband to be sincere, generous, and love me as I am, not to try to change me, but to take me as I am. Change will come with time. It will come spontaneously, not because he wants it. . . . I never felt that I had to change something to please him.

Beyond the traditional expectation of male control of females, some Zawiya women had more broadly traditional expectations of gender roles. A house-wife with a primary education said:

> Generally speaking, it is the man who works, who goes through hardship and brings money. The woman, I mean, does not have much work to do: she just sits and takes care of her home, just cooking and washing and tidying and all. It is not her duty to work or something. . . . If she is a civil servant she'll work, but if she is not a civil servant she'll be sitting at her place, tidying and cooking and washing and fulfilling orders; what he tells her, she does.
>
> Do you have the right to go wherever you want without your husband stopping you?
>
> I have no right until I tell him. If he permits it I'll go, if he does not, I'll stay.

A difference that seemed more associated with education than with rural or urban residence was whether women expressed a desire for material or for emotional support from their husbands. A supportive emotional relationship seems to be a recent expectation. Responses to the questions "What did you want in a husband?" and "How do you know your husband is a good man?" or "How do you know that he cares about you?" revealed this type of information. One Zawiya housewife who had not been to school was asked how she knew her husband cared for her, and she said: "He just brings things home without telling me. He brings surprise presents even if I don't ask for them. He knows what I need and he gets it, and I don't have to ask."

An uneducated woman born in the country but living in Rabat said: "I wanted my husband to be good with me, to have a good job, a large house, not this house here." Her hope that he would "be good with me" might indicate desire for a good relationship, but what she mentions is material support.

Women who have some education want a man who will meet both material and emotional needs:

> From his warmth I knew that he is good. He buys me clothes, gets me presents. If I want something, he buys it for me. . . . My husband takes good care of me. I mean, we assist each other. He loves me. Does not let anyone be disrespectful to me or anything. I mean, I show my pride in him to my women friends, and he shows his pride in me to his men friends.

Two university-educated working women in Rabat mentioned no material conditions for a good husband, focusing only on the emotional. One said, "I wanted my husband to understand me and respect my opinion, and respect me and love me very much, and thank God I found all this."

Yet a university education did not mean that only emotional support was important. One such woman living near Zawiya said that her main condition for her husband was that he be serious, not a playboy. She went on to say that "after marriage, I knew that he loved me because, for instance, when he went to France he bought me things, many things that I didn't think of, and he bought them for me."

What about the future? Although we see some differences between semi-rural and urban, and less- and more-educated women, just how will new gender roles arise? No Zawiya women explicitly challenged the traditional view of gender roles, but several of the more urban and educated women did. Only one of the Zawiya women was educated beyond high school, so it is difficult to separate the influence of education and location. Women with a primary education or more expressed a desire for emotional as well as financial support. While education seems an important factor in changing women's *desires,* will these changes actually occur? Or will the divorce rate continue to rise instead?

In a new introduction to her influential *Beyond the Veil* (1987), Fatima Mernissi raises several points that should be kept in mind while considering these questions. She is describing the important changes in women's lives since she wrote the book in the seventies. First, she notes that Moroccan women are now designing their futures, instead of passively growing old. She relates this to their growing awareness that their problems are not only emotional and personal but that they also have a more general basis, such as the law (1987: xii–xiii). Second, she ties these changes to education: "Access to education seems to have an immediate, tremendous impact on women's perception of themselves, their reproductive and sexual roles, and their social mobility expectations" (1987: xxv). However, she also reminds us of the "split between what one does and how one speaks about oneself" (1987: ix), noting that the former concerns reality and the latter individual psychology and one's sense of identity. Most of Susan's data from young couples are of the latter type: their statements of desired relationships or qualities in a spouse. Finally, Mernissi relates these points to the policies of groups of Islamic conservatives, noting that many are uncomfortable with women's increasing presence in the public sphere, encouraged by education.[11] She points out that this presence blurs both sex and class privilege: education, literacy, and knowledge were previously the prerogative of well-off males, but state-funded education for all has changed that. She sees the calls of some of these groups for women's return to the domestic sphere partially in this light: once home, they would not be competing for hard-to-find jobs.

A striking instance of questioning the present and planning the future occurred at a 1989 meeting of about 100 Moroccan professional women who were discussing their changing roles. After a speaker had described how hard it was for career women to play both their new career and older housewife roles perfectly, someone in the audience noted that it was possible—and necessary—to socialize the next generation of Moroccan men differently, to teach them more egalitarian expectations and participation.[12]

Carrying this further, an educated career woman in Rabat told Susan her plans for her children, and her basis for expecting them to be effective:

> [Our men] are used to having their mother and sisters do things for them. It is difficult to get them used to understanding that they are the same as you at home, that they have got to help you at home. Things like that are a little difficult. . . . Even if he says, "Yes, yes, you are right," and so on, you feel that still [pause]. These things are well-founded in their heads, and that's not good,

but when you understand that it comes from one's socialization, well, you try to be flexible: sometimes let it pass, sometimes not, sometimes say something or [pause]. You hope that your children won't be like that. You try not to bring up your children like that. But for one who is thirty-five or forty, to change him is difficult. . . .

I can do it with a child through socialization, how you bring them up at home. . . . I think of that a lot because I feel it a lot. For instance, when he becomes able to understand that he and girls are equal, he can do kitchen work, set the table, do his bed, tidy his things. Because if he does it since childhood, it will be normal. But if from his childhood you tell a daughter: "Tidy your brother's things, do that for your brother," he will grow up in that direction.

I am not saying the whole truth here, because I am talking about the family, but at school he does not learn what I tell him. He learns that boys and girls are different. That is a problem, but I'll try to teach him what I can at home, doing it so as not to create a psychological problem and make him unstable. . . .

For example, it's thanks to my mother that [my brother] and I get along well. [He] helps around the house. He does everything, thanks to my mother. When my mother used to send him to [her family] for holidays, he came back awful. "I am macho. I am a man. I am this, I am that." But she would take him in hand and he would get straightened out.

CONCLUSION

Gender roles are changing substantially and rapidly in Morocco today—at least at first glance. Closer examination reveals that the changes are uneven, and occurring at different rates for different groups. Some women, and fewer men, favor more change, more egalitarian roles throughout their marriages. This is especially true of educated women who work outside the home. Others support the status quo; these are mainly men for whom change would decrease privileges.[13] Still other women appear to accept, if not support or question, the traditional gender roles; mainly semirural Zawiya women with little or no education fit here. Yet at nearly all levels we find women wanting a more affective relationship with their husbands.

Both education and the media are important influences on gender roles. First, education places youth in more contact with peers and decreases time spent in multigenerational kin groups. Elders, although still respected, thus have a less central role in the socialization of the young. Education has given younger women new goals, increased mobility, and sometimes new jobs. Modern media make viewers in all parts of the country aware of new forms of relationship, and influence, which affect the aspirations of many, especially for a love match. Yet such matches, and the resulting "companionate marriages," contain many flaws and strains. A recent American study of reasons given for divorce notes that problems include an expectation of intimacy, one which is based on an equality for which the sexes are not socialized (Riessman 1990: 73); similar problems are likely to occur in Morocco. Thus whether these aspirations will be met, or if these young Moroccans are buying a fantasy that is unrealistic, and that many of their European and American counterparts have found reason to question, remains to be seen.

NOTES

1. Morocco's population was 46.6 percent urban and 53.4 percent rural, according to the Profil Démographique du Maroc 1988 – 1992 (Royaume du Maroc 1992).

2. The Harvard Adolescence Project, conducted in 1980 – 1983, included field studies of adolescent samples in Australia (Burbank 1988), Canada (Condon 1987), Kenya, Morocco (Davis and Davis 1989), Nigeria (Hollos and Leis 1989), Rumania, and Thailand.

3. Fatima Mernissi's *Beyond the Veil* (originally published in 1975) analyzes the way Islam enforces sexual control by its use of space. In her introduction to the 1987 edition, she stresses the impact of education for women, which has "destroyed the traditional boundaries and definitions of space and sex roles" (1987: xxviii).

4. In a discussion of interviews with women in Casablanca, Naamane-Guessous found television similarly important, although unlike Zawiya girls, urban young women also have access to movie theaters (1987: 36).

5. In urban, upper middle class families, this difference is diminished, with both sexes concentrating primarily on studies and probably a maid doing the housework. For less affluent urban families, the norm is closer to Zawiya.

6. Naamane-Guessous found that 56 percent of her urban sample would accept arranged marriages, even though they dreamed of an ideal man. Only 25 percent wanted to choose themselves, and all had high school or university educations (1987: 68 – 69).

7. Yet in the eighties, 17 percent of Moroccan households were headed by females (Ministere du Plan 1989: 153), and the number is probably rising.

8. In a comparison of career women with high- and intermediate-level jobs, Aicha Belarbi found that those from the high level were more able to relax after work. The others had relatives as household help and felt obliged to assist them (Belarbi 1988).

9. Many American men have similar attitudes (Hochschild 1989).

10. Noufissa Sbai's best-selling novel *L'enfant endormi* (1987), although fictional, presents several possible scenarios for a Moroccan marriage. One is an educated woman who much prefers to support herself as a teacher rather than live with an uncaring and often abusive husband.

11. There are a variety of Islamic revival groups in Morocco, often centered around universities. Their policies are widely known and their adherents visible, but by no means dominant, in the society.

12. Soumaya Naamane-Guessous, author of *Au-dela de toute pudeur,* was on a panel of three Moroccans and three Americans sponsored by the U.S. Information Service in Rabat. As she spoke, describing how difficult it was to be perfectly dressed and efficient during the business day and then return home to Moroccan expectations of an immaculate house, delicious food, and warm hospitality even at 10 p.m. on a weeknight, there was an increasing murmur in the audience. At first Susan wondered if it might be disapproval, but instead it was affirmation: many women were saying to themselves and to friends, "So that's why I'm so stressed out!"

13. The information on men is more impressionistic, derived mainly from women's comments. Verbally, educated men would probably endorse more egalitarian roles, but educated wives' experience seldom included such behavior.

REFERENCES

Belarbi, Aicha. 1988. "Salariat féminin et division sexuelle du travail dans la famille: Cas de la femme fonctionnaire." In Fatima Mernissi, ed., *Femmes partagées: Famille-travail* (Casablanca: Editions Le Fennec), pp. 79–98.

Burbank, Victoria. 1988. *Three Young Girls.* New Brunswick, N.J.: Rutgers University Press.

Condon, Richard. 1987. *Inuit Youth: Growth and Change in the Canadian Arctic.* New Brunswick, N.J.: Rutgers University Press.

Davis, Susan S. 1984. "Adolescence, Education and Social Relations in Morocco." Paper presented at the Forum on North African Literature and Culture at Temple University, Philadelphia, April 11.

Davis, Susan S., and Douglas A. Davis. 1989. *Adolescence in a Moroccan Town: Making Social Sense.* New Brunswick, N.J.: Rutgers University Press.

Fernea, Elizabeth. 1989. Preface to L. Abouzeid, *The Year of the Elephant: A Moroccan Woman's Journey Toward Independence* (Austin: Center for Middle East Studies, University of Texas).

Hochschild, Arlie, with Anne Machung. 1989. *The Second Shift: Working Parents and the Revolution at Home.* New York: Viking Penguin.

Hollos, Marida, and Philip Leis. 1989. *Becoming Nigerian in Ijo Society.* New Brunswick, N.J.: Rutgers University Press.

Mernissi, Fatima. 1987. *Beyond the Veil: Male-Female Dynamics in Modern Muslim Society.* Rev. ed. Bloomington: Indiana University Press.

Ministere du Plan. 1989. *Femmes et condition féminine au Maroc.* Rabat: Direction de la Statistique, CERED.

Naamane-Guessous, Soumaya. 1987. *Au-dela de toute pudeur: La sexualite féminine au Maroc.* Casablanca: Soden.

Riessman, Catherine Kohler. 1990. *Divorce Talk: Women and Men Make Sense of Personal Relationships.* New Brunswick, N.J.: Rutgers University Press.

Royaume du Maroc. 1992. *Profil Démographique du Maroc 1988–1992.* Rabat: Direction de la Statistique, CERED.

Sbai, Noufissa. 1987. *L'enfant endormi.* Rabat: Edino.

Wagner, Daniel, and Jennifer Spratt. 1989. "Education, Literacy, and the Poor." Washington, D.C.: World Bank.

SUDANESE LULLABIES
AND ADOLESCENT SONGS

Collected and translated by Teirab AshShareef

These texts [1] are selected from the repertoire of the Bani Halba, an African-Arab ethnic group who live in Southern Sudan. They are one of the Baggara (cattle-raising) ethnic groups who inhabit a curvelike belt in southern Darfur and southern Kordofan states. According to the last reliable census of 1955–1956, the population of the Bani Halba was about fifty thousand, in the area southwest of the town of Nyala. They have a subsistence economy, animals (mainly cattle with a few goats), land, and hashab trees, which produce gum Arabic. The animals are privately owned by individual households, but land is communally owned and everybody has equal access to it.

The group has a nomadic sector and a sedentary one. The sedentary sector lives on farming and the nomads migrate southwestward in the harvesting season in search of water and grass for their cattle. They spend winter and summer there and then migrate back to the homeland at the onset of the rainy season. The two main sections of the group are the Awlad Jabir and the Awlad Jubara, each having six main subsections. This structure is hereditary and each individual is a member of a household. A group of households forms both a social and an administrative unit headed by a *sheikh* (plural, *mashay-ikh*). A number of sheikhs forms a larger unit headed by a *'umda*. All the 'umad (plural of 'umda) owe allegiance to a paramount head, the *nazir*. The administration of the group is thus organically linked to its social structure.

The Bani Halba are Muslims. The different facets of their life and culture are those of a nomadic Muslim Arab community. Kinship is an important social institution and their group consciousness and sense of solidarity are very strong. Moral values such as courage, hospitality, respect for neighbors, and the like are highly regarded. The different aspects of their life and culture (which includes poetry) are interdependent, and there is continuous interplay between them.

LULLABIES (MAHOHAT AL-ATFAL)

Lullabies (*mahohat al-Atfal*) are a genre of song sung by mothers while rocking their babies to sleep or trying to stop them from crying. The songs use simple words chosen for their sound quality rather than their meaning; hence the frequent use of alliteration and assonance. Short vowels are lengthened to create the melody to the rocking motion. The stanza form is the couplet, the triplet, or the quatrain.

TEXT I

At the time this text was collected, the poet, Fattuma Ibrahim Abd-al-Rahman, was thirty years of age. She was born and brought up at Tabarro, a village in the same area as Am-Labbasa, the village of her residence to which she moved after she got married to the head ('umda) of Qiyat, a branch of Bani Halba.

> *Huya huya huya huya* [2] Oh doggie
> Oh doggie, let the one who is still a child,
> Oh doggie, let the one who is still a child
> Toddle on his knees.
> *Hiya hiya!* my maternal brother [3]
> I hope he'll be prosperous—
> Oh, I hope he'll be prosperous—
> The pupil of his eye is black.
> May God make it easy for him.
> Oh doggie, let the one who is still a child,
> Let the one who is still a child
> Toddle on his knees.
> *Hiya hiya hiyo!*
> *Hiya hiyo hiya!*
> *Hiyo,* my maternal brother
> I wish you were near me and grown.
> *Hay hiya hiya hiyo!*
> *Hiya hiyo!*
> May God stop you from crying—
> May God stop you from crying,
> And bring you milk to drink.
> *Way!* the puppy has come to us;
> *Way!* the puppy has come to us;
> And drunk our neighbor's milk
> And we were ashamed.

TEXT 2

This lullaby was composed by a thirty-seven-year-old poet, Um-Salama Sabil. She was born and brought up in 'Idd-al-Ghamam, the capital of the homeland. After getting married, she moved to Khartoum to live with her husband, who was a soldier at the time.

> When the butter begins to gather,
> It's small like pebbles;
> When it gathers fully
> It's as big as an ostrich egg!
> O my *karyo*,[4] my churn that shakes well,
> Finish the butter
> For morning has come.
> Come on, sleep!
> The sleep of children,
> If you come by day
> I'll give you thin millet bread.[5]
> If you come by night
> I'll give you a calf.
> If you come in the evening
> I'll give you sour milk.
> Come on, sleep!

ADOLESCENT SONGS

Al-Gideiri (literally, he who is my age) is a genre composed and sung by young adolescent girls. It is performed as part of a dance in which both boys and girls participate. The soloist-chorus reciprocity form is essential in the performance of al-Gideiri and verbal repetition is exploited to the extreme. The subject of this genre is adolescent love, its style is emotive, and it makes ample use of natural imagery and metaphor. The couplet is the typical stanza form. The two songs were composed by Fatme 'Umar, who was thirteen when I collected her oral text. She used to live in the village of Am-Janah. Up until then, she had never traveled anywhere, even within the Bani Halba homeland.

TEXT I

> Singer: He's a summer rain that quenches thirst,
> Chorus: The shy one, the twins' brother.

Singer: He's a summer rain that quenches thirst,
Chorus: The shy one, the twins' brother.
Singer: I yearn for the dark-skinned one, but my luck is so bad,
Chorus: The shy one, the twins' brother.
Singer: I yearn for the dark-skinned one, but my luck is so bad,
Chorus: The shy one, the twins' brother.
(repeated)
Singer: I never realized till now
The pain of separation.
I've shed abundant tears,
Chorus: The shy one, the twins' brother.
Singer: He's a summer rain that quenches thirst,
Chorus: The shy one, the twins' brother.
Singer: I yearn for the dark-skinned one, but my luck is so bad,
Chorus: The shy one, the twins' brother.
(repeated and sung)
Singer: O God, I have just realized the pain of separation,
Chorus: The shy one, the twins' brother.
Singer: He's a summer rain that quenches thirst,
Chorus: The shy one, the twins' brother.
Singer: I yearn for the dark-skinned one, but my luck is so bad,
Chorus: The shy one, the twins' brother.

TEXT 2

Singer: Oh Yahaye, the owner of the kuri[6] cow,
Chorus: My life is a gift to you!
Singer: Oh Yahaye, the owner of the kuri cow,
Chorus: My life is a gift to you!
Singer: Oh Musa, the ounce of gold,
Chorus: My life is a gift to you!
Singer: His teeth are as white as silver,
Chorus: My life is a gift to you!
Singer: His teeth are as white as silver,
Chorus: My life is a gift to you!
Singer: Oh Yahaye, the owner of the kuri cow,
Chorus: My life is a gift to you!
Singer: Oh Yahaye, the owner of the kuri cow.
Chorus: My life is a gift to you!
Singer: His teeth are as white as silver,
Chorus: My life is a gift to you!

Singer: Oh Musa, the ounce of gold,
Chorus: My life is a gift to you!

NOTES

1. These texts were recorded during the fieldwork I conducted in the Sudan in May–June 1974 and March–April 1975. The tapes are deposited in the Folklore Archives of the Institute of African and Asian Studies, University of Khartoum, Sudan.

2. *Huya* is an utterance said to drive away a dog. The poet improvises by playing on vowel length and doubling of consonants to make the utterance sound like an ideophone.

3. The expression "maternal brother" is not used literally in Bani Halba dialect, but as a term of endearment. This may be obvious, since the poet is addressing her child.

4. A karyo is a container traditionally used for keeping cosmetics, but sometimes it is used as a butter churn, filled with milk and shaken for a long time. The metaphors of the pebbles and ostrich eggs refer to the process of forming balls of butter.

5. The Arabic word is *kisre,* a type of thin bread made of sorghum. The word in the lullaby is corrupted a little to suit the rhyme scheme, i.e. *kisar.*

6. Kuri is a type of cow similar to the Texas longhorn and is usually owned by the Fallata, the immigrant Fulani of Nigerian origin. It is unusual for a Bani Halba to own a kuri. The poet wants to emphasize her sweetheart's uniqueness.

TO MY SON MEHMET,
I PRESENT OUR FRUITS

by Bedri Rahmi Eyuboglu
Translated by N. Menemencioglu and Sascha B. Cohen

Here: The flesh of pears, stark naked
No leaves to hide their secret places
No coyness when they give themselves.
Like the laughter of an infant child,
Like the rain,
Their gift is all-complete.
Do not take lightly the lust for fruit
My son, my little bull;
In the paradise of fruits alone
Do lust and light commingle.
Listen to the fruit just plucked from the branch:
The earth still sings within it.
Fountains' cool waters flow in its depths.
Bite into fruits one by one, little bull,
Taste their flesh
And enter thus
The fairest paradise of all.
To my son Mehmet I present our fruits
And to God I pray:
Let fruit trees line up before him all his life;
Before the delight of one is ended
Let the next burst into flame on the branch;
Let his dreams be filled
With cool vineyard mists.
Let throwing stones at the unripe almond

Be his crime.
The stab of bramble thorns
His wound.
The sweet poison of the mulberry
His death.

MY RELIGION SERIES

by M. Yasar Kandemir
Translated by Akilé Gürsoy

This is an excerpt from a series of books designed for Muslim children in Turkey. The stated objective of the series is to educate children aged 6–9 and help them love God, the Prophet Muhammad, and the religion of Islam. It has been prepared, states the editor, "with great care for our children, who are the most valuable people in our society." In 1982 this series was recommended by the Turkish Ministry of Education for first-grade students. In 1983 the series was recommended by the Ministry of Religious Affairs, of the Religious Affairs Supreme Council.

TOWARDS RELIGION
BISMILLAH IRRAHMAN IRRAHIM

(In the name of Allah, the compassionate, the merciful)
LA ILAHE ILLALLAH
(There is no God but Allah)

I asked my father:
—Why can't we see God?
My father replied:
—There are other things that you can't see, Ayse. Think of what they are.
I like to think because I am grown up. I can pick apples from trees. Here is an apple. I can see it and I can touch it because it exists.
Today we received a letter from my elder brother. It's nice that he *thought* of us. Now he is taking a holiday in the village. Right now maybe he is playing with lambs.
I do not see him but I know that he exists.
I never saw my aunt. My mother always tells me about her. She shows me

pictures of her. She tells me what they used to do together when they were little girls. By now I know my aunt very well but I have never seen her.

Now I am walking in the garden amidst flowers and roses. I am filled with joy in the face of such beautiful things. I am very happy.

I cannot see happiness with my eyes but I know it exists.

My father and mother love me very much. When they take me into their arms they tell me of their love for me.

I cannot see this love with my eyes. I cannot touch it. But I know it exists.

A very strong wind began to blow in the afternoon. It raised and lowered the branches of huge trees.

I did not see the wind that bent the trees but I felt its existence.

I told my father all these thoughts. He said,

—Well done, my daughter. When one thinks of it one understands God's existence.

Then he read these words of God from the Quran, which is our sacred book: "Eyes cannot see God but God sees all eyes."

Ayse was on a bus trip. When the bus stopped for rest at the foot of a mountain, Ayse looked up and saw snow on top of the mountain.

—It looks so high, its peak is invisible, she said.

A shepherd was grazing his goats nearby:

—It takes mountain climbers ten days to climb up there, he said.

Ayse thought of how powerful God is.

Ayse was seeing the sea for the first time.

—How big the sea is and what a lot of water it has! she exclaimed.

Then she thought of how great God is.

On a blue summer evening Ayse showed her father a shining star in the sky.

—If I take a plane and fly to that star, how long would it take me to reach it? she asked.

Her father replied,

—If you fly day and night without stopping maybe you could reach it by the time you are a grandmother with silver hair.

How big the sky is, oh my God, thought Ayse.

TEACH YOUR CHILDREN
THE LOVE OF GOD'S MESSENGER

by Muhammad Abdo Yamani
Translated and summarized by Farha Ghannam

Teach your children that the Prophet, may the peace and blessings of God be upon him, is the last messenger and the crowning glory of the chosen Prophets.

Teach them that he, may the peace and blessings of God be upon him, was honest and truthful before he became a Prophet and after his Prophethood was a messenger from God to the whole world.

Teach them that he, may the peace and blessings of God be upon him, fulfilled the promise of Abraham, the prophecy of Moses and Jesus, and was the Imam of all Prophets.

Teach them that he, may the peace and blessings of God be upon him, is the one who believed in God's message, fulfilled his mission, advised the Islamic community, and fought for God until victory.

Teach your children that he, may the peace and blessings of God be upon him, was a human being who had a revelation and is the best model for those who fear and remember God and the day of judgment.

Plant in their hearts the love of the Prophet and of those of his people who are good and pure. Remind them that the Prophet said, "The one who loves me, loves God, and who obeys me, obeys God."

Tell them that the believer does not believe until he loves God and his Prophet above anyone else.

These are words about the life of our lord Muhammad, may the peace and blessings of God be upon him, his people and friends, that I have published

This essay is excerpted from *Teach Your Children the Love of God's Messenger*, by Muhammad Abdo Yamani (Jidda: al-Sharika al-Sandia lil-Abhath wal-Taswiq, 1991).

in different periodicals and then collected in this book. My main intention is to motivate parents to inform the young Muslim generation about the life history of the Prophet so that it will be a lamp to light their way and a model that they follow throughout their lives. He is the best model for this umma community. He was the best model for his friends, may God bless them, and will remain the best model for this umma until the day of judgment.

Wise people see the importance of learning from history to inspire the young generation, to increase their interest in the glorious history of the Islamic umma and to reinforce the ethics and values of Islam.

The Prophet came to life, it is said, kneeling on his hands and knees as if praying to God. Everyone was enlightened by the Prophet's presence when he was a child. He was sent to the desert where he was nursed by a woman from Bani Said where his chest was split.[1] He tasted the bitterness of the orphan twice, first by losing his mother and then his grandfather. He worked as a merchant for Khadija, a lady from the Quraysh, and he treated other merchants in the market honorably. He married Khadija. She preferred him over all the lords of Mecca, and bore him female and male children. During this period, when daughters were hated and buried alive, he welcomed the birth of his daughters with the same love as the birth of his sons.

Our children should know this part of the Prophet's life before the emergence of Islam in order to understand his life after his revelation. Let them know of his isolation to worship God in the cave at Hira. Our children should learn how Gabriel was sent down from God with a revelation to the Prophet to say and repeat the word "read" and then say: "Read in the name of thy Lord and Cherisher, who created all" (Al-'Alaq: 1).[2] Thus our children will conclude that their religion is a religion of science and knowledge, for the opening of the message with the word "read" shows the emphasis in Islam on the strong relationship between religion and science. This relationship reveals that science is the basis of knowledge of God, and the knowledge of God is the basis of all other kinds of knowledge; it strengthens and reinforces faith in the hearts of the believers.

Our children should know that he, may the peace and blessings of God be upon him, was selected from the chosen people and was the last messenger. Our children should listen to the words of the Quran, to the Prophet's traditions, and to everything that has been said about him.

Ibn Abbas said that: "He was a light between the hands of God, the sublime, one thousand years before he created Adam. This light was praised by God and the angels. When God created Adam, he cast that light into his body. God's messenger said, may the peace and blessings of God be upon him: God sent me down to earth through Adam's body and he placed me in Noah's body and cast me into Abraham's heart. God continued to transmit me through honorable hearts and pure bodies until He produced me from two parents that did not meet through fornication."

Our children should learn that the scholars who have studied the history of the Prophet agree that he is a descendant of Ishmael ben Abraham, and thus of men with noble manners, with courage which distinguished them from other chosen people. This will reinforce in our children's hearts the noble lineage of the Prophet and his honorable origin and that he was honest and correct when he said about himself: "I am chosen from the chosen."

Our children should learn the names of his grandfathers: He is Muhammad ben Abd Allah, ben Abd al-Mutaleb, ben Hashim, ben Abd Munaf, ben Qusai, ben Kelab, ben Mura, ben Ka'ib, ben Luai, ben Faher, ben Maleek, ben al-Naader, ben Kinana, ben Kuzima, ben Mudraka, ben Elias, ben Mudar, ben Nizar, ben Mu'd, ben Adnan. The descendants of Ishmael ben Abraham, may the peace and blessings of God be upon them.

His mother, a lady from Bani Zahra, is Amena bent Wahab ben Abd Munaf ben Zahra, ben Kelab, ben Mura, ben Ka'ib, ben Luai, ben Ghaleb, ben Faher. Thus, the Prophet has an honorable descent on both sides.

It is stated that Abu Salamah said that Abu Hurira asked: "God's messenger, when were you granted Prophethood? He (the Prophet) said: "When Adam was between the spirit and the body."

He, may the peace and blessings of God be upon him, also said, "I am a slave of God, and the last messenger. I am part of Adam, the annunciation of my father Abraham, the prophecy of Jesus, the son of Mary."

> His Prophethood preceded when Adam was still clay
> he has glory over all human beings
> Praised be the one who distinguished the Prophet Muhammad
> with virtues that can be followed with no limits.

If our children ask when and how he came to be known as honest and trustworthy, we tell them that he was honest from birth till death. He was also known by his opponents for his honesty and purity.

We have to explain to our children how he, may the peace and blessings of God be upon him, used to cure sick minds with mercy and kindness. We should tell them stories that support this, such as the story of the bedouin who came asking the Prophet for something. After the Prophet gave it, he asked whether it helped. The bedouin answered no, which made the people present angry; they wanted to punish the bedouin. But the Prophet asked them to stop. He went to his house and gave more to the bedouin and then asked him if that was enough, and the bedouin answered yes, and he added, "I hope that God will reward you and your people for that." The Prophet then asked the bedouin to repeat what he said in front of his friends to relieve their anger with him. The bedouin agreed and next day, the Prophet, may the peace and blessings of God be upon him, said that "this bedouin said what he said in front of you, so we gave him more and he claimed that he is satisfied now, is that not true?" The bedouin said, "Yes, I hope that God will reward you and your people for that." The Prophet, may the peace and blessings of God be upon him, said that "this man and I are like a man who has a female camel that ran away. Everybody chased her but all they did was to scare her away. So, the owner asked the people to leave him and his camel, saying that "this is my camel that I know better than you do and I am kinder to her."

Another story is the story of a slave girl whom the Prophet, may the peace and blessings of God be upon him, met while she was crying because she lost the money that her masters gave her to buy flour. The Prophet gave her an equal amount of money but she continued to cry because she was frightened that her masters would beat her. So, the Prophet went with her and talked until her masters forgave her.

He was always kind to children. If one of his grandsons (al-Hassan or al-Hussain) climbed his back while he was on his knees praying, he used to stay in that position for a long time so that he would not disturb the children. He, may the peace and blessings of God be upon him, also used to hurry in prayer if he heard a baby crying so that someone would be available to care for the child.

A man said to him: "Oh messenger of God, I wish to fight [jihad] but I cannot." The Prophet, may the peace and blessings of God be upon him, asked him, "Do you have parents?" and the man answered yes. The Prophet said, "Close to God, if you are kind to your parents you are a haj [pilgrim], you are a mu'tamer [minor haj], and you are a mujahed [fighter]." And on another occasion, he said, "You fight by being kind to your parents."

His mercy, may the peace and blessings of God be upon him, was so wide-spread as to cover animals. He said one should be especially kind to animals because they cannot complain or show pain like human beings. Abd Allah ben Ja'afer said that the Prophet, may the peace and blessings of God be upon him, one day entered an orchard in which a camel stood. The camel began to weep when he saw the Prophet. The Prophet came close to the camel and wiped his tears. Then he asked to see the owner and said, "Fear God in this animal that was given to you by God: the camel told me that you let him starve and forced him to work hard."

Our children should know that the Prophet fulfilled God's message, advised the Umma, and fought for God's religion until victory. Let them listen to you when you tell the story of the greatest and most noble fight of the greatest and the most honorable Prophet and messenger. Let them know how much he suffered while he was trying to call his ignorant tribe to God's religion. They were deeply involved in paganism and could not see the light. Tell them that he, may the peace and blessings of God be upon him, started his mission with kind words. He preached kindly and gently to his people and was not harsh, or arrogant. He did not use the sword even though he and his followers were tortured and oppressed by Quraysh leaders and were forced to move to al-Habasha [Ethiopia] and then to al-Madina. At this point God allowed them to fight as He, be praised, said: "To those against whom war is made, permission is given [to fight] because they are wronged; and verily, Allah is most powerful for their aid" (Al-Hajj: 39). The Prophet moved to al-Madina to destroy paganism. He had to punish the Jewish groups in al-Madina because they betrayed him. Then the Prophet managed to establish the Islamic state and al-Madina, which became the center for the spread of Islam to the whole world. Until the end of his life, he fought to spread and establish Islam through the whole world. Our children should know that God said: "The Prophet is closer to the believers than their own selves" (Al-Ahzab: 6). Our children should also learn the meaning of these verses. Therefore, explain to them how considerate the Prophet was and how much he sacrificed for humanity in general. His main concern was to save all human beings from torture in this world and in the Hereafter. Tell them how the Prophet described his relationship with his tribe: "My relationship with you is like that of a man who started a fire into which butterflies and grasshoppers started falling while the man was trying to drive them away. I am like that man; I try to keep you away from the fire, and you keep slipping from my hands." Let this expressive image settle in the minds of the young generation because it will protect them from corruption and forbid them from doing anything against God's will.

Teach your children the love of God's messenger. Mention to them what the Prophet said: "The one who loves me, loves God, and the one who obeys me, obeys God."

He added that "the one who loves my tradition, loves me, and will be with me in heaven."

The traditions of the Prophet, *hadith,* come after the Quran. The hadith help clarify the Quran, explain the rules and their purposes. Some of the Quran's verses were sent down from God summarized, some general, and some absolute. The Prophet's traditions help explain the exact meaning of the verses. For example, God ordered Muslims to pray and to pay *zakah* [alms or charity]. He also set up some general punishment rules for adultery, robbery, and drinking alcohol. The Prophet's traditions explain the meaning of the prayers, their proper times, and the way the prayers are to be performed. They also clarify specific punishments for different misdeeds.

Teach your children that the Prophet was a human being, but one with a revelation. He was created by God, who was kind, merciful, and considerate with his Prophet. God combined in the Prophet honorable manners and noble qualities. Once a man stood in front of the Prophet; he shook and could not move because of the Prophet's prestige. So the Prophet, may the peace and blessings of God be upon him, said to the man, "Take it easy. I am only the son of a woman who used to eat dried meat in Mecca."

This is God's messenger: moral, modest, kind, full of love for his people. This love made everyone love him and his religion and made even his strong enemies into loyal followers.

Teach your children all this; use the telling of the life history of the Prophet as an occasion to enjoy his memory and reinforce our feelings of the great achievements that have survived for more than 1,400 years, and will continue to serve as a guiding light for the whole world.

Please God, strengthen faith and reinforce in our hearts the love of your messenger, may the peace and blessings of God be upon him.

NOTES

1. This incident refers to a belief that while the Prophet was still young, two angels opened his chest and took out envy and hatred and planted instead kindness and mercy in his heart.

2. Translation of Quranic verses is based on *The Holy Quran: English Translation of the Meanings and Commentary,* revised and edited by the Presidency of Islamic Researchers (Jidda: IFTA, King Fahd Holy Quran Printing Complex, n.d.).

ORPHANAGES IN EGYPT: CONTRADICTION OR AFFIRMATION IN A FAMILY-ORIENTED SOCIETY

by Andrea B. Rugh

This study of orphanages examines the causes of recent growth in the populations of this institution to determine whether such growth signifies a change in the basic structure and role of the family, the actual role of the family vis-à-vis these institutionalized individuals, and how these people are regarded by society generally. The findings are: that these institutions in most instances meet the needs of a small minority of young children whose families have abrogated their responsibilities not willingly but for important reasons; that the growth of such institutions does not necessarily reflect a widespread rejection of familial responsibilities; that institutional growth reflects the changing conditions over the past century that have affected the way the obligations of family life are carried out. Orphanage data indicate that the children are victims of special circumstances in which either no parents were willing to claim the children or the family was broken inadvertently due to factors no longer under anyone's control.

Institutionalized orphans are a category of people that, strictly speaking, should not exist in Arab society if the popular notion is correct that Arab family responsibility is all pervasive. Yet institutions to deal with the problems of orphans do exist and with certain reservations appear to be growing in recent years. Does this phenomenon signify changes in the structure and role of the family? How do these institutions meet social needs and how are they shaped by social perceptions? What is the role of the family with relation to these institutionalized individuals? How are they regarded by society?

This essay is adapted from a longer article on orphanages and homes for the aged originally published in 1981 in *International Journal of Sociology of the Family* 2 (July – December): 203 – 233. Reprinted with permission.

This chapter focuses on institutions for orphans in order to shed light on normal family processes at the present and as they are changing over an extended period of time. The study examines three propositions that suggest the role performed by orphanages in a family-based society:

They meet the needs of a small minority of young children whose families have abrogated their responsibilities for important reasons. The growth of the institutions does not necessarily reflect widespread rejection of familial responsibilities.

The institutions can themselves be consistent with the ideal of family responsibility, providing alternative ways of carrying out that responsibility.

The institutions reflect changing conditions and attitudes toward family life in Egyptian society over the last century.

The propositions are not mutually exclusive, and indeed, they overlap. All three may represent varying degrees of accuracy or misrepresentation. The approach used in this study was both historical—looking at changing patterns over time—and functional—examining the relationship of the institutionalized individual to his or her family and to society.

METHOD

Research for the main body of this study was carried out in the fall and winter of 1980–1981. Altogether eight orphanages were visited and their staffs interviewed. The orphanages included ones sponsored by Christian associations (5), civic associations (2), and international donors (1). In addition, a number of officials from the Ministry of Social Affairs were helpful in providing general information, comments on historical trends and current practices, and contacts with the institutions studied. Finally a number of individuals with frequent and close contact with specific institutions—as church workers, social workers, researchers, ex-clients, and parents of clients—discussed their experiences with these institutions. The method of gathering information[1] for this study varied from participatory experiences in institutions, through examination of files and documents, to formal and informal interviews. Each institution had its own flavor, and in each a different combination of approaches yielded the best results. For the general background of the study, my experiences during five years of continuous work and research in a lower-class Cairo community have been invaluable in providing information on norms and values concerning the orphaned.

FAMILY RESPONSIBILITY FOR THE YOUNG

Institutions for children in Egypt are clearly meant to provide for the unusual circumstance. To put this statement in perspective, it is necessary to know how families, given adequate conditions, typically deal with the problem of loss of parents.

Most Egyptians will say that when a child is orphaned by the death of one or both parents, a relative will step in to take care of and support the child through childhood to maturity. With this statement there is the assumption that two distinctly different kinds of support are required. One is financial assistance, and the second is a support that implies attention to the physical and emotional needs of the person. Even when financial assistance is not required, attentive care is expected. Under normal conditions the larger share of responsibility for financial care is expected to fall on men, the attentive care on women.

In Egypt the legal and financial responsibility for orphaned children falls ideally on a male substitute for the father—a father's brother or a father's father. The attentive care falls ideally to a mother substitute—a mother's mother or a mother's sister. There is a contradiction implied in these arrangements when both parents are missing because responsibilities are placed in two distinct households. As a result, accommodations generally need to be made depending upon the age, sex, and independence of a child, as well as upon the availability of households that are willing to assume the responsibility. Without violating the norm, a child may go to live either with his or her mother's sister or father's brother, whichever is most convenient. If neither is available the child can live with another relative who is. "Normality" as a result has a wide range of possible variations.

THE ORPHAN IN EGYPTIAN SOCIETY

In the sense of "children without relatives who have the obligation to care for them," few orphans exist in Egyptian society. There is almost always some relative who should assume this responsibility, according to the norms of the society. The institutional meaning of the term *orphan* must therefore be given a broader meaning: "children who for one reason or another require substitute care outside of the family."

Who then are these children who require substitute care? The majority of children are in institutions for three reasons: (1) They are the products of illegitimate alliances and are abandoned by the natural parents to avoid public knowledge of the relationship. Children found in the streets as newborns are assumed to occupy this category. (2) They are foundlings who are discovered wandering and abandoned at older than the newborn age. In such cases it is assumed that family poverty or disruption caused the abandonment of the child. (3) They are children whose relatives seek their admission because they are unable or refuse to care for them. Poverty is rarely a sufficient reason for the admission of these children but, when coupled with a crisis of some kind, may necessitate their institutionalization. The immediate crisis may be a death, illness, marriage breakup, or family dispute.

There is an additional reason for placing children in an institution which is frowned upon by authorities but nevertheless continues to exist. This occurs when a parent, either mother or father, wishes to remarry after the death of a spouse and finds it difficult to take children into the new marriage. Children, to large degree, define a family unit, and a new spouse is thought (with some reason) to be reluctant to support a unit that he or she had no part in establishing. In fact, the children of an earlier marriage compete with children of the new marriage for the attention and resources of the common parent. In such cases, children may be sent to a relative to raise, to their mother's mother or sister preferably, since they are the closest equivalents to the mother, or to their father's mother or sister if the remaining parent is the father. When no relative of this kind is available, the children may be admitted to an orphanage. Authorities however are reluctant to care for children whose parents simply want to remarry and cannot afford to keep up two establishments at once.

There may be some overlap in the categories of orphans, because little is known about the background of many of them. But the circumstances of their institutionalization have a great deal to do with how they are later viewed by society. The abandoned, lost, or poor child generally evokes sympathy while the illegitimate child, on the other hand, bears the onus of its parents' misconduct. The public tends to generalize social sanctions to all members of a family where immoral conduct occurs. One of the most serious of these sanctions is the reluctance of outsiders to marry members of a family with known misconduct.

Though pity is evoked in the abstract for abandoned children, there is a wariness of becoming closely involved with them as schoolmates, as neighbors, or as workmates. In such situations the generalized disapproval of illegitimacy carries over to all orphans, whether they come from an illegitimate union or not. The public assumes that authorities hide the true reason for the child's presence in an institution. To a large extent this assumption is borne out by efforts of the authorities to conceal from children of unknown parentage the true reasons for their admission to the institution. Children are usually told, for example, that they are foundlings (not illegitimate) and the circumstances of their admission are not revealed, even when institutional personnel themselves are aware of the actual details and sometimes even speak of these details within hearing range of the children. Facts are also made less painful—by calling orphanages "institutions" *(mu'assaat)* or "associations" *(gam'iyaat)* instead of the precise designation "orphanage" *(malga)*.[2] A law in 1960 (No. 260) which clarified the legal status of foundlings reinforced such evasions by omitting the designation "foundling" on the registration certificate and by allowing spaces which identified parentage to be left blank.

In cases of illegitimacy where the parents are known, legal authorities put the need to preserve the reputation of the natural parents before the need of the child to claim a rightful paternity. The same law of 1960 states that the blanks on the registration certificate might be left empty when parentage is known if: (1) there existed an absolute prohibition against the marriage of the father and mother, (2) the mother was married and her husband was not the father of the child, and (3) the father was married and the child was by a woman who was not his legitimate spouse. Presumably, under these circumstances, when children came of age, they would be unable to inherit their rightful share in their parent's property because they had been denied the legal name of the family. Five years later, in 1965 (Law No. 11), these conditions and stipulations were dropped, but their inclusion for even a short period demonstrates some of the issues that are raised in a society where illegitimate unions carry severe social penalties.

When it comes to contracting marriage, children of known parentage occupy a more secure position. Families traditionally insist on knowing the familial background of those whom their children will marry, particularly when the family is self-sufficient and feels it has something to offer to a marriage partner. Families with less to offer insist on fewer attributes in the mates they seek. The ambiguity for the orphan of known parentage is that she or he comes most commonly from a background of poverty, yet has many of the attributes of middle-class status as a result of educational opportunities and upbringing in the institution. This makes it difficult for such an orphan to find a mate with similar characteristics. Several officials commented that prospective husbands sometimes come to orphanages seeking brides because they know the girls are well trained and because they specifically want to find a mate without the entanglement of close relatives to interfere in the marriage relation. Even if this is true, and it probably is true in a few isolated cases, the man is likely to be one who has been rejected by families before and has few attributes that recommend him as a spouse.

Orphaned boys also have a difficult time. Marriage requires proportionally large outlays of money for all classes, for furnishings, a dwelling, *mahr* (dowry), *shebka* (gold gifts), and the traditional minimum of two celebrations: *katab al kitab* (contract writing) and *farah* (wedding). Though the government makes provision for small lump sums to be given to orphans for the purpose of marriage, it is not enough to attract families with the most suitable brides. In addition male orphans do not have access to the usual "negotiators"—female relatives, who can be relied upon to make suitable choices.

Outside official circles, where statements tend to emphasize the positive side of orphanages and the opportunities for orphans to lead a normal life, comments about orphans are more guarded. The test question is always "Would you let your child marry an orphan?" A sampling of comments demonstrates the gray area in which orphans exist. Several people mentioned, beyond the lack of family connections and the low economic backgrounds, what they perceived as disadvantages in the upbringing of orphans. Orphans, they said, are not "filled up" with the loving care that normal children experience and that is required if they are to become loving and generous persons in their own right. Because they are deprived, orphans always "want and want" for themselves and as a consequence do not make good family members. They also do not command the network of services that are normally provided by relatives or familial support to amass the sums needed to acquire household goods necessary for a secure future. If the orphans have been abandoned by their families, a prospective mate thinks twice before subjecting his future children to a pool of relatives known for abandoning its members. Most observers who spoke with candor agreed that one would marry an orphan only if there were serious limitations on one's own side that made it difficult to contract a more optimum marriage. An example of this kind of limitation is a man who seeks a wife to care for his many children after his first wife has died.

The consequences upon the adult life of children who have been institutionalized are difficult to assess. Institutions do not systematically follow up information on their "graduates." Administrators maintain contact with some of their graduates while others, they say, prefer to conceal their connections with the institution. Administrators therefore can provide individual case stories but are unable to summarize what has happened to graduates as a whole. Though it is clear that orphans in Egyptian society face greater difficulties than normal individuals with fully supportive families behind them, enough success stories of orphans who marry and live relatively normal lives exist to indicate that it is not impossible to overcome most of the problems.

EVOLUTION IN INSTITUTIONAL CARE
FOR ORPHANS

The treatment of orphans in Egyptian society has changed over the last century. E. W. Lane, in his 1860 book, comments on conditions between 1825 and 1849 that might lead a family to seek alternative care for children, stressing the role of poverty coupled with the burden of numerous children:

> Hence, it is not a very rare occurrence in Egypt for children to be publicly carried about for sale, by their mothers or by women employed by their fathers; but this very seldom happens except in cases of great distress. When a mother dies, leaving one or more children unweaned and the father and other surviving relations are so poor as not to be able to procure a nurse, this singular mode of disposing of the child or children is resorted to; or sometimes an infant is laid at the door of a mosque, generally when the congregation is assembled to perform the noon-prayers of Friday; and in this case it usually happens that some member of the congregation, on coming out of the mosque, is moved with pity, and takes it home to rear in his family, not as a slave, but as an adopted child; or if not, it is taken under the care of some person until an adoptive father or mother can be found for it. (Lane 1860: 200)

Children born illegitimately similarly were disposed of by abandonment or left anonymously at the door of a wet nurse (morda'a) who, in the case of an affluent family, might receive a sum for the child's support.[3] As time went on, the community role of such women became semi-institutionalized, first as they became known in their communities as specialists for rearing homeless children and later when they were given governmental subsidies for rearing infants to the age when they could enter institutions. Another alternative for the care of orphans, not reared by their own families, was provided in the homes of the affluent where, for charitable reasons or out of a desire to increase the domestic pool of workers, such children were welcome.

Infertility, and the desire to have many children, have also played an important part in the care of homeless children. Lane implies this when he describes the readiness of people to buy the children offered for sale by their parents. Early laws recognized the demand for newborn infants by clarifying how such children should be disposed of. Law No. 23 in 1912 appears to give a right of eminent domain over children to the women who find them. After presenting the foundling to an omda (mayor) or shaykh in the village or the appropriate office in a city and relating the circumstances of its discovery, the person who found the child might keep it if she is able to demonstrate her moral character and an ability to provide for the infant's expenses. The law of

1912 does not specify what the legal status of the child would be or what happened if the finder did not want the child.

It is possible to imagine the conflicts that might arise from finders' claiming prior rights in children, and indeed, by Law No. 30 in 1946 the provision for private individuals to claim foundlings had been dropped. One assumes that in the absence of other provisions, officials were then given the discretionary power to make decisions about the disposition of children.

It was not until the Law of 1965, modifying previous laws, that the process of handling abandoned children was fully institutionalized. The law stated that "It is incumbent on all persons having found a newborn infant in the cities to bring it immediately to one of the centers or sanctuaries that receive foundlings or to the nearest police post to be committed to these centers or sanctuaries." In villages the omda or shaykh was to receive the child and then as soon as possible commit it to the institution nearest the locality.

The growth of formal institutions, as one would expect, preceded the provisions in the laws that related to them. Part of the impetus given to the institutional movement grew out of a desire to provide a more organized and regularized alternative to the ad hoc arrangements for the care of orphans. There was dissatisfaction with cases in which care was substandard or exploitive of children, as for example in cases of children who were brought up and used for household servants. Most institutions are still sensitive on this point, claiming that they do not let their children out to work in homes when they come of age for employment.

The numerical growth in orphanages dramatically increased starting in the decade of the twenties and gathered momentum in the thirties and forties (see Table 1). By the fifties, the enthusiasm for formal care had peaked, and the number of institutions established in the sixties was half that of each of the two previous decades. Only three additional orphanages were reported in the seventies. However, in the early eighties it was not at all difficult to place a child in an institution, suggesting that the number of institutions combined with other programs was sufficient to meet the existing demand.

Orphanages did not have a consistent early inspiration from any single type of sponsor. Between 1890 and 1919, before the dramatic growth in orphanages, there was a scattering of foreign, Christian, Muslim, and general, unspecified community civic sponsors. It appears that "orphans" as a social category had the power to evoke the sympathetic responses of a broad spectrum of society. Even without a single inspiration for orphanages, it was evident that in specific geographical areas there were certain kinds of sponsors who took the main initiative (see Table 2). For example, there are about half again as many identifiable Christian sponsors as all other kinds in Cairo, where roughly 40 percent of the institutions exist, and in Upper Egypt,

TABLE I

Orphanages by Responsible Organizations and Date of Establishment

	Foreign	Christian	Muslim	General	Total
1890–1899				2	2
1900–1909	1				1
1910–1919		2	1		3
1920–1929	2	6		9	17
1930–1939		9	7	17	33
1940–1949		34	3	12	49
1950–1959	1	23	3	19	46
1960–1969	1	11		10	22
Total	5	85	14	69	173

Source: Compiled from *Guide to Nursery Schools and Orphanages for Socially Vulnerable Children,* 1969–1970, Egyptian Ministry of Social Affairs.

TABLE 2

Orphanages by Geographical Area and Responsible Administrative Organizations

	Foreign	Egyptian Christian	Egyptian Muslim	General	Total
Cairo	3	40	5	20	68
Alexandria	2	4	1	8	15
Delta	0	13	5	24	42
Upper Egypt	0	28	3	17	48
Total	5	85	14	69	173

Source: Compiled from *Guide to Nursery Schools and Orphanages for Socially Vulnerable Children,* 1969–1970, Egyptian Ministry of Social Affairs.

where another 30 percent are located. By contrast, in institutions in Alexandria and the rest of the Delta, where the remaining third of the institutions exist, twice as many sponsors are civic and social welfare organizations without specific religious or expatriate affiliation as any other category. Overall, the Christians with their 85 institutions have played the most significant role in the development of orphanage institutions, a role, one might add, that is all the more significant when one considers the small proportion of the population they comprise.[4] A sense of community is present among Christians that perhaps explains the feeling of responsibility they hold toward each other—

somewhat more tenuous than bonds of family but stronger than bonds of geographical place or nationality.

A clear bias exists toward establishing institutions in urban areas. Close to half of the institutions are found in the two largest cities of Egypt, Cairo and Alexandria. These statistics suggest several factors related to the numbers of orphans: (1) that illegitimacy is easier to conceal in the anonymity of the city, (2) that reliance on a monied economy is more likely to produce support failures in urban settings, and (3) that less reliable safety nets in the guise of extensive kin or community support are found in cities. Some people commented that the social problem of orphans does not exist in rural areas, where the problem of illegitimacy is dealt with drastically and where there are always people who will take care of those orphaned for reasons other than illegitimacy.

By the late sixties, the number of orphanages had stabilized at about the level where it remains today, 176 institutions caring for about 7,000 children. That the number of institutions has remained relatively stable in the last fifteen or so years reflects the growing feeling expressed by Social Affairs officials that institutions have not proven fully satisfactory in integrating children into society or in providing them with a full measure of what they would receive if they lived in a family context. Since the fifties new methods of caring for orphans have been adopted in an attempt to make up for those deficiencies.

The first of the new structures established in the late fifties was the foster families program. Today it handles more than 2,000 children, with another 1,000 who are grown-up and living on their own. The program places children in appropriate homes where they are looked after until they reach adulthood. Foster-care families apply for children to the Ministry of Social Affairs which then checks their credentials to assure that they have sufficient means, the appropriate environment, and knowledge of the upbringing of children to make them satisfactory foster parents. In some cases a sum of from 4 to 2 pounds Egyptian per month[5] is paid to the families; in other cases families provide care without reimbursement. Periodic visits by social workers are intended to ensure that children receive satisfactory care.

The foster family program comes closest to providing a substitute for family living. It falls short however of full adoption that would provide legal rights for children. Full adoption is forbidden by the inheritance provisions of Islam. One administrator explained why adoption was forbidden by saying that "It is against the interests of the larger family to give the family name and a share of the property to someone who is a stranger." The Islamic provisions in this way protect the rights of blood relatives against claims by outsiders.

Since the same inheritance rules bind both Christians and Muslims in Egypt, adoption is equally proscribed in both cases. However, though the laws prevent the full incorporation of a child into a family with all the rights and obligations of family members, there is no objection to (in fact there is approval of) the charitable act of raising an orphaned child without the formalization of adoption.

A child living in a family but still identified as an orphan gains the benefits of family living and support but is not wholly free of the social stigma that can potentially affect his or her relations with other members of society. One social worker described how a number of foster families attempted to solve this problem by trying to conceal the origins of the children. According to her version, prospective foster mothers affected a false pregnancy with the aid of gradually increasing thicknesses of sponge rubber until such time as the baby was "delivered" by ministry officials. Others who acknowledged that this process took place made the point that the ministry did not actively encourage such procedures but most agreed that there would be no objection to cooperating with the fiction. Some officials go as far as to falsify registration papers to make the foster parents appear as the real parents. There are also other ways to overcome problems associated with the prohibition against adoption. The social worker explained that the foster parents can either buy property in the name of the child as a gift or can assign up to 30 percent of their property as a gift to be given to the child after their death. This last procedure makes use of legal provisions in Islamic inheritance laws that are acceptable. Since children eventually must learn of their orphan status when registration papers are not falsified, some foster parents resort to revealing the facts slowly so that by the time the children reach maturity they are aware of it. Other parents, according to the social worker, develop the fiction that the children are the offspring of distant relatives who have died. Though not true, this is considered the most respectable way of explaining a child's presence in a home and provides a vague but acceptable background for the child when it is time for marriage.

Most Egyptian observers interviewed agreed that this approach—falsifying the history—comes closest to solving the problems created by being an orphan, and most applauded the humane way in which such solutions were conceived. The social system in effect creates many of the problems for orphans by imposing such strict sanctions against illegitimacy. No solution is seen as entirely satisfactory for these innocent victims except one that by whatever means available transforms them into what they are not, legitimate members of existing families.

A second alternative to the old-style institutional approach is one that appeared in Egypt only in the last half of the seventies. Its inspiration comes from the international movement of SOS Children's Villages, first founded in Austria. In Egypt there are three such villages: one on the outskirts of Cairo, one in the north at Amiriya near Alexandria, and a third in preparation in Gharbiya governorate at Tanta. The purpose is to create in an institutional surrounding an atmosphere that as much as possible duplicates a family home. In the Cairo SOS village, thirty buildings, created on a family plan of living room, dining area, kitchen, and bedroom, house a "mother" and approximately nine children of varying ages. The children are called a family and address each other as brother and sister. One home is reserved exclusively for Christians, with a Christian mother, and the rest are Muslim homes. The mothers cook for the children and attempt as much as possible to relate to the children as a parent would. They live twenty-four hours a day with the children and when they take time off, an "aunt" comes to take over the responsibilities. Funding for the SOS villages comes mostly from abroad, with a system of foreign sponsors that pairs each child with a foreign "parent."

It is difficult to assess the extent to which SOS villages in Egypt retain the character of their European models or have been modified to suit Egyptian conditions and family patterns. Certainly there is a mix of European standards and expectations together with a way of relating to people that is more typically Egyptian. What is important in the SOS institutions and what differentiates them from the older-style institutions is the emphasis upon family-like care and atmosphere. The illusion created at SOS is perhaps only a degree less deceptive than that created by the foster mother with her false pregnancy. The parallels of rationale and beneficial concern are the same. Both new programs also have in common their admission requirements for children. Because they hope to supplant the real parents in their full functional capacity, the programs require that parents be unknown or that they turn over full legal authority for their children to the program directors. As a result, the children benefiting from these programs tend to be those foundlings, wanderers, and illegitimates whose parents are completely unknown, or they are children whose parents are dead or whose remaining relatives are willing to give them up permanently.

By far the largest group of orphans are still institutionalized in the 176 old-style orphanages. For the most part they include the remainder of the children not suitable for either the SOS villages or for foster parent programs, or they are ones for whom no places are available in the programs. The children in the institutions include those with a single parent still living, those from broken homes, those who are temporarily separated from their parents, or those who were not successfully placed in a foster home and are awaiting reassignment. About 7,000 such children are found in these institutions.

Some of the institutions have admission requirements that allow them to specialize in certain kinds of children. For example, one institution caring for 142 orphans takes only three categories of children: (1) abandoned newborns assumed to be illegitimate, (2) foundlings of unknown parentage below the age of four years, and (3) the children of parents in prison. At the time of our visit approximately half of the children were in each of the first two categories and only one child was in the third. When the institution was founded by a civic association it had been advised by the Ministry of Social Affairs that these were the categories of children most in need of care. Since the parents of the children are mostly unknown it is of course impossible to analyze the reasons for their institutionalization or their relations with their families.

By contrast, a private Christian orphanage with 42 children was more characteristic of the "vested interest" institutions. Since their clients were all required to be Christian,[6] it was necessary to know at least a minimum about their family backgrounds. Table 3 shows some of the relevant information about why children were admitted to the institution. Poverty is clearly a major factor in admission to this orphanage. Examination of the case histories of children in this institution reveals that poverty is a supporting cause in all the cases where enough information is available (38 out of 42 cases). It may sometimes involve the poverty of relatives other than parents who assume the responsibility for the children. The immediate cause for admission varies but in the majority of cases there was a significant crisis in the family which when accompanied by poverty provided sufficient reason for admission. By far the most common immediate cause for admission was the loss of the male wage earner in the family. When this happens it is the rapid deterioration in the financial state of the family that leads to admission.

Who assumes contact with the child, acting as guardian or responsible person in relation to the institution? Out of 42 cases, there were 30 females and 12 males who were listed as assuming the responsibility for the children; of these, 24 women and 8 men were the natural parents. Administrative staff commented also that it was mainly women who visited the children. Table 4 summarizes information on the guardians.

What is noteworthy in the summarized data of Table 4 is that we see none of the neat delineations one might expect if the jural-legal relationship of guardian were vested, according to the norm, in males of the father's family. If we exclude rightful parents, the remaining guardians are divided equally between relatives on the mother's side and those on the father's side, and female guardians outnumber male guardians by a ratio of 3 to 2. It is reasonable to assume that poverty is responsible, in these cases, for upsetting norms and encouraging the ad hoc arrangements that result. Under less stringent economic conditions, one would expect more males to come forward and

TABLE 3

TABLE 3

*Immediate and Supporting Causes for Admission
to One Christian Orphanage*

	No. of Cases	Total of Category
Immediate cause:		
Absence of father only		28
by death	20	
desertion	3	
imprisonment	2	
mental illness	3	
Absence of mother only		5
by death	3	
desertion	1	
mental illness	1	
Absence of both parents		3
by death	3	
Both parents present		6
poverty	5	
incapacity of father	1	
Total	42	42
Supporting cause:		
Poverty	35	35
Remarriage of parent		3
of mother	2	
of father	1	
No relative available		5
when both parents dead	1	
unstated	4	
Total	43*	43*

* One father was both poor and remarrying.
Source: Compilation of institutional files.

assume, if not the day-to-day care of the children in their homes, at least the formal legal responsibility for them. It is possible that at these economic levels, male relatives are reluctant to assume legal responsibility for fear they may also be expected to provide financial assistance which they are unwilling or unable to do. A contributing negative factor is that it is usually unlikely that children of these families would be heirs to property that would provide an incentive to relatives to take a greater interest in them. In a case of a girl in

TABLE 4

Guardians: Their Relationship to Orphan and the Circumstances under Which They Assume Responsibility

Relationship	No. of Cases
Mother	24
Father	8
Father's sister	3
Father's brother	2
Mother's mother	1
Mother's sister	1
Mother's brother	2
Mother's father's brother's daughter	1
Total	42

Circumstance	Relationship of Guardian	No. of Cases
Both parents present	Father	4
	Father's sister	1
	Mother's brother	1
Both parents dead	Father's sister	2
	Mother's sister	1
Father absent	Mother (with support from her brother in 3 cases)	24
	Father's brother	2
	Mother's brother	1
	Mother's mother	1
Mother absent	Father	4
	Mother's father's brother's daughter	1
Total		42

Source: Compilation of institutional files.

one institution who had been given only intermittent attention by her paternal relatives, when she reached the age at which she would inherit a piece of coveted land, her father's brother's son claimed his right of marriage and forcibly carried her off from the institution.

The majority of children institutionalized in the old-style institutions, then, divide themselves for the most part into two main categories, those with unknown parentage and those for whom poverty coupled with some severe crisis in the family precipitates their admission to the institution. In the first instance the children find themselves in the contradictory cross fire of sanctions that rigidly protect the sanctity of the family against the possibly disruptive force of extramarital relations, but which in the process prevent the children of these unions (or ones suspected of being from them) from enjoying the normal family life that is being so drastically protected. In the second instance, we see the disruptive force of poverty on the conduct of normal life and the ability of people to accept the responsibilities dictated by the norms and values in the society.

The evolution in institutional care for orphans shows the concern of authorities for moving ever closer to providing the child with what she or he misses by the absence of family. The effort is one that affirms rather than contradicts the authorities' view of the importance of family in Egypt. Families provide needs that cannot be substituted for simply by food, clothing, education, and supervision, as the authorities have discovered. There are additional indefinable qualitative aspects of family care that include among others emotional support, exchange of services, social status, mutual material help, and a sense of belonging, that institutions have difficulty in providing. Public efforts to solve these problems have gone full circle at present and are back to emphasizing foster families as the closest equivalent to true families, much as in the days of informal foster care that Lane reports.

CONCLUSION

To summarize, let us return to the propositions at the beginning of the essay. As expected many of the propositions require modification or, at the least, explication.

"Institutions meet the needs of a small minority of young children whose families have abrogated their responsibilities for important reasons. The growth of institutions does not necessarily reflect a widespread rejection of familial responsibilities." In general this is a true statement. In almost every case cited where the voluntary initiative of the individual was not the reason for admission to an institution, an element of coercion existed in the circumstances of the individual. Families of institutionalized individuals do not appear to abrogate their responsibilities willingly; they are usually forced by poverty, limited space, distance, social sanctions, the conflict of allegiance to a spouse, inability to provide appropriate care, and other reasons to abandon their obligations. When they command sufficient resources they may seek to pay for substitute care and keep up the personal contact by letters and visits. Even poverty alone is not normally a sufficient reason to abandon family obligations. It is almost always accompanied by a crisis of some kind that forces the making of difficult decisions, one of which may be institutionalization.

"Institutions are consistent with the ideal of family responsibility, providing alternative ways of carrying out that responsibility." This statement is only partially true. Unfortunately, children who see themselves as orphans still feel they are institutionalized as a last resort when other alternatives have failed. Orphans can be seen as a coerced group who would choose to remain out of institutions if they had that option.

"Institutional growth reflects changing conditions and attitudes toward family life in Egypt in the last century." Institutional growth does reflect the changing conditions of life that make it necessary to play out family roles and obligations in modified and often rearranged fashion. However, if these may be called surface rearrangements, then the deep structural principles of family obligation appear through the institutional data to remain intact. The attitude that family as a social institution needs preservation has not changed. Nothing in the history of institution building contradicts this attitude. Institutions developed as a substitute for family, either where family did not exist or where the conditions were not appropriate for families to meet their obligations. In a number of cases it was religious associations that assumed the obligations of family, at the community level; in others it was civic associations. One can say also that homes for orphans helped in large measure to defend the institution of family by easing the social contradictions of illegitimacy. Society has not been ready to drop the sanctions against illegitimacy that protect the unity of the family, and therefore the public conscience has responded with institutions to care for the children that are the products of these unions. Each step of the way, those who build institutions have been trying to discover the most satisfactory substitute for family care when it was missing. That these institutions for orphans are presently encouraging family-based care is indicative of the underlying rationale and the refinements that have taken place over the years. This fact recognizes that no publicly provided service adequately substitutes for the full range of family functions.

The data from the orphanages clearly portray institutionalized children as victims of special circumstances. Family has broken down in their cases but usually inadvertently as a consequence of factors that are no longer under anyone's control. Data from this study reveal new conditions and new ways of responding to both old and new conditions but nowhere is there support for the thesis that family as a social institution has lost its potency in modern Egyptian society.

NOTES

1. I want to acknowledge and thank Ms. Neila Rifat and Mme. Samira Megally for their help in eliciting much of the information for this study.

2. The term *malga* literally means a place of refuge for those who have no one to care for them and no place to go.

3. Elderly respondents noted that these were the procedures they remembered in the early decades of the century.

4. Estimates vary on the number of Christians. The government census of 1976 reported 6.3 percent and church officials maintain that the number is 16 percent of the total population. The most reasonable number probably lies somewhere between.

5. These numbers were quoted in an interview with Ministry of Social Affairs officials.

6. There are laws against the proselytizing of those of other religious background.

BIBLIOGRAPHY

Egyptian Government Publications
  1950. *Social Welfare in Egypt.* Ministry of Social Affairs.
  1969 – 1970. *The Guide to Nursery Schools and Orphanages for Socially Vulnerable Children in the A.R.E.* Ministry of Social Affairs. (In Arabic.)
  1975 – 1976. Ministry of Social Affairs. Public Relations Department.
  1976. *Social Welfare in Egypt.* State Information Service.
  1978. *Annual Report of the Ministry of Social Affairs and Its Districts.* (In Arabic.)
Girguis, M. F. 1978. "The Elderly in a Changing Egyptian Society." M.A. thesis, American University, Cairo.
Lane, E. W. 1860. *An Account of the Manners and Customs of the Modern Egyptians.* London: J. Murray Press, 1860. Reprint, London: Dent & Sons, 1954.
Nyrop, R. F. 1976. *Area Handbook for Egypt.* Washington, D.C.: American University, Foreign Area Studies.

Saudi Arabian family at the Spring, Wadi Musa, Jordan
PHOTO BY HEATHER LOGAN TAYLOR

PART III

CHILDREN'S HEALTH

Your children are yourselves, walking upon the earth.

THE QURAN

The health and well-being of children was one of the primary goals of the Middle Eastern governments which emerged as independent nation-states at the end of the western colonial period in 1962. Although cited as a desirable aim long before the onset of western colonialism in the late eighteenth and early nineteenth century, children's health programs were not widely implemented until recently. But with independence, possibilities seemed to change. Free health care for all, like free compulsory education, was a promise which the new nations' leaders made to their citizens, and serious efforts continue to be made in many countries to abide by that promise. Some oil-wealthy countries, like Libya and Kuwait, fund such care for all citizens even if that care must be paid for as treatment abroad. Other countries, with much fewer resources, and even some oil-producing countries seem unable or unwilling to match these standards.

Dr. Hassan al-Ebraheem, director of the Society for the Advancement of the Arab Child in Kuwait, points out that despite a generation of government health-care programs, a million children in the Arab world die annually of treatable diseases. This, he states, "represents a great loss to the Arab nation," and he suggests that new efforts must be made to target the reasons for this reality and to improve the situation.

The essays in this section address issues of child health in different ways. In a society where children are much loved and are culturally, socially, and religiously valued, parents' sorrow at their failure to thrive would be expected. But there are suggestions that historically, in most areas of the world, high rates of child mortality meant that parents did not invest emotionally in small children, and that they were therefore not much mourned. The poignant "Women's Laments for Children Who Have Died," collected in Egypt by Jamal Zaki ad-Din al-Hajjaji, suggest otherwise, however. Steffan Janson presents a comprehensive account of modern achievements in children's health care in Jordan. The Cairo Family Planning Association report on female circumcision has lead to a concerted Egyptian government effort hardly noticed in the West. The goal has been to eliminate this traditional practice. The report became the basis for the current Egyptian law prohibiting female circumcision.

Homa Hoodfar (Egypt) and Akilé Gürsoy (Turkey) deal with cultural and social factors surrounding issues of child health. "Mothers in their social environment are the single most important agents influencing child care and child health," states Dr. Hoodfar. Professor Gürsoy argues that fathers may be a far more important element in the overall pattern of children's survival, at least in Turkey, than has until now been recognized. She suggests that the constructs of motherhood need to be reassessed. The essays offer diverse views of issues related to child health in a rapidly changing and urbanizing environment.

Young girl, Marrakech, Morocco
PHOTO BY DOROTHY ANDRAKE

Soccer game, Morocco
PHOTO BY DOROTHY ANDRAKE

CHILD CARE AND CHILD HEALTH IN LOW-INCOME NEIGHBORHOODS OF CAIRO

by Homa Hoodfar[1]

Mothers in their social environment are the single most important agents influencing child care and child health. Unfortunately, intervention strategies most often fail to recognize their potential as active participants in health care and relegate them to the role of passive intermediaries. This approach is deeply embedded in the ideology of institutions involved in health promotion, including most notably the modern medical profession. As a consequence of this approach, communication between mothers and these institutions is impeded, when in fact there should be a natural alliance between the two groups. This approach has also retarded the development of ways to expand mothers' knowledge in the area of child care.

Improving cooperation between mothers and health-care institutions requires both a fuller understanding of mothers' perceptions of their reproductive role and child-care responsibilities, and a better knowledge of the extent of resources at their disposal for fulfilling these roles. Childbirth and child-rearing practices are affected by cultural values, class orientation, and availability and accessibility of alternatives.

Therefore, studies on women's perceptions and resources should be designed to target specific social groups, and findings should not be generalized. Instead, they should be viewed as guidelines for the development of more appropriate approaches and communication methods for other target groups.

In the present study I have focused on the perceptions, attitudes, and practices of women as mothers, who as the primary managers of child care ultimately determine the well-being and health status of their children. Accordingly, I have tried to depict the daily child-rearing practices and the factors which affect the quality of these practices in two lower-income neighborhoods of Cairo. I have given particular attention to those aspects which relate to child health. The research was designed to contribute to a better understanding of the problems existing in this field.

THE STUDY

The information presented here was gathered over a two-year period (1983 – 1986) of intensive anthropological fieldwork in the greater Cairo-Giza area. The investigation focused on various aspects of household decision-making processes, money management, housework organization, and other family factors that affect the well-being of children and the position and status of women within the household.[2]

Although the study sample includes more than seventy households, a core group of twenty-one informants was targeted for observation and extensive discussion of child-rearing practices. The informants are mothers, sixteen below thirty years of age and five above, who had at least one child under the age of four at the time the research was conducted. Seven older women from the community provided additional primary information. They play an important role, as actual or adopted grandmothers, in providing support and advice to younger mothers.

The neighborhoods studied are located in a typical newly urbanized area of greater Cairo and are densely populated. Municipal services have not kept pace with the rapid population growth. Few of the houses in the research areas are connected to the city's sewage system. There are no regular waste-disposal facilities and many of the buildings are without running water. All of the buildings, however, have electricity. One of the neighborhoods is within walking distance of a well-equipped public hospital with an out-patient clinic and maternity ward. The other neighborhood has good and accessible health centers. There are vaccination centers established by the Ministry of Health located at a short distance from both neighborhoods. There are also many private physicians and pharmacists in the area who are frequently consulted.

The streets in the interior of the neighborhoods are unpaved and very narrow, and only an occasional car passes. Children of all ages play outside and sometimes women sit in the alley to chat or they perform housework while keeping an eye on their children. Most buildings are as high as five floors and very narrow. The majority of the households live in small two-room apartments which often do not contain a defined kitchen space. Some of these small flats are occupied by two households.

For the most part, the population of these neighborhoods consists of first-

and second-generation rural migrants, many of whom have left their extended kin networks behind. There are also some Cairene families. The vast majority of the households live as nuclear families. There is, however, a preference for establishing residence not far from relatives when possible.

Nine of the households from the core group live independently in self-contained two-room flats. Two of them share kitchen and toilet facilities with other households. Eight households live in one room and share facilities, and two households have larger flats. Fourteen out of twenty-one mothers are housewives. Of the rest, two are unskilled laborers and five hold low-level office jobs in the public sector. At the time the research was concluded, three of these five were on leave without pay so that they could take care of their young children.[3] Their educational levels vary: nine of the mothers are illiterate although they have had a few years of education, three can read and write to some extent, and another three can read and write well. Six of the informants have a high school diploma or the equivalent.

RESOURCES AFFECTING CHILD CARE

Child care is the primary responsibility of every mother, particularly the younger ones. The father's role is minimal, especially for the care of babies. It amounts to occasionally holding the baby after he or she is being fed or bathed. As the child grows older the father begins to show more interest in playing with him or her. But it is the mother who feels accountable to her husband for the children's health and general performance.

Every mother carries out her child-rearing responsibilities by drawing on the various resources at her disposal. Her social environment is the broad framework within which she develops and utilizes these resources. They can be grouped into three categories: personal, material, and social. There is a good deal of overlap and interplay among the three categories.

A woman's personal resources include her knowledge, skills, and experience. Her awareness and self-confidence, as well as her receptiveness to new ways of improving her abilities, affect the quality of her child-care practices. Also important are a woman's attitude toward her own reproductive behavior and the degree of self-fulfillment she feels in bearing children and caring for them.

The material resources available to a mother have a significant influence on child rearing and health. The life-style, medical care, and diet a mother chooses for her household are dictated to a considerable extent by the availability of material means. When a woman earns an income or has access to her husband's wages, there is a noticeable positive effect on her household's diet and medical care. However, if a working woman cannot rely on a strong social network, her income earning activities may interfere with her child-care responsibilities. Inasmuch as a working mother's income is crucial in lower-income households, it is difficult to know whether loss of her financial contribution or less time for child-rearing duties has a more negative effect on the health status of the children and the mother.

Child rearing makes constant demands on women's time, energy, and emotions, a fact all women and most men readily recognize. It is not considered practical for a woman, especially if she is young and inexperienced, to shoulder all of the child-care responsibilities by herself. Therefore mothers develop complex support networks, through which they look to other sources who can legitimately assist them in fulfilling their child-care duties. I have categorized these sources of assistance or "resource women" into three broad groups.

In the first group are members of the household. In urban Egypt, this means primarily elder daughters because, in urban Cairo, most households live as nuclear rather than extended families; it is rare for them to include other females. In all families, elder daughters take an active part in raising their siblings. Girls as young as seven years old change, bathe, and feed younger brothers and sisters. Mothers never fail to mention how advantageous it is for them to have an elder daughter. One informant said, "I suffered a lot with my first three children, but the fourth and the fifth I did not even feel, since my daughter was old enough to take care of them. . . . Almost the hardest part was the pregnancy and the delivery."

In some families the eldest daughter is kept out of school in order to help her mother with the child rearing and the daily housework. It happens that while the other children, including the younger daughters, have completed their education, sometimes to the university level, the eldest daughter is totally illiterate or has completed only elementary school. Although the practice of keeping daughters out of school is diminishing, elder daughters are still held responsible for much of the housework and child rearing, so they often do poorly at school or drop out.

The second group of resource women includes female kin, namely mothers and sisters who live elsewhere. My observations reveal that a woman's strongest support comes from her mother and sisters. In-laws play a lesser role except when the wife and husband are related. Younger women prefer to live near their own relatives so that they can rely on their mothers or sisters for support and advice regarding household responsibilities, and child care in particular. Many young women in the neighborhood made it a condition of marriage to stay in the vicinity of their families, and sometimes bypassed many opportunities in order to fulfill this desire. Frequently, one hears that a first child was raised by the grandmother or under her direct supervision. Younger sisters too may perform tasks such as changing, feeding, and carrying the infant.

In-laws often have a less active share in raising children, even when they live in the same building. Their help is under the supervision of the mother, or at her specific request. Otherwise it remains at the level of advice, and there is little pressure to heed it. This is in complete contrast to the very forward role of the mother's mother. Moreover, this also belies the assumption that in a patriarchal community it is the husband's relatives who play a more significant role in the life of the family.

A woman's nonkin network, her neighbors and friends, constitute the third group of her resource persons. The support these neighbors and friends provide is crucial in newly developed neighborhoods where most residents are first- or second-generation migrants, without close kin at hand. The young mothers who live far from their families and close relatives, particularly those who are first-generation migrants, are disadvantaged because they have become separated from their sources of folk knowledge. Therefore they must rely on their social network for the advice and information they need. They see child rearing as laborious, with unending responsibilities, and often are quick to point out that their life conditions are tremendously different from their mother's.

This group of women frequently adopts an older woman in the community as a surrogate mother and source of advice. Their choice is not necessarily based on the older woman's experience and knowledge, but rather on factors such as her physical proximity, her receptiveness, and the general quality of the rapport between the two women. In these relationships children often refer to the elder woman as "grandmother." Generally neighbors living in the same building (usually seven or eight families) are more likely to be incorporated in one another's child-care support network because proximity makes their assistance and advice more easily available in times of need.

More generally therefore, the support networks, who are the mothers' mainstay, are drawn from outside the physical entity of the households. An important characteristic of these networks is that they can include women from all ages and with different levels of education, knowledge, and experience. Most children spend a considerable amount of time in the company of the resource women, often within the physical boundaries of other households where they are fed, bathed, and disciplined. Even if a mother has a high level of knowledge pertaining to child care, her child does not consistently benefit from it if this knowledge is not shared by the members of her support network. Therefore it is not surprising that my observations indicate that actual child-care practices of women with higher levels of education and knowledge are strikingly similar to those of the less informed women in their network. Formal education, when it is above a certain level, however, improves the communication between the mothers and hospital staff and physicians.[4]

Social recognition of one's efforts, achievements, and failure is a factor which plays an important role in the life of the members of these communities. This gives a mother further reasons for widening her network and drawing other people into her efforts for child care. Every mother knows that in the eyes of her husband and the community she can be held responsible for her child's severe illness, injury, or death. She also realizes that she will be blamed much more if she does not have a support network of close relatives who can testify that she did her best, but the fate of the child had been already set.

Most women in the neighborhoods rely on support from members of all three groups. The extent to which she looks to one source more than another depends on her circumstances and her judgment of what is best for her.

DAY-TO-DAY CHILD CARE

Breast-feeding and Infant Diet

All of the women delay breast-feeding for one to three days after birth because it is believed that the early milk, which is yellow and thick, is not good for the child. During this time, children are fed sugared water. Since it is light it washes the baby's stomach and prepares the infant to suckle the mother's breast. Only one of the older informants said that a child should be given the mother's breast from the first day: "Because it is natural it must be good," she said. Her daughter and daughter-in-law do not follow her advice, however.

Even though women are aware that high-protein, high-energy foods are especially important to their diet during lactation, few change their eating patterns when nursing. This is because there is not enough money for additional food expenditures, which do not take priority over spending for household goods and educational costs. Moreover, the general emphasis on sharing does not allow for the nursing mother to buy food for her own consumption without being expected to share it with other family members and friends or neighbors who frequently drop by to visit.

The mothers all insist that they know breast-feeding is best for the child, yet many of them stop it as early as forty days after birth. Some mothers continue breast-feeding for up to six or nine months. Only a few breast-feed for over a year, and it is usually said to be for birth control reasons. Quite a few mothers adopt a mixed method of feeding when the child is about two months old, breast-feeding two or three times a day and using either powdered milk or infusions of caraway, fenugreek, or rice water the rest of the time.

When I asked women why they had stopped breast-feeding, a common reply was "I did not have enough milk and the child was always crying." Others said that as soon as their children tasted food, they would refuse the breast. Another reason frequently given was that it made them tired and that they couldn't cope with it. A few mothers said because they work it was not possible for them to continue, so they switched to powdered milk. Some of the working mothers stopped breast-feeding as early as six weeks, even though they didn't return to work until three months after giving birth. Informants also stopped because they were pregnant and feared that their milk would be poisonous to the child.

An examination of patterns of breast-feeding among mothers of different socioeconomic backgrounds reveals that the higher the mother's educational level the shorter the length of breast-feeding.[5] Working women, particularly those who work outside the neighborhood, tend to stop breast-feeding earlier. Women of higher economic status and who are more modern in their life-style rarely breast-feed for longer than three months. (These women associate themselves with the *afranqi* style and express distaste for the more traditional, or *baladi,* ways.)

Mothers who stopped breast-feeding early were asked, on an individual basis and in group situations, to explain their reasons for stopping. The act of breast-feeding is considered "primitive," "animalistic," and "shameful" by some women, especially when men are around. Some think it is almost a pity that women have to do it, "like any other thing that women have to put up with because of their sex, such as menstruation." These types of responses were often expressed with considerable resentment.

This is in direct contrast to the attitude of most of their mothers, who felt proud of having milk and who sometimes breast-fed their children as long as four years. Similar to these older women, many younger *baladi* (traditional) women feel free to breast-feed anywhere: on a bus, while chatting to their friends, on their doorsteps, or when they are entertaining guests. In the traditional value system the act of breast-feeding is seen as a natural function, and it does not attract special attention.[6]

Breast-feeding does not involve any special procedure. The baby is given the breast every time he or she cries or when the mother is free. A sleeping baby is awakened to be fed if the mother knows she will not be free later. None of the mothers knew how many times a day they breast-feed or at what intervals. None of the mothers washes the breast before feeding the baby.

Besides breast milk, children up to three months old are bottle-fed sugared water or water boiled with sugar and caraway or fenugreek. After the first three months children can be given juice, but no mother could remember the last time she prepared juice for her child. I observed that children as young as six weeks old may be made to taste any kind of liquid that the mother or other family member is drinking.

Most nursing mothers start their children on some kind of solid food after the first three months. One of the most common first foods is *fuul* (mashed beans). The mother crushes the beans between her fingers and then allows the baby to suck them by placing her finger to the baby's mouth. No mother was ever observed washing her hands before feeding the baby. Thickened rice water is another food commonly given to infants.

As children grow they are given an increasing variety of foods. The following list is the main foods that mothers give their children beginning around three to six months: rice water, egg yolk (rarely, wealthier families), boiled and mashed potato, tea, rice cooked in milk, biscuits, bread soaked in tea, yoghurt (rarely), boiled or mashed squash.

Food and beverages for children may be prepared in large quantities and consumed over a period of one or two days. Food may be left covered or uncovered on top of the stove, in a cupboard, or under the bed. Other children serve themselves from it if they wish. The food is sometimes reheated before it is served again or it is given to the baby cold, depending on the nature of the food and the season.

All babies have one or two bottles which are rinsed or washed often with soapy water like all other dishes, but there is no special attempt to sterilize the bottle. Sometimes the mother sucks the nipple (*bazaza*) or the pacifier before giving it to the baby in order to clean it.

Usually, babies have no special dish or spoon. While feeding her baby the mother may have a taste of the food herself or may spontaneously feed other young children with the same spoon or in the case of younger babies with her fingers.

As a rule, no one washes his or her hands before eating, and children are no exception. They may be required to wash their hands and face after eating. It is also quite common for children two years and older to be given five or ten piasters to spend on sweets or biscuits for themselves. Children may be given pieces of vegetables or fruit to nibble on as early as six months.

As soon as the child can sit, he or she joins at the *tablia* (low round dinner table) and starts to feed himself or herself. Adult diets have a major influence on children's food intake. Most mothers say they do not prepare special foods for children once they are over six months, as there would always be something in the meal that a child can eat. At the early stage small pieces of bread are dipped in soup and given to the child to suck. Generally children, like babies, are fed on demand and they are not expected to observe an eating schedule.

There is hardly a proper weaning stage for children. As one anthropologist put it, one gets the impression that children go almost directly from the breast to the tablia.[7]

Children's Hygiene

Bathing and changing the baby are considered basic tasks. Most younger babies are bathed once or twice a week during the summer, and once every ten days or so in winter. The baby's head is rarely washed with soap but only rinsed with water. No special equipment is used for bathing; some warm water is prepared and placed in a plastic or metal basin. This basin may serve many other purposes such as washing dishes or vegetables, laundering clothes including the baby's dirty pants and trousers, and carrying or storing food. Sometimes a large cooking pot is used for bathing; most kitchen and washing utensils are multipurpose.

The child's bottom is usually washed once a day, after a bowel movement, but the rest of the time the baby is only wiped clean. At times, mothers use some kind of cream, especially if the baby has a rash, but most mothers do not think that cream or powder are necessary.

Toilet training should start as early as forty days from birth, according to some of the mothers, and it should be done by holding the child above the toilet seat. However, no mother in the sample did this consistently. No mother employed the traditional method of using her own feet to toilet train a child.[8] Most mothers acquire a plastic potty for their children by the time they are four months old. The potty is placed under the bed, under the kitchen cupboard, or in the corner of a room. It is given to the child on request wherever he or she may be. Because of lack of consistency in training, however, few children are successfully toilet trained before the age of two. It is not unusual for children of up to four years old to defecate in their pants. This is a constant complaint among the mothers.[9]

Young children always sleep with their mothers and no special provision is made for infants to sleep more often in the daytime. Some mothers think that when infants sleep less it means they are healthier. If a baby sleeps a lot, the mother is sometimes advised to wake the infant and give him or her exercise to make the baby's body strong.

Attitudes toward Child Growth

Differences in children's weights are noticed and higher weight is attributed to better health. Weight by itself was not considered something a mother could affect a great deal. Not a single mother among the sample knew her child's birth weight, and only a few mothers have weighed their children a few times at various ages. Most women say that a newborn may weigh from two to nine kilos depending on the mother's weight and what God has arranged.

Although most women did not see that an underweight child needs curative treatment, they were responsive when they were taught to recognize abnormally low weight as a problem. The reason for their responsiveness lies in the traditional belief that plumpness is a sign of good health. This provides an example of how folk beliefs could be exploited in the promotion of good health practices. The use of television and radio for this kind of promotion is most effective in reaching low-income groups, especially in urban areas.

The connection between height and health is much more difficult for most mothers to conceptualize since they see height mainly as a hereditary factor. It is firmly believed that God created a variety of people: black, white, tall, and short. They illustrate this by giving the example of the hand: each of the fingers is different in shape and length, yet they are all fingers and they are all useful. Although they considered a tall person more attractive, this is a matter of luck just like other aspects of physical beauty.

Teething is considered the most difficult period of child raising in terms of health. According to mothers, teething may start anytime from four months to one year. No mother considers a delay an indication of poor health; rather it is believed that children are different and have different rates of growth.

During the teething period children are expected to be sick with constant diarrhea and fever. Also, they do not sleep well and they lose weight. Several mothers said because they wanted the child to get over this difficult stage quickly, they gave the child a "teething injection." Since over half the children in the sample had this injection, I accompanied one mother to the pharmacist when she went to buy it. She was given a box containing ten ampules, each with a one-milliliter solution of calcium and vitamins D and B. She was instructed to take the child to a nurse for an injection every other day. Though injections are more costly, they are often preferred to other types of medication because they are thought to enter the child's blood directly and thus make him or her strong.

Like teething, the age at which a child first sits, walks, and talks is assumed to be different for different children. Generally, children are supposed to sit well by themselves at nine months. Those who do not, whether traditional or modern, are said to have lazy bodies but do not require medical attention. Children who begin to walk at an early age are considered difficult, and their mothers receive a lot of sympathy from others. A child usually begins to talk between nine months and two years. Some say that occasionally children do not talk until they are four or five years old.

Mental Development, Games, and Toys

A child's mental development and learning ability are considered inherent and therefore mothers do not believe they can contribute to their children's growth in this area. But parents feel proud of their clever children and admire them. None of the mothers sees any connection between the learning process and playing games.

Normally, children do not possess any toys except an occasional inexpensive plastic ball. They are allowed to use any household good as a toy and most commonly these are kitchen utensils. Adults make few attempts to stop children from playing with more expensive items such as radio cassette recorders or television sets. None of the mothers in the neighborhood made toys for their children, but grandmothers said that in the old days people used to do so.

Grandparents or other older people in the community sometimes tell little stories to children of two years and older. Now and then, mothers and fathers play with their children by throwing them up in the air and catching them. Mothers say sweet things and express their love to very young children, but this becomes less frequent as children grow older. Children in larger families enjoy more attention from older siblings who cuddle and play with them.

The mothers always show great interest in and are very responsive to new ideas pertinent to child care, particularly when they do not involve much material cost. They are quite aware that their children are their main source of pleasure and fulfillment, as well as their only means of satisfying the wish for continuity. Their children's development is, therefore, of prime interest to these mothers.

CHILD MORBIDITY

Apart from illnesses, accidents are a frequent form of morbidity in the community. Attempts to keep dangerous items out of a child's reach are rare. This is partly due to material conditions and limited space and partly due to lack of knowledge about the possibilities of and ways to prevent such accidents. Children play around their mother as she cooks, cleans, and washes. Often, children upset hot water or gas burners onto themselves or others, sometimes with very regrettable and long-lasting consequences.[10]

Steps and staircases are another major cause of accidents. Fathers usually blame the mothers for negligence and sometimes punish them physically for being irresponsible. But no attempt is made to change physical conditions in order to prevent the repetition of such accidents.

There are two main categories of diseases that every mother considers the greatest threat to her children's health, especially at very young ages. These are diarrhea and *hawa* (colds, flu, and related illnesses). Diarrhea is by far the most common and recurrent ailment among children of all ages. Mild diarrhea is considered inevitable and not so dangerous and there is usually no attempt to treat it.

The women of the community recognize three types of diarrhea: *nazla maaweya, nazlat eshal,* and *nazlat qafaf. Nazla maaweya* is basically a summer disease which can be fatal if not treated in its early stages. It is characterized by frequent attacks of diarrhea and vomiting and the child cannot keep anything in his or her stomach. As soon as the symptoms appear the child is taken to see a physician or pharmacist. All of the women had heard that children should be fed when they have diarrhea, but not a single mother thought they should be breast-fed.

Nazlat eshal is a mild diarrhea that children under two years contract quite often. Bowel movements may come as often as five or six times a day. This kind of diarrhea may persist for as long as a month during teething. Mothers assume there is little they can do to prevent it. It is often ignored in its early stages, and if it continues the child may be given home remedies such as infusions of fenugreek seeds, or rice water.

Nazlat qafaf (dehydration) is another recurrent illness characterized by frequent diarrhea attacks. It is evident from changes appearing in the skin. Mothers explained to me that with a healthy child, it is impossible to pinch the skin away from the flesh, but when a child has qafaf, the skin can be separated from the flesh.[11] Usually when a mother recognizes this illness, she takes the child to see a physician or pharmacist.

Nazla shaabeya, a respiratory illness, is the most dangerous winter illness. Although not considered as serious or potentially fatal as nazla maaweya, it is believed to make the child so weak that she or he may contract any other killer disease. Nazla shaabeya starts with severe coughing, which can cause vomiting, and is often accompanied by fever. It is believed to be caused by hawa (drafts). If the home remedies, usually herbal medicines, do not work and the coughing and fever persist, the child is taken to a physician or pharmacist. It is believed that if nazla shaabeya is not cured it may develop into tuberculosis.

A certain amount of confusion exists about what the word *nazla* means. Young inexperienced mothers, especially those with few social contacts, understand nazla to mean different kinds of diarrhea; otherwise they use the term *taban(eh)*. But to most women the word means any childhood illness, including those which are serious or fatal. Several mothers reported that one of their children had died of what they called nazla, but when these cases were discussed in fuller detail it became obvious that not diarrhea but a bad cold or meningitis had caused the death. I asked the mothers to tell me the exact symptoms of each type of nazla. Many could not and referred me to older or more knowledgeable women in the neighborhood for the answer to my question.

This point is particularly important since both pharmacists and physicians rely heavily on how a mother describes her child's illness. Mothers often go to a pharmacist, or to a hospital, describe the child's symptoms, and ask for medicine. Only on rare and more serious occasions are the sick children examined physically before being diagnosed. Therefore physicians, pharmacists, and other health workers must be more sensitive to linguistic ambiguities, particularly since mothers have various degrees of health awareness and are from different regions.

Mothers are conscious of and often remark on the lack of adequate communication between them and doctors. Many mothers reported that often they do not understand the physician's questions, and just reply yes or no, or say nothing at all. They are embarrassed to ask for clarification and doctors rarely encourage them either by repeating or rephrasing their questions.[12] Obviously, this can lead to inaccurate diagnoses. A mother who realizes that she cannot communicate well with a doctor does not trust his diagnosis or the medicine he prescribes.

It is considered normal for children to develop an occasional fever, or *nazlat sokhonia*. They are usually given *yansoon* (a tea) and sometimes half an aspirin to bring the temperature down. A doctor is consulted only if the fever is unusually high or if it persists for a long time.

Ear infection, also a common malady, is usually caused by water getting in a child's ear while bathing. Often mothers treat the infection with ear drops purchased from a pharmacy or borrowed from a neighbor. A child with a severe infection may be taken to the hospital. (No mother in the sample had ever consulted a private doctor for an ear infection.)

Skin diseases are the most common and unattended ailment in all children up to age seven. The face, hands, head, and legs of many children are continuously covered with pimples, some of which are infected, or by lesions resembling eczema. In the summer this problem is magnified, as it results from a combination of heat, dust, dirt, and the continuous presence of numerous flies and insects. Skin problems are ordinary and treating them is basically futile, in the opinion of most mothers. Visiting the hospital for these infections is thought to be a waste of time. Now and then, iodine (*zahra*) is applied to the infected skin, and in very severe cases the child may be prevented from eating fish, milk, or food cooked in a lot of oil or concentrated butter.

Eye infections, like skin diseases, are considered impossible to combat. Many children have very red eyes but they are expected to heal naturally. During the summer, redness is sometimes treated by holding the child's head down and pouring cold water over the eyes (but only for children over one year old). This may be repeated two or three times a day. Sometimes the infection becomes so severe that the child cannot open his or her eyes in the morning. In these cases, a pharmacist is consulted and the infection is treated with either eye drops or eye lotion. Sometimes the pharmacist may advise a doctor's examination.

There are a few physically disabled and mentally retarded children in the community. Some of them have been crippled since birth and others have become disabled as a result of illness or accidents. The mothers of these children often receive help and sympathy from their neighbors. On occasions when the mothers are tired and frustrated, they are advised not to curse the children or their fate, but to remember that God will reward them with tranquility. These supportive talks often change the mother's mood and she resumes her responsibilities with a lighter spirit. In a sense, the community considers these children blessed, or surrounded by a light of holiness.

Immunization

In contrast to their unquestioning faith in the curative capabilities of modern medicine, the informants have little faith in the value of vaccination. Only two of the educated informants really believe that it effectively prevents disease. The rest of the women remain skeptical about the advantages it offers, except in preventing polio.[13] The lack of trust and ambivalence is primarily due to the lack of attempts to communicate the workings of the immunization process in simple language. On the other hand, the organization of immunization services is not conducive to mothers' taking advantage of these services.[14] Despite this, many mothers do make partial attempts to have their children vaccinated. As one mother put it, "Who knows, perhaps it does work."

Infant Mortality

All the mothers were asked about all the children they had ever borne, whether they were still living or whether they had died. Out of seventy-two children born to the twenty-one mothers in the sample (all born in a neighborhood which is within walking distance of a public hospital), twelve children have died. Of these twelve deaths, eight died before reaching age one, and diarrhea was the cause of death in half of the cases. Diarrhea, despite its relatively easy and cheap cure, has remained the biggest problem to treat in infants.

In the opinion of most women, traditional or herbal medicine has its benefits, but it is not as effective as modern medicine, particularly with regard to children. They are quick to say that in the old days more children died because of the lack of medical care. In serious cases, when they have a choice, they do not hesitate to choose the modern system. But they may employ traditional remedies simultaneously. Even when the two treatments are contradictory they still try to accommodate them both in order to increase their chances of recovery. The success or failure of a given treatment, whether modern or traditional, is observed and remembered for future reference.

People resort to supernatural cures in cases of mental illness, but this rarely includes children. Traditional beliefs such as visiting shrines, placing a Quran above the head, or burning incense in the house may be invoked for the sick child, but not to the exclusion of modern medicine.

It is true that women often talk in very fatalistic terms and refer matters of life and death to God. Observation of their practices, however, reveals that most women try to the best of their ability to save their children. None waits passively for fate to decide the life of her child. But insufficient knowledge due mainly to inefficient dissemination of information sometimes renders their efforts futile. They then resort to the one indisputable explanation of causality: fate. Constantly, when they speak of illnesses and catastrophes, they say, "Il hayaa bitaa' i rabbina" (Life is in the hands of God). This attitude seems justifiable when we look at their life experiences.

In order to explain tragic events, mothers sometimes talk of the evil eye. Most often, it is used as a device for rationalizing misfortune, or for boasting that others are envious of them and their children. But no mother prevents her child from socializing or appearing in front of others, or purposely keeps him or her dirty for fear of the evil eye. In fact, if others are envious of a child, it is considered a compliment to the mother, especially the young mother.

DIFFERENTIAL ATTITUDES TOWARD MALE AND FEMALE CHILDREN

There is strong conviction among all women that it is their daughters who will give them lifetime support. Every single mother wishes to have at least one daughter. Some said, "There is no woman lonelier than the one without a daughter." The lucky woman bears a female child first, who can help with housework and child rearing. Also, the mother and daughter grow together, and before the mother reaches old age, they can enjoy each other's company and support. This attitude reflects the belief that female children are born faceup, i.e., facing the mother, while males are born facedown (Nadim 1980).

But all women believe that not to have male children is disastrous since sons are the guarantors of marriage and their old-age financial security. Every husband wants to have sons who will carry on his name and give him a sense of continuity. In parents' minds, daughters are united with mothers and sons with fathers.[15] In the eyes of the community, a marriage which has not produced a son is not complete because the need of the husband has not yet been fulfilled.

Today, daughters are gaining popularity with their fathers, who sometimes say, "Daughters are more caring and faithful to their parents than sons." While there is a newfound appreciation for daughters, somewhat as a result of changing attitudes in society at large, it is not interchangeable with the pleasure of having sons.

All women said that once they have two or three children with a combination of boys and girls, they wish to stop having children. Many said, however, that if they have only girls, social pressure forces them to continue until they have one or two sons. One woman in the neighborhood who has eight daughters said, "My husband has resigned himself to the fact that God is not giving us a son. Many times I started to use contraceptives, but other women, both friends and enemies, put so much pressure on me that I stopped using contraceptives on my own accord. And yet each time I had another girl."

In discussing the problems and pleasures of child rearing all mothers without exception said bringing up daughters is much easier. Nevertheless parents remain continuously responsible and concerned about their daughters, even when they are married and have children of their own. If the daughter's marriage is problematic or dissolves, responsibility for her reverts back to her parents.

In contrast, boys are very difficult to raise. Girls sit quietly next to their mother, while boys want to run in the street "as soon as they can crawl." As children, boys are troublemakers, but once they become adults they tend to care for themselves and there is no need to worry about them. In other words, boys grow into adults, while girls remain children.

Some mothers say that girls' health is less problematic because they are born stronger, while male children are more susceptible to illness. Although not everyone holds this opinion, none of the mothers takes risks with her boy's health, and in practice all the mothers pay more attention to their male children.

Some of the informants told me that according to Islam, girls should be breast-fed one and a half years and boys up to two years.[16] (Few mothers, however, had continued breast-feeding either their male or female infants for more than a year.) The importance of such a belief lies in the mother's perception that the nutritional needs of male and female children differ.

Based on the data collected for this research, it is not possible to say whether the food intake of girls is lower than that of boys during the breast-feeding period. But once the baby's diet includes powdered milk and supplementary food, it is obvious that families with sons spend more money on dried milk, ready-made baby food, and occasional eggs or yoghurt. Female children are given homemade food and beverages only, therefore their diet costs less. However, that does not necessarily mean that the diet of female children is nutritionally inferior to that of boys.[17] What is clear is that a girl's diet is less varied and includes less milk. Also since food for babies is often prepared and kept for a day or more in unhygienic conditions, it is not always healthy. Eggs and yoghurt are almost never given to daughters, even though every mother considers these items very good for all children over six months.

In terms of sick care, boys were taken to the hospital and private doctors more often than girls. While girls would be given home remedies for mild illnesses, mothers monitored their sons' health more carefully than their daughters'. Umm Mohammed completed secondary school (ten years of education) and has been married for three years. She has a boy and a girl and, relative to others in the neighborhood, her family has a reasonable income and standard of living. At one point, her daughter, who had just started to walk, became ill with diarrhea, supposedly because she was teething. At the time I talked to Umm Mohammed, the daughter had been ill for four months. Her mother and others often comment on her obvious regressive growth, but she has been taken to a public hospital only once.

During the same time period her elder brother was taken to a private doctor and hospital for reasons of diarrhea, spots, fever, and general weakness. When I tried to make the mother conscious of her preferential treatment of the son, she said, "I know that; it is only because he is older and because he is his father's son. When anything happens to him, his father holds me responsible and claims that I am not looking after his son properly. He won't stop nagging that I am not a good wife or mother. So in order to save my own skin, as soon as anything happens, I take him to see the doctor even when it is absolutely unnecessary. My husband gives me money for his son's medical costs much more willingly. Because I don't want arguments, I have to take our daughter to the public hospital, which is cheap but not very useful at all. I give her home remedies and she is all right."

In families where women have full control over the financial affairs or have an income of their own, children have better diets. Mothers tend to spend more readily on their children. One of these mothers expressed her opinion in the following manner: "I would rather spend on food for my children and see them healthy than pay for medicine and doctors." When a mother spends more to enrich her children's diet, boys generally benefit more than girls.

Within my sample, and according to general opinion, boys over one and a half years old contract severe illnesses, particularly diarrhea, much more often than girls. Girls suffer from milder ailments which frequently go unnoticed. This only reinforces the commonly held belief that girls are stronger than boys from birth. Occasionally mothers suggest that boys, more than girls, are subject to the evil eye. Therefore it seems reasonable to them that they should give more care and attention to boys.

Poorer health in male children could also be caused by their eating habits. Once they reach the age of two, boys are given money to buy snacks more often than girls. Predictably, they spend this money on candy and sweet drinks. Little boys learn at a very early age to get what they want by insistence or through aggression toward the mother, and this becomes a continuing trend throughout childhood. Girls, on the other hand, are encouraged to remain passive and listen to their mothers. Consequently, boys eat more irregularly and less nutritiously. They also spend more time playing outdoors in the streets, many of which have remained dirty with piles of refuse despite recent improvement; this probably increases their susceptibility to diseases.

MAJOR FACTORS AFFECTING QUALITY OF CHILD CARE

The level of income, formal education, and economic activity of the heads of households are conventionally considered the most important factors affecting children's well-being, and their health status in particular. The observations made in this research, however, suggest that women's social networks, which are the main vehicle for mobilizing the support of "resource women" for assistance with child-care responsibilities, are at least as important as the other factors in determining the quality of child-care practices. These resource women include elder daughters, relatives (the mother's mother is especially important), and neighbors.

Formal education influences child-rearing and hygiene practices to a much lesser degree. More educated mothers may perceive their child-care responsibilities differently but their actual practices are still dictated more by their life circumstances. This situation is heightened by the fact that the content of formal education has little relevance to the everyday life of low-income women.

This is not to say, however, that formal schooling has had no impact. Women who have achieved higher levels of education are more influenced by modern values. In terms of child care, this influence has not been wholly beneficial. For example, although the more educated women show the highest tendency to vaccinate their children, they also stop breast-feeding earlier, and are more likely to buy manufactured baby foods and to spend more of the household budget on items such as more modern baby clothes.

The working status of mothers and its effect on child care, an often debated issue, was seen here to have both positive and negative effects. Breast-feeding, for example, is not necessarily disrupted if the mother works in the community, as she often takes her child with her. If the baby is left behind with an elder daughter or a relative, the mother may nevertheless return home to breast-feed. Other women, who work outside the community, often stop breast-feeding altogether or adopt a mixed system of breast-feeding and powdered milk. Working outside the community provides these women with an extended social network which gives them better information about doctors, hospitals, different kinds of children's foods, and other new ideas related to child care. These mothers are often consulted on child-care issues and their knowledge is respected.

When women have secure jobs, such as government or public sector jobs, and the household can afford the loss of the mother's income for a period, these women often exercise their right to maternity leave and stop working, sometimes as long as two years. They stay at home until their children are older, when making alternative child-care provisions is less problematic.

The general economic situation of the household and the extent to which a woman has control over the family's cash resources play a significant role in child care. Working women and those women in control of the family resources tend to rely more on private medical care and manufactured baby foods (which are believed to be better), and are better able to provide a more varied, healthier daily diet.

The education and nature of the father's occupation is of little consequence to the way children are raised. All household and child-care activities are seen as part of the female sphere and no man wants to affiliate himself with these female interests. There is very little evidence of change in this regard, since women actively encourage these attitudes of their menfolk. This pattern is further accentuated by the fact that most fathers spend very little time at home.

Women show great faith in the power of modern medicine to cure illness, particularly childhood illness. They rely heavily on public and private health services as well as pharmacists for curative treatment. Poor communication between these women and medical personnel, however, often prevents them from benefiting fully from health-care programs. The dismissive attitude of health workers often disinclines mothers to avail themselves of services offered.

CONCLUDING OBSERVATIONS

In most societies, women have been assigned primary responsibility for child care. The degree of power and prestige women gain in this role depends on the extent to which a given society recognizes and values the activity of child rearing. While it is true that children provide a sense of self-fulfillment, it is reasonable to suggest that mothers are motivated to play their role more competently if it is a source of power rather than a hindrance to participation in more acknowledged and rewarded social activities.

Recent social changes and development policies in Egypt have placed special emphasis on promoting child health and reducing infant mortality. The importance of the mother's role in health improvement programs, however, has been neglected. Resources have been channeled to provide better medical facilities and more extensive formal education, but little attention has been given to expanding mothers' knowledge in the field of child care.

Social changes that were thought to bring improvements in health have been somewhat disappointing. While urban areas have received more than their proportional share of educational facilities, medical care services, and employment generation, levels of infant mortality remain high. In the greater Cairo urban region, where all of these conditions are better than for Egypt as a whole, the infant and child mortality rates are almost the same as the national average.[18]

In this paper, referring to the specific situation of low-income neighborhoods in Cairo, I have shown how mothers carry out their responsibilities for child rearing. While they may not always choose the best practices from a medical point of view, their decisions are based on their own experiences, knowledge, and resources which they are able to mobilize. Health and other social organizations wishing to improve the situation need to recognize the mothers' active role, credit them for it, and work in coalition with them. Recognizing the mothers' active role in child care would result in improved communication between mothers and outside organizations which would lead to overall improvement in the quality of child care in Egypt.

NOTES

1. This research was partially funded by the Population Council, Cairo. For a more detailed account of the study see Hoodfar 1986.

2. For a more comprehensive account of the study see Hoodfar 1989.

3. Female white-collar employees are legally entitled to take two years of leave without pay, apparently without loss of seniority, for every one of their first three children.

4. S. Shami and L. Taminian (1985) made similar observations in resettled communities of Amman, Jordan.

5. Egyptian studies show the inverse relationship of length of breast-feeding to years of schooling of the mothers (Nawar and Hobcroft 1983). In the Middle East generally, the relationship of shortened breast-feeding to various attributes of modernization prevails (Myntti 1978, Firebrace 1983).

6. Among the more *baladi* people the curve of a woman's shoulder has greater relevance to her sex appeal than do her breasts. The latter are considered functional, therefore it is commonplace to observe many of the young village women in low-cut dresses but almost never in sleeveless clothes or even short sleeves. In fact sleeveless dresses are commonly referred to as nighties.

7. Dr. Norge Jerome, personal communication, Cairo, 1985.

8. Traditionally, a mother would place her own feet in such a way as to make a hole between them, and then would sit the child on top of her feet.

9. Davis (1983: 147–167) makes similar observations on toilet-training practices and the general treatment of boys and girls in the Moroccan village where she worked.

10. During the two years of my fieldwork in the two neighborhoods, two women were burned and consequently died because their kerosene burner burst. Many children and adults have burn scars on their bodies. Many of these accidents are the result of the lack of kitchen space.

11. This knowledge was the result of a successful campaign by health authorities exploiting television and radio to publicize the symptoms of dehydration, which claims the lives of many infants every year.

12. For more discussion and consequences of the problem of hampered communication between mothers and physicians see Hoodfar (1984) and Oldham (1984).

13. This awareness of polio too has been the result of a successful campaign during the late seventies. This suggests that once information is provided in an accessible form, the mothers respond positively.

14. For more detailed discussion on the problems of immunization in Cairo see Hoodfar (1986: 56–62).

15. This is the underlying reason why in many broken marriages the daughters stay with the mother while the sons are put in the custody of the father. There are a few such cases in the community.

16. However, this deferential treatment is not substantiated in the Quran. In "The Cow" sura (2: 233), mothers are advised to breast-feed for two years. "Mothers shall give suck to their children for two whole years . . . if the father wishes the sucking to be complete. . . . But if after consultation they choose by mutual consent to wean the child they incur no guilt" [*The Koran,* translated with notes by N. J. Dawood (London: Penguin Books, 1956)].

17. Other studies suggest that girls' diet (as shown by the weight-for-age growth curve) is poorer than that of the boys up to about thirty months of age; after this age their diet improves relative to the boys' since they start to eat from the family pot and can gain equal access (Makinson 1986).

18. Recent studies show that Cairo's infant mortality has been at least 100 per thousand births; some of them show higher rates (CAPMAS 1986). Infant mortality was, of course, differentially higher in the lower-income areas. (See also Committee on Population and Demography 1982.)

REFERENCES

CAPMAS. 1986. *Infant and Child Mortality in Egypt*. Cairo: Central Agency for Public Mobilization and Statistics, Population Studies and Research Center.

Committee on Population and Demography. 1982. *The Estimation of Recent Trends in Fertility and Mortality in Egypt*. Report No. 9. Washington, D.C.: National Academy Press.

Davis, Susan. 1983. *Patience and Power: Women's Lives in a Moroccan Village*. Rochester, Vt.: Schenkman Books.

Firebrace, James. 1983. "Infant Feeding in the Middle East." Report for the International Baby Food Action Network (IBFAN). New Haven, Conn.: IBFAN.

Hoodfar, Homa. 1989. *Survival Strategies in Low Income Neighbourhoods of Cairo, Egypt*. Ph.D. thesis, Department of Anthropology, University of Kent at Canterbury.

———. "Child Care and Child Survival in Low-Income Neighborhoods of Cairo." *Regional Papers*. Cairo: Population Council.

———. "Hygienic and Health Care Practices in a Poor Neighborhood of Cairo." *Regional Papers*. Cairo: Population Council.

Makinson, Carolyn. 1986. *Sex Differential in Infant Child Mortality in Egypt*. Dissertation, Department of Sociology, Princeton University.

Myntti, Cynthia. 1978. "The Effects of Breastfeeding, Temporary Emigration, and Contraceptive Use on the Fertility of Yemen Arab Republic." Regional Papers. Cairo: Population Council. Revised version in *Studies in Family Planning* 10 (Oct. 1979): 10.

Nadim, Nawal el-Messiri. 1980. *Rural Health Care in Egypt*. Ottawa: International Development Research Center.

Nawar, Laila, and John Hobcroft. 1983. "An Analysis of Determinants of Fertility in Egypt." Presented at a meeting of CAPMAS, December 20–22, in Cairo.

Oldham, Linda. 1984. "Child Nurturance and Its Context at Manshiet Nasser, Cairo, Based on a Family Profile." Regional Papers. Cairo: Population Council.

Shami, Seteney, and Lucine Taminian. 1985. "Family Dynamics and Child Health and Survival." Regional Papers. Cairo: Population Council.

BODILY MUTILATION
OF YOUNG FEMALES

Cairo Family Planning Association

Editor's note: The following article is a report of a seminar held in Egypt in 1979 to discuss female circumcision and consider how best to deal with the practice. Reprinted in its entirety, the document includes Ministerial Resolution No. 74 of 1959, which forbade Egyptian clinics from performing such operations. This resolution was the basis for the current Egyptian law against circumcision, which has been in operation for more than a decade.

INTRODUCTION

In its desire to stress the broad and human concept of family planning which has been adopted since 1977 and which does not limit itself to the provision of family planning information and services but extends to the consideration of the social and economic factors which influence the attitude and behavior of individuals toward childbearing;

And in pursuance of its efforts begun in February 1978 regarding the study of family law and its effect on women's security and stability in the family and subsequently on her attitudes toward childbearing (a project which achieved one of its main objectives with the issuing of amendments in family laws by the Legislative Assembly, and which was followed by the Seminar on "Nutrition and the Mental and Physical Growth of the Child"), a topic has been taken up on the occasion of the International Year of the Child in February 1979 because of its relevance to the population problem on the one hand and the health and mental well-being of the coming generations on the other.

The Cairo Family Planning Association has decided to hold a Seminar dealing with a very sensitive and important subject, "Bodily Mutilation of Young Females," a practice imposed on them by old customs and wrong beliefs spread because of ignorance on the one hand and embarrassment in tackling subjects of such sensitivity on the other.

The objective of the Seminar is to point out the historical, social, health, and psychological aspects relating to the subject of female circumcision and to ascertain the prevalence of this custom, the factors contributing to it, and the effects resulting from it in order to formulate a clear policy regarding its harmful effects on woman's health and psychology.

SEMINAR ORGANIZATION

The Seminar was held on Sunday and Monday, 14 and 15 October 1979, at the headquarters of the Egyptian Association for Political Economy, Statistics, and Legislation and was inaugurated by Professor Dr. Amal Osman, Minister of Social and Insurance Affairs. Representatives of the following organizations participated:

Arab League, UNICEF, WHO, Sudanese Embassy, Ministry of Social Affairs, Medical Departments of the Cairo Governorate, Nongovernmental Organizations, The General Federation of Social Welfare Associations, Cairo and Ain Shams Medicine Faculties, American University in Cairo, National Center for Social and Criminological Research, National Center for Industrial Security, Shoubrah High Institute for Social Work, Academy of Arts, Federation of Radio and Television, representatives of newspapers, General Organization of Information, Federation of Writers, and the Italian Cultural Center, the Eritrian Liberation Front, and Mrs. Joan Swingler, of the IPPF Central Office.

THE FIRST SESSION, OCTOBER 14, 1979

Dr. Amal Osman, minister of Social Affairs, and Mrs. Aziza Hussein, chair of the Cairo Family Planning Association, presented inaugural statements.

Professor Anwar Ahmed, former Under-Secretary for Social Affairs, chaired the session where the following papers were presented:

1. "Religious Background for the Customary Practice of Female Circumcision." Professor Anwar Ahmed, former Under-Secretary for Social Affairs.

2. "Health Damage Resulting from Female Circumcision." Dr. Roushdi Ammar, Professor, Obstetrician, and Gynecologist, Ain Shams University.

3. "Official Authorities on Female Circumcision in Egypt." Dr. Afaf Attia Salem, Director of Maternal and Child Care Department, Ministry of Health.

4. "Health Damage Resulting from Female Circumcision." Dr. Maher Mahran, Professor, Obstetrician, and Gynecologist, Ain Shams University.

SECOND SESSION

Mrs. Aziza Hussein chaired the second session on Monday, 15 October 1979, where the following papers were presented:

5. "Historical and Social Background for the Customary Practice of Female Circumcision." Professor Marie Bassili Assaad, Social Research Center, American University in Cairo.

6. "Field Experiences Regarding Customary Practice of Female Circumcision in Egypt." Mrs. Neemat Aboul Seoul, Director, Nursing School, Kasr El Aini Hospital.

MAIN CONCLUSIONS

During the final session, chaired by Professor Anwar Ahmed, the following conclusions and recommendations were approved:

1. The medical point of view is that female circumcision is a kind of mutilation and distortion of bodily organs having a special function. When we add to this the absence of any health benefit occurring from this operation, we come to the conclusion that female circumcision is harmful and therefore its confrontation and opposition become imperative.

2. The operation of female circumcision may cause a psychological trauma that may accompany the girl for the rest of her life.

3. Religions have not recommended female circumcision. Regarding Islam, the Quran does not mention it. No definite evidence exists to prove that the Prophet had ordered or recommended female circumcision. Islam leaves female circumcision to the discretion of society in the context of the public interest. The trend among Islamic scholars is that, if, for health and psychological considerations, female circumci-

sion should be discontinued or prevented, this will not contradict religious jurisdiction.

4. No scientific evidence exists to prove that there is any relationship between female circumcision and the girl's femininity and/or chastity.

5. The Conference approved the recommendations made in the Sudan WHO Conference held in February 1979, presented by Dr. Taha Ba'shar, the representative of the WHO Regional Office.

a. To establish a national policy which aims at combatting female circumcision.

b. To form a national organization that will work for the abolition of the practice of female circumcision.

c. To promote health and cultural awareness about the harmful effect of female circumcision, and to attempt to inform the public about the Islamic standpoint on this issue.

d. To hold training courses in health fields, particularly for midwives, to clarify the harmful effects of female circumcision.

RECOMMENDATIONS

As a consequence, the following recommendations were made:

1. To organize a national campaign in which religious scholars participate, in order to arouse consciousness about the health, psychological, and social damage resulting from female circumcision and informing the public about the religious stand toward it.

2. To inform and educate the parents.

3. To use the mass media and information agencies in educating the public.

4. To provide simplified booklets for the doctors, health and social workers, and the public including instructive materials about female circumcision.

5. To encourage women's associations to educate women about the harmful effects of female circumcision.

6. To give attention to the role of women's organizations and those responsible for women's committees in political parties in leading the fight against female circumcision.

7. To profit from rural and urban women leaders' efforts as well as from the efforts exerted by the students of National Service in publicizing the need to eliminate the custom of female circumcision.

8. To exert efforts to convince midwives to work on eliminating the custom, and simultaneously provide them with alternate work so they do not continue to gain from practicing such operations.

9. To carry out further scientific research on the custom.

10. To include in medical faculties and nursing schools appropriate courses and programs on the harmful effects of female circumcision.

11. To include in the Ministry of Education schools curricula instructive material in courses on the physiology of reproduction, family planning, and religion, showing the damage caused by female circumcision.

12. To formulate the legislation necessary to forbid female circumcision.

13. To exert efforts to inform and educate doctors and others in health and social welfare sectors about the facts surrounding female circumcision and the harmful effects resulting from practicing this custom.

14. To undertake educational efforts to emphasize what has been scientifically proven, that there is no relationship between female circumcision and the girl's chastity or femininity.

A QUESTION OF OUR CHILDREN'S BODIES
THE MEDICAL AND PSYCHOLOGICAL INJURY
CAUSED TO A GIRL BY CIRCUMCISION

(Article by Bahira Mukhtar, from the newspaper 'Al Ahram, 19 October 1979, translated by IPPR, London.)

This seminar, in raising several fundamental issues, highlighted the social and medical risk that attends female circumcision operations. The seminar exonerated religion from responsibility. This was stated by M. Anwar Ahmed, former Under-Secretary for Social Affairs, who said that there was no specific mention in the Quran of the circumcision of girls. He said also that although there was a requirement under usage sanctioned by tradition (Sunna), the theological jurists were not in agreement about it, and that the hadith (sayings and traditions of the Prophet Muhammad) said to support female circumcision were of doubtful validity. It has been said by some, he added, that the operation dignifies a woman, that it adorns her in the eyes of her husband, and that circumcision as a religious act is a matter of public interest; but health considerations call for its banning, and this does not conflict with religious edicts.

Marie Assaad, senior researcher at the Social Research Center, American University in Cairo, said that circumcision of girls is not found in Christianity or Judaism. She added that investigations had confirmed that the custom was of African or Pharaonic origin.

Dr. Rushdi Ammar, of the Ain Shams University medical faculty, said, "A girl receives a real psychological shock, particularly when this operation is done at an age when the girl is fully aware of what is being done to her." This was supported by Dr. Camilia Abdul Fattah, Professor of Psychology at Ain Shams University, who explained that submission to custom and to the tradition of female circumcision is the psychological explanation for why women and young girls accept circumcision operations, even though there is a risk to their lives. In so doing, the young girl is prepared for the day, enjoys it and its rituals of dancing, special songs, distinctive food and new clothes, and being decorated with henna; she receives presents, especially money which, particularly among the poorer classes, she is unable to resist.

The local study showed that, in the majority of cases, those circumcised had little education. Among the poorer classes the significance of circumcision lay with pleasing the husband as well as with being associated with cleanliness and moral reserve; in the upper classes it was a desirable tradition. The girl submits to the operation, since she knows that it is to the general satisfaction of the man, for the thought prevails that female circumcision is one of the qualifications without which she will not be accepted as a wife.

It is impossible to eradicate the psychological effect of the betrayal perpetrated upon her in the midst of the ceremonies: the shackling, the sight of the instruments of her mutilation, the pain and the complications, the offer of simple material bribes, for, however young the girl, she can compare between what she is being offered and what she is paying in the way of dignity and health.

The medical damage is considerable and very varied, says Dr. Rushdi Ammar, Professor of Gynecology and Obstetrics. Hemorrhage takes place, and infection leading to suppuration, septicemia, and eventual disfigurement of the area.

The urethra is sometimes damaged, and other complications occur.

In some cases, at childbirth and at the age when young girls are circumcised, it is difficult to ascertain the sex with the naked eye when sexual organs are externally examined, and, in certain cases, the circumcision operation may be carried out on a boy, presupposing that he is a girl, his sex being confirmed later on.

A survey of 331 women from the popular quarters has shown that circumcision does not affect the marital relationship, which relies more on the psychological aspects. Dr. Rushdi Ammar, however, recommends that circumcision of females not be carried out except in rare cases determined by a specialist.

Dr. Afaf Attia Salem, director of MCH at the Ministry of Health, representing the official side, announced that the following, Ministerial Resolution No. 74 of 1959, was promulgated: "The carrying out of female circumcision operations in Ministry of Health clinics is prohibited for medical, psychological, and social reasons; it is not authorized for midwives to undertake any surgical operation including circumcision."

Dr. Afaf went on to say that, since the Ministerial Resolution was issued, these operations have been carried out under cover, away from Ministry supervision, in the clinics of private doctors, and by unlicensed midwives.

The important social research done by Marie Assaad, senior researcher at the Social Research Center, American University in Cairo, concerned two age groups: the first group of fifty-four married women between the ages of twenty and fifty, of whom the majority was illiterate; and the second group of ninety-four unmarried girls and young women, Muslim and Christian, between the ages of twelve and twenty.

The study showed that 90.8 percent of the married women had had a circumcision operation, 46.9 percent had had one already performed on their daughters, that 34.7 percent intended to have it performed on their daughters, and that 94 percent had sisters who had had the operation. Twenty-six of the operations had been performed by midwives, eight by gypsies, six by barbers, six by doctors, and three by trained nurses. Operations had been performed on daughters by midwives (twenty-one), barbers (twelve), doctors (fifteen), nurse (one).

Of the married women, 93.8 percent said they were happy with their husbands, and gave as their reasons for circumcising their daughters the following, in this order: reduction in sexual desire, family tradition, medical purposes. The women gave similar reasons for their own circumcisions when they were young, with the exception that, for them, family tradition came first and that they were following the traditions of the Prophet. The mothers' generation was more influenced by tradition.

Public opinion about female circumcision is of great significance within the community. Moreover, some old traditions die hard in spite of changes in concepts and times. With the emergence of new scientific facts, 40.7 percent of the wives said that men supported female circumcision, 29.6 percent said that they were opposed, eleven cases said that they did not know if men thought about it, 5.6 percent said that the matter was up to the man and that some accept it and some do not.

A woman who has not been circumcised has a higher level of sexual desire, one that is insatiable, according to 77 percent of the married women. Wives expressed their insistence on having this operation performed on their daughters who should, in their view, be exposed to the selfsame fate as their own.

Of the young, unmarried women, the study showed that they had been circumcised between the ages of three and twelve, the greater proportion being done by midwives, with an increase in the number of doctors. These young women stated that they suffered greatly from the same psychological and medical complications . . . that occurred with the mothers, and the majority stated that they will not circumcise their daughters.

LIFE AND HEALTH OF
JORDANIAN CHILDREN

by Staffan Janson

This chapter will discuss the life conditions of suburban Jordanian children. In recent years a number of articles have been published dealing with the life of children in occupied Palestine during the Intifada,[1] but practically nothing has been published about the everyday life of Jordanian children. This essay is based on available, mainly statistical, information about maternal and child health in Jordan. The information is drawn from governmental bodies, universities, UNICEF, and nongovernmental organizations. To a large degree, this discussion is also based upon my own experiences dealing with mother and child health in Jordan for three years between 1986 and 1989. During these three years I headed the Institute of Child Health and Development (ICHD), a joint Swedish-Jordanian project with the goal of developing maternal and child health care. The institute also comprised an assessment unit for children with various handicaps, especially mental retardation and behavior disturbances. I also worked as an advisor to the United Nations in the development of a community-based rehabilitation program for Palestinian refugee children.

There are only a few reports on child health in Jordan published in English,[2] and they are not generally available. Many of the results from the ICHD also are presented here for the first time.

My experience of Jordanian children is mainly confined to suburban children. This is, however, where the majority of children live. Urbanization has been extremely fast in Jordan. Amman, the capital, for example, has grown from 45,000 to 1 million inhabitants since World War II.

As I have been dealing with health problems, most of what is written in this article is based on medical knowledge. I believe, however, that this is a fruitful starting point for further discussion of the conditions of life.

GEOPOLITICAL AND DEMOGRAPHIC
BACKGROUND

The Hashemite Kingdom of Jordan is located in southwest Asia, east of the Jordan Rift Valley. It borders Syria, Iraq, and Saudi Arabia and has access to the Red Sea through the Gulf of Aqaba. The land area is approximately 91,000 square kilometers. Jordan has three climatic zones: the Jordan Valley agricultural area, the Hill area with the major urban centers, and the semiarid desert.

The Emirate of Transjordan was created as an independent country on the East Bank of the Jordan River in 1921 during the British mandate period. It became a sovereign state in 1946. The West Bank of the Jordan River was formally united with the kingdom in 1950 but fell under Israeli occupation after the 1967 Israeli-Arab war. In 1988, after the Palestinian uprising in the West Bank and Gaza, Jordan formally severed legal and administrative ties with the West Bank, thus abandoning its claims to the territory.

Since its establishment four decades ago, Jordan has gone through three destructive wars and political and economic challenges that often looked insurmountable for a country so young and so limited in natural resources. Despite this, Jordan has achieved high literacy and immunization rates, a low infant mortality rate, and a well-functioning health system.

Jordan's economic well-being is dependent upon trade and political relations with neighboring Arab countries, especially Iraq. Due to its own very limited natural resources, job opportunities are limited within the country. One third of the Jordanian labor force works in the Gulf states and brings money back to Jordan. The economic recession, which began in 1983 with the weakening of oil prices and a slowdown in the neighboring economies, continued through the eighties.

The average annual income per household in 1987 was 3.491 Jordan dinars. This corresponded to 10,000 U.S. dollars. After the economic devaluation in 1988–1989, the average annual income was reduced to almost half that value. That money was expected to support a family of seven persons.

At least 11 percent of urban households in the Amman region had an income below the poverty level in 1985, according to the World Bank definition of an urban household poverty income level of 2,670 U.S. dollars per year. Unemployment in 1988 was estimated by economists at 16 percent.[3]

Expenditures for defense and security constituted nearly 30 percent of the total state budget in 1988. Expenditures for financial administration accounted for 31 percent, while expenditures on social services, health, and medication amounted to 17 percent.[4]

TABLE I

Population Data and Health Indicators, Jordan, 1988

Total population	3.1 million
Total area	91,110 square km
Population density (per square km)	2 – 65
Fertility rate (live births per 1,000 pop 1988)	6.6
Crude birth rate (births per 1,000 pop 1988)	45
Crude death rate (deaths per 1,000 pop 1988)	10
Population annual growth rate	3.4%
Life expectancy at birth (1988)	
Male	67
Female	71
Infant mortality rate (deaths per 1,000 live births)	35
Under 5 mortality rate	45
Urban population as percentage of total population (1988)	64%
Age structure as percentage of total population	
0 – 5 years	18%
6 – 15 years	30%
16 – 64 years	49%
65 years and above	4%
Adult literacy rate, male	85%
Adult literacy rate, female	75%
Percent of population with access to safe water	87.7%
Physician-to-population ratio	1 : 837
Nurse-to-population ratio	1 : 2,553
Hospital beds per 1,000 population	1.9
Per capita GNP	$1,150

Source: L. Bisharat, UNICEF regional office, Amman, 1988.

The economic crisis that became apparent in 1988 is perhaps one of the toughest challenges to face the Jordanians since the war of 1967.

Jordan's population in 1988 was estimated at 3.1 million. Sixty-four percent of the population lived in urban areas of 10,000 or more. The two major influxes of Palestinian refugees in 1948 (400,000 people) and in 1967 (350,000 people) dramatically increased the size of the population. However, the rate of natural increase is now higher than ever, at 3.4 percent. This is due to a constantly declining crude death rate (now 10 per 10,000), a constant high fertility rate (6.6 live births per 1,000 in 1989), and a low infant mortality rate, now said to be only 35 per 1,000 live births. As a result of the high fertility and recent reduction in infant and child mortality, Jordan has a very young population. Almost 18 percent of the population is under five years of age and

48 percent is under fifteen years of age. Over 75 percent of the total population is under thirty years and less than 5 percent over sixty-five years of age. Therefore the overwhelming bulk of Jordanians are children or young adults in their reproductive years.

Adult literacy has doubled in the past two decades, from 32 percent in 1962 to 80 percent in 1989. The literacy rate is estimated at 75 percent for females and 85 percent for males. Today practically every child goes to school and older children usually even speak some English.

One hundred percent of the families have radio and 95 percent own television sets. Consequently educational messages transmitted on TV and radio reach virtually the entire population. This has recently been used successfully in campaigns for oral rehydration therapy and in promoting breast-feeding.

Average family size is seven with a mean of two to three children under seven years. Average age of marriage for women in urban areas was estimated at twenty-two in 1988, compared to sixteen in rural areas. First pregnancy is usually one year after marriage.[5]

HEALTH FACILITIES FOR MOTHERS AND CHILDREN

National health expenditure is 6 percent of the GNP (Gross National Product). The ratio of physicians to the population reached 1 : 837 in 1988—a figure comparable to that of wealthier industrialized countries. There is an acute shortage of nurses in the country, particularly in rural areas. The national ratio is 1 : 2,553. The majority of nurses working in Jordan are expatriates.

The number of primary health care centers doubled during the years 1987–1988, to reach very remote areas as well as low-income urban areas. The number of government health centers run by the Ministry of Health reached 400 in 1989. This is in addition to 170 village clinics, 160 mother-and-child centers, 68 dental clinics, and 16 school health-team centers. There are also specialized health centers such as those for tuberculosis control. The percentage of infants fully immunized against DPT and polio (three doses) has reached 90 percent (Table 2). These figures are comparable to the best coverage in the western world.

The percentage of babies delivered by trained personnel has reached 50 percent. According to a survey conducted by the Ministry of Health and UNICEF in 1988, nearly half of all infants are born in hospitals and an equal number of women are examined by either a physician or midwife during pregnancy.

TABLE 2

Immunization Rates in Jordan, 1988

	%
Polio (three doses)	98
Triple-vaccine (DPT) (three doses)	98
Measles below 12 months	87
Measles below 24 months	94

Source: L. Bisharat, UNICEF regional office, Amman, 1988.

TABLE 3

*Trend of Infant Mortality Rate
in Jordan*

Year	Infant Mortality per 1,000 Live Births
1961	151
1972	90
1974	74
1976	78
1977	69
1986	55
1987	45
1988	35

Source: Jordan Ministry of Health and UNICEF, 1988.

Jordan has achieved the world's fastest annual rate of decline in infant mortality over the last ten years (Table 3). The rate of 35 deaths per 1,000 live births is significantly lower than rates in neighboring Mediterranean and North African countries and is a clear indicator of improved health status in Jordan.

Saudi Arabia, a much wealthier nation, has higher infant mortality. The growth pattern of Saudi rural children resembles that of children in most developing countries, with moderate stunting due to malnutrition. In Saudi Arabia that pattern is probably due to the focus on a highly technological system of medical care contemporary with relatively low maternal education and incomplete preventive services unequally distributed among the population.[6]

In Jordan about 88 percent of the population is provided with clean water and 98 percent with adequate sanitary facilities. Mortality from diarrhea is

1 death per 1,000 live births per year for children under five (down from 5 per 1,000 in 1985) and 3 per 1,000 for children below twelve months of age.

Over one half of the women have used oral rehydration solution, and 55 percent of the women who know about or have used it can properly describe its preparation.

MATERNAL MORTALITY

Although no study on maternal mortality in Jordan has ever been conducted, maternal mortality is estimated at 4 deaths per every 10,000 live births (mortality before, during, and after delivery).

BREAST-FEEDING

According to a survey conducted in 1987, 2.9 percent of the mothers never breast-fed their children. The highest rate (4 percent) was found among economically advantaged families, followed by families living in refugee camps, low-income and poor families in urban areas.

The most common reason for not breast-feeding is a new pregnancy and a perceived poor milk secretion. In a survey of 930 women in 1988, Abulaban[7] showed that the majority of women (91 percent) breast-fed their children at some time, but weaned their infants from their breasts early. Only 27 percent of the women in the urban area thought that breast milk was satisfactory for children up to four months of age, while 80 percent of the rural women thought it should be enough. There was no relation between education and breast-feeding. Of the highly educated women, 43 percent gave supplementary food before four months of age according to instructions they received from physicians. Well-off women usually have their babies in private hospitals. The majority of these places are run by obstetricians and pediatricians educated in Europe twenty to thirty years ago. They adhere to outdated policies with early formula feeding and separation of mother and child.

The rate of contraceptive use for 1988 was estimated at 31 percent, compared to 23 percent in 1976. Our own data on 500 pregnancies in Suweileh between 1987 and 1989 are very close to the national mean, with an overall contraceptive use rate of 32 percent. Eleven percent used oral contraceptives and 11 percent intrauterine devices only, 1 percent other methods, and 8 percent used more than one method. Contraceptives are not used by Jordanian women until they have had at least one pregnancy. Women of higher parity are more likely to use contraceptives than women of lower parity.

Abortion is not legal in Jordan except in cases where the mother's health is threatened. Women with the means to pay for illegal abortions obtain it on occasion.

NEW HAZARDS FOR CHILDREN

Following the significant reductions in mortality from diarrhea diseases and the immunizable childhood diseases, acute respiratory infections have now come to the fore as a major cause of morbidity and mortality.

A retrospective analysis of inpatient mortality during 1987 and 1988 in the pediatric ward and the neonatal and premature unit at the largest governmental hospital in Amman (al-Bashir, mainly accessible to the middle class and the underprivileged sector of the population) showed that deaths and mortality are clustered mainly in the first year of life and particularly in the first month of life.[8]

Sixty-seven percent of deaths are during the neonatal period and 92% in the first year of life. In the pediatric ward (referral from own maternity excluded) 35 percent of the admitted have neonatal problems including sepsis, anomalies, and cold injuries. It seems paradoxical to have cold injuries in a warm country like Jordan, but improper handling of the newborn and young infant seems to be a common problem. In areas at a high altitude like Amman, winter can be very wet and cold, with even a few days of snow. The majority of houses are not equipped for this climate.

In the above-mentioned study from al-Bashir, further important reasons for death in infancy were found to be:

Lower respiratory disease/pneumonia   19%

Diarrheal illness   11%

Heart diseases   8.5%

Neurological diseases and complicated cerebral palsy   6.5%

Communicable infectious diseases like tetanus, measles, and bacterial meningitis   6%

It is obvious from these figures that former major killers like diarrhea and communicable infectious diseases now have been replaced by neonatal problems, malformations, and lower respiratory diseases.

CHILDHOOD DISABILITY

There is reason to believe that Jordan, being in transition to a modern state, might have a higher prevalence of handicapped children than western countries, since effective preventive measures have not yet been implemented at the same time as more children, even those disabled, are surviving. A recent study of the prevalence of handicaps affecting children in the Gaza district supports this view.[9]

We have specifically looked into the etiology of severe mental retardation in a group of 203 retarded Jordanian children, born 1975–1985.[10] It was found to be related to two main factors:

1. Aftermaths of high perinatal morbidity or meningitis in infancy, often giving rise to a combination of severe mental retardation and cerebral palsy.

2. A high degree of intermarriage and a high frequency of retarded siblings, indicating that genetic causes of mental retardation are common.

As can be seen from Table 4, low birth weight is in itself a risk, even when not complicated by any other disease. Due to different factors such as malnutrition and infections during pregnancy, low birth weight and/or prematurity is twice as common in Jordan as in Sweden. Asphyxia (inadequate oxygenation at birth) accounts for the largest proportion of children with the combination of mental retardation and cerebral palsy. A lack of professional birth attendants able to resuscitate newborns both at home and in the Jordanian hospitals is a part of the reason for bad outcome at the deliveries.

Although the coverage of antenatal care in Jordan is satisfactory, many mothers do not attend on a regular basis. In a study done at al-Bashir Governmental Hospital in Amman [11] we highlighted services for pregnant mothers. Mothers were cared for alike, irrespective of their problems. High-risk mothers did not get any specific attention and, where pregnancy complications were identified, a large proportion of the mothers were not given proper follow-up. It was also obvious that for those mothers who got proper antenatal care, much of the investment was lost due to scattered services and a practically nonexistent connection between antenatal care, delivery, and neonatal ward. There is unfortunately a risk that service programs tend to be valued for their own sake unless the staff is very well trained and guided by an outspoken preventive ideology. Many problems could also have been prevented if the mothers had been taught to be more alert to signs and symp-

TABLE 4

Etiology of Mental Retardation in 203 Children

Etiology	Number of Cases	% of Total
Prenatal		
True microcephaly	15	
Mb Down	8	
SGA / LBW without reported asphyxia or other disease in the neonatal period	10	
Neurometabolic disease	4	
Congenital hydrocephalus	3	
Total	40	20
Perinatal		
Asphyxia / cerebral hemorrhage	44	
Kernicterus (blood-group incompatibility)	4	
Neonatal infection	2	
Total	50	25
Postnatal		
Sepsis / meningitis	36	
Brain trauma (accident)	4	
Severe dehydration	2	
Morbilli-encephalitis	2	
Tetanus	1	
Drowning	1	
Intoxication	1	
Postoperative anoxia	1	
Total	48	24
Unknown etiology total	65	32

SGA: Small for gestational age.
LBW: Low birth weight.

toms. There is a great need to educate mothers in pregnancy, as was shown earlier by Abbas and Walker.[12]

THE SUBURB OF SUWEILEH

The Suweileh area is situated northwest of Amman, 900 meters above sea level. It is usually cold in winter with days of snow. Fifteen percent of the houses have central heating. The others are kept warm with kerosene heaters, a major cause of burns in small children. Many houses have their front door on the street, where people, cattle, and cars mingle. The area contains a mosque, primary schools, and two junior high schools, one private and one public. There is also a community center with a kindergarten, library, and occupational-training center for women. This center, which is unique in Jordan, is run on a voluntary basis by the Sociological Institution at the University of Jordan. There are a few playgrounds, dangerously situated adjacent to main roads.

The majority of the families are Muslims. Only 7–8 percent are Christians. The Muslim man is allowed to marry up to four wives, but a second wife in this mainly urbanized society is uncommon nowadays. In our region only 3 percent of the men had second wives, and only 1.5 percent had two wives living under the same roof.

One third of the families had a decently equipped kitchen and furniture comparable to western standards. Seventy percent had carpets, rugs, and mattresses directly on the floor.

The wives usually stayed at home (88 percent) or worked full-time (9 percent), usually as teachers. Ten percent of the women were illiterate and had no formal education. On the other hand, 25 percent had a college diploma or a university degree, underlining the sincerity of the Jordanian schooling system in supporting the education of both sexes. The close relation between child health and good education of mothers is well understood by the authorities.

In comparison, 4 percent of the men were illiterate and 40 percent had a diploma or a university degree. Twenty-one percent were unskilled workers and 8 percent were unemployed. Families had, on average, four children and one other relative living in the house. In general seven persons lived in a two- to three-room concrete house.

There is a long tradition of consanguinity both in the Palestinian and the bedouin society. The general explanation for this tradition is the importance of keeping estate, wealth, and livestock within the family or at least within the tribe. The Quran does not directly support intermarriage, although it states that a man has the first right to his female cousin.

In our region 16 percent of the children's parents were married to a first cousin, 21 percent to a second cousin, and 7 percent to another close relative. Well-educated men married a relative less often, reflecting their greater freedom of choice, while well-educated women still married a cousin as often as the poorly educated. Much has been said about the negative consequences of intermarriage, but little is actually known. There are definitely clusters of heritable diseases like congenital cataract (eye disease) and muscular dystrophias. In our study mentioned above [13] we found a definite higher frequency of intermarriage among parents with children with severe mental retardation. At present we are engaged in a study to discover the effect of intermarriage on the health of the total population.

What can definitely be stated, however, is that other risk factors like neonatal complications and accidents at present overshadow the importance of possible consequences of consanguinity for the health of the Jordanian child.

Distance to health services, especially if the family has many children, seems to be very important. The health centers should therefore be placed as centrally in the community as possible. Eighty percent of the families living within a distance of 300 meters attended our services irrespective of being poor or rich. On the other hand, only 13 percent of poor families living far away (more than 800 meters) attended. The typical family attending our services consisted of a 34-year-old father, a 29-year-old mother, and three children of preschool age. The families were of Jordanian, Palestinian, Armenian, or Caucasian background.

By the end of 1989 we had followed closely 498 pregnancies, out of which only 6 percent delivered at home. Premature births (less than thirty-six gestational weeks) were only 5 percent, which corresponds to western figures. Eighty-four percent had a normal delivery. Of the 501 children (three pairs of twins) only 4 had asphyxia and 1 was injured during delivery. Twenty-nine children had infections or other diseases complicating the neonatal period. Six children died within the first month due to congenital malformations or severe infection.

Nutritional levels of children in Jordan remain unsatisfactory. The first major incidence of malnutrition occurs when the children reach the age of six months and is associated with unsatisfactory weaning practices. Weight loss is quite frequent at this stage.[14] When breast milk production is unsatisfactory, poor people cannot afford formula but give milk powder, low in iron, with subsequent anemia. The supplementary foods first introduced are cooked rice with milk, biscuits with tea, and sauce from meat. Biscuits represent a specific problem as they introduce refined sugar early in infancy. In Jordanian schoolchildren, dental health has deteriorated during the last twenty years.[15] Suspected factors include consumption of refined sugars and the absence of active cleaning of teeth. Dental decay is especially harmful if it starts early in life. We made an unprecedented study of preschool children showing that regular sweets consumption early in life is common (Table 5).[16] Dental decay (caries) is unfortunately so common that in the age group 3−6 years 71 percent have acquired caries, most of them severe.

Jordanian parents do not appear to be aware of the importance of dental hygiene for children, especially with regard to toddlers and young children. Introduction of sweets comes early and is uncontrolled. All children eat

TABLE 5
Regular Consumption of Sweets

Age Group (Years)	% Eating Sweets Regularly
0.5 – 1	13
1 – 2	57
2 – 3	84
3 – 6	96

Source: S. Janson and H. Fakhouri. "Dental Health in Jordanian Preschool Children." *Swedish Dental Journal* 17 (1993).

sweets and biscuits whenever available. There is no program of dental prophylaxis whatsoever in Jordan.

CHRONIC DISEASES AND HANDICAPS

In a society where malnutrition and communicable infectious diseases are reduced and no longer life-threatening for the bulk of the children, other problems come to the fore. Such problems are chronic diseases and handicaps which in the past were not attended to or caused children to die. Like in the industrialized countries, services for children suffering from such illnesses in Jordan have been initiated not by the government but mainly through private initiatives. There are several small homes and schools for the mentally retarded, a few homes for the physically handicapped, and a Cerebral Palsy Foundation working with the neurologically handicapped child. Dr. Samira Baban, the head of the CP Foundation, recently estimated that although the foundation has been operating for ten years now, they are still reaching only one third of the neurologically handicapped children in Jordan.

It has often been said [17] that in Arab culture disability traditionally has been seen as something shameful, a trial or an ordeal to be faced by the family that has a disabled person in its midst. Thus, Arab families have been loath to admit that they have a disabled child, for fear that this would be considered a disgrace which lowers the family's standing among its neighbors. Furthermore, some people feel disability is a divine tribulation visited upon the family with the aim of testing their belief in God, and that one is bound to accept such a misfortune with faith and forbearance. However, I have not encountered such attitudes and neither has the CP Foundation of Jordan. When people think that there is some real help available, they will come with their children for consultations. When there is no help available, attitudes like the ones mentioned above perhaps are the only remedy. In our experience, the most difficult problem was to explain to parents that usually there was no instant healing for their children, but many possibilities to give them a better life through continuous physiotherapy, sometimes long-term medication, and by changing attitudes toward the handicapped.

The royal family has supported sports for the disabled. This probably has done a great deal to change attitudes toward the handicapped in the Jordanian society.

PSYCHOMOTOR DEVELOPMENT

Diagnoses of mental retardation and neurological handicaps are generally delayed in Jordan. One reason for this is the lack of interest in psychomotor development of the child by professionals. There is consequently no screening program for hearing, vision, or neurological handicaps. Our study shows that there are a lot to be found if one is interested, and many things can be diagnosed early.

There are reasons to believe that Jordanian children develop along the same stages and at the same time as western children. Because there are no normative data on psychomotor development for the population of Jordan, we tested this by applying a simple psychomotor screening program adapted from the MCH Centers in Sweden. This is built upon items drawn from Gesell, Griffith, and the Denver test. The screening program has worked well in Sweden for fifteen years and on two million children. Between 100 and 250 Suweileh children were studied in different age groups, between two weeks and eighteen months, and about 70 children in the age groups of four and five and a half years, by our local pediatrician, Dr. Hind Dawani. Differences in performance between Swedish and Jordanian children started to appear around the age of eighteen months. The most striking differences were that, while 85 percent of Swedish children know about the parts of their body, only 46 percent of the Suweileh children properly do so. In a non-handicapped population practically every Swedish child can eat with a spoon at this age, while 20 percent of the children in Suweileh could not. Other gross and fine motor performances showed no deviation.

The results correspond well to the clinical experience of our doctors and nurses. The reason for the delay of body awareness and the retarded ability to feed themselves could be that Jordanian women, due to a heavy work load and big family, do not have time to teach their babies to eat and be aware of themselves. Another possible reason is that children in Jordanian culture are not treated as separate persons as early as in Sweden. This seems paradoxical, as there usually is a new baby in the family when the index child is eighteen months old, and the older child could benefit from feeding itself, but our experience is in accordance with what has been said above.

At four years of age, speech, gross motor, and fine motor performance are similarly developed in Jordanian and Swedish children, while abstract entities like quantity and orientation in space (like above-under, in front of, and behind) are significantly less well understood by Jordanian children. At five and a half years these differences have vanished and even antithetical items like little-big and long-short are understood well by 95 percent of the children. Still, only 45 percent of the Jordanian children could accurately copy drawings like a cross, circle, triangle, and square.

The results from four and five and a half years of age indicate that there is a lack of abstract stimulation for children in the investigated population in Suweileh, but the children catch up before five and a half years of age. Only their skills in drawing and copying are still behind. As children in the western world have been tested on their performance for at least thirty years now, we know that such skills, especially abstract and fine motor skills, are mastered better in every decade, probably due to earlier and more intensive stimulation. Swedish children begin school at seven. Few demands are made for technical skills. Rather the emphasis is on sociability. Jordanian children develop abstract reasoning skills and fine motor skills later. They begin school at age six in a very demanding school system, where they are expected to read and write within a few weeks of starting school.

ACCIDENTS

Another very important condition for the life of Jordanian children is the high risk of getting involved in an accident. This has rarely been discussed in public, and there are no statistical figures to rely on. Accidents are probably one of the main killers over one year of age. Street traffic is very heavy where small children are playing. It is common to see children of three or four years even crossing highways on their own. Jordan has a society for the prevention of road accidents, to which I have been invited several times, but measures to prevent childhood accidents still seem far in the future. The authorities also have acted very inconsistently. A safety-belt law was instituted by one minister and taken away by the successor. The importance of child safety is not at all understood. In an ongoing study at the surgical ward of the Princess

Basma Teaching Hospital in the north of Jordan, we noted such absolutely unnecessary accidents as children falling off platforms of trucks and drowning in water tanks.

At our MCH Center in Suweileh, during a winter week in 1987, we asked 100 mothers with a total of 444 children under sixteen years of age if the children had been involved in any accident during the last seven days. This was the case in 30 of the 100 families. Most cases were mild. Cut wounds and burns dominated. The average number of children in the families with accidents was 8.4, in contrast to the families with no wounded children, with an average of 3.8. This is a significant difference, suggesting that injuries are more common where possibilities for observation by the mothers are fewer. More accidents were reported in families where the mother was illiterate and where mothers were full-time workers. There were no clear differences between poor and well-off people. The overall problem therefore seemed to be supervision of small children in a dangerous environment.

As most of the injuries could have been prevented, we started an accident home inventory, connected with an educational program for the families.[18] During 1988, fifty families with a total number of 207 children, including 114 preschool children, were visited. Educational level, professions of parents, and housing were representative for the whole area. Only eighteen of the fifty families reported that the children had ever been exposed to an accident. We know that long-time recall gives only minimal figures, but it can provide some other valuable information. Burns and falls were the most common accidents, and they occurred with equal frequency among girls and boys. The overall frequency of accidents was higher for boys.

Children were exposed to many dangers. In practically every house there was an exposed gas tube. Kerosene heaters present a very big problem as they usually are placed in the middle of the room. Children step over them or get burned from hot water put on top of the heaters. Staircases without rails both inside and outside the house were common. People stored their drugs reasonably safely, but 25 percent of the families nevertheless had dangerous drugs where they were easy to reach by preschool children. Only nineteen of the fifty families stored chemicals in a suitable way.

Only 50 percent of the families had a safe garden for the children to play in, or a safe roof. Ten families with unsafe surroundings stated that they watched their children all the time (which is usually not possible), and in the remaining fifteen families the children played in unsafe gardens, on unsafe roofs, or in the street. Twelve families lived on streets with very little traffic, twenty-nine families lived on streets with moderate or heavy traffic, and the remaining nine families in streets with definite risks for accidents. The common way of building houses in this area unfortunately is to place the front door so that it opens directly onto the street. Only well-off people have a yard around the house with a fence. Easily accessible flat roofs with low fences are extremely dangerous.

PSYCHOLOGICAL PROBLEMS

Psychosocial problems and psychosomatic diseases often reflect the conditions of life. Our clinical experiences of Jordanian children showed that psychological problems exist, but the picture was very scattered within the society. Children from large, poor families might show signs of understimulation or apathy due to anemia and frequent infectious diseases, while well-off people showed typical problems of the small, core family with spoiled, demanding children and a variety of psychosomatic diseases. Children in our region did not seem to react with psychosomatic disease to an authoritarian upbringing but reacted in this way where the parents had a bad relationship.

Every week we had a conference where the MCH staff had the opportunity to discuss psychosocial and psychosomatic diseases with a social worker and a psychologist. The staff was supervised by a Swedish psychologist, but the local staff had all their basic training in Jordan or Lebanon.

The problems of seventy-one consecutive children discussed at these team conferences during 1989 were registered (thirty-four boys and thirty-seven girls; thirty-three children were infants and thirty-eight were one to six years old). The most common topic was biological problems. This usually concerned multiple problems in poor families with handicapped children, such as children with muscular dystrophia, cerebral palsy, congenital vision and hearing defects, or different degrees of mental retardation. The care required by handicapped children can be a significant burden for a poor family with few resources, especially when they receive no help from their relatives. They usually are not able to find the right way to receive aid or are queuing endlessly at places where they are badly received and finally end up with an inadequate and expensive investigation, usually not followed by any treatment. Social and psychologic support is practically nonexistent.

Different types of developmental delay are also common, either on a biologic or cultural basis. People of Jordan highly appreciate formal schooling and are often worried by signs that could indicate future learning disability. Developmental delay on cultural grounds seen in smaller children was often a consequence of mothers' depression and, in older children, of understimulation. In big families, children between the ages of four and six get squeezed between the youngest children and the school-age children. In rural areas there is usually something to do, like sheep tending, even for this age group, but suburban children and children in the refugee camp go idle during the last years before they start school.

Another problem, giving rise to much discussion, is a failure to thrive in children who initially were looked upon as malnourished. This is probably a fairly common but misinterpreted problem. Among our group of seventy-one children we had six cases of definite failure to thrive. For six of the children, the background was a depressed mother with many children. The following examples illustrate this topic.

Case Report 1

A three-week-old girl. Third child. Caesarean section at gestational week 34. Birth weight 2,030 grams and practically the same weight when coming to us at three weeks of age. Dehydrated and starved, cried all the time; mother was depressed. No breast milk. The mother was not supposed to breast-feed until nine days after birth, due to the rules at the hospital and infection in the wound.

The family is poor and the father is unemployed.

The mother said that this girl was more important to her than a free Palestine.

The family received some economic help through our social worker and continued support for breast-feeding. The child put on 300 grams in one week and the mother got successively more breast milk.

Case Report 2

Eight-month-old girl. Youngest of six children of a mother of thirty-two and a father of thirty-three. Born in hospital, birth weight 2,500 grams. Lost a lot of weight as the mother was sick after birth and couldn't take care of her the first ten days.

When the girl was three months old, she weighed only 2,100 grams. She was admitted to a hospital for investigation but the family could not afford it so they took her back. Diagnosed as malabsorption. She was then judged by us and we could not find any obvious signs of severe disease. Mother and child were depressed and the child was diagnosed as having failure to thrive. The mother started to come regularly to our clinic and we learned that the girl was the consequence of an unwanted pregnancy which the mother was unaware of until the child started kicking at five months.

Through continued support of the mother, the child started to grow and made a decent recovery.

ABUSE AND NEGLECT

Mild flogging seems to be a regular phenomenon in the Jordanian family, but abuse is very seldom heard about. We brought up this topic several times with our local staff, but they always stated that abuse is not a part of their culture. In the three cases where we noted abuse with a high degree of certainty, the fathers were mentally ill or divergent.

Case Report 3

A well-educated but poor family with seven daughters. The father is mentally ill and paranoic from time to time. He has lost his post as a civil servant. The mother of thirty-one is pregnant. She came in wintertime with two of her youngest children who had chilblains. The girls got their frost damage during two days of snow when the mother had to leave them to go to the hospital with an older girl who had a complicated arm fracture caused by the father. He did not take care of the younger ones. Instead, he abused the mother for not having looked after the children.

This case illustrates something which is well known in Sweden, namely that the risk for abuse of children is big in families where the mother already is maltreated by the husband. It is true that the woman has a strong position in the Jordanian home, but in our experience maltreatment of wives is a common phenomenon.

DEPRESSION IN MOTHERS

Many of the problems of younger children seem to be a direct consequence of mothers' depression.

Three different psychological phenomena at the time of delivery are usually distinguished in the literature.

1. Puerperal psychosis. A severe mental illness, sometimes named breast-milk psychosis, as it is concomitant with lactation. Puerperal psychosis is rare. One or two per thousand deliveries are usually so severe that they require admission to hospital. In 500 pregnancies followed by us we had one such case.

2. Postnatal depression. Much more common, affecting 10–15 percent of all mothers, usually treated in outpatient departments. There are no reports on postnatal depression in Jordan, but we saw several cases, which will be discussed below.

3. Postnatal blues. Transient irritability, tearfulness, and depression occurring in the first week following childbirth in 50 percent or more of newly delivered mothers.

Our clinical experience is that this was also very common in Jordan.

As practically nothing is known from the past about Jordanian mothers' experience of pregnancy, delivery, and the postnatal period, our social worker at the ICHD, Hiam Insheiwat, has started to investigate this. In April 1990 she interviewed twenty-nine mothers using a semistructured questionnaire. The mothers were referred to her by the local midwife, mainly due to social and economic problems or worry about the pregnancy. Each mother was questioned the first week after delivery and a second time three weeks later.

Of the twenty-nine mothers, fifteen had a normal delivery without complications. Nine had vaginal deliveries with complications like the use of vacuum extraction, extensive bleeding, severe blood-pressure fall, or fever postpartum. Five mothers had caesarean sections.

The mothers' own descriptions of their delivery experiences are presented in Table 6. The important thing about this table is not the exact relation between the answers, but that such a large group of mothers expressed such experiences of severely difficult delivery. These women are supposed to be brave and strong and expected not to lament. Some of them were extremely afraid of another pregnancy. It is easy to understand if these women develop depression and subsequent problems in bringing up their children.

When the mothers were asked to judge their own well-being at the first interview, thirteen felt bad or very bad about the delivery and the postnatal period, ten mothers felt good, and six neither good nor bad. When inter-

---
TABLE 6
Mothers' Descriptions of Delivery

Description	Number of mothers
Very painful, afraid of dying	5
Very difficult, very painful (compared to expectations or to previous deliveries)	7
Quick but very painful	4
Less difficult and painful than previous deliveries	4
Ordinary (said by mother with more than five children!)	1
Easy and nice	4

viewed three weeks later, only three mothers rated themselves as depressed; eighteen now felt all right.

There were fifteen girls and fourteen boys delivered. We found no relation between the sex of the child and the mother's depressed feelings.

Ten of the mothers touched their babies or breast-fed them directly after delivery. The four mothers who delivered at home are in this group. Four mothers touched their babies or breast-fed them two to four hours after delivery. Ten mothers touched their babies or breast-fed them the second day after delivery. These mothers were usually delivered in private hospitals, where they still have a rule not to give the baby to the mother until the day after delivery, and where babies often are given sugar water or formula before breast-feeding. Two mothers touched their babies or breast-fed them on the third day after delivery. They were mothers with complicated deliveries. On the whole, mothers who could breast-feed their babies early felt better in the postnatal period.

Fortunately enough, the majority of women were well supported by female relatives in their homes during the postnatal period. The woman's own mother or mother-in-law was the usual person to help. Some relatives came from far away to help, for example, from the West Bank, Syria, or Saudi Arabia.

CONCLUDING REMARKS

Children compose the majority of the Jordanian population. Today 75 percent of them live in urban or suburban areas. Two thirds of the population has a Palestinian background, and most have relatives in the West Bank or in Gaza. To ask them where they come from is very important, and they proudly refer to places west of the Jordan River, which they usually have never seen. Palestinian families are aware of the unpredictability of life. They are prepared to leave at any time and they know that the best way to bring about change is to get a good education. Formal schooling is looked upon as very important, and in Jordan today both sexes can get at least a good basic education.

Unfortunately the school system is very conservative and demanding from the first day. Many children, especially those from large and poor families, are not prepared for this. Due to intellectual understimulation, technical skills of writing and drawing as well as their abstract thinking lag behind those of other children. Children between four and six are in a particularly exposed group. This is even more obvious in the refugee camps.[19]

For twenty years Jordan has been in transition between an agricultural and a modern urbanized society. In two decades, it has passed stages that took

100 years in Europe. Great achievements have been made in the health sector during the last 15 years. Immunization rates of children and pregnant mothers are the best in the whole region, and the mortality rate is lower than in any other comparable country. During the last 5 years Jordan also has learned to master diarrheal diseases.

Tasks to accomplish in the period to come are assuring safe motherhood and a good start in life. There is a clear need for the development of knowledge, attitudes, and procedures which will help to reduce neo- and perinatal problems, particularly since about 40 percent of all births still take place at home.

There is also added concern about postnatal care, because children who suffer from low birth weight/immaturity, birth accidents, and/or congenital abnormalities and survive form the majority of the disabled and handicapped population later in life. The severity of their handicaps can be reduced and sometimes even negated if detected early or corrected early.

One must also focus on the very dangerous surroundings in which particularly suburban children live. Preventive thinking needs to permeate the whole society in order to diminish accidents, dental decay, and many secondary handicaps resulting from preventable or treatable diseases.

The everyday life of Jordanian children is quite different from that of their parents. Rita Giacaman[20] gives a lively description of West Bank village children and their life-style:

> Children spend most of the day outside playing with twigs, mud, Coca-Cola cans, plastic bags and stones among other natural and synthetic items. They are left unattended, barefoot and almost always dirty. They are free to move around without fear, and no one prohibits them when curiosity instructs them to tear an object apart and examine it. Such objects, if found, have already been deemed useless.

In the suburban area, there are very few natural places for children to play, and the living space for younger children is very limited. Especially in well-off families we have noticed many children with irritability and a lot of aggression, overloaded with toys but geographically bound to an apartment or a small yard. The need for stimulation and affection of these children seems to be satisfied when they are living among many relatives, but more problematic when living in a small core family. This successively more restricted and artificial way of living in the suburbs contrasts with the life-style of children in smaller villages, who tend to be much more free to move around, and where nature provides both their toys and playground.

ACKNOWLEDGMENTS

This essay is based on experiences and observations made during a three-year stay in Jordan, 1986–1989. I am greatly indebted to Dr. Hind Dawani, Dr. Aiman Abulaban, and all the staff at the Institute of Child Health and Development in Suweileh. Without their professional skills and eagerness to document their work, this article could not have been written. I would also like to thank my Swedish workmates in Jordan, nurse Anna Bodin and psychologist Birgitta Aberg, who implemented our program with great patience.

NOTES

1. R. Giacaman, *Life and Health in Three Palestinian Villages* (London and Atlantic Highlands: Ithaca Press, 1988).

2. Jordan Ministry of Social Development, *Jordan Child Study* (Amman, 1984). S. Hijazi, *Child Growth and Nutrition in Jordan* (Amman: Royal Scientific Society Press, 1977).

3. L. Bisharat, "The Situation of Children and Others in the Hashemite Kingdom of Jordan" (stencil, Amman: UNICEF regional office, 1989).

4. Ibid.

5. Z. al-Kayed, Working paper (Amman: Jordan Ministry of Health, 1987).

6. F. Serenius, *Child Health in Saudi-Arabia* (thesis, Uppsala University Press, 1988).

7. A. Abulaban, "Breast Feeding Knowledge and Practices in Jordan" (working paper, Annenberg School of Communications, University of Pennsylvania, 1989).

8. S. al-Azab, "Highlights on Infant and Child Mortality in Jordan: Experiences of al-Bashir Governmental Hospital, Amman," in *Perinatal Brain Damage* (proceedings of a seminar, September 1989, University of Jordan).

9. C. Saunders, "A Study of the Handicapping Conditions Affecting Children in the Refugee Camp Population of the Gaza Strip" (stencil report, Faculty of Education, University of Calgary, 1984).

10. S. Janson et al., "Severe Mental Retardation in Jordanian Children," *Acta Ped. Scand.* 79 (1990): 1099–1104.

11. S. Janson, "The Importance of a Comprehensive Maternal and Child Health Care Program in Jordan," in *Perinatal Brain Damage* (proceedings of a seminar, September 1989, University of Jordan).

12. A. Abbas and G. Walker, "Determinants of the Utilization of Maternal and Child Services in Jordan," *Int. J. of Epidemiology* 15, no. 3 (1986): 403–406.

13. Janson, "Importance of a Comprehensive Maternal and Child Health Care Program."

14. S. Hijazi, A. Abulaban, and J. C. Waterlow, "The Duration for Which Exclusive Breast Feeding Is Adequate," *Acta Ped. Scand.* 78 (1989): 23–28.

15. M. al-Habashneh, "Dental Health of Children in Jordan" (stencil, Jordan University, 1981).

16. S. Janson and H. Fakhouri, "Dental Health in Jordanian Preschool Children," *Swedish Dental Journal* 17 (1993): 123 – 127.

17. A. al-Khatib, "Disability in Jordan" (stencil, Amman: UNESCO, 1989).

18. S. Janson, M. Alcco, A. Beetar, A. Bodin, and S. Sham, "Accident Risks for Suburban Preschool Jordanian Children," *J. Trop. Paediatr.* In press.

19. B. Eckerberg, "Psychomotor Development of 100 Children 4 – 6 Years in Palestinian Refugee Camps" (stencil, Stockholm: Swedish Save the Children, 1987).

20. Giacaman, *Life and Health in Three Palestinian Villages*.

CHILD MORTALITY AND THE CHANGING DISCOURSE ON CHILDHOOD IN TURKEY

by Akilé Gürsoy

Much has been written on the discovery and the conceptualization of childhood as a social construct after Philip Aries' classic work *Centuries of Childhood* (1965). In the decades since, issues of "child rights" have preoccupied the agendas of international organizations such as the United Nations. In line with these recent developments, Turkey also has witnessed the development of literature and research related to child-rights themes.

Since the turn of the century, childhood in Turkey has been viewed not only within traditional and religious frameworks but also from a nationalistic perspective. In the early years of the republic (1920s), the situation of children was seen as an integral part of nation-building and progress, and discourse on childhood expressed the nationalistic desire for high fertility and an emphasis on child health and survival. Since the establishment of the Republic, the future power assigned to Turkey's children has been a frequently voiced assumption. Special attention has been devoted to education, especially to that of girls. April 23,[1] the date of the establishment of the republic in 1923, was officially proclaimed Cocuk Bayrami (Children's Holiday) partly in recognition of the fact that it is children who will inherit the republic.[2]

After the seventies, however, in contrast with the themes of desired high fertility, child health and survival, and children as part of nation-building and progress, we begin to hear the discourse of problems of *overpopulation* and the issues of child rights, often expressed as the problem of "unlived" childhoods.[3] Since that time Turkey's national discourse on children has shared the concerns of the United Nations and other international development organizations that view child health and survival as issues related to *child rights* rather than to *nation-building*.

The problem of high infant and child mortality remains an issue. My own anthropological research and fieldwork in a low-income neighborhood of

Istanbul suggests the need for reevaluation of the theoretical paradigm that views childhood issues primarily in relation to mothers rather than in a broader cultural context. The emphasis on mothers as a primary problematic reflects an extensive and implicit conceptualization of motherhod that has penetrated scientific discourse and methodology (Gürsoy Tezcan 1992).

Today Turkey has a population of over 55 million people. In 1987 there were an estimated 20 million children under sixteen and 7 million children under five (UNICEF 1989:94).[4]

UNEXPECTEDLY HIGH INFANT AND CHILD MORTALITY RATES

Infant mortality rate (IMR)—the number of newborn children dying prior to one year of completed age, per 1,000 live births—is a commonly cited criterion of development and has received increasing attention over the past twenty years (World Bank 1980, 1985; OECD 1979; Sümbüloglu 1982:236; Mosley 1984; Sivard 1985; UNICEF 1985, 1987, 1989). In recent years the World Health Organization and international public opinion have focused considerable attention on infant and child health and deaths. In 1982, James Grant, World Director of UNICEF, stated that out of the 125 million children born that year, 17 million would die before reaching their first birthday, and he called all countries to joint action against this state of affairs (Grant 1982). In 1979, the Thirty-second World Health Congress revised the Alma Ata Meeting decisions of the previous year, and the outlines of an international strategy were published under the title *Health for All by 2000*. Within this perspective, twelve global objectives were defined. One of these objectives was directly related to IMR: "Infant mortality rate will be less than 50 per thousand for each identifiable sub-culture in each country" (WHO 1981). Several studies look specifically at the different IMRs in different sub-cultures (Sawchuk et al. 1985).

It is assumed and generally borne out in statistics that there is a negative relationship between a country's (or community's) level of economic well-being and IMR. Whereas developed countries have an average IMR of 10 per 1,000, underdeveloped countries have IMRs ranging from 180 to 45 per 1,000. It is clear from Table 1, however, that there is not a consistent relationship between IMR and level of income. Turkey, with a GNP per capita of $1,110,[5] three to five times higher than countries like Burma, Sri Lanka, Madagascar, or Kenya, has a higher IMR than these countries (see Table 2).

Nearly all Middle Eastern countries share the same problem that Turkey faces: high IMR in relation to GNP per capita. Countries like Syria, Iraq,

TABLE I

IMR and GNP per Capita of Middle Eastern and Four
Industrialized Countries (1987)

Country	Infant Deaths per 1,000 Live Births	GNP per Capita (US$)
Turkey	78	1,110
Afghanistan	173	
Ethiopia	155	120
Chad	133	80
Somalia	133	280
Yemen	117	550
Bangladesh	120	160
Pakistan	110	350
Sudan	109	320
Oman	109*	6,490*
Egypt	87	760
Indonesia	85	490
Libya	84	8,520*
Morocco	84	590
Saudi Arabia	72	6,950
Iraq	70	3,020
Iran	65	
Tunisia	60	1,140
Syrian Arab Republic	49	1,570
Jordan	45	1,540
Lebanon	41	
United Arab Emirates	27	14,680
Kuwait	19	13,890
Israel	11	6,210
USA	10	17,480
United Kingdom	9	8,870
Sweden	6	13,160
Japan	5	12,840

* Figures for 1986 (UNICEF 1987:92).
Source: UNICEF 1989:94–95.

and Egypt have a higher IMR than nearly all other countries with similar GNP per capita. The United Arab Emirates and Kuwait have the fourth and fifth highest GNP per capita in the world, yet their IMRs are respectively only forty-first and thirty-third lowest in the world (Table 1).[6]

Furthermore, Turkey seems to have a higher IMR than all its neighbors: in 1987, the IMR in the Soviet Union was reported to be 25, in Syria 49,

TABLE 2

Countries with GNP per Capita Lower or Same as Turkey's and IMR Lower than Turkey's (1987)

Country	IMR	Life Expectancy at Birth	GNP per Capita (1986)	Adult Literacy Rate (1985) male/female	Total Population in Millions	% of Population Urbanized
Turkey	78	65	1,110	86/62	52.5	47
Burma	71	61	200		39.1	24
China	33	70	300	82/56	1,088.6	21
Thailand	40	66	810	94/88	53.3	21
Cape Verde **	67		460			
Maldives **	68		310			
Papua New Guinea **	61	55	720	55/35	3.7	15
Philippines	46	64	560	86/86	58.0	41
Samoa **	33		680			
Solomon Islands **	44		530			
St. Vincent **	33		960			
Costa Rica	18	75	1,480*	94/93	2.8	51
Chile	20	72	1,320*	97/96	12.5	84
Dominican Republic	66	67	710	78/77	6.7	58
El Salvador	60	64	820	75/69	4.9	44
Guatemala	60	63	930	63/47	8.4	41
Guyana	31	70	500	97/95	1.0	33
Ecuador	64	66	1,160*	85/80	9.9	54
Honduras	70	65	740	61/58	4.7	41
Jamaica	18	74	840		2.4	51
Nicaragua	63	64	790		3.5	58
Paraguay	42	67	1,000	91/85	3.9	46
Sri Lanka	34	71	400	91/83	16.6	21
Botswana	68	59	840	73/69	1.2	21
Comoros **	81		320			
Congo	74	49	990	71/55	1.8	41
Mauritius	25	69	1,200*	89/77	1.1	42
Kenya	73	59	300	70/49	22.1	22
Zimbabwe	73	59	620	81/67	8.8	26

* Countries with GNPs slightly higher than that of Turkey, but IMRs substantially lower.
** Countries with small populations.
Source: UNICEF 1989: 94–102.

in Iraq 70, in Greece 12, in Bulgaria 15, and in Iran 65 (UNICEF 1989: 94–95).[7]

The issue is that in Turkey, as in most Middle Eastern countries, or the USA, neither the GNP per capita nor other criteria of development seem to justify the high incidence of infant death. Countries with a mortality rate for adults and children over age five similar to that of Turkey have a much lower IMR (Adlakha 1970: 31, 56, 181). The causes of the particularly high infant and child mortality rates in Turkey remain unexplained. It is not clear whether they are due to certain child-specific diseases or health conditions that uniquely affect Turkey, or malnutrition, or whether the health-care practices that exist for adults do not exist to the same extent and effectiveness for infants and children (Shorter and Macura 1983: 21).

Aksit and Aksit also comment that "We are aware that the historical relationship between income and mortality during economic development can be highly variable, yet it is puzzling that Sri Lanka with one-third of the Turkish per capita GNP has half the Turkish infant mortality" (1989: 571). Similarly, Tunçbilek and Ulusoy consider infant mortality to be one of Turkey's major problems, particularly given the contradiction with other socioeconomic and demographic variables (1988: 3). Caldwell argues that the difference in child mortality rates between small countries or regions like Kerala or Sri Lanka and predominantly Muslim societies is mainly due to the differential degree of female autonomy experienced in each (1986).

Even though IMR seems to be a simple health statistic that reflects material culture and environmental conditions, it is also a silent but meaningful indicator of a country's (or community's) life-style, of the value given to different generations, age groups, and genders, and of many unspoken balances of power that exist in that society. The importance of conditions beyond the material and environmental has emerged in research such as that by Schepher-Hughes in a Brazilian shantytown in 1982 (Schepher-Hughes 1985).

LITERATURE EXPLAINING THE SOCIAL DETERMINANTS OF IMR

Literature shows that generally, in developing and developed countries, research on infant and child deaths has concentrated on intermediate variables affecting child health through their medical/physiological effects. Studies have been carried out to measure the effects of nutrition, of breast-feeding, and of morbidity (Brown 1984, Delaney 1983, Hoffman and Lamphere 1984,

Martorell and Ho 1984, Tezcan 1985). The role of respiratory and intestinal diseases and infectious illnesses has been examined (Black 1984, Bradley and Keymar 1984, Foster and Anderson 1978).

Socioeconomic environmental factors and level of technology have also been the focus of study. Generally, a significantly positive relationship has been found between the total number of pregnancies a woman has had, the total number of her children, the number of members of the household, and infant mortality. A significantly negative relationship has also been found between the amount of schooling the mother and father have had, the level of family income, and infant mortality (Adlakha 1970, Briscoe 1984, Gürsoy Tezcan 1986, Schultz 1984, Tunçbilek and Ulusoy 1988, UNICEF 1985, Ware 1984). Scientists often try to explain mortality by stating the existence of a relationship between mortality figures and selected socioeconomic variables. The manner in which these variables affect mortality and the way they are interconnected with national and global policies and ideologies are, however, left unexplained (Mosley 1984: 25, Schepher-Hughes 1985).

Mosley and Chen have proposed a framework for research on child survival which shows how the causal linkages can be traced back from death to health status, thence to a variety of intermediary factors, and finally to a layer of determinants which they place in one category called "socioeconomic." It has been remarked that, even though they have received a great deal of research attention, the socioeconomic determinants remain a black box to this day (Mosley and Chen 1984, Shorter 1987: 1).

FIELD RESEARCH ON CHILD MORTALITY IN ISTANBUL

My research was aimed at the specific problem of identifying policies, cultural practices, and conditions that may be reasons for the higher than expected IMR in Turkey. What, for example, are the implications of national policies and of local cultural factors operating together to determine child health in Turkey? In view of the rapid and increasing urbanization in the country, an area was chosen which would be representative of this trend. Within the selected area, which had a relatively homogeneous low-income population, a multivariate approach was adopted for a more refined measure of mortality experience. Observations were made and intensive in-depth interviews were conducted with women with different child mortality experiences. In this way I hoped to identify the family circumstances, proximate kin, and cultural factors that lead to infant deaths.

GÖÇKENT: THE RESEARCH AREA IN ISTANBUL

The area of Göçkent (a pseudonym) was chosen as the location of research because it was assumed to be inhabited by a community with a higher than average infant and child mortality rate. Göçkent had received migrants from nearly all parts of Turkey for the past 20–25 years. Therefore, it was also assumed to be similar in many respects to some of the more recently settled *gecekondu*[8] areas of Istanbul, and also to be illustrative of differentials within Turkey. As a whole, migrants are a select group from their home regions and not a pure cross-section of the country, but nevertheless, we expected to obtain strong clues for the cause of the unexpectedly high child mortality in Turkey.

The gecekondu areas are populated mostly by members of the urban working class and by the unemployed and underemployed. Housing is generally of low prestige and durability. In Göçkent, some dwellers own their homes, officially or unofficially, while others rent, making it a combination of squatter settlement and slum (Epstein 1975: 261–262). Göçkent is situated in a densely populated area of Asian Istanbul. It is inhabited by an estimated total of about 200,000 people, of whom nearly all are rural migrants who came to Istanbul in the last ten to twenty years from central and eastern Turkey and the Black Sea Coast, including a small group of gypsies.

The household survey and the subsequent in-depth interviewing took place in a particular district within the official boundaries of the *muhtarlik* (local headman's jurisdiction), constituting about 28,000–30,000 inhabitants within the larger Göçkent suburb. This district has a main road with a number of groceries and markets; a few butchers; a lot of furniture, electrical goods, and kitchenware shops; construction material and carpentry shops; barber, clothing, and shoe shops; and a large number of private doctors' offices and pharmacies. The availability of shops selling things like furniture and electrical goods points to the presence of a consumer market in the district. Within the boundaries of the district there are three mosques, about twenty men's coffeehouses, several beer shops or billiard halls (which are also local social and business centers), and a physical activity center for men. During the research, one apartment in the district was converted into a mosque, bringing the total number of mosques to four. The district has a health center offering free services and the nearby state hospital catered exclusively to citizens with state health insurance.

THE RESEARCH METHOD

The primary research methodology was to carry out in-depth interviewing and observation-based research for a limited number of households. However, in order to be able to generalize the findings for the community involved and to be able to present these findings numerically, a combination of methods was chosen that would allow both a rich personal historical insight into the microworlds and daily lives of individual women and their families, and a quantification of these findings. Therefore, rather than simply conducting a classic ethnographic study in which households or individuals are selected purposely (according to various criteria) in small numbers, the research team first conducted a representative sample survey in Göçkent.[9]

The sample of 1,025 households for this survey was distributed over nine randomly selected streets from the municipality plan. The suburb is characterized by adjacent buildings or flats where tenants and landlords (who represent different economic and migration patterns) live next door to each other. Therefore, in selecting the sample of households rather than using a random sample of dwellings over a wider area, I was able to choose a small but complete area where every individual dwelling was investigated; by so doing, I aimed to include all the different types of inhabitants on those streets. Information was collected from nearly all the dwellings on these streets. In this survey, carried out in November and December 1986, respondents were asked the number of people actually inhabiting the house, their ages and dates of birth, how they were related to each other, and whether there were any pregnant women at the time. Second, they were asked whether anyone had died the previous year and, if so, their age and the cause and date of death.

To gain insight into cultural issues as well as precise and comparable data for all the families, the survey used a smaller sample (a subsample) of the original 1,025 households. This was a one-in-four sample selected by taking every fourth household in the original sample list.[10] In each household one woman was selected, giving priority to (1) a woman under forty-five who had children, and if not, then (2) a woman older than forty-five with children, and if not, then (3) a woman married or single with no children. In this way, we interviewed a total of 251 women. The statistical analysis of the factors associated with child mortality excluded the women (married or single) who had no births, because there was no born child ever at risk of dying. For this study's purposes, the 229 women who were married, widowed, or separated and who had *at least one birth* were selected.

RESULTS OF THE SURVEY

The results of the preliminary survey indicated that most of the demographic patterns in Göçkent were similar in their broad features to those found in other parts of Turkey. Household size showed a mean of 4.7 persons, age distribution was about 50 percent under age twenty, sex ratios were normal.

The same is true of household composition: 71 percent of households were nuclear families, composed of husband, wife, usually children, and sometimes semipermanent guests. Some sets of nuclear families living in the same apartment block might in fact be classified as semiextended families, where a nuclear family resides in the same building with other related groups eating most of their meals together, spending time together, and going to their individual apartments only to sleep. Some of these families have been classified as extended families, depending on how the respondent actually described and named her type of family. Some researchers have distinguished temporary from permanent extended families, depending on who is the breadwinner in the household. In our survey, however, the extended family household is defined as a household unit consisting of at least two generations of adults, sharing housing and pooling economic resources.

The traditional patriarchal model of the extended family household consists of the father, mother, son, son's wife, and children. This form of family unit undergoes various permutations according to the life cycles of its members (Timur 1981: 117–132). Thus, in the survey sample, a total of 21 percent of the households are patrilineal extended families, 3 percent are extended families where the wife's relatives are present, 3 percent are broken homes, and 1 percent are inhabited by single dwellers (seven middle-aged men and five women lived alone). In three households, the husband was a polygynist with two wives present in the same household.

As regards infant mortality rates, however, Göçkent had a higher rate than that given for Turkey. According to the first survey (1,025 households) Göçkent had an IMR in 1986 of 148 per 1,000. Out of 164 live births in the previous year, 16 babies died before completing their first year. The most frequent cause of infant death was described as involving "high temperatures, infantile convulsions and sudden death." Nearly half these babies died before completing their first month (Gürsoy Tezcan 1988). From these preliminary results, it was clear that Göçkent had lower-than-average child health, compared to both national and Istanbul statistics. This was to be expected since the sample had targeted some particularly poor migrant families.

WOMEN AND CHILDREN IN THE GÖÇKENT SAMPLE

In the in-depth interviewing stage detailed information (more than 500 separate variables) was collected from each woman. The range of questions included information on migration patterns, forms of livelihood, economic well-being, levels of education, assessment of social skills, health status of the women and their household members, fertility, religious devoutness, worldview, and child-rearing practices. As infant mortality is also indicative of other problems of early childhood, the questionnaire was not limited to asking questions about infancy alone, but at the next stage of the research detailed questions were asked about all children born and their survival or early death.

Results of the in-depth interviews show that in our sample of 229 women the mean age is 31, ranging from 11 to 60 years; the average age of first marriage is 17.6, ranging from 11 to 32 years; and the mean length of time is 13 years of marriage.

This is a sample of low educational level. The women have an average of three years of education; 29 percent of the women have no schooling, 18 percent did not finish elementary school (which is required by state law), 45 percent are primary-school graduates, and only 8 percent have any education beyond primary school. Thirty percent of the women describe themselves as illiterate. This number contrasts with only 3 percent for their husbands, as high as 85 percent for their mothers, and 36 percent for their fathers. Although the literacy rate is much higher than that of their mothers, it does not compare so well when we take into account their situation vis-à-vis their husbands, or when taking into consideration literacy levels between mothers and fathers.

The majority of husbands are workers in the construction sector. Some are street vendors, taxi drivers, and a few are in the service sector. Most are employed and only a few are employers with their own businesses. The majority of the women (78 percent) have never worked for money. Six percent work at home sewing or knitting, 7 percent work as maids cleaning houses, and 10 percent are involved in work at institutions like factories and can be called laborers.

On average, women in our sample have 4.3 pregnancies (ranging from 1 to 14), 2.7 living children (ranging from 1 to 7), 0.48 deliberate miscarriages or abortions (ranging from 0 to 6), and 0.37 miscarriages, some of which may in fact also be self-induced abortions (the range being 0 to 5). Thus, on average, women have a total of 0.85 *düsük:* i.e., both self-induced miscarriages and abortions as well as involuntary miscarriages, ranging from 0 to 7.

Of the twenty women pregnant at the time of the interview, twelve said that they had become pregnant unintentionally and fourteen said that they had used some kind of contraceptive precaution prior to becoming pregnant. Most of these methods, however, were traditional and are considered ineffective from a medical point of view. Recent Turkish data on reproductive behavior shows that 70 percent of the women have stated that their last pregnancy was an involuntary one.[11]

The 229 women in our sample had a total of 631 living children. The majority of these children were under ten years old during the interviews; 48 percent of these children were female, 52 percent were male; 79 percent were the outcome of wanted pregnancies, 21 percent were from unwanted pregnancies. In 20 percent the mother thought she was using a type of contraceptive, and in 12 percent the mother tried unsuccessfully to abort the baby.

As regards some of their views and attitudes in relation to their children and issues related to education, religion, and family expectations, the majority of this sample was in favor of giving their children a religious Quranic education; 79 percent of the women said that they either were already or that they would want to send their children to Quran courses. The majority of the women (59 percent) confidently counted on their children to take care of them in old age; 43 percent specifically counted on their sons and daughters-in-law as opposed to their daughters. Only 7 percent of the women said they thought nobody would take care of them in their old age. Most women (46 percent) found television useful for their children; 40 percent thought television had both useful and harmful elements; 9 percent of the women thought that television was simply harmful for children. The type of harm mentioned included keeping children from schoolwork, harm to eyesight, as well as moral issues and wrong messages. When asked about what problems they felt were pressing for their children, most of the women in our sample mentioned the danger of traffic in the streets, the need for children's playgrounds, and the difficulty of providing for good education and a future for their children.

QUANTIFYING CULTURE AND CHILD MORTALITY

After initially searching for associations of single variables with child mortality, as measured by the child mortality index (CMI), I condensed the voluminous data into several categories of variables, each expressing a particular concept. Table 3 shows the correlations of some of the categories with the CMI. In a multiple regression analysis, using these fifteen categories, the most influential factors affecting child mortality were found to be (1) the husband's education, (2) household composition, (3) the woman's attitude toward abortion, and (4) the amount of alcohol and smoking in the household. The first two and the last of these variables have already been found in other studies to be influential in regard to child mortality. The above study contributes a further variable, a woman's attitude toward abortion, to the set of variables shown to affect the IMR.

Thus, one immediately striking research result is that *only one* of the most important four variables seems to be a personal characteristic of the mother

TABLE 3

Correlations of Compound Variables with Child Mortality Index

Compound Variable	Correlation Coefficient	Significance (p)
Age of woman (high, older)	−0.0084	0.450
Place of origin of woman, parents, i.e. rural background (high, rural)	+0.0057	0.466
Proportion of woman's life spent outside Istanbul (high, more years outside Istanbul)	+0.0566	0.197
Property ownership (family capital, i.e. land, house, apt., etc.) in Istanbul and in place of origin (high, more property)	+0.0207	0.378
Consumer goods available in household: TV, radio, video, music set, etc., total of 16 items (high, more items in household)	+0.0374	0.287
Religious devoutness: praying, fasting, reading Quran in Arabic, children's religious education (high, more religious)	+0.0366	0.291
Health status of woman and household members (high, worse health)	+0.0812	0.110
Bread consumed daily per person (high, more bread consumed)	+0.1194	0.036
Woman's father's literacy and formal education (high, more educated)	−0.0240	0.359
Woman's mother's literacy and formal education (high, more educated)	−0.0867	0.096
Woman's own literacy and schooling (high, more educated)	−0.0421	0.263
Drinking and smoking by members other than the woman (high, more of these consumed)	+0.1158	0.040
Woman's attitude toward abortion (high, conservative)	+0.1389	0.018
Household composition (high, coresidential patri-local extended)	+0.2205	0.000
Husband's literacy and formal education (high, more educated)	−0.2621	0.000

herself (i.e., her attitude toward the legitimacy or acceptability of abortion). The other three variables, namely, her husband's education, the presence or absence of agnatic in-laws, and heavy drinking and smoking in the household, are all environmental factors within which the mother tries to nurture and raise her child(ren).

THE RELEVANCE OF MOTHERS', FATHERS', AND OTHERS' CHARACTERISTICS FOR CHILD HEALTH

The Father's Education

In our research the most significant variable related to child mortality was found to be the father's education. As expected, the higher the level of education, the lower the mortality. In our study, the women's comparable formal education does not emerge as one of the most important variables. In Göçkent, the husband's education may be a more important determinant because the women are considerably restricted in their movements and subject to the authority of their husbands in making daily decisions.

Furthermore, more education for the husband may mean easier access to important institutions like hospitals and to relevant health-related knowledge. Also, it might mean that the men are less dependent on the worldview imposed by their own families. More than the content of the education they have received, their years of schooling may offer an external reference point for the men and thus a break from the patriarchal constraints which also affect their wives and children. The emancipation of men by educational experience may serve women by allowing men more freedom to support the women in their own lives, which includes their reproductive choices and how they raise their children.

Other research has also demonstrated the significance of education as a variable related to child mortality. In a cross-national study by the United Nations (1985), it was shown that mother's education was a more powerful explanatory variable than father's education in rural areas (Aksit and Aksit 1989). It is suggested that in urban areas variation in father's education was more extensive and associated more with class and status differences, and perhaps for these reasons, the father's education rivaled the explanatory effectiveness of mother's education.[12]

The importance of changes in men's worldview have been commented upon in other research. Kandiyoti, for example, comments that the breakdown of classic patriarchy results in the earlier emancipation of younger men from their fathers and their earlier separation from the parental household. For the generation of women caught in between, this may represent personal tragedy, since they have paid the heavy price of an earlier patriarchal bargain, but are not able to cash in on its promised benefits (Kandiyoti 1988: 282).

Household Composition: Patrilocal Extended Households

Our in-depth interview results show that not only women who presently live in patrilocal extended[13] households but also women who initially gave birth (or became pregnant and miscarried) in a patrilocal extended family tended to have a higher rate of child mortality compared to women who had the termination of their first pregnancies in a demographically nuclear family. Another criterion in assessing the extent of "patrilocal residence" for a woman was the presence of her mother-in-law during the in-depth interview. When developing this compound variable we took into account the fact that generally we had no problem in interviewing the women in the sample privately. Many women even expressed appreciation that we were doing research on child health. Some mothers-in-law, however, were apprehensive when we said that we wanted to talk to their daughters-in-law privately, and some would not allow full or even partial privacy during the in-depth interviews.[14] We took such problem cases as being an indication of severe interference with the young women, and an indication of control of the daughters-in-law and the extent to which they are blocked from outside influences. These young women were classified separately.

This finding indicates that living patrilocal, with in-laws under the same roof, poses serious handicaps for at least some of the married women when it comes to their nurturing and mothering capabilities toward their children. This is true not only in individual situations of decision-making but also in the more general sense of a daughter-in-law's overall secondary and servile position in a patriarchal and gerontocratic family. This position, combined with a patrilocal extended household and the severity of constraints and interferences a woman encounters from her in-laws, determines the survival and well-being of her children. Here the question is not only one of individual health-related habits and/or curative actions, but also one of overall mental health for the mother and her child within the patrilocal extended household.[15]

In research related to child health as well as in popular thought in Turkey, the extended family and the influence of the older generation on child health has, in general, been considered a positive one. In fact, close ties among the family members have been one of the prime points of pride and cultural identity in Turkey. The transmission of experience and know-how in child rearing has been considered valuable and beneficial for child development.

Even though health practitioners have sometimes questioned the validity or even the harmfulness of traditional ways of bringing up children (often imposed upon the young mother by elderly women, i.e., the mother-in-law), this questioning has been limited to considerations of individual traditional practices such as feeding, bundling, or specific ways of healing as in diarrhea, the perceived illness of the child, the imposed timing of taking the child to the doctor, and so on (see Aksayan 1983, Cin et al. 1975). Surprisingly little attention has been given to the overall psychological well-being or the psychic situation of the young mother within the patrilocal extended family context, or to her nurturing responsibilities and capabilities within the extended family.

It is often remarked upon that in traditional families, "Especially the young bride is expected to serve all the adults within the patriarchal household. Once she bears a son, however, her status increases, and it reaches a peak when the son grows up and brings in a bride, the cycle thus repeating itself" (Kagitçibasi 1982: 12). Abadan-Unat (1981), however, has noted that in recent years the position of "the woman" has improved more than that of "the young woman," who is still subject to strict social control (Kagitçibasi 1982: 11). Clearly defined sex roles, division of labor, and separate social networks may all help the women endure the status difference and yet at the same time serve to reinforce and perpetuate this difference (Kagitçibasi 1982; Kandiyoti 1977, 1982; Benedict et al. 1974; Karpat 1976).

With the birth of a baby, much of the conflict inherent in the extended family's dynamics seems to be transferred to and articulated as issues related to the child. An additional difficulty for the mother in claiming her motherly rights is the embedded belief related to reproduction which views women as only vessels (fields) into which the seeds of the man are planted. Thus, the child is the outcome of and belongs to the patriarchal family and the mother is reduced to the state of being a carrier of the child only (Delaney 1986, 1987).

I argue that, given the inherent conflicts of intrafamily relationships (i.e., those with in-laws), close proximity with in-laws becomes detrimental not only for the formation of the conjugal bond between husband and wife but also for the psychological well-being and independence of the young mother. This damages her nurturing capabilities and negatively affects the survival of infants and children. The extreme form of this proximity is living together under the same roof, as is the case in households defined on a coresidential basis as patrilocal extended households.

Of course, detrimental influences may also occur when the young mother is living with her husband separately in what is defined as a coresidentially nuclear family. The nature and the frequency of the interferences and the nature of the psychological bond between the husband and his parental family will determine the extent of independence of the husband and the extent of control the young mother has in bringing up her children and controlling or having a say over the resources of the household.

I do not want to dismiss the role of the mother-in-law as valuable teacher, helper, and friend to young women (see Mernissi 1975: 69–80), or the fact that there may be many exceptions where mothers- and daughters-in-law genuinely live together harmoniously. Neither do I wish to diminish the valuable role of the family as a protective shelter for individuals in a society where hardly any other form of emotional, social, or welfare security exists. I do not wish to imply that in every case where there are forms of oppression within the household the result will be poor child health and mortality.

Nevertheless, I would venture to say that oppression encountered by women in their marital families does significantly contribute to poor child health and mortality by reducing the mothers' ability to nurture their children physically and emotionally. The young woman who is too restricted in her movements and activities, or too busy dealing with the frustrations of living together with her in-laws in a severely patriarchal and gerontocratic culture, becomes unable to provide her infant with the essential care it needs, especially during the initial years of childhood.[16] The higher incidence of infant and child mortality encountered in patrilocal extended families seems to support this hypothesis. What our research has pointed out is the fact that children born into patrilocal extended families have had a higher incidence of mortality compared to children born into nuclear families where there is no visibly interfering mother-in-law.

Literature from the Middle East and elsewhere suggests that the relationship between extended household structure and higher IMR is not unique to Göçkent. In researching the relation between household structure and child mortality in low-income areas in Amman, Deeb found that the presence of another woman (usually a mother-in-law) was associated with a high childhood mortality, despite the fact that these extended households were characterized by a higher total income than nuclear-family households (Deeb 1987: 152). A similar finding was reported by Caldwell (1979) among Nigerian women, where it was found that children living in extended households experienced higher mortality than children living in nuclear households. Caldwell argues this is because mothers in extended households are restricted in their decision-making by traditional beliefs imposed by in-laws.

To my knowledge, no other research on Turkey has tried to explore the relationship between household structure and child mortality. Our research data indicate that children born into patrilocal extended, coresidential households in our region have a higher incidence of mortality compared to children born into nuclear families.[17]

The Relevance of the Mother's Attitude toward Abortion

The third significant variable related to child mortality was the woman's attitude toward abortion. Women with more conservative attitudes toward abortion were also those with higher child mortality indexes. This variable is also an indication of the woman's attitude toward taking a radical initiative for her own reproductive course, and the degree of her conformity with (or her internalization of) values that subject the course of her reproductive life to decisions made within the patriarchal family logic and within the context of secular or religious societal reference points.

To my knowledge, there is no other research that has tried to build a relationship between women's attitudes toward contraception and abortion and child mortality. However, in this study, the compound variable which gives an insight into women's attitudes to abortion also gives an idea of the women's perception and acceptance of their own initiative and control as regards their reproductive life. Many of the conservative arguments given by women in our sample for not accepting abortion were that since the woman has conceived, she must go ahead and give birth. This is opposed to other women who stated that a woman should act as she feels is suitable to her own particular condition.

The fact that this variable had more significance than women's formal education seems to suggest that in a society where women are mostly confined to the home and family relationships, and where their reproductivity is crucially important, how women perceive themselves in relation to their reproductive life is more influential for child mortality than years of formal education. It is significant that women who had the strictest conservative attitude toward abortion (i.e., women who stated that women should go ahead and give birth under whatever condition once they become pregnant) also had the highest incidence of child mortality.

The Prevalence of Drinking and Smoking by Household Members

Households where an adult (other than the mother herself) was found to be drinking and smoking above average were found to be households where the mother had an above-average child mortality experience. Again, our research points to the importance of conditions created by proximate people other than the actual mother of the child. Although most of the previous research has concentrated on alcohol and cigarette consumption of the mother, it is interesting that in our sample poor child survival is linked with the smoking and drinking of household members other than the mother. In the case of heavy drinking, this obviously implies the negative psychological effects of living closely with people with drinking problems, as well as the expenditure of the household budget for smoking and drinking.

All four significant findings point to a need to rethink the exclusive focus on mothers' characteristics for explaining child health and mortality. In fact, the variable of mother's attitude toward abortion calls for the introduction of new, culturally relevant factors. Furthermore, we still need in-depth research into how factors like degree of education influence child health.

CONCLUDING REMARKS

Our research has shown that only one out of the four most influential factors contributing to a high child mortality experience is linked to the individual attributes of the mother (i.e., her attitude toward abortion). The other three factors (i.e., the father's education, household composition, and smoking and drinking by household members *other* than the mother) are all factors beyond the mother's immediate control. The results of this study point to the need for a review of the theoretical paradigm that necessitates an almost exclusive linkage of child health to a focus on mother-child bonding.

This important issue also brings us to question the recent concerns in the USA over issues of mother rights versus child (or fetal) rights, where once again a social issue which is linked to extensive cultural dynamics is conceptualized in isolation. In fact, the part which touches the mother seems to be only a portion of a much larger and dynamic complex where mother and child are delegated respective positions.

Recent trends show that Turkey too is being influenced by the predominant discourse which focuses on child (or fetal) rights versus mother (or women's) rights.[18] Some of this debate seems to revolve around the newly emerging practical and ethical issues created by the possibility of artificial insemination, but when these moral considerations are translated into wider practice they touch the daily lives and choices of many individual men and women. Such discourse about the individual woman versus her child, of course, will have a complex resonance in the Turkish context, where *individualism* and *familism* have different historical, cultural, and class bases, and different contemporary implications.

NOTES

1. April 23 has been accepted by the United Nations as the International Day of Children.

2. In a book aimed at the American reader, Ekrem writes, "How would you like to be governor for a week? If you are a Turkish child you may be one, as the government is encouraging Turkish children in civic education. For one week every year,

the school children take over the local government of all the provinces. Boys and girls are elected as governors, mayors, police chiefs, etc. and perform the functions of these officials while their elders watch them closely to see that no mistakes are made, and so train the youngsters in the art of government. . . . On [April 23] thousands of school children meet at the huge auditorium at Ankara where they parade and take part in all kinds of athletic events while their fond parents watch them from the stands. Girls in gym suits, their hair cut short, their legs bare, march erectly, and I must add that they are applauded more than the boys" (Ekrem 1947: 122).

3. Renowned Turkish child psychiatrist Yörükoglu begins his prize-winning book on child mental health with an apology to all children who could not live out their childhood (1980). Similarly, a teacher of Turkish, in an introduction to an anthology of children's poems, comments that it is the fate of children in villages or in cities not to have lived their childhood. The author expresses surprise that at an age when present-day children ride bicycles and play marbles, the famous Ottoman poet Sinasi (1826–1871) became a blue-collar officer at the Tophane offices. Similarly the poet Abdülhak Hamit Tarhan (1852–1937) began work at the Babiali chamber of translation when he was only twelve. The writer interpreted this as "these children being forced to take on adult responsibilities." In line with the above observations, another Turkish journalist commented in the fifties: "I never had a childhood. Those who do not have a childhood do not have a youth either. Shall I tell you something? They do not have old age either" [Ataç Nurullah, *Günce* 1953–1955 (Ankara: Türk Dil Kurumu, 1972), p. 59].

4. Turkey had an estimated fertility rate of 3.8 and an average life expectancy of 63 years; the crude death rate was 9 per 1,000, the crude birth rate 30 per 1,000. The annual population growth rate was estimated at 2.2 percent for 1973–1984 and the infant mortality rate at 80 per 1,000 (UNICEF 1987: 98). Figures given for IMR and GNP per capita for the same periods of time differ from one source to the other. I quote the figures given in the original texts, therefore these figures differ accordingly throughout this article. The dependency ratio was estimated to be over 79 percent for the eighties. Dependents are defined as those below age fifteen or above sixty-five. In 1985, the adult literacy rate was 86 percent for men and 62 percent for women. More significant, between 1984 and 1986, secondary school enrollment was 56 percent for boys and 33 percent for girls. The GNP per capita was $1,325 [*Official Gazette* (Ankara), May 22, 1989: 29].

5. The World Bank (1980) gives it as $1,160 for 1980, and official Turkish government sources (*Resmi Gazete*) give it as $1,325 for the same year. Furthermore, the question remains whether some of Turkey's GNP is not captured by statistics and is therefore underrepresented.

6. The USA shares the same discrepancy, with a high IMR (10 per 1,000) despite a high per capita GNP. Infant mortality in the USA is characterized by high rates relative to other industrialized nations, and there are persistent and substantial infant mortality differentials between population groups (Eberstein et al. 1990: 413). Furthermore, child health receives low political priority as far as research and health-service funding goes in the USA (Price 1992: 128–146).

7. The GNPs per capita for Turkey's neighbors are: Soviet Union $4,550, Syria

$1,570, Iraq $3,020, Greece $3,680, and Bulgaria $4,150. There are no recent figures available for Iran's GNP per capita.

8. *Gecekondu,* literally meaning "landed overnight," refers to the newly constructed regions on the peripheries of cities. Developed by migrants, such housing is often characterized by poor quality and illegal constructions. The spread of gecekondus has accelerated since the fifties but especially since the eighties.

9. This preliminary survey was necessary since the muhtarlik (office of the district headman) did not have complete, up-to-date records of births and infant deaths in the district. Neither did the immunization campaign center located in the vicinity and supported by UNICEF have such records for children in the community they served. Hospital records would have created a bias, in that the study would have access only to children who had been taken to the hospital and would miss those who had died at home and were not taken to the hospital.

10. Before the systematic selection was made it was enriched in favor of families with recent infant mortality by selecting all the women who had an infant death during the last year (sixteen). The one-in-four selection was done without removing the sixteen. My purpose was to be sure to have enough representation of mortality as well as survival to be able to study the variation well.

11. Peker observes that couples have been found to be informed and willing to limit their number of children, but that they are insufficiently and ineffectively served by the state or other health services [M. Peker, "Population and Population Policy in Turkey, 1980–88," abstract of paper presented at the Second National Social Science Congress, June 1989 (Ankara: Türk Sosyal Bilimler Dernegi), p. 75].

12. Hobcraft and McDonald's cross-national study found that in Latin American countries, mother's education had more explanatory power, while in some Asian and Islamic countries father's education and occupation and mother's work status emerged as rival predictor variables (Aksit and Aksit 1989: 571–572). In our sample also, the husbands' formal education seems to surpass the women's formal education as well as other criteria in explaining child mortality.

13. In our interview sample four different types of households were classified: (1) 68 percent of the households were found to be nuclear, (2) 27 percent extended [in fact, the husband's relatives lived in 25 percent of the households (patrilocal extended) and both the husband's and the wife's relatives lived in 2 percent], (3) 3 percent included the wife's relatives, and (4) 2 percent were fragmented households with a mother and children but not an adult couple.

14. In fact, one particular mother-in-law sabotaged the interview, would not allow her daughter-in-law (who was part of the sample) to speak to the interviewers at all, and I had to contend with interviewing the mother-in-law to be able to get some information about child health. Another mother-in-law (whose own daughters were also in the house) kept on telling us how stupid her daughter-in-law was, that she would never be able to answer the questions correctly, that she had caused all the health problems of her grandchildren, that she was ill-intentioned. Although we insisted on absolute privacy during the interview, some mothers in-law kept coming in and checking on us.

15. Tunçbilek cites consanguineous marriages as another factor causing infant

mortality rates to rise (1988: 64). This study is not concerned with the issue of genetic diseases but with the social relations, within which consanguinity plays a role as part of the extended family and patriarchal ideology.

16. The same can be argued for families where there is a drug problem; too preoccupied with dealing with the negative effects of the excessive drinking in her household, the mother cannot give adequate attention to her child.

17. Not only in the interview sample but also in the survey sample of 1,025 households, an interesting difference became apparent regarding the family structures of the households which experienced infant mortality in the one-year period in 1985 – 1986. Extended patrilineal families constituted only 22 percent of all households within the survey sample, but 38 percent (as opposed to the general 22 percent) of households which experienced infant mortality in 1985 – 1986 lived in the form of extended patrilineal families.

18. In the last few years, one of the best-selling books in Turkey has been a translation of the novel *Letter to an Unborn Child,* by Oriana Fallaci, in which the Italian author writes on the issues of the mother's right to give birth and care for the fetus and the child, in contrast to society's direct interferences for the sake of the child's rights.

REFERENCES

Abadan-Unat, N. 1981. "Social Change and Turkish Women." In Abadan-Unat, ed., *Women in Turkish Society* (Leiden: E. J. Brill).

Adlakha, A. 1970. *A Study of Infant Mortality in Turkey.* Ann Arbor: University Microfilms.

Aksayan, S. 1983. *Çocuk sagligina iliskin geleneksel inanç ve uygulamalar* (Traditional beliefs and practices related to child health). M.A. thesis, Hacettepe Universitesi Saglik Bilimleri Enstitüsü, Hemsirelik Programi Bilim Uzmanligi, Ankara.

Aksit, B., and B. Aksit, 1989. "Sociocultural Determinants of Infant and Child Mortality in Turkey." *Soc. Sci. Med.* 28, no. 6: 571 – 576.

Aries, P. 1965. *Centuries of Childhood.* New York: Vintage Books.

Benedict, P., E. Tümertekin, and F. Mansur. 1974. *Turkey: Geographic and Social Perspectives.* Leiden: E. J. Brill.

Black, R. E. 1984. "Diarrheal Diseases and Child Mortality and Morbidity." In Mosley and Chen 1984.

Bradley, D. J., and Anne Keymar. 1984. "Parasitic Diseases: Measurement and Mortality Impact." In Mosley and Chen 1984.

Briscoe, J. 1984. "Technology and Child Survival: The Example of Sanitary Engineering." In Mosley and Chen 1984.

Brown, K. H. 1984. "Measurement of Dietary Intake." In Mosley and Chen 1984.

Caldwell, J. C. 1986. "Routes to Low Mortality in Poor Countries." *Population and Development Review* 12, no. 2 (June 1986).

———. 1979. "Education as Factor in Mortality Decline: An Examination of Nigerian Data." *Population Studies* 33, no. 3: 395 – 413.

Cin, S., et al. 1975. "Gecekondu bölgelerinde sosyal arastirmalar: 1. Gecekondu aile-sinin sosyal yasami ve çocuk ölümleri" (Social research in gecekondu areas: 1. Social life of the gecekondu family and child deaths). *Journal of Faculty of Medicine, University of Ankara,* Supp. 100.

Deeb, M. E. 1987. *Household Structure as Related to Childhood Mortality and Morbidity among Lower Income Areas in Amman.* Ph.D. thesis, Johns Hopkins University, Baltimore.

Delaney, C. 1987. "Seeds of Honor, Fields of Shame." In David Gilmore, ed., *Honor and Shame: The Unity of the Mediterranean* (Washington, D.C.: American Anthropological Association Special Publication).

———. 1986. "The Meaning of Paternity and the Virgin Birth Debate." *Man* (Journal of the Royal Anthropological Institute) September.

———. 1983. "Symbolism of Procreation and Implications for Education and Population Planning." Unpublished manuscript.

Eberstein, Isaac W., Charles B. Nam, and Robert A. Hummer. 1990. "Infant Mortality by Cause of Death: Main and Interaction Effects." *Demography* 27, no. 3 (August).

Ekrem, Selma. 1947. *Turkey, Old and New.* New York: C. Scribner's Sons.

Epstein, D. G. 1975. "The Genesis and Function of Squatter Settlements in Brazilia." In J. Freid and N. J. Chisman, eds., *City Ways* (New York: Crowell Co.).

Fallaci, O. 1989. *Dogmamis çocuga mektup* (Letter to an unborn child). Ankara: Verso.

Farah, A., and S. H. Preston. 1982. "Child Mortality Differentials in Sudan." *Population and Development Review* 8, no. 2 (June).

Fikes Courtney, J. 1985. *Huichol Indian Identity and Adaptation.* Ph.D. dissertation, University of Michigan, Department of Anthropology.

Foster, G. M., and B. C. Anderson. 1978. *Medical Anthropology.* New York: John Wiley and Sons.

Grant, J. P. 1982. *The State of the World's Children 1981 – 1982.* New York: UNICEF.

Gürsoy Tezcan, A. 1992. "Infant Mortality: A Turkish Puzzle." *Health Transition Review* 2, no. 2 (October).

———. 1988. "Demography Briefly." *Journal of Contemporary Management* (Marmara University, Istanbul) March.

———. 1986. "Türkiye'de bebek ölümleri ve düsündürdükleri" (Reflections on infant mortality in Turkey). *Türk ekonomisi ve Türk ekonomi ilmi* (Türkiye Ekonomisi Arastirma Merkezi Yayini, Istanbul) 2, no. 2.

Hoffman, S. L., and B. B. Lamphere. 1984. "Breastfeeding Performance and Child Development." In Mosley and Chen 1984.

Kagitçibasi, C. 1982. Introduction to *Sex Roles, Family, and Community in Turkey,* ed. C. Kagitçibasi, Indiana University Turkish Studies 3.

Kandiyoti, Deniz. 1988. "Bargaining with Patriarchy." *Gender and Society* 2, no. 3 (September).

———. 1982. "Urban Change and Women's Role in Turkey: An Overview and Evaluation." In *Sex Roles, Family, and Community in Turkey,* ed. C. Kagitçibasi, Indiana University Turkish Studies 3.

———. 1977. "Sex Roles and Social Change: Comparative Appraisal of Turkey's Women." *Signs* 3, no. 1.

Karpat, K. 1976. *The Gecekondu: Rural Migration and Urbanization.* London: Cambridge University Press.

Martorell, W., and T. J. Ho. 1984. "Malnutrition, Morbidity and Mortality." In Mosley and Chen 1984.

Mernissi, F. 1975. *Beyond the Veil: Male-Female Dynamics in Modern Muslim Society.* Boston: John Wiley & Sons.

Mosley, W. H. 1984. "Child Survival: Research and Policy." In Mosley and Chen 1984.

Mosley, W. Henry, and Lincoln C. Chen. 1984. *Child Survival: Strategies for Research.* Cambridge: Cambridge University Press; New York: Population Council.

OECD. 1979. *Social Sciences in Policy Making.* Paris: Organization for Economic Co-operation and Development.

Price, J. Laurie. 1992. "A Medical Anthropologist's Ruminations on NIH Funding." *Medical Anthropology Quarterly* 6, no. 2 (June).

Sawchuk, L. A., et al. 1985. "Evidence of a Jewish Advantage: A Study of Infant Mortality in Gibraltar, 1870–1950." *American Anthropologist* 87: 616–625.

Schepher-Hughes, N. 1985. "Culture, Scarcity and Maternal Thinking: Maternal Detachment and Infant Survival in a Brazilian Shantytown." *Ethos* 13, no. 4: 291–317.

Schultz, T. P. 1984. "Studying the Impact of Household Economics and Community Variables on Child Mortality." In Mosley and Chen 1984.

Shorter, F. C. 1987. "The Production of Health in (Cairo) Households, Observations Concerning Analytic Frameworks." Paper presented at ME Awards workshop "Assessment of Health Interventions," Aswan, October 1987.

Shorter, F. C., and M. Macura. 1983. *Turkiye'de Nufus Artisi (1935–1975).* Ankara: Yurt Yayincilik, AS.

Sivard, R. L. 1985. *Women: A World Survey.* Washington, D.C.: World Priorities.

State Institute of Turkey. 1988. *Statistical Yearbook of Turkey 1985.* Ankara.

Sümbüloglu, K. 1982. *Saglik alanina özel istatistiksel yöntemler.* TTB Ankara Tabib Odasi Yayini, No. 4. Ankara.

Tezcan, S. 1985. *Türkiye'de bebek ve çocuk ölümleri.* Tip Fakültesi Halk Sagligi Anabilim Dali, Yayin No. 26. Ankara: Hacettepe Üniversitesi.

Timur, S. 1981. "Determinants of Family Structure in Turkey." In N. Abadan-Unat, ed., *Women in Turkish Society* (Leiden: E. J. Brill).

Tunçbilek, E., and M. Ulusoy. 1988. "The Relationship Between Infant Mortality and Consanguineous Marriages." In *Infant Mortality in Turkey: Basic Factors* (Ankara: Hacettepe Institute of Population Studies).

UNICEF. 1989. *The State of the World's Children 1989.* Oxford University Press.

———. 1987. *The State of the World's Children 1987.* Oxford University Press.

———. 1985. *1985 World Statistics.* New York: UNICEF.

———. 1983. *1983 World Statistics.* New York: UNICEF.

United Nations. 1985. *Manual X: Indirect Techniques for Demographic Estimation.* New York: Department of International and Social Affairs, Population Studies, No. 81.

Ware, H. 1984. "Effects of Maternal Education, Women's Roles and Child Care on Child Mortality." In Mosley and Chen 1984.

WHO. 1981. *Global Strategy for Health for All by the Year 2000.* Geneva: World Health Organization.

World Bank. 1985. *World Development Report 1985.* Oxford University Press.

———. 1980. *World Development Report 1980.* Oxford University Press.

Yörükoglu, A. 1980. *Çocuk ruh sagligi* (Child mental health). Ankara: Türkiye Is Bankasi Kültür Yayinlari.

WOMEN'S LAMENTS FOR CHILDREN WHO HAVE DIED

Collected by Jamal Zaki ad-Din al-Hajjaji
Translated by Susan Slyomovics and Suzanne Qualls

Fatima Barbari 'Abdallah

Fatima is a professional paid lamenter who chants and sings improvised songs in connection with death rituals. She was recorded by Jamal Zaki ad-Din al-Hajjaji December 30, 1988, when she was sixty-five years old. She is from the village of il-Awamiyya, Upper Egypt, and she is illiterate.

LAMENT FOR HER DEAD DAUGHTER

I want my daughter to wash my corpse,
To drape my garment and arrange the shroud.
I want her to reach my age: she will rest
My head on her lap, and she will groom me.
I want my daughter to turn
My dead body piously toward Mecca.
  Pain came to me filling my ribs.
My beloved cannot hear my complaint,
She does not know my loss.
I dressed her in red and she exhaled
The fragrance of rose. I made her beautiful.
No one was with me.
Come near me. Let me wrap your head.
I will loosen the rishrish on your shoulder.
Come near me. Let me braid your hair.
I will unbind your hair.
I will loosen the hair across your back.
(*Rishrish* are silver or gold beads braided into the ends of the hair.)

LAMENT FOR A DROWNED CHILD

O father of children, your children lie broken,
A flood descended drowning them.
If only they were absent instead of dead!
We would swear silence until they returned.
I went to the graveyard in torn garments,
    no stairs, no window there.
I was drawn to the graveyard, longing drew me,
    no stairs leading me to them.
Watchman of the river, o sleeper!
I swear by your youth, release the floating corpse.
Watchman of the river, o drowsy one!
I swear by your youth, bring out my drowned child.
I will give you whales and fishes,
I will give you he who casts the net.
Everyone left and I stand by the Nile.
Captain! Where has my son gone?
They left me a remnant of a house,
    as if I were a scrap forgotten by the carpenter.

Fathiyya Mahdi

Fathiyya lives in Luxor, Upper Egypt. Three of her nine children have died.
She is not a professional lamenter but learned her art from hearing her mother's laments. She was forty-seven years old in 1988.

LAMENT FOR A YOUNG SON WHO FELL FROM A ROOF

My son's wrist bindings are white.
I save them to help me with my fate.
A pearl necklace was cut from me.
Where is the beloved who searches for it?
A pearl necklace was cut from me.
Where is the dear one who searches well?
My precious bracelet fell from the roof.
Your mother searches, your father is helpless.
I saw your father coming into the courtyard.
My powerful amulet fell from me.
I saw your father running into the courtyard.
My powerful amulet fell into the well.
I saw children playing with palm leaves,
wearing caps, heads shaven.

I saw children playing outside—
I covered my eyes and said, "God's will."
A row of children in the alley met me.
I covered my eyes and said, "It hurts me."
Say God's name over him, O tomb's worm,
     Say God's name over him when he rises and cries!
Say God's name, O short-tailed maggot,
     Say God's name when he gets up at night!
Mother, look at the gravedigger lowering me.
     My father walked away and left me.
Your white skin is like paper in candlelight.
Your beautiful face, praise its creator!
If I say, O my son, my heart is torn,
the dust weeps: YOUR BELOVED IS WITH US.
If I say, O my son, my guts are cut up,
the dust weeps: YOUR BELOVED IS AMONG US.
My children are the rings for my hands,
the silver kohlstick for my eyes—
Children are beautiful, their bodies beautiful.
Happy mother who lives for them,
I search for you in all corners.
I tell myself that they were here,
there were three, and where is the third?
The evil eye possessed you.
When you fell you said, "O master,
O pardon, O Lord, I am only a young boy."

Working boy, Cairo, Egypt
PHOTO BY HEATHER LOGAN TAYLOR

PART IV

CHILDREN AND WORK

Work hard because who does not work is worthless.

ANCIENT EGYPTIAN PROVERB

The regulation and abolishment of child labor has been an almost universal liberal or reformist cause since the Industrial Revolution in Europe in the late eighteenth and the nineteenth centuries. Yet demands for labor far outstripped the supply of adult workers in early years of industrialism and economic dislocations of families led to a continued dependence on the work of children by family as well as the labor market itself. English poets such as William Blake and Robert Browning dramatized the plight of these child laborers, which was also a topic of sermons and newspaper articles. Eventually child labor laws were passed in the late nineteenth century in England, as well as in the United States and the rest of Europe.

Child labor also came under criticism in the Middle East and laws forbidding it can be found on the books of a majority of countries in the area. But perceived necessity overcomes legality, and child labor is still present, as the following essays demonstrate. Despite rising wages, inflation means lower- and middle-class living in many Middle Eastern countries is only possible now if all members of the family work. The migration of men from the Middle East to search for work outside their own countries is a phenomenon noted by economists since the end of World War II. Turkish workers are in Germany, North Africans in Spain, France, and Belgium, and Egyptians and Yemenis in the oil-rich countries of Kuwait, Saudi Arabia, Libya, and the Emirates. Women have gone to work outside the home in increasing numbers simply to help put bread on the table. Since 1955, the percentage of women in the labor force outside the home has nearly doubled in Algeria, Lebanon, Morocco, and Libya, tripled in Tunisia, and quadrupled in Iraq. Yet children still may have to contribute to family income to assure survival of the family group which may be endangered by illness, death, and conflict as well as by rising economic costs. The survival of the family group is seen by the majority of Middle Easterners as essential to the survival of the individual among both poor and rich families. This attitude is demonstrated by the figures in the collection of tables found in sociologist Helmi Tadros' essay, "Children's Contribution to Social Security and the Family in Egypt." The expectation that children should assist parents throughout their lives should not be surprising, given the fact that no other institution or system of welfare in both the rural and urban Middle East has yet offered an alternative source of security, much less one of personal identity.

Increasing urbanization and access to free schooling, according to analysts, affects the societal *perception* of the importance of child labor, and it is true that the traditional concept is currently in question, as Aicha Belarbi's essay indicates. Still, as Professor Belarbi points out, in Morocco "material needs . . . push families to speculate on their children's potential as an economic investment," on a short-term basis (as child workers in the labor force) or on a long-term basis (family sacrifices to send children to school).

The effects of the short-term approach can be seen in Eftetan Farag's description of the lives of five working children in Cairo, and in Daisy al-Amir's short story, *The Rungs of the Ladder.* Jenny White chronicles in some detail a day in the life of a teen-age Turkish girl, who does piecework in a home-based business. As Professor Belarbi points out, child labor today is a result of forces expressed to a greater or lesser degree in almost every country in the late capitalist world. These forces are clearly beyond the control of individual parents and children; thus *family* labor continues and may well increase.

Boys with a cartload of corn, Cairo, Egypt
PHOTO BY DIANE WATTS

THE CHILD AS
ECONOMIC INVESTMENT:
PRELIMINARY REFLECTIONS

by Aicha Belarbi
Translated by Moncef and Wafaa Lahlou

To approach the child as an economic investment for the family is to deal with two different domains. The first refers to the family as a unit for reproducing human beings. The second is much vaster—the economic domain: the world of production, distribution, and consumption of material goods. Production and reproduction are the two essential components of every human society, components that maintain a dialectic relationship and so determine the history of each society.

If one takes the evolution of human societies into consideration, one notes that in a subsistence society when production seems to be static or blocked, reproduction is very high; the family unit accumulates all social and economic functions, and the patriarchal family system is dominant. With economic development, the increased production of goods has an effect on the socioeconomic and cultural status of the family and consequently also on family structure, indeed, even on society. The child is integrated into the production cycle according to the specific social class to which he belongs.

Economists define the components of production as capital and labor. Capital, which is a good that contributes to the creation of other goods and to the act of creating capital, is called investment. From that, it can be concluded that in the economic domain there is always investment.

According to political economy and the Larousse Dictionary, an investment is a decision made by an individual, a business, or a community to use its own resources (or borrowed funds) for the growth of its own stock of produced goods. The Quillet Encyclopedic Dictionary gives a simpler definition: the idea of investment encompasses all expenses set aside in the present for a return of greater value in the future.

Following this definition, one has to wonder to what extent this economic concept can be used to address the child as an investment for the family.

Would the child be the capital invested by the parents, the capital that has to be profitable in the short or long term? Should the fact of having children be an economic investment for the family? Should the expenses set aside by the family to feed, dress, educate, and care for their children always be geared for profit or some important future gain? On the issue of the child as investment, could it be said that, in making a decision, the investor is conscious of the profitability of his capital? It becomes necessary here to introduce all the notions of economics, accounting, and forecasting, notions that most families do not understand.

This essay aspires to answer these various questions and to test this notion within Moroccan society. Concerning methodology, the subject will be treated in two ways:

1. The psychosociological approach, in which an attempt is made to demonstrate society's and the family's perception of the child. Is the investment that the family makes for the development of the child devoid of economic value since it is wholly aimed at a human being who has his own vision of existence and who will very probably be enticed to move far away from home one day? Or is this person invested in because he must later provide for himself and his family?

2. The sociological approach, which allows us to pull out the socioeconomic structure that the child lives in and see if the child is effectively considered as capital within the various existing socioeconomic levels in society. The reference to the concept of socioeconomic levels is a methodological choice and not a reference to social classes; the existing typologies in this domain are quite varied and refer to many theoretical frameworks that are often borrowed from elsewhere. A scientific study of Moroccan social classes would not be sufficiently elaborate to serve as a frame of reference for this research.

At any rate, a hierarchy of socioeconomic levels is easily discerned: well-to-do, average, and underprivileged. This essay will deal only with the well-to-do and the underprivileged levels, and will be particularly concerned with living conditions of the respective families and what they project onto the child.

The family has undergone profound changes. Most of these changes have been imposed from without, whether they concern the function, the form, or the goals and expectations of the family. To establish a comparison, we will begin by looking at the extended family, which was the dominant type in Morocco for many centuries. This type of family was at the same time a unit of reproduction, production, consumption, and education. The patriarchal family was overwhelmed by colonization (the introduction of a modern economy, urbanization, formal education, and a dismantling of preexisting social hierarchies).

The child in the patriarchal extended family participates according to his capabilities within the same economic, cultural, and social life as his ancestors; and his place in society is justified only by the role he plays. In this kind of family, different chores are distributed among the children: economic tasks (herding livestock, errands, house chores, professional apprenticeship) and educational tasks (the oldest are the educators of the youngest). The economic division of tasks is reinforced by another division, according to sex, of specific chores for boys and girls. The boy becomes an extension of the father outside the home and the girl becomes the extension of the mother inside the house. The learning of tasks is done automatically by the members of the family with precocious cooperation in economic activities. The child in this type of family produces just like everyone else; the tasks he accomplishes evolve as he ages. He provides for his own needs, indeed, even the family's, at a young age. The patriarchal family that colonization dismembered has suffered profound changes with regard to its function and form, and it has undergone a revolution in its goals and aspirations.

The child is a producer in the patriarchal extended family among well-to-do and underprivileged families.

The Well-to-do Families

The well-to-do family has a very high income and consumes ostentatiously. An inquiry into household consumption in 1971 shows that 10.5 percent of families constitute a group with the highest level of consumption. The formal education of the child lasts a longer time because the parents have the means to get along without his labor. In this way, the child enters into productive life at a later age. Within this type of family, he is more a consumer than a producer. His parents hope that he will have a profession that is worthy of their social level, and expect him to establish a home and family and to be more of a moral support for them than a material provider for the family.

The Underprivileged Families, Working Class and Underclass

Out of an active population of 4 million people, hidden unemployment is in the 30 percent range, and 9 percent are chronically unemployed.

Ninety thousand to 100,000 people annually leave the countryside for the cities, adding to the misery already present in the urban areas.

Of the families whose income is the lowest, 51 percent consume the same amount as 10 percent of well-to-do families.

Malnutrition is just one of the difficulties parents encounter while trying to provide the bare necessities for their children. A study by the Minister of Health in March and April of 1971 confirms that 41.5 percent of children between the ages of zero and four are malnourished; 4.6 percent of these children have symptoms serious enough to require hospitalization. The rural areas and the shantytowns are also seriously affected.

Infant mortality rates are very high, especially in the countryside and the shantytowns.

The education rate [those who enroll in primary schools] is very low— only 47 percent of the children who qualify by their age; the attendance rate among those who do go to school hovers around 37 percent; the primary school drop-out rate exceeds 50 percent. All these facts together conspire to throw the child into the working world at a very young age. The child's physical constitution is not appropriate for supporting the work that is imposed on him. The 1971 census shows that 7.2 percent of the children under fifteen are considered to be in the active portion of the population, working in the different areas of production: 73 percent in agriculture, 13 percent in domestic services, 18 percent in the crafts industries, 4 percent in other areas.

The child works to provide for himself and to help the family. On another level, the child is a sought-after work-force resource because he will accept very low wages and complain very little.

Child labor is pushed to outrageous limits, such as when children find themselves kicked out of their own homes or neighborhoods. This is the situation for certain rural families who place their daughters in city homes as servants. It can be said that these parents are "investing" in their children. The more children, the more hands for work and the more income for the family. If the child works outside the home, there will be fewer mouths to feed, too. In this case, the child indeed becomes capital, and it can be said that the parents are investing in the child.

Material needs therefore push families to speculate on their children as economic investment. This can be for short- or long-term profitability. Either the child is placed in the world of work at an early age, or sacrifices are made and the child is sent to school. However, children from the general, i.e. poorer, population are handicapped by the need to complete more studies in order to attain a decent standard of living.

The poorer child may thus reject school. The capitalist modes of production may not accept him. Either unwilling or unable to adapt himself to the so-called traditional modes of production, he becomes neither producer nor consumer. He is not a producer because he does not provide for himself or others; and he is not a consumer in the true sense of the word. He is a consumer on the edge of society. On a material level he survives, and nothing more. On a cultural level he is force-fed the wastes of an outdated western culture.

In these terms, the profitability of the parents' investment in the child is insignificant, if not worthless. In the first case, the child is quickly integrated into the world of work at an early age; in the second case, the family supports the child and suffers much deprivation, betting on his education which often turns out to be a dead end. To blame either the family or the child would only further complicate what is already problematical. For the basic causes of this situation are not the desires of children or families, but the political, socioeconomic, and cultural choices made by those who govern.

NOTES

This article was originally written in 1979.

CHILDREN'S CONTRIBUTION TO SOCIAL SECURITY AND THE FAMILY IN EGYPT

by Helmi R. Tadros

Household heads were asked if any of their children, whether living with them or not, helped them financially, in work, or in kind. If the answer was affirmative, additional questions inquired about the number and sex of those children and the nature of help offered (Tables 1, 2, and 3).

Household heads were also asked if they helped any of their children who were not living with them, financially, in work, or in kind. If the answer was affirmative, they were asked the number and sex of those children and the nature of help given (Tables 4, 5, and 6).

According to the distribution of scores on the intergenerational relations scale in connection with the study areas, the important social demographic characteristics of respondents and coverage by social insurance programs reveal the following:

• Interdependence between generations proved strongest in the resettled areas, followed by rural areas, with the urban district coming last.

• Females rated higher than males, and the better-educated were more likely to undermine the strength of intergenerational relations.

• The married viewed these relations in stronger terms than the divorced and widowed, who in turn rated higher than the singles.

• Extended families scored highest, followed by nuclear families, whereas those living alone came last.

This material is excerpted from *Cairo Papers in Social Science* 7 (1984).

TABLE 1
Household Heads Receiving Help from Their Children

	Resettled		Rural		Urban	
	%	No.	%	No.	%	No.
Receiving help	56.6	435	22.6	162	22.4	163
Not receiving help	43.4	333	77.4	555	77.6	564
Total	100.0	768	100.0	717	100.0	727

TABLE 2
Children Offering Help to Household Heads

	Resettled		Rural		Urban	
	%	No.	%	No.	%	No.
Not applicable		333		555		564
Sons	81.9	684	89.1	196	76.9	223
Daughters	18.1	151	10.9	24	23.1	67
Total	100.0	835	100.0	220	100.0	290
Children per household head		1.9		1.4		1.8

TABLE 3
Nature of Help Offered by Children

Type of Help	Resettled		Rural		Urban	
	%	No.	%	No.	%	No.
Not applicable		333		555		564
Financial	9.7	84	79.6	183	81.2	251
In kind	0.8	7	4.3	10	14.9	46
Work	89.5	775	16.1	37	3.9	12
Total	100.0	866	100.0	230	100.0	309

TABLE 4
Household Heads Offering Help to Their Children

	Resettled		Rural		Urban	
	%	No.	%	No.	%	No.
Offering help	23.8	183	15.3	110	6.2	45
Not offering help	76.2	585	84.7	607	93.8	682
Total	100.0	768	100.0	717	100.0	727

TABLE 5
Children Receiving Help from Household Heads

	Resettled		Rural		Urban	
	%	No.	%	No.	%	No.
Not applicable		585		607		682
Sons	31.7	96	13.8	24	37.8	28
Daughters	68.3	207	86.2	150	62.2	46
Total	100.0	303	100.0	174	100.0	74

TABLE 6
Nature of Help Offered by Household Heads

	Resettled		Rural		Urban	
Type of Help	%	No.	%	No.	%	No.
Not applicable		584		607		682
Money	42.0	157	24.5	45	64.6	51
In kind	54.3	203	75.0	138	35.4	28
Work	3.7	14	0.5	1		
Total	100.0	374	100.0	184	100.0	79

• There is negative association between total family income and bonds between the generations, i.e., the higher the income, the weaker is the bond.

• Respondents not covered by insurance programs scored about twice as high (49.5 percent) as those covered (21.8 percent) in their perception of intergenerational relations.

All of the tables have shown statistically significant chi-square values ($p < 0.01$).

Respondents were asked whether they would seek financial help from their children if they were in need. Affirmative answers were given by 93.7 percent in the resettled areas, 89.0 percent in the rural, and 80.2 percent in the urban. The majority stressed that this help would come from a son and not from a daughter. Proportions favoring a son's financial help were in the following descending order: 94.6 percent in the resettled villages, 91.3 percent in the rural, and 70.8 percent in the urban. Those who favored accepting a daughter's financial help were 0.7 percent in the resettled areas, 0.8 percent in the rural, and 7.1 percent in the urban. The remainder had no preference.

Among the main reasons given for objecting to a daughter's financial help were:

• It is opposed to tradition, especially in Egypt's rural areas.

• A daughter is usually married to a nonkinsman; hence it would be degrading and embarrassing to her and to her parents if the latter would accept her help.

• The son, even if he is married, is still the money earner and the master of his immediate family; hence he is free to offer any help to his parents.

WORKING CHILDREN IN CAIRO: CASE STUDIES

by Eftetan O. Farrag

The employment of children less than age twelve is prohibited by the Egyptian labor code, except in the case of the agricultural sector. Yet, even the most casual observer will notice that many young children in Egypt work in numerous economic activities other than agriculture, a phenomenon which is confirmed by official statistics.[1] Young boys especially make up a large proportion of the labor force in the country's multitude of small, informal workshops. Young girls tend to work in the home, out of the public arena.

Child laborers in Egypt are almost always underpaid and sometimes unpaid. Frequently, their work is not conceived as labor at all, but disguised as some form of apprenticeship or training. Also, since their employment is usually illegal, it is difficult to protect the children from exploitation and diverse forms of oppression. That this is the case leads many reformers in Egypt to call for the strict application of the labor code as the only way to protect children against abuse in the labor market.

The reasons leading to a high degree of child labor in Egypt are complex and multifaceted and include: overpopulation, a high rate of adult labor migration abroad, the failure of the Egyptian education system to provide schooling for large numbers of children, and an increasingly high number of school dropouts. Child labor is thus mainly due to the prevailing socioeconomic conditions in the country and, as such, can hardly be legislated out of existence. The current "problem" of child labor can only be solved by major transformations of Egypt's economy—at best, a long-term prospect.

In the meantime, greater attention should be given to improvement of the working conditions under which Egyptian children labor and to the development and implementation of new policies to protect their rights in the existing labor market. However, a program to improve or alleviate the conditions that confront child laborers must take into consideration how these children perceive their own situation within the world of labor.

The cases presented here are extracted from a study designed to investigate the life conditions of working children, with a special focus on how the children themselves view the labor scene and their participation in it.[2] During the course of the research, fifty boys were interviewed and observed at both their homes and workplaces in different parts of Cairo. The four cases of working boys presented here are a good representation of the rest of the sample. The presentations of their lives emerge through the combined co-operation of the children themselves, their families, their employers, and their coworkers.

SALEM

Salem is thirteen years old. He has been working for two years in a weaving workshop. He is underweight, pale, and probably undernourished. He is the fifth in a family of eight children, six sisters and one brother. None of the children has been to school except his elder brother, who dropped out of the fourth grade of primary school.

The father is sixty-one years old, widowed, and works collecting garbage for a salary of sixty pounds per month. The mother died six years ago. The father has not married again. Three of his daughters are married and live away. The eldest daughter (thirty-nine years old) lives close by in the neighborhood and spends part of the day taking care of her father and the young children. The other two, since they live in Tanta and Assiout, visit their father only occasionally. The three sisters' financial status can hardly provide for their basic life necessities, so they cannot provide any support for their father and the rest of their family. The elder boy (eighteen years old) used to contribute six pounds weekly when he was also working for the same weaving workshop. However, when he was drafted into military service twenty months earlier, his contribution ceased.

These circumstances explain the poor conditions in which the family lives. Their house is one three-by-three-meter room rented for four pounds monthly in the entrance of an old building at the dead end of a narrow alley. The room is stuffy, due to its poor ventilation, for there is only one small, high window overlooking a dark stairway. It is crowded with very old furniture: a wooden bed; an old sofa covered with a torn rug, the rest of which covers part of the floor; a high wooden cupboard on the shelves of which all the clothes of the family are thrown, along with some shoes; a two-shelved table with a fourteen-inch black and white television and a big radio cassette on the top shelf and some cassettes, pans, and a boiler on the lower shelf; a gas shelf-stove on another table; and a fan on top of the cupboard. Under the bed there is a low round table (for their meals) as well as many other articles and blankets. Outside this multipurpose room there is a narrow corridor with shelves on its walls, leading to a toilet with a shower in the corner. The father sleeps on the sofa, the three sisters on the bed, and the two boys on the floor.

The family's income is about 130 pounds per month: the father's salary is 60 pounds, the child Salem gets 10 pounds per week, and his sisters make a pound a day selling sweets to the children of the neighborhood. This income can hardly provide for even basic necessities. Their meals are composed of foul and molas for breakfast, taameya or kushary (a lentil and macaroni dish) for lunch, and cheese or halawa for dinner. Once a week (or sometimes every two weeks) they have a hot meal with meat or fish. During the workdays the owner of the workshop provides sandwiches for Salem's lunch. He also provides the child with medication when needed. For the father and the other children health services are provided by a small clinic attached to a mosque in the neighborhood. Clothes are purchased from a used clothing shop nearby, in addition to some winter clothes provided free of charge by the district's social center.

In spite of all these hardships and contrary to what might be expected, all members of the family seem to be contented and happy. The father is always smiling and kind to his children. Love, friendship, and warmth seem to characterize the relationships between all the members of the family.

The workshop where Salem works is located in Abdeen on Sarayat Street, which is a back street parallel to Port Said Street. It occupies an old stone and concrete building of two flats of about 200 square meters each. On the ground floor there are five old weaving machines, a store room, and a bathroom. On the second floor there are four threading machines, a closet for different tools, and an office for the manager, who is also the owner. The two floors are well ventilated through high windows and wall fans. However, there are no precautions against fire except two fire cylinder pumps. The building has two entrances. The main entrance leads directly from the narrow street to the weaving machine section, while the second entrance is located on another, wider street and leads to the back yard, where there is a stairway to the second floor. A mechanic's repair workshop is located in the back yard, where there are some old weaving machines and unused spare equipment left here and there. The back yard is dirty, unpaved, and covered with grease and mud. Near the second entrance there is a small first-aid box containing some cotton, a few bandages, plaster, and Mercurochrome. The weaving machines are operated electrically, and the threading machines are operated manually. One of the weaving machines is not working, awaiting some spare parts.

The weaving machines are operated by two adult workers, the threading machines by two boys, Salem and a fifteen-year-old boy. Each of them operates two machines. They are also responsible for cleaning the whole workshop once a week. There is also a clerk/account officer who is a relative of the manager. A part-time repair mechanic comes three times a week or whenever needed. The workshop uses cotton and polyester for the production of textiles of two different colors. It operates from 8 a.m. until 5 p.m., with one hour (12–1) for lunch and rest, on a one-shift basis, producing about 110 meters a day, six days a week. Adult workers receive fifty pounds and each boy ten pounds per week.

The founder of the workshop started the business in the mid-twenties. His son, the father of the present manager, added the second floor, remodeled, and replaced the machines with new electric ones in 1961.

The manager thinks highly of the child Salem. He considers him sincere and honest. He believes that he is bright and was able to learn his job quickly. According to his promise, he will raise his wage to thirteen pounds a week starting next month. However, he does not like the boy Rashid, who operates the other two threading machines. He thinks he is naughty, dishonest, and lazy. Rashid was assigned to his job four months ago and was the fifth to replace Medhat, Salem's older brother who left to join the military. The manager believes that good children like Salem and his brother Medhat are not easy to find nowadays. He also likes the two brothers because their father worked as a night guard for the workshop for six years and was always honest and trustworthy. Once he caught two workers who came at night to rob the workshop's storehouse. When he caught them they wanted to bribe him, but he refused and, with the help of a neighbor, called the police, who arrested them.

In general the manager is considerate and kind to all his workers. He helps them in solving problems, grants bonuses for good production, and gives gifts on occasions of marriage or birth and during the feasts. On the other hand, he insists on a penalty whenever a worker comes late, or is absent without permission or justified excuse, or when the worker produces faulty material. He also visits them at home on certain occasions. Examination of his records reveals that all the workshop's employees are registered for social security except the two boys because they are underage. He stated that, to compensate, he pays each child a bonus of forty pounds a year in two installments. Salem confirmed this statement, but Rashid, the other boy, denied it. The manager hopes that Salem will continue working after he reaches the age of eighteen. Then he will be treated like other adult workers, receiving fifty pounds a week. The manager will pay two thirds of his social security, while Salem will pay the remaining one third. The total amount represents 33 percent of the monthly salary.

When asked whether the workshop and the employees are insured against fire, electric shock, damage, injury, or death, the manager admits that there is no insurance, but claims that the workshop is small and costs are very high. He also cites the repeated failure of the electric power supply and the serious shortage of raw materials needed for production.

Salem likes his work, and his relationship with his employer encourages him to perform better. He is proud and satisfied with his contribution to the family income. He sees himself as an indispensable part of the family. He might have dreams of his own, but the hard work and the struggle to survive do not leave him much time to think of personal aspirations. He is quite sure that one day he'll have a family of his own, and that any father would be proud to give him his daughter in marriage.

MAHROUS

Mahrous is a slim, small boy of eleven years. He works in a glass factory in the Abdeen district. He is the third child in a family that includes a father (forty-three years old), a mother (thirty-nine years old), a married sister (eighteen years old), and a sixteen-year-old brother who completed his preparatory education and at present is enrolled in a voluntary military two-year training program in communication. The fourth and fifth children are two girls of six and eight years.

The boy is considerably less physically and intellectually mature than other boys of his age. He seems more impulsive, gregarious, and, at times, provocative. He is restless most of the time, and cannot concentrate for long periods. Occasionally he has difficulty expressing himself, followed by serious stuttering and stammering. He can barely read or write, except for his name and those of his father, mother, and siblings.

The boy was enrolled in a primary school at a village near Beni Suef for three years before his family migrated to Cairo two years ago. Because their arrival in Cairo was during the school's midyear vacation he failed to reenter school in Cairo. Because the boy was not doing well in school before migrating to Cairo, the father did not care too much for his schooling and preferred to push him to go to work.

In their village the father, though illiterate, was described by his wife as a good farmer. He earned his living by cultivating vegetables on two feddans that belonged to his father-in-law and were later acquired by his wife, as well as working for other landlords in the village. They lived a relatively smooth life. The mother raised sheep to sell, gaining some money that helped in supporting the raising of five children. However, as the father was suffering from a chronic case of bilharzia, his health started to deteriorate rapidly until his farming work was seriously hampered. With the growing up of his children and the marriage of his daughter, financial requirements kept soaring, and the family suffered serious difficulties. The mother was forced to sell her two feddans to meet the pressing needs of the family. Finally they decided to migrate to Cairo.

At the beginning they lived for four hectic months with some relatives in a slum area in the Arb Ghaneim district near Maadi. Finally the father—through his relatives' help—was able to find a job as a *bawab* (gatekeeper) in a small primary school on the road between Maadi and Arb Ghaneim. His very small salary of fifty-five pounds was inadequate to cover even the barest necessities of the family's life. He consequently forced his eldest son to quit school and join the military vocational program, and sent Mahrous to work for the glass factory. He also gave way to pressure from his school headmaster to take his daughter Sakina to work as a servant in the headmaster's house for sixty pounds a month. Even the youngest girl, Khadra (six years old), is now working for the owner of a small cigarette and sweets shop in a nearby dead-end alley.

The family lives in a one-room dwelling in a compound (*wekala*) near the citadel, composed of thirteen rooms surrounding a big yard, where donkey-driven carts are kept at night. In the room there is nothing but an old broken sofa, a table, and a straw mat (*hasira*) on which all the family members sleep. Outside the room there are some utilities (e.g. a kerosene heater), a short dining table (*tablia*), two pans, a tray, and a wooden box where they keep their clothes.

Some clothes are hung on nails on the walls of the room. Outside the entrance of the room there is an old bicycle which Mahrous uses for commuting to the glass factory (twelve kilometers) every day. There is one dirty bathroom and toilet that serves about sixty people dwelling in the thirteen rooms of the wekala. The whole place is extremely unhygienic because of the donkeys living among the human beings in the middle yard. Flies as well as many other insects roam everywhere. The smell is unbearable.

The relationship between the father and mother as well as between the parents and their children is very bad. Most of the time they quarrel, using terribly insulting terms, and using their hands and legs; otherwise they hardly speak to each other. Mahrous and his two young sisters show no respect for their mother or father. Lately the mother has been able to find occasional work in the homes of some families living in Helmeia. The total monthly earnings of the family do not exceed 140 pounds, and what remains after paying the rent on the room (15 pounds) hardly covers their meals, which are most of the time composed of bread, an onion, molas, old cheese (*mish*), boiled beans (*nabet*), and falafel once a week. Occasionally the mother and younger girl bring some food or clothes from the families they work for. The whole family is looking forward to the elder son's completion of his training, when he is expected to work for the army for a monthly salary of 120 pounds.

Mahrous does not think much of his job. He took it because it was the first thing available to him. He feels alienated in Cairo. He says that he used to love the village, where he had the opportunity and the space to run and play in the fields. Back at the village he had friends and he used to know and was known to everybody. Ever since he came to Cairo he has had to work hard, has no time for himself, and eats very poorly. He can still remember being in school. Although he was not very clever, he liked being around children his own age and learning things like reading stories and writing his name. He was forced to quit school and move out of a place he loved to a place he hates and fears. Working in the glass factory gives him headaches and sometimes makes him very sick from the excessive heat. The employer hands his salary to either his father or mother, and Mahrous does not keep anything for himself. Accordingly, work brings him no pleasure, no satisfaction, yet he feels the inevitability of it and is resigned to it.

HAMED

Hamed is a nine-year-old boy who works in a print shop handling, counting, piling, and separating cards for the printing machine. This machine is handled by an elderly man who used to work for one of the newspapers in Cairo, but is now retired. The job does not require any skills from Hamed. He just has to be attentive and follow instructions closely. The workshop is located in Bostan Street off Tahrir Square. There are two other boys working in the shop, and three adult workers other than the owner, who supervises the work and takes the orders from customers to print cards, short books, or articles sometimes, but mainly calling cards and office cards.

Hamed is very shy and apprehensive of strangers. The owner helped the progress of the interview with him, and took the first steps toward assuring him that there was no harm in talking to me. Hamed started working when he was six years old. His father is serving a sentence in prison, and his mother works selling vegetables and lemons on the sidewalk, in front of a fish shop. He has never been to school, and he has three sisters who also have never been to school. One sister, Nadia, is fourteen and stays at home tending to the younger sisters, four and three years old. Nadia cleans the house and cooks rice and vegetables for the family to eat at the end of the day. Hamed seems to love her very much, as she is always very kind to him. He was not given a choice when his mother made it known that he had to start being useful. She took him to a butcher's shop in the nearby district, where he was hired to clean up the floors and wrap the meat cuts for customers. The butcher was a very severe man whom Hamed hated. According to Hamed, the butcher abused him physically, and was always threatening to kill him if he complained to his mother. Hamed did not know how much he was paid. The butcher gave it to his mother along with some meat every now and then. One day last year he got so scared of the butcher and fearful his mother would make him stay with him, he ran away with five pounds, the price of meat he had been delivering next door. He had no intention of going back. He said that Nadia was the only one he was sorry to leave. He roamed the streets, sleeping in side-street garages and train stations for almost ten days; then he met one of the boys who work with him now at the print shop. The boy took Hamed with him to work and begged the owner to hire him. The owner insisted, as a condition of employment, on notifying his mother. Hamed went home with the print-shop owner, who was a respectable man, and managed to persuade his mother to forgive him and take him back in. He was happy to be home with his family again, especially with his sister Nadia. He feels very grateful to the owner of the print shop and seems to identify with him as the father he wishes he had. The man is actually a very kind man, religious and compassionate. He treats the boys with firmness and kindness, and seems to be willing to teach them the secrets of the business. He and the elderly man (Mansour) who operates the printing machine urge the boys to learn to read and write. Two of them actually do; only Hamed and another twelve-year-old boy are illiterate.

When I visited Hamed's home, the mother was not very encouraging, at first doubting perhaps the reason for my interest in her son and her life. Toward the end of the first visit she relaxed and agreed to a second visit. The nature of the father's crime was never divulged. She dwelled upon her poor luck and her struggle to keep up the family. Her son's job helps the family a great deal and his earnings of fifty pounds a month are now indispensable. She earns almost seventy pounds and is able to feed the family, and save to buy them new clothes twice a year. Neighbors are kind; they give them old clothes, and sometimes money in the feasts. They live in a room located under the stairs of an old building. The room is large, dimly lit by one light bulb, and contains a kitchen, sofas, and a rug on the floor where Hamed sleeps. There is a very small toilet attached to the room, with no shower but a tap and a big basin for washing clothes as well as bathing people. Nadia keeps the room very clean and the little girls, although wearing old rags, were clean.

Hamed revealed that he is satisfied with his accomplishments and hopes to master his job and perhaps run the printing machine one day. He has time for play only after 8 p.m. when he finishes his work and has a meal with his family. He has a few friends in the building, who play ball with him. Two of them go to school and one boy across the street works in a carpenter's work-shop at the end of their street. The school friends sometimes tell him about school and show him books.

The family seems to be close, and they treat each other with love and care. Hamed seems much closer to Nadia than to his mother. He does not remem-ber his father very much. Hamed seems happy with his job as compared to the hell he went through at the butcher shop. He wishes that he could learn to read and write, but says he cannot go to school and let his mother down. He has to earn a living.

AZIZ

Aziz is a twelve-year-old boy learning to become a carpenter. Aziz started working last year when he finished his fifth year of primary education. His father is a carpenter and works at the workshop with Aziz, which is owned by another carpenter who is currently working in Saudi Arabia and left the shop in the care of Aziz's father. Aziz is the only boy in his family. He has four sisters, two older and two younger. His mother is pregnant with their sixth child, who they hope will be a boy.

The father had planned this career for his son ever since he was born. He believes that learning to become a skilled carpenter will secure a prosperous future for Aziz. He himself was taught the skill very young by his own father, who migrated in the sixties to Cairo from Damietta to start a carpentry busi-ness. They owned a small workshop in one of the alleys in Shobra district, but unfortunately Aziz's uncle lost it in the early eighties. According to Aziz's father, he was a drug addict and is now dead, leaving his family of five mem-bers to the care of Aziz's father. He came to work for his friend, the owner of this workshop, six years ago and is hoping to save enough money either to buy the place or become a partner. Aziz's father is in his forties, and appears to be a competent carpenter. He manages the workshop, and teaches the workers. There are three adult workers and four children, including his son. Aziz addresses his father as "Osta" at work, just like the rest of the workers.

He is treated exactly like the others in the workshop, occasionally being beaten or harshly spoken to. "It is the only way these kids learn and master their skill. I am teaching him the way we learned as kids." This was the father's response to comments on the treatment of the children. The children are paid five pounds a day and the adult workers ten to fifteen, depending on their skills. Aziz gets paid, but his father saves the money for him. According to the father, Aziz is now making more money than a university graduate, who might still be looking for a job and not earning any money. To him, Aziz has all the benefits of education as long as he can read and write. He is now learning the trade of his family, and one day he'll thank his father for it.

Aziz was interviewed alone, and among other things, he appeared to miss school very much. He was a good student and would have liked to stay in school. The idea of defying his father never occurred to him. He was prepared for this role ever since he was a toddler. Aziz is well fed and wears a clean outfit, but he does not have time anymore for fun and games during the day. If he is caught playing ball during working hours, he is beaten and punished. Only on Sundays, when the shop is closed, can he play, and mostly it is with other working children who take Sundays off. Schoolchildren keep different hours, and according to Aziz, he doesn't like to play with them anyway.

Aziz has very low self-esteem and often feels incompetent, inadequate, and worthless. He does not like woodwork and seems to be learning nothing. He sometimes feels guilty for not obliging his father by becoming a good carpenter. He says he tries, but feels helpless and does not believe things will get better in the future. Aziz seems unable to make decisions of his own and often says, "I can't do it," even before he tries. He says that he believes other workers in the shop laugh at him behind his back, because he is very stupid and cannot seem to learn anything. He seems to be concerned about what others think of him and strives to be accepted by his coworkers, who he believes tolerate him only for his father's sake. It seems Aziz is caught between what he wants and what his father wants him to be. Wanting to please his father and failing to do so are making him think poorly of himself.

The interview with the mother revealed that she agrees with the father in wanting her son to become a carpenter. If it were not for this skill her husband would never have succeeded in keeping his family, as well as his brother's family. The older girls in Aziz's family have both been to school the same amount of time Aziz has. They are now sixteen and fifteen and learning housework and preparing for a married life. The younger two sisters, ages nine and seven, are still going to school, and plan to follow the path of their elder sisters. The whole household is preparing for the expected baby. They live in a three-bedroom apartment located in a street near the workshop.

Their home is tidy and full of many electric appliances (video, television, washing machine, refrigerator, radio cassette recorder, and so on). They seem proud of their possessions and hinted that had the father been a university graduate they would never have been able to afford this kind of life.

NOTES

1. Arab Republic of Egypt, *Labor Force Survey* (Cairo: Central Agency of Public Mobilization and Statistics, 1984).

2. Eftetan O. Farrag, *Child Labor in Cairo: Profiles of Working Boys.* M.A. thesis in Sociology-Anthropology, American University in Cairo.

THE RUNGS OF THE LADDER

by Daisy al-Amir
Translated by Caroline Attieh

Author's note: The following story about a child servant is fictional, but it is based on real circumstances, which, thankfully, no longer exist in most parts of the world, including the Middle East.

She could not resist turning her head to catch a fleeting glimpse of the things in the shop windows. Yet the two children kept tugging at her arm. They wanted to get home as soon as possible. The schoolday was over. As for her . . . she wondered when her term of work would be over.

A few months ago her father had come to collect her yearly wage. She wished she could see him . . . simply to talk . . . to tell him how sad she was . . . how upset she was . . . how she missed home and wanted to see her mother . . . how she hated him. She said this last aloud and then put her hand over her mouth, to keep her lips from uttering such words.

One should respect one's parents. One must love one's parents. Yes, one must respect and love them . . . but this, what she was doing, was that her duty? Was it only the duty of the children?

Years ago, when she was only a little girl, her father had taken her to work as a maid in a household. She was too short to reach the kitchen sink, so the housewife showed her how to stand on a wooden box to reach the tap. Yet her small hands and fingers were sometimes unable to hold a plate or glass firmly; when utensils slipped and broke, she knew what would follow, a beating from the lady of the house on her head, her back, her feet, and her face.

Why all those slaps? Since her hands were the cause, why wasn't the lady content to just hit her hands? A beating was painful, and what could she do if it covered other parts of the body? If she wept the beating was worse and if she kept silent curses followed. Where else could she go? She had no room of her own. She slept with the children. In the daytime she was responsible for all the duties of the household. How could they expect her to manage household affairs and know the proper place of knives, spoons, plates, and towels when she moved to a different house every year?

It was the agency that told her which house to go to. If she asked about her father, why he didn't come to see her and reassure her about her mother, more slaps would come. Beatings for silence, beatings for talk. When would the time come when the beatings stopped?

The two children held to her hand tightly. She turned her head toward the beauty parlor and would have stopped, had it not been for the children tugging on her arm insistently, wanting to hurry . . . home. She wondered: why should she hurry? The house was not hers, the family was not her family. Its visitors were not her friends. She wished that the door of the beauty parlor would open slightly but the children pulled her away. Oh, how she wished to know what was going on inside. She saw the ladies going in and then coming out looking different, with beautiful faces and shiny wavy hair. What were the secrets of the beauty parlor, she wondered? If only her mistress would ask her to accompany her there . . . if . . . only she could see what went on in that mysterious place.

She does not know when she was born, she has not counted the years of her life. Parents who did not even ask about the type of household in which their daughter worked were not likely to have registered the day or year of her birth. But she had heard her mistress shout that she was grown up and should take more responsibility. Responsibility? Was there any chore that she did not already perform? Cleaning the house, cooking, washing and ironing clothes, taking care of the children from the moment they awoke until their bedtime. All this and she was still unaware of responsibility?

She remembered the day when one of her mistresses surprised her in front of the mirror combing her hair. The woman pulled her . . . pulled her hair and then mercilessly whacked it with scissors. She closed her eyes to hide her tears but this angered her mistress who then began to whack her hair with one hand and slap her with the other. When her tears reached the floor her mistress had said, "My hand is tired. Oh, how obstinate you are." But her present mistress was not so harsh. She did not beat her and even gave her some money each week, the first she had ever handled herself.

The children pointed out that they had passed their house, so she retraced her steps with them and went in, afraid they would tell their mother about her absentmindedness. She was afraid that beatings and shouting might begin again. She motioned to the children not to reveal her mistake but they rushed into their mother's arms. She hurried to the kitchen to get their meal, which she had prepared before the outing, as she did every evening.

She didn't realize that children forget easily, since she herself was unable to forget that she hadn't seen her parents and brothers and sisters in a long time. She did not even know how many siblings she had now, or where they were. She had not forgotten her lingering wish to see her parents, and this desire became more persistent every time she began work in a new household. What kind of people were the members of her family? Did they not think that she missed them? Did she miss them or only miss having a home of her own? If they would only let her spend a week there, . . . only a week, she would be willing to wait on her parents, to serve in her own home. What did it mean for a person to have a home? She didn't know the feeling, yet had always wished to. Whenever she served food to household guests she would hear her mistresses speak of their homes with arrogance and pride. How could she get this persistent thought out of her mind . . . a house that was not hers . . . people that were not her relatives . . . guests that were not her friends . . . children to whom she had no ties . . . wages she did not receive . . . pain that was unforgettable . . . complaints that could not be expressed . . . but complaints to whom and from whom and from what? To all people and from everything, yet there was no person to whom this could be said, no time or place to say it.

The children's tutoring was over and they went to bed. She remained to serve the guests, wash the dishes, and clean up the kitchen before silently entering the children's room and spreading her mattress on the floor between the two beds. She lay down with the single hope that the children would not wake her before morning when the work would begin anew.

She wished she had paused by the beauty salon, for perhaps one of its clients would have gone in or come out, thus opening the door so that she could glimpse what was going on inside. She touched the strands of her own hair. It hadn't been sheared for a long time. It touched the bottom of her neck. Tomorrow she would do as her mistress asked, do it sincerely, obediently. Her new mistress was sympathetic. She spoke to her and treated her in a way that made it very unlikely that she would whack off her hair again. But if she felt like doing such a thing, who would prevent her? Her father? Her brother? Her parents? The owner of the agency? The children? The neighbors?

This was not the first time that she felt a sense of not belonging, but she did not know why tonight it was more painful than it had been in the past. Everything around her belonged to a place and people who were not her own, yet all she wanted was her new mistress's goodwill so that she would not have to move on to another household in another year. New work and new moods. She wanted to stay until these children grew up and married and had their own children, and then . . . ? Such thoughts of marriage and childbearing had not crossed her mind before today. She told herself she had no right to think of such things.

That world was not her world and she told herself she had no right to think about what happened in it. That world was a ladder with rungs that were not for her tired feet. When her hair brushed her cheek, she touched it again, happy that it had not been cut off. She did not know when she fell asleep, but awoke at the usual time when the first rays of the sun came into the room. She prepared breakfast and cleaned the sitting room. When she awoke the two children, they smiled at her. This made her feel optimistic, for this was a beautiful day which she had now begun with the smile of two innocent children who loved her. And she remembered . . . she remembered all the children she had brought up and taken care of . . . how were they doing now? Where had they gone? The paths of their lives had already been laid out for them. She knew that and they did too. And she? . . . She too was once an innocent and loving child. But today she was growing up and her hatred was growing up with her. And the remnants of innocence and love: did she have any such? She knew since she was more experienced that her work was increasing and so were her household responsibilities. Her father usually asked for higher wages now, and the new household would accept this request. She wished her new mistress would agree to increase her annual wage. Because here she was never beaten, nor was she cursed and she saw . . . yes, she saw and actually touched some money of her own.

Before taking the children to school, she went as she customarily did to her hideaway in one of the kitchen cabinets. There she counted the sum of money she was gradually putting together from her secret weekly income.

On the way to school, the beauty parlor door was open and one of the boys was scrubbing the pavement. She wished she could stop and look inside, but the children would be late. On the way back the door was closed and loud music could be heard from within. If the door had been open could she have stood and gazed inside? Her mistress would undoubtedly ask her why she was late. The beauty parlor had done well to close its door, she thought, removing the temptation for her to linger.

The beauty parlor became her daily obsession. Every time she walked by it, even if the door was wide open, she had no chance to look inside, for she only left the house on specific errands. If she stood and peered into the shop, wouldn't her mistress be upset when she knew the reason for her lateness? Would the mistress then cut her hair? She touched her hair and looked at it in the reflection of the shop windows. She had a lot of hair, long and lustrous. She wondered what the hairdresser would do if she let him set it. What would her hair look like then? Her mistress's hair was curly and rough before she went to the hairdresser's, but shiny and tidy afterwards. What could the hairdresser do with her hair if she went to him?

Every day she added up the money she had put together. What should she do with it? Buy a new dress? Wear the old clothes her mistress had given her, the clothes collected from her sisters and their daughters? Those dresses were not her size. Some were too long, others too short, and the colors were not of her choice. However, her hair was her own, implanted in her head, and no one could change it. Still, she had to tie it back with a ribbon or any scrap of rag so that it would not fall over her shoulders. That was the request of her mistress. Thus she had no right to choose what to do with her hair which was . . . her private property, wasn't it?

Her mistress told her that the family was going to spend the weekend in the mountains. She, the maid, was to stay in the house to clean it and roll up the carpets in preparation for summer. She was afraid to say that staying alone in the house was a prospect that frightened her, so she kept silent. . . . Then she said to herself: This was the first time that she had been left alone in the house. Wasn't this good? That she be without supervision, independent and free?

However, at the end of the day her mistress said that the maid of the children's aunt would be staying to supervise the house-cleaning process. She warned about disobeying the older maid, who was temperamental and very particular about cleaning matters. She did not know whether she should feel relieved to have company or whether it would be better to have remained alone, working without instructions and supervision.

Saturday came. The family made their preparations to leave. The children smiled at her before they left and continued to wave good-bye until the car disappeared from sight. Tears came to her eyes. She wished she were accompanying the family, for they were going to stay in a hotel and her work would have been simply to watch the children. Cleaning the carpets was a new experience, and she wondered about the aunt's maid. She had been told that she was temperamental. Would the two of them get along, she wondered.

She did not have to wait for very long, for she heard the door open. The aunt and the maid came in. The maid was tall and thin with sunken eyes and a sorrowful expression. She wore a long, flowing dress, a remnant no doubt of the aunt's wardrobe. She compared herself to this maid and realized that she was happier; she herself looked better and was younger. As soon as she arrived, the elderly maid began to cough. How could she herself help her? And why had her mistress made her fearful of this person who had such a deathly appearance?

The aunt sat down in the salon and began allocating tasks. When she realized that some of the cleaning materials were unavailable, she sent the young maid to the shop. She took the piece of paper, not knowing what was written on it, and left the house. As she passed the beauty parlor, she saw . . . she rejoiced . . . and she smiled. The door was wide open and a lady was coming out. She moved close and smelled perfume. She looked into the salon. It was full of ladies and the place was noisy. No one noticed her come in for everybody was busy, a young woman, girls, men and women. Some were washing hair in what seemed to her an upside down way . . . another was rolling hair on little colored discs. Girls were working on the feet and hands of ladies. People sat in front of mirrored walls. Women stood beside men and spoke to them in whispers or in scandalously loud voices. She shifted her glance. At a gesture of the hand, a lady moved from one chair to another. Loud noise came from a source she could not determine. Some of the chairs had a big globe above them . . . no, it was half a globe.

What was happening here? Why all the noise, the machines, the people? She felt she was beginning to discover the secret of the beauty parlor. Suddenly a boy approached her and asked her what she wanted. She reached up her hand and touched her hair, but it was not styled, so she said nothing. He looked at her with scorn and then turned to a table covered with magazines. These he proceeded to hand out to some of the ladies. She stood there at the entrance for a long time. But no one asked her to sit in front of a mirror . . . or to put her head in a sink, cover her shoulders with a towel.

A blond lady entered hastily and shouted to one of the men, "I'm in a hurry, quick, change the color of my hair." The man who was already working on another head answered, "I cannot; you changed its color already once this morning." She answered rudely, "But what difference does it make to you as long as I pay you and I pay for the dye? My husband wants me to be more blond." The man left the head he was working on and looked at the rude lady turning over the strands of her hair. "Your hair will be ruined," he said. "Coloring twice in one day will burn it." The blond took him by the shoulder and shook him. "My husband won't take me out in the evening with such hair," she said. "Do you understand what that means?" He motioned her to sit. Another person hurriedly came forward carrying a brush and bowl and began to cover the strands of the woman's hair with a white paste.

The dialogue between the blond and the man had caught the little maid's attention. Now she saw that some of the ladies had left their seats for a table near the door where a man sat. They opened their handbags and left piles of money, then went back to the young women and men and put something in their pockets. What were they putting in? She thought she was beginning to understand what was going on in the beauty parlor, but she didn't understand this gesture. One of the boys was helping a lady with her coat and she too put a piece of paper in his hand. Since the boy and lady were close to her, she saw exactly what the boy had received: money. All this was the cost of his helping her on with her coat. She remembered all the money she had saved from all those weeks of her service. All of it, all of it did not equal this amount.

The blond lady shouted that they should hurry for the honking of the car in the street was her husband. The noise and movement increased in the beauty parlor with laughter and conversation. Cups of coffee were brought to those ladies present. She slid out through the doorway. The wind brushed her face and lifted up her hair. She pulled at it. It was attached to her head, she knew its color, its length, and its texture. The blond woman changed her hair color twice in a day, but there was someone who paid. Her husband waited to take her to a party, while she, . . . who was waiting for her? What awaited her? Where could she find enough money to fix her hair? How had she lost all this time while money was paid to her father? She had neither time nor money, no party, no concerned husband. So what did she share with these women in the beauty parlor? The rude lady's hair was not hers. It was her man who decided on its color and who had the right to do so, for he was paying for it and he would take her to the party. As for her, her hair was her own property, but she couldn't have it fixed. She didn't have the money. She didn't have time. She didn't have a party to attend. Why was she here? How had she managed to get into this place that was for only a certain type of women? These were women she was supposed to serve and ensure their comfort. They were comfortable ladies. She was their tired captive.

She remembered the house where she worked, the carpets, the aunt, and the sorrowful maid. She wondered what punishment awaited her. She saw her own image in the reflection of a shop window. She looked at herself, at her billowing dress, and at her disheveled hair. Suddenly she put up her hand and held tightly to her lustrous hair, to protect it from the scissors that would come to whack it off.

AN UNMARRIED GIRL AND A GRINDING STONE: A TURKISH GIRL'S CHILDHOOD IN THE CITY

by Jenny B. White

PART I. EMINE'S DAY

MORNING

At eight o'clock in the morning, Hatice[1] emerges from the bedroom she shares with her husband. She shakes her sixteen-year-old daughter, Emine, awake. Emine throws off her quilt, rises from the couch-bed in the sitting room, and heads for the kitchen. She moves quietly past her two younger sisters sleeping together on the mattress bed and steps around her seven-year-old brother, who is curled up on a small mattress on the floor in a corner of the room.

I stir under my blankets on the second couch-bed in the cramped sitting room and prepare to resume my role as visitor and observer. Except for my presence, this is a typical day for Emine, a young girl in a squatter district in the hills surrounding Istanbul, city-born daughter of migrants from a village on the Black Sea.

Emine spoons tea leaves into the top of the double boiler, fills the bottom with water from the tap, lights the gas stove, and sets the tea water to boil. Still dressed in the thin cotton jogging pants and sweatshirt in which she slept, she begins to prepare breakfast, cutting thick slices of bread and toasting them on a thin sheet of metal laid over the burner flame. She boils eggs, pours jam and black olives out of jars into little glass serving bowls, and takes out the tiny tulip-shaped glasses and saucers for tea. She arranges these items, along with knives, forks, plastic plates, and a large jar of sugar, on an enormous round aluminum tray.

Hatice emerges from the bathroom down the hall and assists her. Ergin, her husband, enters the bathroom. Emine wakes up the other children, helps them wash and dress, and neatly folds up the quilts, mattress, and bedding, and carries them in enormous armloads into the bedroom to be stacked neatly on top of the chest and wardrobe and then covered with a decorative cloth. The couch-beds are pushed in; the mattress bed is covered and backed with large rigid cushions. The debris of sleep is cleared away, and the family gathers for breakfast.

A square cloth is placed on the floor and cushions positioned around it. Emine places a low round wooden board with short legs in the middle of the cloth, then places the large round aluminum tray on it. The family sits on cushions around the tray, pulling the cloth over their laps to catch crumbs. Hatice prepares each person's tea, first adding two teaspoonfuls of sugar to each tiny glass, then adding tea concentrate from the top of the double boiler, and finally topping the glass up with hot water from the bottom can. She proffers tea to every member of the family and tops up each glass as it is finished. The family breakfasts on toast, eggs, margarine, jam, and black olives. Emine bustles about fetching fresh toast from the kitchen but eventually settles down to eat.

After breakfast, Ergin goes to the workshop attached to the back of the house, the younger children tumble about in the sitting room, and mother and daughter clear away the breakfast things and do the dishes. They change into their day-clothes, simple midcalf-length skirts and knitted sweaters topped by knitted vests. Hatice goes into the bathroom, squats on the tiled floor before two large round low plastic tubs, and begins to wash the laundry. Emine sweeps the house, then begins preparations for lunch.

Women and children from the neighborhood drift in and out and work stops briefly for conversation. Emine goes out of the house and around to the workshop in the back. She sits at one of the two leather-punching machines and begins to edge precut diamonds of leather with evenly spaced holes. These will eventually be crocheted together into skirts and tops by neighborhood women who work for Ergin on a piecework basis. Emine's friend Güllü is seated at the other machine. Güllü, also sixteen, works about eight hours a day, five and a half days a week. She receives $7 a week, which she gives to her mother. Emine, because she is a family member, is not paid for her work in the workshop. Emine was taken out of school in the fifth grade. Her mother says she had wanted to leave of her own accord, but Emine tells me it was because her father needed her to be in the shop while he looked for buyers. "I work, but I have no value," she complains. Then, laughing, she adds, "I'll marry right away!" as if that would be revenge for her father's lack of appreciation.

Emine confides that she would like to own the business someday. She has learned the ropes and even accompanies her father sometimes on trips to the merchants who buy their finished clothing. "There are women merchants too," she says. The business, however, is named after her seven-year-old brother. Hatice says that they plan to educate their son, so he may not be interested in the business. In that case, they would hire a manager. Emine, in any case, will marry and leave the household. There is a framed photograph of the boy hanging on the workshop wall, and one in both the sitting room and the parlor, next to a photograph of Ergin's parents. There are no pictures of the girls.

Women and children of all ages drift in and out of the workshop, to ask for new work, pick up materials, bring completed outfits, or just to chat, some knitting or crocheting as they stand. One of the young girls relieves Güllü at the machine for half an hour. "She'll do that. She's a friend," explains Güllü. The girls discuss the progress of their trousseau preparations, describing in detail the different pieces of embroidery and stitching they have completed, the covers for couchbacks and armrests, the table runners, mats, doilies, scarves, and other covers. The conversation shifts to Turkish music and the singers everyone likes best. Emine takes out a publicity photo of Emrah, the teenage Arabesque music idol. "Look, he's winking," she says. The girls trade scraps of foreign languages they know. They talk about their old school days, what schools they went to and until what grade. A girl comes in and says she heard that a woman at the far end of the neighborhood had given birth to a bearded baby.[2] The girls joke that this is the end of the world.

When Ergin approaches the workshop from outside, the two girls at the machine jump to their feet. Emine rushes to put on her headscarf of thin purple cotton with beaded edging. Güllü wears her hair open, unlike the other girls that come in to visit. In the house, Emine takes off her headscarf occasionally, but only when her father is not around, and puts it back on when a man comes into the house. A piece of white plastic sacking is tacked neatly around each hole-punching machine so that merchants who come to pick up the finished clothing cannot see the girls' legs. Ergin's goal is to build a separate office attached to the front of the house, facing the street, to receive the merchants, so that the workshop at the back can be used solely for production.

AFTERNOON

At two o'clock, Hatice calls us to lunch from the balcony overlooking the entrance to the workshop. We go around to the front of the house, take off our shoes at the entrance, and walk barefoot down the hall to the sitting room. Güllü has joined us. Hatice is in the kitchen. The youngest girls spread the cloth and distribute the cushions on the floor. Emine goes to help her mother in the kitchen. Her brother lies on the couch alternately watching the proceedings and demanding attention from his sisters. Emine begins to bring in the pots of food, which are placed on the floor around the cloth and tray. Lunch is hot yoghurt-based soup, potatoes and tiny meatballs in a thin tomato sauce, and a great deal of bread. This is followed by a plate of rice eaten plain, and a bowl of cold yoghurt soup. Ergin joins us when the food has been laid out and leaves when he has finished eating.

The girls clear the remnants of the meal, although it is mostly Emine who cleans the kitchen. Hatice explains that the other two girls, aged eight and nine, are still too young but that they help sometimes. Emine and Güllü return to the workshop and Hatice sits with her children and a neighbor in the sitting room. Hatice and the two young girls take up knitting and sit and chat with the neighbor. A gentle breeze wafts in through the open balcony door. On hot days, the women and girls sit on woven cloth mats and cushions on the floor of the balcony. Not even their heads can be seen from the street below. The two young girls are impatient and drop their knitting on the couch, disappear briefly, only to return and begin again. They spend a great deal of time thwarting their younger brother's attempts to pull their hair and other mischief. On this particular day, a Turkish video movie forms the backdrop for our conversation. Women and young girls, some relatives, some neighbors, enter without knocking, sit for half an hour, chat, and leave. Hatice makes tea and serves it. Later, her son nestles up against her and rests against her breast as if he were still nursing. She stretches out on the couch and encourages him to take her breast in his hand and sleep. This he does. As the movie ends, she gets up, leaves her knitting on the couch, and goes to prepare dinner.

EVENING

Emine comes from the workshop to help. She sets the "table" and brings out the pots from the kitchen, placing them on the floor, along with the tea in its double boiler. Thick bread slices are placed liberally on the tray at everyone's place. We begin to eat: thin tomato-based soup, followed by a plate of beans, then a dish of eggplant, split and stuffed with a small amount of ground meat, and ending with a plate of white rice. Water is drunk with the meal, and tea afterwards. Ergin arrives home halfway through the meal, sits down, and joins us. Emine clears away the dishes and tray and disappears into the kitchen to clear up.

Ergin turns on the television. This forms a backdrop to the evening's activities and conversation, but is rarely watched for more than a few minutes at a time. Hatice sits on the couch facing the television, knitting. The children move around. Ergin has brought home some fuzzy gold-colored yarn that he wants one of the young girls to knit into a square to see how it looks. She does it desultorily, picking it up and putting it down. Occasionally, her sister or Hatice picks it up, knits a few rows, then puts it down again. They complain about the way the yarn handles and looks. After his daughter has knit a five-inch square, Ergin says to her, "Knit thirty sweaters and I'll pay you." The girl looks dubious. He continues, "Knit thirty sweaters and I'll give you one gold bracelet." He is joking. No one pays any attention to his offer.

The young boy has been flitting around the room teasing his sisters and mother. Now he approaches the video recorder, which is covered with an embroidered cloth. On top of the cloth are various bric-a-brac. The boy grasps hold of the cloth and yells, "Look!" Hatice looks up briefly from her knitting and utters a halfhearted admonition, "Don't." She looks back at her knitting as, with a flourish, the boy pulls the cloth and the things on it onto the floor, whooping. Ergin and the girls laugh. The objects scattered around the floor lie that way until the next morning, when Emine picks them up while she is sweeping the house.

Later, the children have fallen asleep in various parts of the room. Hatice motions to Emine to get the mattress and covers, and begins to pull out the couch-beds. When these are prepared, the sleeping children are placed in them or on the mattress on the floor and covered. The parents retire to their own bedroom, and Emine goes to the bathroom to change into a cotton jogging suit.

NIGHT

Emine goes out onto the balcony and doesn't emerge for some time. I go out to see. She lies on the rag rug of the balcony floor, looking silently at the night. I sit too, silently, looking at the lights in the distance, the road of or-

ange lights snaking along the crest of the hill opposite. This squatter settlement is at the very edge of the city. It is very quiet except for the wind and
the leaves. Occasionally a car light emerges from behind the house and illuminates the thin metal rods rising from the unfinished construction next
door. In a little while, Emine goes quietly into the room, past the three sleeping children, to steal a cigarette from the bric-a-brac cabinet. One of the girls
wakes up. Emine tells her she is looking for a comb, and goes back onto the
balcony. Later, she tries again and, this time, succeeds. I see the flare of the
match as she sits there, her back against the wall of the house.

I ask her about Fatma, the young girl who had been working with her in
the workshop the last time I was here, and who now was replaced by Güllü.
She says Fatma has been forcibly engaged to her cousin. She is nineteen, he
fifteen. Also, the two don't like each other. Fatma stopped working at the
workshop because her fiancé didn't want her to. Fatma's father, explains Emine, is a nasty, violent man, and he did this in order to prevent her from
marrying anyone else. Later, Emine whispers a secret, that Fatma is actually
in love with a young man in the neighborhood. She points out a silhouette
against a lighted window a few houses down. "That's him. They communicate occasionally by phone, but only as friends."

She adds that the boy actually loves someone else.

"Who?" I ask.

"Me," she says, laughing.

"And who do you love?" I ask.

"I love work," she says. She wants to be a working woman, she explains,
a woman merchant. She wants a business bigger than this, and she wants to
move to the shores of the Bosporus near Besiktas.[3]

"Why?" I inquire.

"Because," she says firmly, "they are backward here. They won't let you
wear pants or be without a scarf on your head."

Emine's friend Nermin, like Güllü, generally does not wear a headscarf,
and Nermin commutes every day to a job as secretary in a small business on
the Bosphorus. Unlike the other neighborhood girls who dress in wide skirts,
long-sleeved sweaters, and vests, she wears blue jeans, short-sleeved sweaters,
and other modern attire. She is different in other ways as well, once receiving
Emine and myself in her nearby home late one evening when her parents
were absent (although her brothers were present in another room). She
put on very loud music and danced both to modern pop and, winding a
scarf around her hips, to Turkish music in a sprightly and attractive oriental way. Emine was fascinated by this behavior, but it evidently also made
her uneasy. She watched the dancing intently, not moving, but would not

dance herself and wanted instead to listen to and moon over the young pop idol, Emrah.

Nermin also has a file of letters from and photographs of foreign men she has met on arranged group tours to the Turkish coast. Although she knows a little English, she gives me the letters to translate. "They're all lies, aren't they?" she asks. I tell her that the writers on the whole probably are not people she would like to be with for any length of time. She doesn't seem surprised. She says she receives phone calls from this man or that, even from the United States, and claims that her parents allowed her these trips and contacts: "Why not?" She adds with conviction, "I am going to find a foreign man to marry."

PART II. AN UNMARRIED GIRL AND A GRINDING STONE

Emine's day is in many ways typical of that of other young girls in Turkish families that have moved to Istanbul from the countryside. In 1989, over half of Istanbul's six and a half million people lived in squatter[4] neighborhoods such as Emine's. As in the village, the residents of a neighborhood generally know one another. While the men often work outside the neighborhood as civil servants, drivers, or in factories, the women stay within its borders. Women's participation in the labor force outside the home in Istanbul squatter areas is as low as 6 percent.[5] The women visit each other freely within and, more rarely, between nearby neighborhoods. In other words, the women consider themselves to be housewives, in Turkish literally "sitting at home." Yet even when they are sitting, as is evident from the description above, girls' and women's hands are always busy. "Good" women are defined by their abilities, their skills, and their labor. A girl needs a reputation as a good woman in order to marry. Girls become adults and acquire social identity only when they marry, and have full community status only when they have a child. The opinions of unmarried women, even if they are advanced in age and education, are not given as much weight as those of their younger but married sisters. The first thing young girls learn, then, are the labor skills which will define them both personally and socially.

Young girls help their mothers with the housework and take care of younger siblings. The presence of an older sister frees younger girls from some of this labor, at least until their sister marries. Women's labor in general is not bounded by individual identity, and what is put down by the mother can be taken up by the daughter or by a neighbor or friend. As girls grow older, they take over more and more of their mother's household labor. They learn how to serve a glass of tea or water with the proper gestures and ceremony, how to keep the house clean, how to cook time-consuming Turkish dishes, and how to take care of younger children. These skills are on display when a man's family goes to view a prospective bride. Great attention is paid to the girl's manner of serving coffee from a tray. Some families, it is said, leave some of the roasted chickpeas served them under the couch cushions. If at the next visit the chickpeas are still there, the girl is considered to be too untidy to be a good wife. As a bride, the girl will be required to display these skills in her husband's household and often in that of his parents as well. Her quality as a bride will be judged accordingly.

There is a saying in Turkish, "Delikli tas yerde, gelinlik kiz evde kalmaz," which means: Just as a grinding stone (literally "stone with a hole") can't stay on the ground (unused), a girl of marriageable age can't stay home. In other words, like a grinding stone which is always in use grinding *bulgur* (cracked wheat), a woman of marriageable age invariably becomes a bride. The latent labor function of a grinding stone is inevitably transformed into social use, just as the labor skills a girl has learned transform her into a socially acceptable bride.

To prepare for their marriage, young girls begin at an early age to prepare their trousseau. This involves skilled and intensive labor, fine stitching, embroidery, and crochet work. The trousseau is displayed at marriage and, again, reflects on a girl's quality as a bride.

Marriages tend to be arranged, although it is rare that a boy or girl is forced to marry someone he or she dislikes. In the case of Fatma's engagement to her much younger cousin, friends and neighbors thought badly of her father for forcing an engagement with a boy so much younger and, moreover, with someone Fatma disliked. The preferred marriage partner is a cousin, relative, or someone from the same village. Consequently, although a girl leaves her parents' household, she may still live among people who know her and who will treat her well.

Before they are engaged, young girls indulge in romantic fantasies about young men in the neighborhood, but these remain platonic relationships since after age seven or eight, neighborhood boys and girls rarely come into social contact with one another. It was said that Fatma's father arranged her engagement because he had heard rumors that she was interested in a young man from the neighborhood, and he wished to preempt what he considered an unsuitable marriage with a nonrelative.

In any case, a girl's movements are circumscribed by an intensive pattern of labor activities in the house and sometimes in a workshop. At a very early age, girls may begin to contribute to family income by taking in piecework or by helping with their mother's or sister's piecework. Sometimes they work in the family workshop or in a neighborhood workshop. Family labor in workshops generally is unpaid. The labor of family members, like girls' and women's household labor, is seen to be their natural contribution to family life, and the proceeds of family loyalty are paid out in accordance with family tradition: bride wealth, trousseau, engagement and wedding celebrations, furnishings for the new home, as well as premarriage expenses and, more rarely for girls, education. Ergin will indeed give his daughter a gold bracelet—at her wedding—as he jokingly promised in return for her knitting.

The other workshop employees are paid very little and unpaid labor is donated by neighbors and friends. The minimal, even token salaries are justified by pointing out that the young girls are only working to earn money for trousseau materials. There is a high turnover as the girls leave at marriage, often at age sixteen. Girls are taken out of school after the third grade more readily than boys. Their parents often insist that their honor (*namus*) is threatened in a mixed-gender environment at school or on the street coming from and going to school. However, as with Emine, the girl's labor is often immediately put to use in the workshop. She does piecework or another money-earning activity such as cleaning middle-class homes. She might also provide child care and household labor to free her mother for other work.

Since exposure to strange men and possibly compromising circumstances in strange homes affects their reputation, it is in only the poorest families that girls and women leave the neighborhood to work. Nermin is an exception in this as in many other things. Her job, however, is a respectable one, as secretary at a small and reputable business on the shores of the Bosphorus not too far distant from the neighborhood.

Girls and women prefer to remain in the neighborhood. They form an almost limitless pool of cheap labor for enterprises such as that of Ergin, in which a local man obtains orders and materials from outside the neighborhood, distributes the raw materials to neighborhood women through the female members of his family, and pays the women a set amount for each finished item. He delivers the finished products to the merchants (or a merchant may also send a representative to the workshop; therefore the need for plastic aprons on the hole-punching machines in Ergin's workshop and his wish for an office separate from the site of production) and keeps for his family the difference between what he has charged the merchant and the cost of labor.

If production expands, a small storefront may be rented nearby, and young neighborhood girls or boys (depending on the type of business) might be hired to supplement the labor of family members. While boys generally are hired as apprentices, girls are hired on a more informal and temporary basis, since they are expected to leave such employment at marriage when it becomes their husband's duty to support the family. Women continue to do piecework, however, since it is done in their own home and since it generally is not thought of as work, although it is remunerated, but rather as part of the labor activities which express women's social identity.

In a city the size of Istanbul, however, the value of traditional skills and behavior is challenged by exposure to new ways. Squatter settlements have grown in size and complexity and no longer have a homogeneous population emigrated from the same region of Turkey. The families of Emine's friends exhibit a wide range of permissiveness with regard to modest dress and behavior, working outside the neighborhood, and travel. Emine herself sees other lifestyles; she need only travel down the road into the city with her father. She meets female merchants, role models that would not have been available in the village. While Emine is less radical than Nermin, or even Güllü, in dress and lifestyle, she has ambitious dreams and rebels subtly and quietly against her parents' expectations.

The freedoms and new perspectives afforded by city life are tantalizing and create conflicts within families and within communities that try to protect the way of life that has been transplanted here from the village. Old ways clash with new dreams as the girls negotiate a path between honor and ambition. In traditional family life, girls learn labor skills and emotional independence in preparation for their roles as brides in a strange and potentially hostile environment. Ironically, it is perhaps these very skills and this independence that will allow them to respond successfully to the challenges of urban life.

ACKNOWLEDGMENTS

This chapter is based on research carried out in Istanbul, Turkey, from 1986 through 1988, and funded by grants from Fulbright-Hays and from the National Science Foundation. The conclusions, opinions, and other statements in this publication are those of the author and not necessarily those of the sponsoring institutions.

NOTES

1. In the interest of privacy, all names have been changed. In Turkish, the letter c is pronounced j; "Hatice" is pronounced "Hateeje."

2. This story was very widespread in Istanbul in July of 1987 and was said to have been started by an article in the *Tan* newspaper.

3. Besiktas is an area with established working-class neighborhoods, close to the

spectacular scenery of the Bosporus. Emine would have passed this area traveling from the squatter settlement to visit merchants in the old city.

4. Squatter neighborhoods today generally consist of a mixture of legally and illegally built housing. In 1987, Emine's neighborhood was formally annexed by the municipality, although it had already received bus service and utilities some time before.

5. Tansi Senyapili, *Gecekondu: Cevre Iscilerin Mekani* (Ankara: ODTU Mimar Fakultesi, 1981), p. 92.

Boys at summer camp, near Amman, Jordan
PHOTO BY HEATHER LOGAN TAYLOR

PART V

CHILDREN'S EDUCATION

Educate your child for tomorrow.

THE QURAN

Education has always been highly valued in Middle Eastern society. The Quran, holy book of Islam, advises a parent to "educate your child for tomorrow." Although the Prophet Muhammad was unlettered, he continually urged his followers to read. This emphasis on the importance of education has become comparable to the American attitude, which, as John Kenneth Galbraith stated years ago, has been to see education as the cure for many problems of underdevelopment and poverty, the way to individual mobility in a rapidly changing world.

Historically, two or three years of religious education were deemed sufficient for most Muslims, as well as for Christians and Jews. A small number of specially talented persons, mostly men but including some women, went on to study in secondary schools and even to the great religious university centers, financed through local religious and charitable foundations. In the eighteenth century, western missionary schools were established for the elite who could pay to learn the new languages of the ruling colonial powers (France, Italy, Britain, Spain). Some young men and women were subsequently sent to Europe by their families to become acquainted with western secular knowledge, particularly in sciences, and hence to be armed to compete in the new world of the colonial Middle East.

But free, compulsory secular education for all children, male and female, is a new phenomenon in the area, a promise made to all citizens by the majority of independent governments which emerged at the end of the colonial period. President Gamal Abdel Nasser set up a system in the 1950s whereby a talented child, by succeeding in a series of open examinations, could obtain a graduate college degree, without cost. This policy was admired as a way to develop manpower and was widely copied in the area. Schools were built.

School children in Cairo, Egypt
PHOTO BY DIANE WATTS

Teachers were trained. New textbooks, using local rather than European languages, were published. By 1985, the literacy rates in Egypt for females fifteen and older had increased from 33.8 percent to 48.4 percent and enrollment in secondary schools had jumped from 26 percent to 81 percent.

Today, governments and citizens are beginning to reassess the educational system and to recognize its failures as well as its successes. By the end of the eighties, statistics showed that even in Egypt, 17 percent of all children did *not* benefit from elementary education and nearly 30 percent of boys and girls were still outside the secondary school system. Although in 1988 Morocco expended a third of its annual budget on education, students were still scrambling for places in the overcrowded government schools, and the quality of the schooling was generally perceived to be uneven. This has been true of all the poorer Arab countries to some degree. Kuwait, among the oil-rich countries, has been able to establish early childhood education. The nursery school curriculum, outlined by A'isha al-Haj Hasan and Lu'lu'a al-Qattami, illustrates the Kuwaiti approach. In Saudi Arabia, however, education is still not compulsory, although incentives are built into the system, as Jerine Bird points out in "Revolution for Children in Saudi Arabia." The excerpt from a Turkish first-grade text underscores some basic Turkish values: obedience to parents, a division of labor based on age and sex, and the necessity of hard work to do well—in school or anywhere else.

Education has become more problematic in the West Bank, where

Elementary school, Aswan, Egypt
PHOTO BY DIANE WATTS

Palestinian schools have been closed by the Israeli government for long periods during the Intifada or uprising in the territories. Abdalla al-Kurd and Barton R. Herrscher record the response of parents and teachers, who have organized alternative forms of schooling.

In Yemen, the growth of education reflects changes in the nation's economy, particularly a reduced demand for child labor, according to Susan Dorsky and Thomas Stevenson. But in the nineties, they say, this pattern is changing. Iran's educators since the 1979 Revolution have been taking a second look at the goals of its education and reassessing both textbooks and curricular materials. Adele Ferdows looks at changes in gender roles in new Iranian textbooks, and Patricia Higgins and Pirouz Shoar-Ghaffari analyze changing perceptions of Iranian identity in the same new books.

Most recently in the last decade, another educational movement has arisen. Great numbers of private schools have opened, partly in reaction to the overcrowding in public schools in many countries; most are religious schools which are responsive to the modern Islamic movements in the region. Some are expensive preparatory schools for children of the wealthy elites.

Thus, the populist ideal of free schooling for all so often cited since 1952 in almost every country has not yet been achieved. New economic and political pressures are affecting not only how education should be structured and what subjects should be taught, but also *who* is being educated. This has profound implications for the next generation of Middle Eastern adults.

EARLY EDUCATION IN KUWAIT: A BRIEF DESCRIPTION OF THE NURSERY CURRICULUM

by A'isha al-Haj Hasan and Lu'lu'a al-Qattami
Translated by Ahmed Sweity

The aim of this curriculum is to develop the various physical, social, mental, and sensory abilities of children. Hence, some basic directions that help children to build and develop these various abilities have been designated. They are as follows:

RELIGIOUS EDUCATION

A. Memorizing short chapters of the Holy Quran such as al-Fatiha, as-Samad, al-Kawthar, to strengthen memory.

B. Learning about religious duties such as praying, fasting, and pilgrimage.

C. Learning social behavior such as cooperation, truthfulness, security, helping the elderly, obeying parents, general cleanliness of body and the place for cleansing, to strengthen independence and fusion with others.

SOCIAL EDUCATION

A. Self-reliance: One of the most important elements of social education is training the child to depend on itself to help itself by itself. This is done by means of the following exercises: putting on and taking off the uniform, putting on and taking off shoes, combing hair, cleaning teeth and nails, eating food, washing hands and face, and going to the bathroom.

B. The family concept: Learning kinship relations (father, mother, grandfather, grandmother, paternal uncle, and maternal uncle), and the concept of life stages (childhood, youth, old age).

This essay is from *The Annual Book for the Model Nursery,* begun in 1974, published by al-Khalidiyya in Kuwait.

C. The school: Knowing the school facilities (classes, administration) and those employed in them such as directors, headmistresses, secretaries, and workers.

D. The road: . . .

E. The neighborhood: Learning what exists in the quarter (schools, mosques, society, and gardens) and about other things from which people of this area benefit, such as restaurants, entertainment houses, exhibitions, museums, and so on.

F. Official holidays: Learning about weekend holidays, religious and national feast days.

G. Social occupations: tailor, carpenter, blacksmith, mechanic and so on.

MENTAL EDUCATION

1. The Sciences

    A. The four seasons: Tasks: Observing the weather and the garden and their changes according to the seasons, variations in clothing, and methods of heating and cooling.

    B. Plants: Learning the way they grow, their seasons, and about some of their visible parts (using onions, potatoes, lentils).

    C. Animals: Learning types of animals and their characteristics (domestic animals, some wild animals).

    D. The magnet: Some of its uses.

    E. Floating: Its benefits.

    F. Human beings: The external organs.

    G. Nutrition: Learning about plant and animal varieties of food such as vegetables, grains, fruits, meat, fish, eggs, milk and its products; observing their visible forms, distinguishing taste and smell.

2. Counting and Arithmetic

    A. Cardinal counting

    From 1 to 5 for younger children (first group).

    From 1 to 50 or to 100 for older children (second group).

    B. Analyzing and synthesizing the number 5 (first group).

    $$1 + 1 + 1 + 1 + 1 = 5$$
    $$1 + 2 + 2 = 5$$
    $$1 + 1 + 3 = 5$$
    $$1 + 4 = 5$$

    C. Ordinal counting:

    From 1 to 5; for example, the first, the second, the third.

    D. Knowing some geometric shapes

    The triangle, square, rectangle, circle, and their uses.

3. Reading
   A. Oral reading: Working to increase the child's linguistic acquisition by means of stories, plays, songs, and oral conversation so that the child is able to express what it wants and to understand what is requested from it.
   B. Visual reading: The reading of some written words, concentrating on the learning of short words with simple pronunciation and words important for children's speech such as Papa, Mama, rooster, chicken, lion, rabbit, elephant.

PHYSICAL AND MOTOR EDUCATION
Training the senses and muscles through physical exercises.
   A. The senses: Training all the child's senses by means of games that aid in developing perception: of colors, shapes, areas, and volumes, that help in developing eyesight; of voices and sounds of human beings, animals, instruments, and the natural environment to develop the sense of hearing. Smells are used in developing the olfactory sense, food in developing the sense of taste, and the surfaces and shapes of objects to help in developing the sense of touch. The best training methods for these are Montessori methods for sensory training.
   B. Physical education: Developing muscles such as those of the fingers, neck, back, and legs by means of physical exercises, sorting grain, and play-acting the various social occupations such as carpenter, farmer, and musician. This is in order to link physical with social education.

AESTHETIC EDUCATION
   A. Developing aesthetic appreciation: Showing children beautiful scenes of nature such as flowers and trees as well as colored pictures and having children exhibit beautiful fashion on their dolls.
   B. Drawing and works of art: Training children to mix colors and to recognize their beauty and use them in suitable places according to their imagination. These are accompanied by increasing artistic activities on paper and cardboard, using cloth and mud, and cooking. This allows the child to apply what it chooses from the pictures it saw in its environment, and is based on the condition that the child is given complete freedom in drawing and formation.

EMOTIONAL EDUCATION
This is based on the knowledge that emotional education is the first and foremost objective in developing the child's personality. This is done by means of developing the spirit of love (i.e. to love and to be loved) through play.

OUR FUTURE HOPES

Our future hopes are to open more model nurseries in various areas of the state to provide the opportunity for all levels of society to take advantage of these educational services for the prekindergarten child.

God is the ruler of our affairs and success.

REVOLUTION FOR CHILDREN
IN SAUDI ARABIA

by Jerine B. Bird

In a scant thirty years the opportunities for children in Saudi Arabia have expanded dramatically. The first public schools for girls opened in 1961. Those first little girls to enter school at six were thirty-eight years old in 1993. What their children now take for granted was for them a unique experience which their mothers and aunts had not had. In 1991 there were more than 2.5 million students in school in Saudi Arabia.[1] School attendance is not compulsory but there are incentives built into the system, even stipends, to encourage the attendance of every child, and education is available throughout the sprawling kingdom, from large cities to the most remote mountain villages.

The success of this enormous emphasis on developing and expanding educational opportunities can best be demonstrated by the steep rise in literacy rates. Although reliable figures are difficult to find and, at best, somewhat subjective, in 1970 (ten years after the first public schools for girls opened) Saudi Arabia had one of the lowest literacy rates in the Middle East: 15 percent for men and 2 percent for women. In a scant twenty years the rate rose to 73 percent for men and 48 percent for women.[2] The commitment of the government can be demonstrated by the fact that by 1979–1980 more than 25 percent of the entire annual budget for the Saudi government was devoted to education.[3]

Development of educational facilities in one generation for both boys and girls may serve as a model for other societies, but the kingdom is also unique. Saudi Arabia had one enormous advantage that few other countries may ever have—seemingly unlimited monetary resources. But the Saudis also had extremely limited human resources and no tradition of formal education. It would be fair to say that few countries faced as much potential resistance to modern education and change since Saudi Arabia represents one of the most isolated and culturally pristine conservative societies. How did it happen that the best in education in a roughly western sense became the number-one goal of the Saudis' development planning beginning in 1960?

ISLAM

The primary influence in Saudi Arabia is, without question, Islam. Most Saudis are Wahabis, a sect in the Sunni wing of Islam, which has its roots in the heart of the Arabian Peninsula. This sect calls for a return to the five basic tenets of Islam. Saudis take very seriously the responsibility of being custodians of the holy cities of Mecca and Medina and are proud to host the pilgrims, the hajjis.

The Wahabi faith provides its adherents with a very liberating notion (from the Quran): "Every man and every woman must determine the truth (or 'black from white') for himself or herself." This implies a need for tolerance which one would not expect in a fundamentalist type of faith, but it has, in fact, produced a very diverse array of life-styles behind the walls of family compounds.

There is no central creed other than the five tenets of Islam: (1) confession of faith, (2) prayer five times a day, (3) contribution to charity, (4) fasting during Ramadan, and (5) pilgrimage to Mecca. The diversity in the application of Islam in day-to-day life in Saudi Arabia is not visible to outsiders because it is such a private society.

Of the two major branches of Islam, the Sunni and the Shia, only an estimated 5 percent of Saudis, concentrated on the eastern coast of the peninsula, are Shia.[4] The great majority are members of the Sunni wing and are Wahabis, the Puritans of the Muslim world, a sect which emerged in the late eighteenth century, calling for a "return to the true faith." The Wahabis, from the central Arabian peninsula before the area was consolidated by the Sauds into a nation, were considered by other Arabs to be not just conservative but primitive. However, this new form of Islam denied the right of any clergy to stand between the believer and God, placed the local mosque in the hands of its own worshipers, and emphasized not just the right but also the obligation of the believer to determine "truth" or right from wrong for himself or herself. This is a radical and revolutionary notion which can be a great asset for a community in the process of change. It is in some ways an eighteenth-century Islamic statement comparable to Luther's stand against Rome.

Fazlur Rahman describes the Wahabis as placing great emphasis on the text of the Quran and the hadith, which one could expect to result in ultra-conservatism. However, by the rejection of *taqlid* (authority in religion) and insistence that the true believer must exercise independent reasoning (*ijti-had*), "the door was opened for more liberal forces to interpret the test more freely than the principle of analogical reasoning."[5]

Furthermore, the absence of a religious hierarchy or centralized religious authority to lend power to a political entity has made it easier for the Saudis to accept and indeed embrace the advent of modern technology in the kingdom which has made life much more comfortable.[6] Each group in the community (usually a family unit or group of family units) could accept or reject selectively innovations which might impact the social or family framework. Watches, radios, and cars are owned today by most Saudis, but even the radio was initially seen as a device of the devil by religious leaders.

When Abdul Aziz introduced radio stations in the early thirties, the chief qadi of the Hejaz was incensed and insisted that sacrifices must have been made to Satan in order to accomplish this deviltry. The king was exasperated and took the qadi to the radio station in the palace to show him that there was no evidence of blood or bones. The qadi continued to pester the radio operators so Abdul Aziz challenged him with "Would Satan carry God's word from here to Riyadh?" The sheikh replied angrily that, of course, the devil would not carry God's word even an inch. Then the king led him to the radio station and watched the qadi as he heard the words of the Quran intoned by the imam in the Great Mosque of Riyadh over the radio connection. The qadi was incredulous and concluded that the radio was a miracle of God.[7]

The only significant public violence over technological change came fifteen years later when television was introduced. There was actually a small protest group organized when the first station was nearing completion in Riyadh. The soldiers killed one Saudi protester, whose American-educated brother later took revenge and assassinated King Faisal. This delayed its introduction only briefly. The Arab American Oil Company (Aramco) had, in fact, been allowed to broadcast programs for the benefit of its foreign workers in the eastern province years earlier. The station was required to keep a very low power level making reception poor or nonexistent in nearby Saudi towns. The programming was carefully controlled to uphold Muslim values (i.e., no kissing!—there was lots of film on the cutting-room floor) and the broadcast language was English. Slowly, as it became apparent that Saudis were watching *Leave It to Beaver* and *The Lone Ranger* with no interference from religious authorities in the nearest village, the power level was increased. Soon the programming was dubbed in Arabic with the English sound available on the radio. Many Americans were amused to see the Lone Ranger speaking Arabic and didn't bother with the English sound.

Most technology could be adapted to Saudi sensibilities. Public municipal bus transportation, for example, was introduced with great success by incorporating a special section of the bus for women only, and even providing a separate entrance and fare box. Many young girls are today able to attend school and university because there is transportation available which does not violate the principle of complete separation of the sexes. While not specifically required by the Prophet, this has become a cultural habit related to religion.

EARLY SCHOOLS

But the introduction of schools, probably predictably, began in urban areas and was at first very slow to expand. There is only limited written history of the advent of formal schooling in Saudi Arabia. A century ago the country consisted largely of bedouin who roamed the peninsula and villagers living in quite isolated settings. There are a number of reports of the existence of *kuttab* (mosque schools) in the villages and towns of the nineteenth century, especially in Jidda, the western coastal port city which always had the most contact with the outside world. Until 1924 when the first Department of Education was created, the *kuttab* was the only type of school available.[8]

Initially the mosque school was intended solely as a method of conveying religious education. Rote learning was the major method of teaching with relatively little emphasis on reading and writing.[9] Throughout the Arab world memorization has been a common element of education. A deputy minister from the Sudairy tribe in southwestern Saudi Arabia told me of his memory of school: "Look at my ear lobe," which was somewhat extended and black as if severely bruised. "I can thank my teacher in the mosque school in my village for this. He pulled me from one end of the mosque to the other until I was able to recite my Quranic verses perfectly." He seemed to regard the experience as almost an initiation rite into his own community—one which sustained him during his years in America (where he earned his Ph.D. in political science). Bonding with his tribe and nation was perhaps a result of the ordeal.

The value of such memorization is not thought of solely as discipline, but also as a method of conveying the wisdom of the Quran in a way that will remain with the individual throughout his lifetime. Emphasis is placed on declamatory style and students are honored for both this style and the length of their memorized passages. On Friday mornings, Saudi children today can watch on television some cartoon shorts, interspersed with prize-winning students who recite in dramatic style excerpts from the Quran—the updated version of the recitals in the mosque of earlier years.

The influence of the hajjis (religious pilgrims) from throughout the Islamic world no doubt was a major factor in the further development of the early schools. An example of this influence is the establishment in 1873 of the Saulatiyya School, founded by a woman, Mrs. Saulat al-Nissa, an emigrant from India. It provided an education in traditional religious subjects and reading, writing, and what are described as "rational and intellectual subjects." Algebra, arithmetic, and astronomy were included in the program. There was an examination system which posed remarkable questions such as:

> 1. Give the rule governing the four rational numbers and its procedures. What is that number if increased by a quarter and a sixth of its value, and if its total is subtracted by 5 comes up to 10? Show in detail how the number is obtained.
>
> 2. Show the double-error control system and its method. Indicate how the preceding question can be verified through the double-error control system.[10]

In 1901, during the time of the Ottoman presence in Jidda, Hajji Abdullah Alireza, a prominent businessman in the community, established the Falah schools, considered by Robert Lacey, author of *The Kingdom,* to be the first modern schools in Arabia.[11] Hajji Abdullah gave a substantial part of his resources to the schools and they were free of tuition.

The Hejaz, on the western coast of the Saudi Arabian Peninsula, was the area which had the most contact with the outside world. Jidda, its port, welcomed the pilgrims who came to make the "haj" and was the economic center for the peninsula. By 1915 there were seventy-eight state elementary schools, a few private schools, and some mosque schools but some did not survive the war and were not replaced. The first Saudi government elementary school for boys was established in 1925. There were 2,300 students in the entire country in 1930, and about 20,000 by 1949.[12]

Establishing the notion that schools were a valuable asset to the society was an uphill battle. When Charles Crane came to Jidda in 1931 in the hope of negotiating a geological survey agreement with King Abdul Aziz, he suggested sending one of the king's sons to the West for education. "Abdul Aziz thought this a bad idea. What was required in Arabia, he explained, 'and more especially for members of the ruling house, was an education which should fit them to be leaders of men. . . . In order to be a leader of men, a man has to receive an education in his own country, among his own people, and to grow up in surroundings steeped in the traditions and psychology of his countrymen.' "[13]

This, in fact, describes well the education of members of the royal family. Until eleven or twelve they were required to spend time memorizing the Quran; then they would be assigned to a bedouin tutor to learn the skills of survival in bedouin life and then in time would return to sit in the *majlis* (literally the "place of conferring" but actually the gathering of the host, his relatives, and friends where problems are discussed and decisions made). King Khalid and Crown Prince Fahad both had such an education.

By 1925 the General Department of Education was founded by the Saudi government.[14] In 1926 a training college for teachers was established, followed by a religious law college seventeen years later. It was not until 1936 that the first government secondary school opened, called the King Abdul Aziz Secondary School, located in Mecca.

Al Azhar University of Cairo, the oldest university in the world, was the university frequently chosen by those few privileged Saudis who pursued higher education. It was those pioneer graduates who staffed the Taif School of Islamic Fundamentals (Dar al-Tawhid). A very innovative intellectual climate together with the bonding of teachers and students in this isolated setting produced "the Club." Every Friday night these students and teachers gathered for speech contests, recitations of poetry, and even performances of plays. The Club's influence expanded when the town fathers were included in the audience, and these dignitaries came to look forward eagerly to the Friday-night assembly. Unfortunately the Club disappeared, but Dar al-Tawhid survives even today as a secondary school with a standard government-mandated curriculum.[15]

By 1950 the General Department of Education, with a very small budget, claimed to have 196 elementary schools, 942 teachers, and 23,835 students. In 1952 the department was raised to ministry level with a significantly expanded budget. Nine years later the doors opened for the first time at a school for girls.

EDUCATION DEVELOPMENT UNDER FIVE-YEAR PLANS

In 1970 the first of a series of five-year plans was initiated which in a formal structure spelled out the goals of the government, the rationale for establishing those goals, and the allocation of resources to accomplish them. In order to make such a comprehensive plan it was necessary to establish some baseline statistics, not an easy task in Saudi Arabia. Traditionally there was no recording of births; as much as 50 percent of the society was thought by some authorities to be nomadic, making census-taking difficult; and there were government sensitivities about a count which seemed to them too low.

Taking the best estimates available, however, demographers say that the population in 1970 (Saudis only) was not more than 4.5 million to 5 million.[16]

Saudi figures for school enrollment in 1970 were 545,000. By 1989–1990 this figure had grown to 2.3 million, an average increase of 10.5 percent per year. While it was estimated that in 1970 about 33 percent of the boys and 20 percent of the girls (of appropriate age) were in elementary school, by 1990 the figures increased to about 86 percent of the boys and 82 percent of the girls.[17]

The increase in physical facilities is another measure of progress. Even by 1974 in Riyadh the authorities had grossly overcrowded facilities and 75 percent of the elementary schools and nearly 50 percent of the intermediate and high schools were in inadequate mobile classrooms or rented office or apartment space.[18] A high priority was placed on new school construction in the five-year plans. Between 1970 and 1980 an average of 2.2 new schools were added every day of the year and by 1990 there were 8,489 schools reported by the Ministry of Education and 6,923 by the General Presidency of Girls' Education.[19] In 1970 there had been only 3,100 schools in all, so there was a five-fold increase in schools in only twenty years.

When the initial efforts were made to provide universal education, it was evident that the bedouin life-style presented a unique obstacle. For some time the Ministry of Education offered special incentives to young teachers if they would travel to the bedouin during the school year in order to provide the children with a coherent school program. Few Saudi teachers could tolerate this life. In 1976 Prince Khalid al-Fahd, Deputy Minister of Education, recognized the severity of the problem with a proposal to double the salaries of teachers who served in remote areas.[20] With the steadily declining number of bedouin continuing to live a truly nomadic life, however, the problem became less acute. More and more bedouin were spending at least a part of the year in or near a village.

Financial incentives in the form of stipends paid to each child who attended school made it attractive even to poor families to place their children in school. Not only is there no tuition and books are free, but also children are still paid stipends to encourage school attendance.

Schools have become a social melting pot for the country. While youngsters in the past could grow up knowing only their relatives and close family friends who shared the same value system and life-style, now they might share a classroom with those of widely differing backgrounds. Income levels, occupations, varying degrees of conservative values, all contribute to the melting pot.

SCHOOLS FOR GIRLS

Because there is little of importance which occurs in the public arena in Saudi Arabia and very few foreigners see anything beyond that which takes place in public, very few foreigners have a true sense of the degree or nature of change in the society. Women are still usually veiled in public, or at the very least wear the *hijab* form of dress (long dress, long sleeves, high neck, hair covered completely with a turbanlike garment, no makeup, jewelry, or perfume). Even little girls of eleven or twelve proudly don the *abbaya* and are seen only as small black shapes bouncing along the sidewalks of residential areas on their way to school.

Social change in Saudi Arabia has a distinctive character which seems truly unique and is the product of the dominant Wahabi sect of Islam. The technocrats in government are usually the leaders in modernization, but often they must move more slowly than they would like, and find an Islamic rationale for action. Astonishing steps can be taken which threaten at least a portion of the community; a step backward may then be taken without really acknowledging that the first move was too far too fast; and then very shortly thereafter the forward motion will be resumed without comment. But always, the trend over any decade time span has been forward. Perhaps the most significant premise of the progressives in the community is that nothing is undertaken without an explanation or defense in religious terms. Islam is pervasive and offers its faithful answers for all activities of life and any change must be consonant with the Quran.

Little church hierarchy, no formal theology, relatively little church money and power to serve as a conservative brake provided the Saudis with a fluid, flexible environment. Rather than hail the education of girls as a necessary step in order to be modern or keep up with the West, the king could remind the citizens that the Quran demands that all the faithful must seek knowledge; education would prepare girls to be better mothers and homemakers and developing the religious or spiritual sensitivities of the girls would strengthen the spiritual life of the community. Clothing this innovation in Islamic values made it acceptable.

As the chief sheikh, the king also recognized that while he could make this education for girls available, he could not impose it. It was necessary for each family to determine "truth" for their own girls. What he could and did do was offer both example and incentive.

The first school for girls was opened in 1956 at the initiative of Iffat, the wife of Faisal (who became king in 1963).[21] Dar al-Hanan (House of Affection) was initially established as an orphanage, but such a concept was not easily accepted in Saudi Arabia, where no child is an orphan—there is always a family member to take on the responsibility. Iffat managed to recruit the children of friends and some from the royal family in order to get the school into full operation. Amir Faisal and his wife Iffat had already popularized the idea of education by inviting friends and relatives to join them in a school in

Taif which came to be known as the Model School. These private schools established a good climate of acceptability in at least the more sophisticated circles. Cecile Roushdi has guided Dar al-Hanan over more than thirty-five years and today it is the premier school for girls, with a large, modern campus and a curriculum from traditional subjects to computer technology.

The sensitivity of the whole idea of public education for girls was acknowledged when its administration was placed in the hands of a religious body rather than the Ministry of Education. Curriculum was acknowledged to be the ultimate battlefield. In the early years there was an especially heavy emphasis on Islam but, as one teacher explained to me, there is little that cannot be taught as a part of religion. Certainly Arabic language skills and even health education could be regarded as a part of Quranic studies. The pervasiveness of Islam even extended to these first classes in geography.

A young Egyptian teacher in a private girls' school in the late fifties told me of her delight when she found in the market a balloon which had a rough map of the world printed on it. She used it as a tool for demonstrating how the earth turns as it revolves around the sun (an orange). One of the older girls in the class challenged her teacher's assertion that the world is round: "My father," she said, "says that the earth is flat." Since her father was a prominent religious leader, the teacher retreated and did not use the balloon demonstration for a while. But this too did not last. In time, and without any fanfare, the king was heard to pronounce while visiting with friends during the evening *majlis* that the earth was round, and there was no protest.

The decision to open schools for girls was met with varying degrees of resistance. Buraida, north of Riyadh, traditionally a very conservative town, opposed the introduction of public education for girls with threats of violence. King Faisal was determined and sent troops to the city to protect the teacher and any girls who dared to attend. For some months the teacher and her daughter were alone at the school, but after two years the town elders who had so vigorously opposed the school returned to the king requesting another school be provided as the first was already too crowded.

Of course the mosque schools and all the other early efforts to provide schools were for boys only. The education of girls was left to the discretion of each family. A tutor might be provided to teach the rudiments of reading and Quranic studies but little more. As one would expect, the more sophisticated members of society, those who had had significant experience outside of the kingdom, were most likely to regard the education of their daughters as important.

The very limited practice of sending young men to Cairo for higher education was expanded after World War II to the revolutionary experiment of sending them to the United States. No doubt the presence of the Americans at Aramco influenced this, but the Saudi royal family provided an example as well. These young men returned to Saudi Arabia and formed the nucleus of the decision-making apparatus in the Saudi government. There appeared to be no dramatic changes in their life-styles in terms of family and social relationships—until one observed their decisions about the education of their daughters. It was the daughters of these men who were the first to leave the country, who were allowed, indeed encouraged, to attend university in the United States.

These young women were, inevitably, watched carefully for signs of Westernization, but, true to their concern for family, they returned after their education was completed, once again wore the veil, acceded, at least on the face of it, to family decisions regarding their futures, including marriage, and seemed to resume a fairly traditional life-style. Again, there was a difference, for these women became involved in community life, either by taking a job in their field (usually education or social welfare) or by assuming a role of leadership in the women's centers.

By 1973, only thirteen years after the introduction of public education for girls, eleven young women graduated from King Abdul Aziz University. They knew that they could not attend the graduation ceremony, but when they learned that their names were not even listed on the program they protested. While they could not call upon the chancellor personally, they could and did telephone him. He was deluged with calls, not only from the young women graduates themselves but also from their fathers, brothers, and uncles. He, in turn, telephoned the woman who headed the women's section of the university and asked that plans be made for a special ceremony for women only.

It is hard to describe the atmosphere of that eventful evening. It was held outdoors inside a walled compound under a clear star-studded sky. More than five hundred women came, delivered to the gate by their drivers. They entered the festive area in their abbayas and full-face veils which they immediately shed, revealing elegant long gowns and masses of gold jewelry. It seemed almost like an Arab wedding celebration. Beautiful carpets covered the dais and defined the aisle. The first few rows comprised enormous overstuffed sofas and chairs and gave way to hundreds of folding chairs in neat rows under the trees.

The academic procession was colorful, with women professors of many nationalities in their academic robes, stoles, and headgear, and the eleven graduates in green robes and mortarboards the color of the Saudi flag. As the solemn procession walked down the aisle the assembled women emitted the spine-tingling "oo-lu-lu" (*zaghrouta*) traditional for times of joy. The usual speeches were delivered and diplomas presented. Probably the majority of the women present had had no formal education and many, no doubt, could not read. But the electric atmosphere of the audience conveyed their appreciation for the historical significance of the occasion and they enthusiastically shared the victory of these first eleven. I learned several days later that in the competitive examinations taken by the hundreds of graduates (both men and women), the five highest scores were earned by women.

This was only the first of many such celebrations. In 1979 the graduation of 215 girls from the Girls' College in Jidda was covered in the newspaper, reported by a woman journalist in her bylined column. The speaker for the occasion was an Egyptian visiting professor who said, "I didn't study when I was small because our parents feared that we would be ruined. We have to understand their sentiments. But, we have all passed through this difficult stage." [22]

There were some very special problems to be dealt with in developing schools for girls. Staffing and curriculum are the focus of problems in many school systems, but in Saudi Arabia there were some additional complications. Staff had to be female (in a society where women had not had any public working role) and the curriculum had to satisfy the conservative religious element which still held that women should stay at home.

It was extremely difficult to recruit Arab women teachers from other countries, for they regarded the restrictions that would be placed on them as both demeaning and threatening. Authorities learned that a married woman whose husband could also be employed was often more disposed to accept a position. Saudi teachers were, of course, preferred, so there was immediate employment for any qualified Saudi woman, and recruitment campaigns in other Arab countries were launched with enticing incentives in an attempt to staff the schools. If the foreign teachers were single, they had to be provided group housing in an appropriate situation and be provided transportation to and from school as well as for any other movement outside their quarters. The logistics of such situations were very cumbersome.

Since it was especially difficult to find Arabic-speaking women who could teach science or mathematics (both subjects tend to be regarded even in western countries as less appropriate for women), this affected the curriculum decisions. Of necessity the subjects covered in the early years were limited, but reading and writing were emphasized and opened many doors. The real crunch came when there was demand for curriculum expansion to include higher mathematics and science at the secondary and university levels, which by that time could probably have been introduced without strong objections, but too often Arabic-speaking teachers could not be found.

Special emphasis was put on creating teacher-training institutes in order to attract more Saudi teacher candidates, and in one five-year period alone

(1975–1976 to 1980–1981) the number of such institutes more than doubled. The government also offered a more generous pay scale and other incentives, but recruiting remained a major problem.

Novel remedies were devised which elicited much negative comment in the western press. On the university level women could take courses for which there was no woman professor by assembling in a room with a large television screen and observing the lectures given by male professors. Not only could they follow the lectures but they could even participate in the discussions or questioning period by using a telephone on the wall which connected them with the classroom.[23]

Saudis not only discuss with friends their concerns about the problems encountered in the development of educational institutions in the country but also write in newspapers. Abdul Rahman al-Musaibih wrote in 1980 in *Al-Jazirah* of the problems encountered with "local teachers" whom he asserted were showing "a trend of indifference" despite all the "privileges and potentialities the state has provided for them."[24]

By 1981, in spite of the many difficulties, the curriculum for girls at college level had expanded to include education, arts and humanities, medicine, medical sciences, social service, science and meteorology, agriculture and veterinary, economy and business, administration, and Sharia law.[25]

There is strong public pressure to decrease the number of foreigners working in the country. Many foreigners are employed in work which could be done by women, such as clerical tasks, computer operations, planning, and administration. In the seventies almost all men of employable age were economically active, leaving the only hope for Saudization in the arena of additional women in the work force.[26]

Mahamed Jokhdar, a prominent Jidda businessman and graduate of UCLA and USC, expressed it this way: "We have serious manpower shortages and if we don't give women an opportunity to contribute to society I don't see how we can hope to achieve the goals of our second Five Year Plan. Yes, I am optimistic. I believe women can retain Muslim traditions, be good wives and mothers, and still participate as useful citizens."[27]

All Saudi schools follow a familiar three-level, twelve-grade plan: elementary, intermediate, and secondary. At the elementary grade four, as stipulated by the Ministry of Education, a student spends 30 percent of class time on Islam, 30 percent on Arabic, 17 percent on mathematics, 7 percent on science, and the balance on art and physical education.

By ninth grade the student would devote 24 percent of the school day to Islam; 18 percent to Arabic; 12 percent each to history/geography, science, mathematics, and English; and the remaining time to art and physical education.

At the secondary level the student chooses between an arts section or science section, but all students are required to complete 18 units of Islamic studies, 14 units of Arabic, 8 units of social studies, 6 units of physical science, 5 units of mathematics, 5 units of computer studies, and 8 units of English. Graduation requires 168 units minimum with 67 in the general program, 78 hours in the concentration program chosen by the student, and 23 units in English or computers or other electives.

Curriculum development, including writing and publishing textbooks and educational aids, is a major activity of the Ministry of Education. Secondary schools were first provided with slide projectors, film-strip projectors, and then later with video and TV sets. They also now have broadcasting equipment. The language labs in schools have been used exclusively for teaching English, but are being expanded to include other languages. A new policy calls for creating educational resource centers which will incorporate the traditional library and other audiovisual aids. In 1985 a new art education curriculum was introduced in the first three grades of elementary school; a new modern mathematics curriculum at the third-grade level and the English language texts at the secondary-school level were replaced. There are science labs in 264 of the intermediate and secondary schools and language labs in 134 secondary schools. The Ministry of Education designs and prints geographical maps and scientific illustrations and, in 1985 alone, distributed 342,000 of these to schools. American universities have had a major influence on the educational system in Saudi Arabia as a result of the large number of advanced degrees in education earned by Saudis. More than 413 master's and Ph.D. dissertations were catalogued and microfilmed by the Saudi Embassy in Washington, D.C., in the field of education alone between the mid-seventies and 1990.[28]

In addition to the public schools there are a number of private schools, some of which are solely for foreign students. The Ministry of Defense, National Guard, and Ministry of Labor and Social Affairs also operate schools at all three levels plus, in some cases, kindergarten and adult education (for literacy). The number of Saudi students in these schools totaled almost 40,000 in 1989. These numbers do not appear in the Ministry of Education totals and so appear to be additional to the numbers cited above.

EXPANDING COMMUNITY RESOURCES

Of necessity, government authorities established nursery schools in government buildings, particularly schools, in order to accommodate women employees who had young children. It became the goal across the country to provide nursery facilities in order to attract the women needed as teachers. Children were, for the first time in Saudi society, playing with children from outside their family and close-friends group. The newspapers in the late seventies began featuring columns devoted to new facilities for children, opportunities for young mothers to return to school where nursery facilities were provided, and problems associated with all the changes in the community.

Letters to the editor or to the signed columnists in newspapers discussed concerns of mothers who protested the lack of an area in the mosque reserved for women with children, others who urged the establishment of nurseries within mosques, parents who criticized the lack of proper care of books by students, and even those who protested the overabundance of automobiles driven to school by teenage boys.

Youngsters, particularly those of preschool age, have been benefiting for twenty-five years from the programs offered through the women's centers of the kingdom. The first center was pioneered by King Faisal and Iffat's daughters, who inaugurated the first program in a modest house in a residential area of Riyadh in 1963.[29] A large variety of programs soon evolved, including child-care classes for young women, training programs for Montessori teachers, child-care facilities for mothers coming for programs at the centers themselves, health classes, nutrition classes, and literacy classes. The first centers were largely funded privately with subsidies from the royal family, but eventually parts of these budgets were met from government funds. Kindergarten was not available in public schools until recently and is still not offered in all schools, so preschool education really started in the centers.

The opportunity created for community building through the participation of women and children from a variety of backgrounds was one of the particular strengths of these neighborhood centers. It offered them both an opportunity to enlarge their horizons, develop skills, share their concerns, and enjoy themselves in an environment which was acceptable to almost all members of the community in time.

Sports clubs were another resource for children which appeared rather early. Little boys played soccer on every vacant lot and on little-traveled streets before sports facilities were available. There is a special government ministry devoted to the health and welfare of youth in the kingdom and it promotes the development of sports facilities, in the beginning only for boys. Physical education for girls was slow in coming, but once again there was a model set in the progressive private schools, and the five-year plan of 1980–1985 specifically addresses the need for facilities for girls similar to those established for boys.[30]

IMPACT OF EDUCATION CAMPAIGN
ON THE COUNTRY

How does one measure the impact on the society as a whole of this massive emphasis on education for girls? I asked a simple village woman what kinds of hopes and dreams she had for her daughter. Did she have any qualms about this new habit of sending girls to school? She responded by admitting that she sent her daughter to elementary school only with great reluctance but said that she now takes great pride in her daughter's achievements. The daughter is a schoolteacher and brings home a sizable income in a perfectly honorable way. Although she is twenty there are no plans for immediate marriage, and it was apparent that when the daughter marries this household would miss the extra income she provides. And, the mother continued, the bride-price (for men pay this money to the family of the women in Saudi Arabia) would be substantial since, after all, she is an educated woman and will be an appropriate wife for an educated man.

So it is safe to deduce that education has certainly contributed to the fact that women are not marrying as early as was the practice only thirty years ago—a very significant change.

The combination of a faith which requires each individual to find the truth for himself or herself, plus an education enabling the student to read the Quran as well as commentaries, has already had a striking effect on the community. A girl grows up today in Saudi Arabia accustomed to the fact that family members will choose her husband for her. However, she knows both her obligations and her rights as a Muslim woman. She knows that marriage is a legal contract and that she can be very specific in her requirements. She may require that she be permitted to pursue her education after marriage, that she be granted a divorce if the husband ever wishes to take another wife, indeed she may specify anything that does not directly violate the instructions of the Prophet. She also knows that she has the right of refusal and that the Prophet spoke against any forced marriage.

It has become popular for girls to take a special interest in Islam. It is possible to major in Islam at the university level, and a young woman with such an education is likely to become a religious teacher when she graduates. She may have groups of women with whom she meets on a regular basis to discuss, even debate, accommodations to modern life which are appropriate and where the limits are.

In 1980, twenty years after the introduction of public education for girls, I visited a very prestigious private school for girls in Riyadh, the nation's capital. I found behind the high walls a school building with wide balconies overlooking a modern interior courtyard filled with light. The classrooms were beautifully equipped. The girls spoke good English, from kindergarten through secondary school. When I asked what her ambition was, one young secondary student answered, "I am going to be an engineer."

High, even revolutionary, expectations could certainly be assumed from this girl's comment. It would also be reasonable to assume that false hopes may be raised that could have unpleasant repercussions in a society that continues to be very conservative. Still, there are Saudi women petroleum engineers and computer programmers who work in special settings, often separate from any men. It is difficult to find any attitudes among young women that could be described as feminist. Almost universally the young woman of today in Saudi Arabia still feels that her first obligation is to her role as wife and mother—her first loyalty is to her family. She wants to share in an active way in the development of the country and so demands that she be able to study science, mathematics, and business administration, just as her brothers do. She seems content for now to work in facilities separate from men. Indeed she may have no desire to compete with men, and may say that there is plenty of work that she can do without joining the male work force.

A study was published in 1982 of the attitudes of young Saudi men who were studying in the United States. A questionnaire was designed and sent to 2,896 Saudi men studying in the United States in March 1980. One part of the questionnaire dealt with the issue of women in the work force. More than two thirds were willing to accept women in order to reduce the number of foreign workers needed in Saudi Arabia. Furthermore, more than two thirds said they would hire Saudi women if it were not contrary to Saudi law.[31] In a scant twenty years, the attitudes toward women had obviously changed dramatically.

There has not been the kind of generation gap and tension-filled relationship between mother and daughter that one could have reasonably expected. Women born well before this revolution in education seem to hold no grudge against their daughters who have such exciting opportunities and even encourage them to forge ahead. The mother of a young Saudi woman friend of mine who has an advanced degree from a U.S. university told me of going by camel from the mountainous area of Taif to Jidda each year, a rugged seventy-mile ride. She described the practices that surrounded childbirth at that time, and it was like stepping back into another century for both her daughter and for me. But there seemed to be no awkwardness between mother and daughter—only genuine love and pride in both directions.

Shirley Kay and Malin Basil, in both words and drawings, depict very well the life of a child in the new modern world of Saudi Arabia.[32] The family remains the heart of all activity. Even though the habit of having living quarters for all the extended family in the same building or compound has given way to single-family dwellings and new careers in other parts of the kingdom, still the attachments are very strong. Children have grandparents to hover over them, older cousins fuss over them, and a strong sense of security develops in this atmosphere of caring. Entertainment is almost entirely within family walls. Television, with accompanying video machine, has become common even in homes with modest incomes. Videotape libraries provide a wide variety of programs. Card games are popular with all age levels, and electronic games have taken the country by storm.

Homework is taken very seriously, with much competition between the boys and girls. Boys tend to be spoiled more than girls since the girl is still constantly reminded of her responsibility for the good reputation of the family and the boy can be more lighthearted. There are more opportunities for competitive physical sports for boys than for girls but this too is changing gradually. One great outing for children is an evening at the amusement park where there are the typical thrilling rides. Even black-veiled little girls can be seen driving bumper cars with great verve. Special days and evenings are reserved for families only. At those times mothers, daughters, aunts, and female cousins may join in the fun. Picnics are another popular family outing. One can see the typical picnic scene (with Saudi food favorites instead of hot dogs) at parks along the corniche in Jidda or in the desert outside Riyadh, but with the addition of a portable television set. The women and older girls are garbed in their black abbayas but may not bother with a face veil in this setting. There seems to be an unwritten rule requiring substantial space between families, providing the needed privacy.

Life for children in villages is perhaps free of some of the restraints of the city. Certainly the bedouin child (though few remain) has the most freedom of movement. For even the most remote villages and tribes, however, the advantages of education are available, and as a result, life-styles are changing there too. For the children of this generation there is unprecedented opportunity for education, for sports, for good health care, and for participation in the development of the community.

NOTES

As the wife of an American diplomat Jerine Bird lived in Saudi Arabia for ten years between 1962 and 1982. She had extensive contacts with government leaders. Much of this essay is based upon research in Saudi government documents and the newspapers and periodicals of the time and is supplemented by the limited information available in western publications.

1. Helen Chapin Metz, ed., *Saudi Arabia: A Country Study* (Washington, D.C.: U.S. Government Printing Office, 1993), p. 292.

2. Ibid, p. 96.

3. "Billions Raise Literacy Level," *Arab News* (Sept. 23, 1981).

4. Fazlur Rahman, *Islam,* 2nd ed. (Chicago: University of Chicago Press, 1979), p. 84.

5. Ibid, p. 198.

6. While the royal family has maintained close relations with even the most conservative religious leaders and even appointed them to government positions, there is no formal religious hierarchy to exert power and authority.

7. Robert Lacey, *The Kingdom* (London: Hutchinson & Co., 1981), pp. 243–244.

8. Elvin J. Cottrell, ed., *The Persian Gulf States* (Baltimore: Johns Hopkins University Press, 1980).

9. Richard F. Nyrop, *Area Handbook for Saudi Arabia* (Washington, D.C.: U.S. Government Printing Office, 1977), pp. 119–120.

10. Abdulla Mohamad al-Zaid, *Education in Saudi Arabia* (Jidda, Saudi Arabia: Tihama Publications, 1981), pp. 16–20.

11. Lacey, *The Kingdom,* p. 188.

12. Nyrop, *Area Handbook,* pp. 98–99.

13. Ibid, p. 230.

14. Ibid, p. 98.

15. Mohamad al-Zaid, *Education in Saudi Arabia.*

16. Ibid, p. 63.

17. Saudi Arabia Facts and Figures, *Achievements of the First and Second Development Plans, 1970–1980* (Riyadh: Kingdom of Saudi Arabia Ministry of Planning, 1982).

18. Ibid, p. 101.

19. *Statistical Card of Girls' Education* (Riyadh: Saudi Arabia Presidency of Girls' Education).

20. "Saudi Arabia Finds a Way to Shift Teachers," *New York Times* (April 11, 1976).

21. Willard A. Beling, ed., *King Faisal and the Modernization of Saudi Arabia* (Boulder, Colo.: Westview Press, 1980).

22. "Saudi Scene," *Saudi Gazette* (Jan. 1, 1979), p. 5.

23. "Closed TV Circuits Studied," *Saudi Gazette* (Feb. 26, 1980).

24. Abdul Rahman al-Musaibih, "Comment," *Arab News* (Nov. 4, 1980).

25. "Girls' Education Makes Headway," *Arab News* (Sept. 23, 1981).

26. J. Stace Birks and Clive A. Sinclair, *Country Case Studies: Kuwait, Qatar, Libya, UAE, Bahrein, and Saudi Arabia,* International Migration Project Working Papers (Durham, England: Durham University, Economics Dept., 1977–1978).

27. "Doctorates for the Distaff," *Aramco World* (May-June 1979), p. 30.

28. *Index of Master's Theses and Doctoral Dissertations of Saudi Graduates from Universities in the United States* (Washington, D.C.: Royal Embassy of Saudi Arabia, Cultural Attache).

29. Willard A. Beling, ed., *King Faisal and the Modernization of Saudi Arabia* (London: Croom Helm, 1980), p. 162.

30. *Third Development Plan, 1980–1985* (Riyadh: Kingdom of Saudi Arabia Ministry of Planning, 1985), p. 375.

31. Joy Winkie Viola, *The Development of Human Resources: A Case Study of United States—Saudi Arabian Cooperation* (Boston: Northeastern University, 1982), pp. 64–65.

32. Shirley Kay and Malin Basil, *Saudi Arabia Past and Present* (London: Namara Publications, 1979).

TURKISH FIRST-GRADE TEXT

From Jinn Ali Starts School,
Cin Ali Publications, Ankara

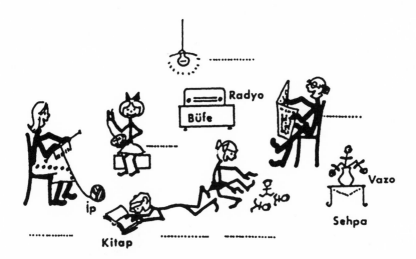

After washing their hands and brushing their teeth, the family sits in the living room. The father reads the newspaper. The mother knits. The older sister does needlepoint. Suna plays with her dolls. And Jinn Ali looks at the pictures in the books.

Jinn Ali loves books very much. During the time when his elder sister has less work, he takes his story books and goes to her. "Elder sister, please read this to me!" he begs her. He has the story read to him.

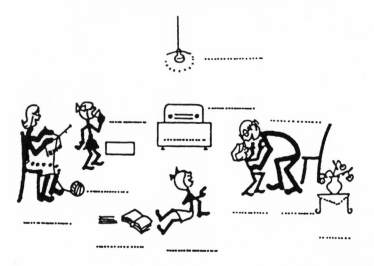

And sometimes, when his father is not tired, he hugs his father. "My father, tell me a story!" he cries, begging, and has him tell him a few stories.

Sometimes he hugs his mother and has her tell him a story. Jinn Ali is a well-behaved and intelligent child. He never makes his mother or father sad. Whatever they say, he does.

Jinn Ali wanted to study a lot. Often he said, "Oh, if only I could study too like my elder sister!"

ALTERNATIVE EDUCATION UNDER THE INTIFADA: THE PALESTINIAN RESPONSE TO ISRAELI POLICY IN THE OCCUPIED TERRITORIES

by Abdalla al-Kurd and Barton R. Herrscher

The Intifada is the strongest and most persistent response in the history of the Palestinian people to the Israeli occupation of the West Bank and Gaza Strip. In an effort to crush the uprising, Israeli military authorities, since the beginning of the Intifada in 1987, employed a variety of forms of collective punishment, including the demolition of homes, the confiscation of lands and water resources, the destruction of olive trees, etc. Among the most comprehensive and pervasive of these measures has been the obstruction of Palestinian education, at all levels and in all areas of the West Bank and Gaza Strip. This interference involved extended closure of schools and universities—all five major universities in the West Bank and Gaza Strip have been closed several times since the beginning of the Intifada; kindergarten through high-school level schools have also been closed for extended periods during much of this time.

These closures affected approximately 320,000 school-age children and about 18,000 university or college students. In short, almost the entire population was denied access to consistent, formal education over a period of years (Jerusalem Media and Communication Centre 1989).

Interference in the educational system also included military attacks on schools and the occupation of school premises for military purposes; the harassment and detention of countless educators, school administrators, and students; and the banning of grass-roots alternative education programs (Jerusalem Media and Communication Centre 1989).

Our purpose is to examine the process by which alternative or "popular" education was developed and implemented by the Palestinian people in response to Israeli policy in the occupied territories. Alternative education, as used here, refers to a system of education conducted by the population in general, especially educators, outside the traditional educational institutions.

It arises in response to specific needs within the society. In this case, when traditional educational institutions were closed by Israeli mandate, alternative education filled the void.

PALESTINIAN SYSTEM OF EDUCATION

Under normal conditions, general education in the occupied territories takes the following form: elementary school for six years, from age six to eleven, preparatory for the next three years, followed by three years of high school. An exit exam at the end of the preparatory period determines whether students will go on to secondary school or enter vocational school.

The first nine years of schooling is mandatory. The first year of secondary school consists of general studies. Students scoring high in scientific subjects are allowed to enter the science branch, while the remainder enter the humanities. The exit exam for secondary school students, the Tawjihi, is the sole determinant for the continuation of higher studies in general.

While the structure of the Palestinian general educational system roughly paralleled that of its Israeli counterpart, the conditions under which the two operated were quite different. The Israeli military appointed an officer of education to oversee the operation and administration of Palestinian schools. His responsibilities included hiring and firing of teachers and administrative staff, allocation of funds, and determination of curriculum. The effect of this was negative. For example, since 1976, no West Bank school has hired a librarian or a lab technician, and since 1982, no Palestinian teacher has been sent to study abroad on a government-sponsored scholarship (Lesch 1992).

To Palestinians, education is of utmost importance. After the loss of their lands and other property, they have tended to invest in "moveable property," i.e., higher education. Palestinians have concentrated on education for practical reasons, to help support their families, and to satisfy personal ambitions. The loss of their lands, homes, water resources, and other basics essential to the pursuit of agriculture left them two choices: either to remain in refugee camps for the rest of their lives, or to seek higher education as a means of improving their situation.

PALESTINIAN UNIVERSITIES

Prior to 1967, the Gaza Strip was under the protection of Egypt, and the West Bank was under Jordanian rule. Both of these countries have their own colleges and universities which were attended by Palestinians seeking higher education. When the territories were occupied by Israel after the 1967 war, only junior colleges and teacher training institutions existed as Palestinian institutions.

After 1967, Palestinian universities were established. Israel claims credit for the establishment of these institutions—Bir Zeit, Najah, Bethlehem, Jerusalem, Gaza, and Khalil universities—but the reality is somewhat different. Israel played no role in the planning and financing of these institutions of higher education but did permit the creation of Palestinian universities. This coincided with its plans for the territories, which might be phrased as follows. It was assumed that a well-trained, well-educated population with no opportunity for commensurate employment would be forced to emigrate (Aruri 1985).

Olga Kapeliouk, an Israeli professor of Semitics at Hebrew University, attributes the growth of universities in the West Bank and Gaza Strip to many causes. "The occupation cut off the West Bank and Gaza Strip from the Arab and Western countries where young Palestinians used to study. . . . The Israeli military authorities make it difficult for young Palestinians to study abroad. Inhabitants with identity cards issued after the occupation may easily lose them if they leave the territories for more than twelve months" (Kapeliouk 1985).

Kapeliouk notes that restrictions imposed by neighboring Arab states such as Egypt and Jordan, which have traditionally received a large number of Palestinian students, as well as the increased cost of studying abroad have also contributed to the growth of these institutions.

Another major reason for the growth of institutions of higher education in the occupied territories, as indicated by Kapeliouk, has been the economic organization and structure of the area. Israel kept a very strong grip on the economy of the occupied territories, using them primarily as a market for its goods and products, and as a source of cheap labor. Indigenous agriculture and industry were simply not permitted to develop, and educated graduates hoping to find jobs and opportunities commensurate with their skills had to look outside the territories (Kapeliouk 1985).

Higher education in the occupied territories developed in response to these conditions, but more especially because of the efforts and enthusiasm of its teaching personnel. Many professors have chosen to return to their native land, if possible, for patriotic and other reasons, to teach and work in the area and to serve their people even under very difficult conditions. This commitment and dedication has been a crucial factor in the growing success of these institutions (Kapeliouk 1985).

There has also been a general realization within the Palestinian population that in order to regain their land and their rights, they have to compete with Israeli society, and higher education has become one manifestation of this competition. "Palestinians realized that they have to close the cultural and educational gap that characterized the early Zionist-Palestinian confrontation" (Tahir 1985).

Palestinian institutions of higher education, unlike many western institutions which maintain some independence from their society, are closely tied to Palestinian society. Institutions of higher education in the occupied territories are not only centers of learning but are also symbols of survival and of resistance to the military occupation. These institutions became irrevocably connected to their society and now hold a key position in the social and political life of the region. In theory, Palestinian universities, where the student unions are elected and function democratically, provide an opportunity for students to be immersed intellectually and politically in the democratic process, which carries over into their expectations after graduation (Kaufman et al. 1993). For this reason, these institutions occupied and continue to occupy a place of critical importance in the West Bank and Gaza Strip, especially when no organized national institutions existed to plan and coordinate the socioeconomic infrastructure of the area. Their effectiveness is further enhanced by their relative autonomy, which results from their being independently financed and operated (Heiberg and Ovensen 1993).

PALESTINIAN ALTERNATIVE EDUCATION

As the Palestinian Intifada became institutionalized, during the early months of 1988, the Israeli authorities officially banned Palestinian education. The entire educational system was shut down by the military occupation authorities. This closure affected all private, public, and United Nations Relief and Works Agency schools, as well as the universities and community colleges. The mass closure of Palestinian schools spurred the institutions and the community itself to develop alternative means to educate the students. As explained by Dr. Gabi Baramki, the acting president of Bir Zeit University and a prominent member of the Council of Higher Education in the West Bank, the coordinating body for Palestinian universities in the occupied territories, "The complacent irresponsibility and hostility of the Israeli authorities proves that they are not fit to be entrusted with the education of youth. Therefore, it is our responsibility to find alternative means."

In most West Bank towns, the community itself began organizing "popular committees" to govern the lives of the Palestinian inhabitants under the circumstance of the Intifada. As early as April 1988, towns like Ramallah, al-Bireh, Beit Sahur, Beit Jala, Nablus, Jenin, and Tulkarm started neighborhood committees which began teaching elementary, preparatory, and secondary students in private homes, mosques, churches, clubhouses, community centers, etc. In addition to the regular curriculum, classes were added in first aid and survival strategies for the Intifada—how to recover from tear gas, what to do in the case of arrest, small-scale gardening—all very practical skills for these circumstances (Nasser and Heacock 1990).

In April of 1988, a meeting of high-school principals in the West Bank and the Council of Higher Education was held to consider the plight of the 13,000 high-school seniors who had taken only the first half of the required exit exam, the Tawjihi. Without the second part, these students would be ineligible to attend universities. Internal regulations could be modified, but this would require the approval of the Association of Arab Universities, a multinational accrediting agency. Upon request of the council, approval was granted, and the problem for this group of students solved (Taha and Johar 1990).

During the early phase of the Intifada, in response to a call from the Unified National Command of the Uprising to defy Israeli closure orders, faculty, staff, and students attempted to return to their classes and carry on with normal university functions. When Israeli authorities surrounded the institutions and prevented them from doing so, university personnel and students then pursued other means of protest: staging sit-ins at the Israeli checkpoints, beeping automobile horns and carrying signs while they marched through town, demanding the reopening of the universities. At Bethlehem University, students and faculty were able to enter the university at first and make use of some of the facilities. Lectures were held for small groups of students on topics relevant to the uprising, e.g., psychological warfare, taxation regulations, etc. Before long, however, university buildings were occupied by the Israeli military and used as detention centers or military headquarters, and many were damaged by the occupying forces.

By the end of May 1988, a need had evolved for some kind of underground structured alternative educational system to meet the growing needs of the student population. It became especially urgent after the Israeli military banned popular committees in August 1988. The restrictions on education imposed because of the Intifada were having a critical effect on all students, from first graders to university seniors. Perhaps most urgently in need of attention were the children who were missing the opportunity to learn the essential basic skills (reading and writing) at this critical stage of their development (Arikat 1990).

The Unified National Command identified the shutdown of the education system as deliberate "de-education," and a policy of enforced ignorance upon the Palestinian people, leaving "no recourse but to rely upon ourselves to educate our youth; popular education must continue and universities must find ways to resume education there, especially for students in their final years" (*Jerusalem al-Fajr,* May 8, 1988). The group then called upon Palestinian educators to develop an alternative system, while pressing for the reopening of the schools.

As a Najah University professor put it, "We have to keep the educational system alive, and we must adjust to the conditions of the uprising because apparently the Intifada is not going to stop unless a political solution emerges. Israel argues that closure is necessary because the universities are hotbeds of agitation, though this has been visibly disproved by the continuation of the uprising despite the closures." Yet he conceded that creating an alternative system away from the facilities of the university was a difficult task, especially since it was declared illegal by the military authorities.

Classes were organized by faculty members, and the physical sites of the classes were designated by individual professors for the convenience of the students. In many cases, classes were held in the homes of the teachers. In general, the professors were familiar with the students and vice versa. Classes were announced by word of mouth and were intensive in nature. Students were required to pass an exam in order to pass these classes. The majority of the classes were senior-level courses as seniors have been particularly hard hit by the closure of the universities.

Classes were also convened in churches or mosques, in community centers, in the consulates of some western nations such as the United Kingdom and the United States, and at the homes of students. Most students hid their books to escape detection at the various checkpoints. For example, between one student's home in Shaufat, a suburb of East Jerusalem, and Ramallah, where she attended classes (a distance of eight miles), there were three Israeli military checkpoints. At each stop she was searched and questioned about where she was going and why. It sometimes took an hour and a half to travel the eight miles.

As a result of this grass-roots system of alternative education, hundreds of Palestinian students have graduated on schedule. This at-home system of higher education had psychological effects on the students. They learned not only how to cope but actually how to produce under severe pressure. "It is really painful, what we have to go through to get our education," a Bethlehem student said, "especially those of us who come from the [refugee] camps and have had to work so hard to get here. But we are determined. We have grown to appreciate education more and more."

With respect to the curriculum, certain subjects were added which were taught as one-time seminars. But, the basic academic curriculum was not altered, except for courses that required specialized facilities or equipment. In those cases, the lecture component of the course was taught, leaving the laboratory aspect for a later date (Taha and Johar 1990). Yet the Intifada resulted in a new educational development. Since this experience, educators have shifted their attention from a purely academic orientation to a more technical and practical one. In short, education has become even more oriented to what the society has needed.

The instructional delivery system was drastically changed, however. For example, many classes were conducted in an independent study format, in which students were expected to do most of the work on their own with minimal supervision from their instructors. Long assignments were given to the students as classes met much less frequently and less predictably than under normal conditions. The location of the sessions changed according to the circumstances, and, of course, was kept secret.

Many K–12 schools chose to distribute home instruction packages to parents so that they could teach their children at least the basic skills that they would receive in school. Although these materials were prepared by education experts and were quite good, there were several serious problems. First, the number of students to be served was very high, 320,000, so the alternative system was able to reach only some 20 percent of the total student population effectively.

Other real problems were psychological and therefore more far-reaching in nature. Extended periods of time without schooling have a very negative effect on children. Education is not only reading books. Children are affected in their habits of listening, respecting others, working with their friends, and behaving in a group. The habits of schooling are broken.

Another problem is the inertia that sets in after a certain length of absence from school. When the opportunity to study is denied, the motivation to go to school is diminished. This disheartening effect was worsened by the general knowledge that conditions are actually worse for university students, so that even if one completes secondary studies, dreams of pursuing further education may be impossible to fulfill.

In addition to the home-study work for general education, classes were also conducted, mostly for senior high school students. Attendance at these classes, however, was negatively affected by the factors mentioned above, as well as by the economic effects of the Intifada, which compelled many students to leave school and look for work to try to assist their families financially. Moreover, many of the students were detained by the authorities or injured in clashes with the Israeli forces.

THE ISRAELI RESPONSE

After Israel outlawed popular committees and alternative education, the Israeli government started a crackdown on violators of the new laws. For example, on September 1, 1988, Israeli troops raided the College of Science and Technology in Abu Dis near Jerusalem and detained three professors and twelve students. On September 5, 1988, soldiers also invaded the building of the Society of the Friends of al-Hajah in Nablus where alternative education classes were being conducted. The society was ordered closed, and its director was arrested for violating military orders (*Jerusalem Post*, September 6, 1988).

Similar Israeli raids were conducted with some regularity until 1993, while the schools remained officially closed. For example, on April 16, 1989, St. George's School, a private English school in East Jerusalem where Bir Zeit University students were taking make-up classes, was entered, and the principal ordered not to allow West Bank students to use the school premises (*Jerusalem Post*, April 19, 1988). In early May 1989, Israeli troops also raided a building in Ramallah and a teacher and two students were arrested for studying (*Jerusalem al-Fajr*, May 8, 1989).

As one Palestinian student leader explained, "The Israeli crackdown on alternative education is nothing new. It is actually an assertion of authority and a harassment measure that we have been subjected to all along." In fact, the crackdown was widely viewed as merely a more blatant policy of an already existing state of deprivation that the Palestinian people had been living with for a long time.

The Israeli crackdown on education, however, was unprecedented in recent history. Even in South Africa, the white minority government kept the black schools open. Israel's policy of making education criminal was against the Fourth Geneva Convention and the Universal Declaration of Human Rights. Israeli law prohibited interference with private education; even if Israel's reasons for the closure of Palestinian educational institutions were considered valid, this hardly justified interfering with privately conducted education.

On May 1, 1989, a group of Israeli professors from Hebrew University held a press conference in Jerusalem to state unequivocally their position that the continued closure of Palestinian universities was unjustified, and to demand their immediate reopening (*Jerusalem Post*, May 2, 1989). This group, which represented some 400 Israeli professors, spoke out in particular against the Israeli raid on St. George's School in East Jerusalem, referred to previously.

This group of professors insisted that Israeli authorities had the responsibility to see that students in the occupied territories attended school. Along with the general outrage was a sense of disbelief that such a thing could be happening in "democratic" Israel. In reference to the document issued by the Israeli police commander to the principal of St. George's School in Jerusalem, forbidding the use of the school for alternative education classes for Bir Zeit students, one professor stated, "I didn't believe that such a document could be written by an official in Israel" (*Jerusalem al-Fajr,* May 8, 1989).

In general, the Israeli group of professors acknowledged that there must be a balance between security and the need to maintain education, but stated that there was no plausible reason to justify the continued closure of education institutions (Abdallah 1990).

Yet for all that, the Israeli educational establishment—the Ministry of Education, the teachers' unions, and Israeli university authorities—offered no protest. One reason for this may have been that Palestinian educational institutions have traditionally been branded "nationalistic," which in many peoples' eyes translates into being anti-Israeli.

While Israel used the existence of Palestinian institutions of higher education to document its liberality and concern for academic freedom, the official Israeli position was that these campuses were breeding grounds for Palestinian resistance, places where students disseminated PLO propaganda and ignited demonstrations throughout the occupied territories (Aruri 1985). Free-lance writer Lisa Wolf, in her article in the *New York Times,* quoted Israeli army spokesman Raanan Gissin as saying, "It is not a threat as we regard organized terrorist squads, but it is a bastion of hard-core resistance. We must make sure the situation does not degenerate into chaos" (Wolf 1987).

On the other hand, Wolf noted that according to a number of Israeli officials, "The government recognizes the absence of serious planning on campus; the hoopla . . . is essentially benign."

"The students are not a political threat," said Michael B. Oren, a fellow of the Truman Institute and an expert on Arab-Israeli relations. "They wave flags, and have demonstrations and large theoretical discussions about the future of the Palestinian state, but all it amounts to is rhetoric . . . they can't even operate as real revolutionaries, because Israel has the West Bank completely infiltrated" (April 1987).

Israeli officials, when confronted with questions about the mass closure of schools and universities, replied that it was a necessary security precaution dictated by the unusual circumstances of the Intifada.

THE FUTURE

The international response was overwhelmingly negative with regard to the continued closure of the schools in the occupied territories as a means of maintaining order and guaranteeing security.

The U.S. response was also against the closure of schools, and on May 16, 1989, a resolution was introduced in the House of Representatives by Congressman Howard C. Nielson of Utah, demanding that Israel take immediate steps to reopen schools in the West Bank.

That message was underscored by Secretary of State James Baker in a speech before the American-Israeli Public Affairs Committee on May 22, 1989: "For Israel, now is the time to lay aside, once and for all, the unrealistic vision of a greater Israel . . . allow schools to reopen. Reach out to the Palestinians as neighbors who deserve political rights" (Peretz 1990).

The end of the Intifada came with the signing of the Oslo accords in 1993, but provisions for the continued development of the system of alternative education are ongoing. The universities in the occupied territories are monitoring the situation in an effort to arrive at viable and effective solutions to new challenges. The academic councils of many educational institutions are developing programs to accommodate students who are behind in their studies, especially high school and university students in Gaza and Jericho. The possibilities afforded by mobile libraries and tutoring by faculty are also being examined, though funding is still a problem. The development of an alternative educational system was a vital and creative moment in the history of Palestinian education, and it offers a model for other nations and other peoples. In spite of the odds, educators made a significant difference in the social and political lives of Palestinians living in the occupied territories during the Intifada. They now are turning their energies and attention toward developing new curricula for the new Palestinian educational institutions.

BIBLIOGRAPHY

Abdalla, Ghassan. 1990. *The Intifada and Israel* (in Arabic). Acre: Palestine Educational Institute.

Anabatawi, Samir N. 1986. *Palestinian Higher Education in the West Bank and Gaza: A Critical Assessment.* New York: Routledge and Kegan Paul.

Arikat, Sa'eb. 1990. *The Intifada and Changes* (in Arabic). Jerusalem: Dar al-Awda for Studies and Publications.

Aronson, Geoffrey. 1990. *Israel, Palestinians, and the Intifada: Creating Facts on the West Bank.* New York: Kegan Paul.

Aruri, Naseer H., ed. 1985. *Occupation: Israel over Palestine.* Belmont, Mass.: Association of Arab American University Graduates.

Ashmore, Robert. 1986. "Palestinian Universities under Israeli Occupation: A Human Rights Analysis." *American Arab Affairs* 16 (Spring).

Gavison, Ruth, et al. 1986. "Report on the Condition of Universities in the Occupied Territories." *American Arab Affairs* 16 (Spring).

Goldring, Beth. 1987. "Palestinian University Development Shaped by Occupation." *Jerusalem al-Fajr,* July 12.

Graham-Brown, Sarah. 1984. *Education, Repression, and Liberation: Palestinians*. London: World University Service.

Heiberg, Marianne, and Gier Ovensen. 1993. *Palestinian Society in Gaza, West Bank, and Arab Jerusalem: A Survey of Living Conditions*. Oslo: Institute for Applied Social Science.

Israel's War against Education in the Occupied West Bank: A Penalty for the Future. 1988. Ramallah: al-Haq/Law in the Service of Man.

Jarbawi, Ali. 1989. *The Intifada and the Political Leadership of the West Bank and Gaza Strip* (in Arabic). Beirut: Dar al-Talia.

Jerusalem Media and Communication Centre. 1989. *Palestinian Education: A Threat to Israel's Security? The Israeli Policy of School Closures in the Occupied West Bank and Gaza Strip (December 1987–January 1989)*. Jerusalem.

Johnson, Penny. 1989. "Palestinian Universities under Occupation." *Journal of Palestine Studies* 68–72 (Spring 1988–Summer 1989).

Kapeliouk, Olga. 1985. "The Palestinian Universities under Occupation." *Arab Studies Quarterly* 7, 2/3 (Spring/Summer).

Kaufman, Edy, Shukri B. Abed, and Robert L. Rothstein. 1993. *Democracy, Peace, and the Israeli Palestinian Conflict*. Boulder, Colo.: Lynne Rienner Publishers.

Lesch, Ann Mosely. 1992. *Transition to Palestinian Self-Government: Practical Steps toward Israeli-Palestinian Peace*. Indianapolis: Indiana University Press.

Nasser, Jamal, and Roger Heacock. 1990. *Intifada: Palestine at the Crossroads*. New York: Praeger.

Peretz, Don. 1990. *Intifada: The Palestinian Uprising*. San Francisco: Westview Press.

Report on Human Rights Violations during the Palestinian Uprising 1988–1989. Tel Aviv: Israeli League for Human and Civil Rights, 1989.

Shehadeh, Raja. 1989. *Occupier's Law: Israel and the West Bank*. Washington, D.C.: Institute for Palestine Studies.

Sullivan, Anthony Thrall. 1988. *Palestinian Universities under Occupation*. Cairo: American University in Cairo Press.

Taha, al-Mutawakel, and Ibrahim Johar. 1990. *After One Thousand Days of the Intifada: The Intifada and Culture* (in Arabic). Jerusalem: General Union of Palestinian Writers.

Tahir, Jamil M. 1985. "An Assessment of Palestinian Human Resources: Higher Education and Manpower." *Journal of Palestine Studies* 14, No. 3.55 (Spring).

Wolf, Lisa. 1987. "The Palestinian Campus: Bir Zeit University Is an Oasis of Higher Education for Arab Students on the West Bank." *New York Times Magazine*, April 19.

CHILDHOOD AND EDUCATION IN HIGHLAND NORTH YEMEN

by Susan Dorsky and Thomas B. Stevenson

Arab Muslim societies tend to separate male and female spheres more sharply than most other contemporary societies. Some also define sex roles quite rigidly. Not surprisingly, differential treatment of girls and boys is often pronounced from birth onward. The differentiation is more marked in nations without longstanding secular government and without substantial exposure to more developed countries and their associated ideologies. The Yemen Arab Republic [1] (also known as North Yemen; hereafter referred to as Yemen) is such a nation. Until 1962 Yemen was led by theocratic rulers and, especially in the tribal north, exposure to foreign ideas was minimal. While Yemen's revolution instituted many changes and increased contacts with developed countries, in the tribal north where a largely conservative perspective on sex roles and related issues endures, the pace of change has lagged behind the rest of the country.

Yemen is geographically diverse and Yemeni culture varies regionally. This essay will deal with childhood and adolescence in the market town of 'Amran in Yemen's tribal north. It will speak mainly of conditions in 1978 and 1979 when the two authors conducted doctoral dissertation research,[2] but will also draw from subsequent research by Stevenson in 1982 and 1986–1987. We are interested here in providing a context for understanding the pronounced differences in, and changing beliefs about, the formal education of girls and boys. Attitudes in towns tend to be more conservative than in either cities or villages; still, the conditions in 'Amran are in many respects typical of the processes of change throughout highland Yemen. To provide this setting, we will begin with a brief historical overview, and then examine the lives of children and their roles in the family and community from birth to the close of childhood.

BACKGROUND AND SETTING

In the last quarter century, the Yemen Arab Republic has undergone a profound transformation. Until the 1962 revolution Yemen was ruled by an imam, a *sayyid* descended from 'Ali, who sought to maintain the country's religious purity and his political position by keeping the country and its citizens isolated from the rest of the world. Foreign contact was limited. A poor country with a widely dispersed population, prerevolutionary Yemen had only a rudimentary infrastructure. Rugged terrain contributed to the lack of roads, communications, and health care.[3] Yet, in the forties and fifties there was a surprisingly large number of schools, most of which offered religious education.[4]

The overthrow of the imam and the formation of a republican government initiated substantial changes, the most fundamental of which was the transformation of the economy from one based primarily on subsistence agriculture to one founded on commerce. This transition was accompanied by the rapid growth of urban areas and the institution of health care and secular education systems. While urbanization and education have reshaped some aspects of childhood, these changes have not altered the extremely strong role of religion nor altered many conservative attitudes.

Despite extensive postrevolutionary urban expansion and development, Yemen remains a predominantly rural country. As in most traditional agricultural societies, children were a source of labor both in the fields and in the extended family household. While it would be an overstatement to portray children's lives as work-filled, during the imamate era childhood and life in general were hardly carefree. Weir remarks that "the population lived in material conditions of spartan simplicity."[5] It is common for adults to recall having been hungry as children. Meat was eaten only once or twice a week and in hard times a thin gruel was the base of the diet. Certainly children played games, although many of these are all but forgotten. What is recalled by adults is how hard everyone worked in the production and processing of food and the obtaining of water and wood for fuel.

Children contributed to the household economy from an early age, watching younger siblings, carrying meals to the fields, and helping in harvesting and threshing. In some areas, a boy's transition to adulthood was celebrated with circumcision.[6] Female circumcision was also performed in some areas.[7] Young men might serve in armies, either of their tribe or the imam, from as early as age fourteen. Marriages were not delayed; newly married couples were often in their early teens.

In many rural areas educational opportunities were limited. Literacy and education were primarily associated with the religious elite, the *sada* (singular *sayyid*). However, Steffen et al. note that by the late fifties Yemen had about 680 primary schools.[8] Generally these were religious schools (*katatib*, singular *kuttab*) where teaching centered on reading, writing, arithmetic, and reciting the Quran.[9] In addition, particularly after 1948, there were some schools offering secular education in the major cities—Ṣanʻa, Taʻizz, and Hodeida.

The 1962 revolution and the institution of a republican form of government led to a change in these conditions. Following the civil war (1962–1969) foreign aid financed the building of an infrastructure. A cash economy emerged, creating a demand for money to purchase consumer goods. In the seventies, this led to huge numbers of Yemeni men migrating to the neighboring oil states and repatriating not only large amounts of money but also new ideas. While agriculture remained important, by the mid-seventies commerce had become the mainstay of the economy. Many rural agricultural market towns, like ʻAmran, fifty kilometers northwest of Ṣanʻa, expanded rapidly into commercial and population centers. Apart from business opportunities, one important attraction of towns like ʻAmran was the availability of schools.

ʻAMRAN

ʻAmran is situated in a large fertile valley. Until the late fifties ʻAmran was a walled town of about 350 houses laid out in an intricate network of narrow dirt streets. In addition to agriculture, the town's economy was supported by commerce in the weekly market and in government offices. During the civil war of the sixties, refugees and others seeking new economic opportunities moved into ʻAmran, launching a period of rapid urban growth. By 1975 the population had doubled to about 6,000. Freed from threat of attack, new neighborhoods sprang up outside the protection of the town's gates. By 1986, the population had grown to over 10,000 and the sprawl of new houses and stores pushed the town's residential areas up to those of neighboring villages.

In the walled town and other older neighborhoods, traditional Yemeni architecture prevails. Four- or five-story mud-brick row houses line narrow, secluded streets and alleys. Rooms on the lower floors of these homes are used for keeping livestock and storing grain and firewood; the upper floors contain the kitchens and living rooms of nuclear and extended families. Owing to the declining importance of agriculture, foreign influences, and the preference for nuclear-family residences, many houses built since the mid-seventies tend to be one and, rarely, two stories, often surrounded by a walled garden.

In all houses one room is set aside for men's gatherings. In traditional houses this room is the one affording the finest view. Generally men sleep alone except for when they desire their wives' presence for sex. Women, girls, and small children sleep together. Adolescent boys sleep apart.

CHILDREN AND CHILDHOOD

As in other traditional Arab societies, children are highly valued in Yemen. Bearing and raising children are prescribed by the Quran. Having children is a key to adult status for both sexes, and eventually the children provide return on investment, although the content and timing of the return is not the same for daughters as for sons—nor are the potential risks and heartaches.

Both women and men express a preference for male children. Stated reasons usually focus on sons' continued affiliation with the family of origin in contrast to daughters' eventual marriage and affiliative shift. While the role of agriculture has declined and sons are no longer necessary for farm labor, they remain important for their economic contributions and to the continuance of the family line. The value of daughters is the labor they provide before marriage, the linkages that are forged through their arranged marriages, and the emotional support they are likely to give. What daughters provide is significant but, in the view of most 'Amranis, not as important as what sons provide.

Male births are more celebrated than female births. From the congratulatory statements given new mothers onward, the fuss is greater over sons. A son's birth involves a circumcision ceremony, an affair that formerly included numerous male guests, each of whom was obligated to bring a gift for the new mother. Now the event is just for the immediate family and the mother's father and brothers. Only these men and the new father bestow gifts on the boy child's mother. Because they are more highly valued, sons are considered likely targets for the evil eye and are accorded greater protection from harm than are daughters.

Women tell folktales and anecdotes that address male preference for sons. Typically these involve men who discriminate harshly against a female birth or at least threaten to do so, but see the light or are somehow punished in the end. There are some women who, after giving birth, pretend to their husbands that the new baby is a girl just for the pleasure of later being able to announce that what the men had hoped for had actually occurred.

While all infants are swaddled, it is not uncommon for a mother to discontinue the practice if her baby appears to dislike the tight confinement. Boys are more likely than girls to be perceived as highly active and chafing against restraints, and so are unswaddled sooner. Whether they are objectively more active and willful or just perceived as such is unknown.

Generally Yemeni mothers are very indulgent of young children of either sex. They often redirect children's attention rather than ordering them to put something down or stop doing something. Some mothers try to startle a resistant child into stopping bad behavior by telling the child that a lunatic is coming. While striking children is not approved, some mothers pull children's ears or hit them as a form of discipline. Striking a child in the head or face is particularly disapproved. One educated young mother told of having been so upset when her husband had hit their firstborn in the head that she took their son and returned to live with her parents. She knew permanent damage could result from such blows and took extreme measures to protect her son, returning to her husband only after he had been pressured by others to promise never to strike their children in the head again. He had, she said, honored his promise to her.

Children are not believed to be capable of self-control or significant learning until at least the age of four, and even then the capacity for self-control, rationality (*'aql*), and responsibility are minimal. In women's view, males are much slower to develop in these areas. What they do not appear to recognize is that the time lag can be accounted for by differential treatment of boys and girls. For example, male toddlers are permitted to hit and kick their mothers or sisters practically until they tire of doing so or can be distracted from the aggression. Not only are older sisters expected to tolerate painful abuse from younger brothers, but they must also start pitching in and helping their mothers in many ways from an early age. Modesty, self-sacrifice, and helpfulness are expected from girls although lapses are not at all unusual until they are about twelve years old. Especially when there are younger siblings, girls are expected to assist their mothers, while boys are largely free of such responsibilities. Boys have more leisure time and are less closely supervised than girls.

While both girls and boys have limited access to the public social worlds of adult women and men, girls have far greater exposure to adult women's gatherings than boys do to women's or men's gatherings. Being more confined to the home and immediate neighborhood, girls spend much of their time with women of several generations. While perhaps not actively involved in the conversations, they can and do listen and learn a great deal about women's lives and concerns. Largely apart from adults of either sex, boys' socialization is more horizontal and their grasp of what will be expected of them as men is more delayed. Their childhood is more prolonged than that of girls, and in fact, many women perceive at least some men as remaining childlike, in the sense of being irresponsible, even into their thirties.

As soon as they can walk children begin to spend time in the dirt alleys and streets around their houses. Usually they are supervised sporadically by their mother or an older sister. Play is unstructured and draws on the creativity of the children. Toddlers use the street rather like a sandbox. Young children rarely venture far from home except in the company of an elder sibling. Often these trips are to nearby shops for sweets.

Toddlers spend most of their time with their mother or siblings. Fathers generally leave the house early, return at midday to eat, go off to chew *qat,*[10] and often return late. Despite, or perhaps because of, limited contact, both fathers and children relish their time together. Fathers especially like to spend time with their younger children. One man said the few minutes he spent drinking his morning tea on his doorstep with his young daughter and son hanging all over him were the high point of his day.

Young children's play activities in the neighborhood are limited,[11] much of them in imitation of adult life. Girls pretend to hold parties or bake; boys roughhouse using sticks as daggers. In the late seventies a common pastime was using large packing boxes as play houses and shops. Sometimes, slightly older children would sell real sweets from such temporary, cardboard stalls.

In the seventies imported toys were expensive and found only in specialty shops in the major cities. Often these were of poor quality and did not last. In rural areas, toys, imported or of local manufacture, were uncommon. The most ingenious were small cars made of wire and directed by a steering wheel on the end of a three- to four-foot piece of wire. In the middle eighties, while there were many more, better quality manufactured toys, such as dolls and tricycles, available in the major cities, they remained rare in 'Amran. A new development in 'Amran was that boys, and sometimes girls, played soccer using small balls or occasionally empty plastic bottles.

The introduction of television broadcasts in the late seventies did not alter children's play patterns. Broadcasts only began in the late afternoon and programming was oriented toward adults. While it appeared some men were more likely to spend time in the evenings with their families watching television, younger children usually fell asleep. In the mid-eighties, some programs for young children were broadcast in the early evening. In addition to some cartoon shows, the Kuwaiti version of *Sesame Street* (ifta simsim) was shown and appeared to be popular.

The neighborhood is an important focus of activity and point of identification. As children get older, they socialize with a wider range of children in their neighborhood. While Yemeni society is divided into ranked, endogamous groups—religious elite (sada), tribesmen, and marketeers—ascribed status differences may not reflect economic standing. Neighborhoods are mixed. Play groups cross-cut status differences, but children are aware of status and allusions to rank are not uncommon.

The neighborhood remains the focus for girls longer than it does for boys. Few boys have responsibility for housework or sibling supervision. They are encouraged to be adventuresome and they venture farther from home and interact with boys from different neighborhoods. Mothers send sons on errands—to take food or messages to fathers in the fields or market or to pick up the odd item needed for a meal. While girls may run errands in the marketplace, they are expected to do their business quickly and discreetly and return right home. Girls with brothers old enough to run the errands are unlikely to enter the market often.

FORMAL EDUCATION

In 1978–1979, 'Amran had one elementary (grades 1 to 6) and one intermediate (grades 7 to 9) school. The elementary school was built in the early seventies and replaced a much smaller one that had been located in a room above one of the town gates. The intermediate school was built a few years later. Both were designed to serve children from 'Amran and nearby villages. The intermediate school was the only one in the region and a number of male students came from some distance and lived in unfinished shops while attending. Before 1979, when secondary classes were initiated in 'Amran, intermediate graduates wishing to complete their secondary schooling (grades 10 to 12) had to move to San'a to do so.

By 1982 a second elementary school had been built and the secondary school was in full operation.[12] Most neighboring villages had built their own three- or four-room schools and 'Amran's elementary schools served only local children. In 1986, and typical of the rest of Yemen,[13] enrollments in 'Amran were extremely high and schools conducted morning and afternoon sessions for many classes. In a few neighborhoods, parents hired their own teachers and classes were held in unused stores. While only a small portion of students who matriculate in elementary school complete secondary school, 'Amran's intermediate-secondary school, which still serves youth from throughout the area, had an enrollment well beyond capacity.

Boys begin school around the age of six or seven. Some girls also begin at about this age but there seems to be a wider age range during which girls matriculate. The boys enrolled in school vastly outnumber the girls. Both sexes have a high drop-out rate. This seems especially true at the completion of elementary school.

When we first conducted research, boys attended school in the morning, beginning about 8 a.m. and finishing about noon. Girls' classes began in the afternoon, starting about 3 p.m., and were shorter, finishing at the latest by 6 p.m. A few girls attended boys' classes in the morning as well as the afternoon all-girl sessions. An obstacle to female school attendance in the seventies was the fact that women pay formal visits; they need the services of their daughters to watch younger children. While daughters were enrolled in school, their attendance was less regular than boys'. Interestingly, women often expressed fervent hopes that their daughters would become sufficiently educated to enable them to be economically self-sufficient if necessary. Yet their own desire for respite from being confined at home led them to interfere with their daughters' schooling on at least an occasional basis. Thus many girls began school late or attended irregularly or were in and out of school contingent upon mothers' changing needs. By the mid-eighties this had changed since girls attended classes in the morning with boys.

Like most Yemenis, many 'Amranis consider education a reward of the revolution, and in fact those boys coming of age in the late seventies were referred to as the "children of the revolution." Education was a part of the modern world that the imam had kept from the people. This notion was reinforced by the expanded range of subjects taught by a large number of expatriate, primarily Egyptian, teachers. In addition, texts were written by non-Yemeni and classes followed the Egyptian curriculum.[14] In the eighties a Yemeni curriculum and texts were introduced.

In the seventies classes were conducted along the patterns of Quran schools. Class work emphasized recitation, repetition, and memorization. This may have changed in the eighties. For example, al-Iriyani notes that in the eighties "pupils derive the content of the lesson from the discussion."[15] Physical punishment, usually the swat from a switch to the palm of the hand, was and continues to be used on both boys and girls.

Owing to rapid changes in political economy, both men and women tend to see education as increasingly important for their sons.[16] At the same time, there seems to be some awareness by uneducated parents that educating their children creates a barrier between them. While in the late seventies enrollment in elementary and to a lesser degree intermediate school did not reflect status differences, sons of high-status families were more likely to move to Ṣan'a' to complete their secondary education. Old status markers were no longer sufficient for traditionally high-ranked families. They recognized that education was essential to acquiring government posts and to keep ahead of traditionally low-ranked merchant families who now had unprecedented economic opportunities for upward mobility.

The following class distribution of secondary school graduates illustrates this. In 1977 there were nine graduates, all male: two sada, five tribesmen, two marketeers. In 1978 there were thirteen graduates: one male sayyid, eight tribesmen, and four marketeers (three male and one female).

Boys also see school, especially learning to read and write, as essential for their future. In the eighties it became clear that literacy was necessary to obtain most higher-paying positions. There was also increased recognition of the value of vocational training. This incipient awareness is based in part on the employment histories of preceding classes of students. In 1986 almost all the 1977 and 1978 graduates held government positions. By contrast, self-described illiterate workers in the 'Amran Cement Factory had relatively low salaries. Still, boys who are unsuccessful in schoolwork—measured by either low marks or having to repeat a grade—or are needed to help with the family business are likely to drop out at the elementary-intermediate or intermediate-secondary transition.

If education was important for sons, at least in the late seventies, parents were more ambivalent about its value for daughters. While men and women also saw a certain amount of education—generally the completion of elementary school—as a benefit to their daughters' chances for a good future or enhancing their suitability for marriage to educated males, there was less conviction about this. There were also serious concerns about preserving family reputation. To some families, especially those trying to hold on to traditional status by maintaining an unimpeachable public image, having a daughter in school beyond the age of ten or eleven involved possible loss of honor. For some other families, whose chances of marrying their daughters into families of higher status were inconsequential, education did not seem as important. In many cases parents could not really begin to imagine what the future held for their children, so while they may have expressed vaguely idealistic goals for their daughters, their own life experience did not permit them to behave in ways that would advance those goals.

Like their parents, many young schoolgirls of the late seventies had vaguely formed high educational goals but no realistic idea of what would be involved to pursue them seriously. Nor did they have many role models of female employment outside the home. Aside from a few female schoolteachers and nurses, there were no professional women in 'Amran.[17] Adult women must cover their faces when outside the home, and even fully veiled are not supposed to shop in the marketplace. If they must pass through the marketplace, they are expected to do so quickly and discreetly. Husbands, children, or other relatives do the shopping. How, mothers ponder, could our daughters work given these restrictions? Decency and family honor must come first. Awareness of this obstacle to female employment contributes to lack of parental investment in daughters' education.

In 1978 second- and third-grade schoolgirls were surveyed about their educational aspirations and hopes and expectations for their futures. The age range of these girls was approximately seven to thirteen. Second-graders generally said they wanted to have jobs as teachers or nurses when they grew up, but in most cases, they expected to continue in school for only two years. These girls all expected to marry and expressed the hope they would marry within the family. All third-graders said they wanted to complete elementary school (sixth grade). The only girl who said she wanted to go farther in school was a sister of one of the town's two females to have attended high school. She said she wanted to go to college because her father wanted her to be educated like her older sister. As with the second-graders, most third-grade girls wanted to hold jobs as adults, most as a teacher, one as a doctor. All but one said she wanted to be able to attend school after marriage. A few of these girls' mothers could read the Quran; the rest of the mothers could not read. Most had fathers and brothers with some literacy, but few reported receiving help with schoolwork at home. All of these girls expect to be married and, like the second-grade girls, say they would prefer to marry a relative because of the greater security. Most said they would prefer living in an extended-family household rather than a nuclear one and none wanted to have more than two or three children. The majority thought they would rather remain in 'Amran after marriage while about one third were attracted to the idea of life in the capital.

At the time of our research there were two females who had attended high school, both of whom eventually graduated. The girls had to reside through the week in the capital because that was the closest school they could attend. One lived in the capital and worked in a bank; the other returned home to live with her parents before completing school. She had no job and stayed home almost all the time. No other girls attended secondary school for many years.

RELIGIOUS EDUCATION

In addition to free public education, the traditional Quranic school (*kuttab*) is still available for boys. Since religion is included in public schools, the number of pupils enrolled in Quran schools appears to be low. Some parents are willing to pay the fees to insure that their sons acquire some proper religious training; others say they enroll their sons less because of the importance of religion than because they believe success in learning or memorizing the Quran will improve the student's success in public school. Boys, who have already spent the morning in school, are not overly enthusiastic about the additional afternoon classes. By local convention, 'Amran women do not enter the mosque and girls do not attend the *kuttab*. [18]

INFORMAL EDUCATION

School does not occupy as much of the day or as important a place as it does in more developed countries. Children have a great deal of time and energy to channel in other directions and their nonschool, informal education is at least as important in their formation as is their formal schooling. Here there are significant sex differences. As mentioned earlier, girls have many more chores related to domestic life and child care than their brothers. Because of their duties and because of the high cultural value placed on female chastity and modesty, girls spend most of their time in or near their homes. They are frequently in the company of women and girls of all ages and are exposed to a wide range of female interactions and topics of conversation. When they are free to play with other girls it is very common for them to have younger siblings tagging along. They have been trained to sacrifice their own needs to those of the very young siblings, but, like children everywhere, often become involved in their own play and ignore the siblings. The opportunities for play are most frequent in the afternoon when their mothers are out visiting. Older girls play make-believe games, do play chants, and drum, sing, and dance in imitation of traditional, low-status singers (*muzayyinat*).

Older boys who do not work have fewer responsibilities and consequently more free time. Most of this is spent with male age-mates often in sports-related activities or in a number of game rooms in the market area. Boys have less contact with men than girls have with women. When they become teenagers they can spend time in the men's tea shops and, on occasion, in men's social gatherings engaging in the national pastime of chewing *qat* leaves.

Fathers are more distant and authoritarian toward sons than they are toward daughters, although they do expect obedience from both and require modest behavior from daughters. While boys are pampered by mothers, it is not considered suitable for boys beyond a certain age to spend too much time with their mothers or other women. Their socialization is more horizontal and age-group based. Fathers, it is believed, are better equipped than mothers to control boys' behavior. Fatherless boys are considered to be at risk to become overly willful and even unruly and to be especially delayed in the acquisition of a sense of responsibility. This is related to the high tolerance mothers and other women have for physical aggression in male toddlers, even when the aggression is toward the mother herself, and to the absence of responsibility placed on boys.

CONCLUSION

It is clear that formal education has become a significant component in the lives of Yemeni children. Current demand exceeds available space, and owing to Yemen's high birth rate and the growing percentage of children attending school, this promises to continue to be the case. However, while school will occupy more of children's time and attention, ties to family and neighborhood will remain strong. Changes in patterns of informal education also seem likely. Television exposes children to a variety of roles and has the potential to broaden the horizons of people in the most remote villages.

The growth of education reflects changes in Yemen's economy. There is less work for children and a reduced demand for child labor. It also hints at changing attitudes toward the roles of boys and girls. While the number of girls enrolled is below that of boys, there has been an increase that seems likely to continue. Moreover, the recent union of the two Yemens suggests there may be further changes. Perhaps this will lead to new roles for women and to a further emphasis on girls' education.

POSTSCRIPT

In summer 1992 we returned to united Yemen for a short stay. One of the most dramatic changes was the return of more than one million migrants and dependents from Saudi Arabia and the Gulf states in the wake of the 1990 Gulf crisis. The 350,000 new students increased already serious overcrowding.[19] Most schools have two shifts and two students to one chair. Parents must purchase schoolbooks which are prohibitively costly for some families.

The fifteen-year trend of increasing enrollments was reversed for females in 1990. Between 1977 and 1991, male matriculation rose from 25 to 61 percent. Female matriculation grew from 12 percent in 1977 to 21 percent in 1990 but fell to 17 percent in 1991. The decline was concentrated in the former Yemen Arab Republic where poor returnees may have chosen to use their limited resources on sons' rather than daughters' education.

During visits to 'Amran several changes were noted. Now all schools are sexually segregated. This is one way Islamic fundamentalists appear to have influenced educational policy. Our informants viewed this practice positively. Students can complete secondary school in 'Amran but some 'Amran families living in the capital claimed that Ṣanʿa schools were vastly superior.

Attitudes toward boys' education remain fairly constant. Informants still see it as a way to get ahead, especially when it leads to enrollment in either the War or Police College. Several 'Amrani government-employed university graduates were pointed out as role models.

Susan Dorsky did follow-up interviews with adult women who were children and teenagers when she first knew them. They appear to have taken two very different tracks, the traditional wife-mother track for those who quit school at an early age and the educated woman track.

Traditional young women's lives differ in some respects from their mothers' lives fifteen years ago. Now women can shop in the market (*suq*) without shame; most use gas models of the traditional oven, so they need not chop wood, make dung cakes, or suffer the discomfort and ill health caused by the old smoky conditions. Plumbing has improved and washing machines are common, as are VCRs. However, visiting patterns seem to have narrowed, with many confining their visits to a family circle except for major social occasions. Enthusiasm over visiting also did not appear as keen as in the past. Some traditional-track women appeared to feel cheated or deprived when they compared their lives to those of educated women. They spoke of the financial rewards and greater independence of working women and their sense that educated women's lives held interest and dimensions unknown to them.

As for 'Amran's first two female high school graduates, one had moved to Ṣanʿa, earned bachelor's and master's degrees, was a director of a bank, owned a fine house, and was well known and respected. Less successful was her counterpart, who had remained in 'Amran and did not attend college. She held a low-level job in a bank and was relatively poor. Both had married, although when interviewed, one was divorced, the other separated. Each had only one child, a son. Both resided with their widowed mothers and siblings.

These two had a friend from a higher-status family who had wanted to study with them but whose father had made her quit. The family's prestige, he had explained, would have been damaged by her studying beyond primary school. She had several children and like her friends had had marital difficulties. The family was far from affluent. Her husband was said to treat her badly, but, uneducated and unemployable, she was dependent upon him. She had a very bright, intellectually curious cousin living in Ṣanʿa who had completed secondary school and longed for a college education, but that was viewed as unseemly by her high-status father.

Reinterviews of young women who were in primary school during our 1978–1979 stay revealed few surprises. The only one who had attended both girls' and boys' primary classes is now a student at Ṣanʿa University. Still single, she has her heart set on completing college. From a very poor family, she lives in Ṣanʿa, and visits her family when possible. Another had completed secondary school and was doing the government-service teaching required of females before they can enter college. Both of these young women had college-educated older relatives. Neither had a living father and neither had married. Neither came from traditionally highly ranked families. Several childhood playmates of these career-track women were also interviewed. They had quit school, married young, stayed in 'Amran, and had several children each. Talking about their childhood and their lives now, they seemed somewhat dissatisfied and mildly embarrassed, as if, at least at that moment, they felt they did not measure up, and regretted the choices they or their families had made for them.

ACKNOWLEDGMENTS

Thomas B. Stevenson's field research in 1978 – 1979 was supported by the Social Science Research Council, the American Council of Learned Societies, and a Wayne State University Graduate Fellowship. His research in 1986 – 1987 was supported by a Fulbright Islamic Civilization Research Grant. His 1992 research was supported by an Ohio University Research Committee Award and an American Institute for Yemeni Studies Fellowship.

NOTES

1. On May 22, 1990, the Yemen Arab Republic (North Yemen) and the People's Democratic Republic of Yemen (South Yemen) united as the Republic of Yemen.

2. Dorsky 1981, 1986; Stevenson 1981, 1985.

3. El Attar 1964.

4. Zabarah 1982: 15 – 17.

5. Weir 1987: 274.

6. Weir 1985: 139 – 140.

7. Dorsky 1986: 137.

8. Steffan et al. 1978: 109 – 110.

9. Al-Iriyami, Ḥamid, 1987: 376.

10. Qat (*Catha edulis*) is a shrub grown in mountainous regions of Yemen. When the tender young leaves are chewed, the user experiences first a stimulant and then depressant effect. Although it is expensive, the majority of men and a sizable portion of women chew *qat* daily.

11. One 'Amran neighborhood mosque had set aside part of its religious endowment (*waqf*) land and had built a small playground with a swing, some spring-mounted animals to ride, and a jungle gym. This was used only by children from the neighborhood. Playgrounds of this type were extremely rare throughout the country.

12. A vocational secondary school, serving the northern region, had also been built. Although near the center of town, the school was nearly invisible and it seemed few students from 'Amran attended.

13. Al-Iriyani, H. M., 1990.

14. Al-Iriyani, H. M., 1985: 184.

15. Ibid.: 182.

16. Myntti (1978: 25) notes that education had a strong urban focus and that in some areas was seen as a stepping stone to professions such as medicine, science, engineering, or aviation. Such clear-cut educational objectives were not articulated by most 'Amranis.

17. In the eighties, the local bank employed a number of women. While their presence was certainly common knowledge, few women or girls ever enter the bank. Most of these workers commuted from Ṣan'a. Myntti (1985: 44) observes that women account for 4 percent of the urban work force. Most of these have some education and a number were university graduates.

18. H. M. al-Iriyani (1985: 179) describes the prerevolutionary education of both boys and girls in religious schools. This practice seems not to have reached the tribal highlands. Myntti (1985) suggests that it was only daughters of the religious elite who attended these schools.

19. Stevenson 1993.

REFERENCES

Al-Iriyani, Ḥamid. 1987. "School and Education—Formation and Development." In W. Daum, ed., *Yemen: 3000 Years of Art and Civilisation in Arabia Felix* (Innsbruck: Pinguin-Verlag), pp. 375–388.

Al-Iriyani, Hooriya Mohammad. 1985. "The Development of Primary Education and Its Problems in the Yemen Arab Republic." In B. R. Pridham, ed., *Economy, Society, and Culture in Contemporary Yemen* (London: Croom Helm), pp. 178–189.

———. 1990. "Education and Development in the Yemen Arab Republic." Paper presented to the conference "Contemporary Yemen: Processes of Change," School of Oriental and African Studies, University of London, May 21–23.

Dorsky, Susan. 1981. *Women's Lives in a North Yemeni Highlands Town.* Ann Arbor: University Microfilms.

———. 1986. *Women of 'Amran: A Middle Eastern Ethnographic Study.* Salt Lake City: University of Utah Press.

El Attar, Mohamed Said. 1964. *Le Sous-développement économique et social du Yémen: Perspectives de la révolution Yéménite.* Algiers: Edition Tiers-Monde.

Myntti, Cynthia. 1978. "Women in Rural Yemen." Unpublished manuscript prepared for USAID, San'a.

———. 1985. "Women, Work, Population and Development in the Yemen Arab Republic." In J. Abu Nasr, N. F. Khoury, and H. T. Azzam, eds., *Women, Employment and Development in the Arab World* (Berlin: Mouton Publishers), pp. 39–58.

Steffen, Hans, W. Dubach, U. Geiser, R. Schoch, E. Egli, and M. Fürer. 1978. *Final Report of the Swiss Airphoto Interpretation Project of the Swiss Technical Co-operation Service, Berne,* vol. 1. Zurich: Swiss Technical Co-operation Service.

Stevenson, Thomas B. 1981. *Kinship, Stratification, and Mobility: Social Change in a Yemeni Highlands Town.* Ann Arbor: University Microfilms.

————. 1985. *Social Change in a Yemeni Highlands Town*. Salt Lake City: University of Utah Press.

————. 1993. "Yemeni Workers Come Home: Reabsorbing One Million Migrants." *Middle East Report* 181 (March–April): 15–20.

Weir, Shelagh. 1985. *Qat in Yemen: Consumption and Social Change*. London: British Museum Publications.

————. 1987. "Labour Migration and Key Aspects of Its Economic and Social Impact on a Yemeni Highland Community." In R. Lawless, ed., *The Middle Eastern Village: Changing Economic and Social Relations* (London: Croom Helm), pp. 273–296.

Zabarah, Mohammed Ahmad. 1982. *Yemen: Traditionalism vs. Modernity*. New York: Praeger Publishers.

GENDER ROLES IN IRANIAN PUBLIC SCHOOL TEXTBOOKS

by Adele K. Ferdows

Every society has its own definitions of the roles of its male and female citizens according to which socially accepted role stereotypes develop. These stereotyped gender roles are absorbed by the members of the society through socialization.

The learning and internalization of concepts of masculine and feminine gender roles in society takes place through different channels. Textbooks used in schools comprise one very important component of this learning for children and youths. Various studies of gender roles in western countries have concluded that the majority of school books used in Italy, France, and the United States continue to depict women in stereotyped roles as submissive, passive, and confined to household duties and motherhood responsibilities.[1]

In every country, of course, the content of textbooks reflects what the government wants the children to learn. It is through textbooks that desirable attributes of the citizen are clearly defined. The Iranian government's attempts to create the ideal citizen are no exception.

The purpose of this essay is to analyze the content of textbooks in an attempt to comprehend the norms and values related to the position and role of women and men which are conveyed and reinforced through public education in Iran. Two major questions need to be addressed for a meaningful analysis. First, what are the gender norms and values that are communicated by the schools through textbooks? And, second, what is the actual impact on students? This study is limited to the identification and analysis of the norms and values regarding gender roles transmitted through elementary and secondary school textbooks. Whether the transmitted values are actually being accepted and internalized by the students is the subject of further research.

EDUCATIONAL GOALS OF THE ISLAMIC
REPUBLIC OF IRAN

Since 1979, a major sociopolitical and cultural revolution has transformed Iran. This cultural transformation has taken place as a result of calculated and deliberate efforts of the new political leadership.

A major goal of the new Iranian educational system in the postrevolution period has been to convert the entire sociocultural body from a secular and western orientation to an Islamic one. Islamic ideology and worldview clearly shape the educational goals laid down by the government of Iran. Furthermore, it is generally believed that in order to transform the institutions of society, the beliefs and values of individuals must be altered. The major responsibility for this change in values is delegated to the school system, where teachers carry the heaviest burden, not only teaching the new beliefs and norms but also being the ideal Muslim role models for the next generation.

One important point must be made clear regarding the educational aims of the Islamic Republic. Schools not only teach Islamic subjects and history, and the advancement of human achievement and knowledge under Islam, but also western languages and history, as well as the sciences, which are stressed as vehicles for progress and development toward self-sufficiency and independence.

In May 1979, shortly after the Islamic authorities took power, all educational institutions, except universities, were segregated on the basis of gender. It must be noted, however, that most schools in Iran had been segregated prior to the revolution with the exception of private and international schools, and a few coeducational elementary schools. After 1979, teachers were also segregated so that only females taught in girls' schools and men in boys' schools. However, due to a shortage of female teachers in math, physics, and the sciences some male teachers still teach in girls' schools, and there are a number of female teachers in the first and second grades of the boys' elementary schools.

EDUCATIONAL REFORM

The Islamic regime has attempted to Islamicize education by revising school textbooks. Immediately after the revolution in 1979, Ayatollah Khomeini instructed the educational authorities to rewrite fundamentally the textbooks used at all levels, sanitizing them of western colonialist and degenerate topics left over from the former regime, and to replace them with Islamic and revolutionary subjects and themes.[2]

The first revisions took place in 1982 and again, more recently, in 1988. New textbooks were prepared or existing textbooks completely modified to present a Muslim perspective on gender roles. In the new texts, Islamic rules of social relationship and responsibility replaced western concepts.

Since 1911, Iran's educational system has been highly centralized, with the Ministry of Education in Tehran determining the curriculum, textbook development, and structure of the entire educational system and teacher-training institutes. The Islamic Republic has retained the pre-1979 system. The school system consists of five elementary school grades (ages 6–10), a three-year middle-level (*rahnama'i*) cycle (ages 11–13), and four high-school grades (ages 14–17), with a total of twelve grades.

Since public schools, unlike colleges and universities, were never closed, the revisions and changes in the content of textbooks occurred only gradually. In 1987 a special bureau, the Center for Textbooks, was instituted within the Ministry of Education and charged with the task of changing the content of elementary and high-school texts, with the active participation of the clergy.

The curricular contents of elementary and secondary schools are uniform throughout the country with a very high dose of religion and ethics, the Quran, and Islamic history. In addition, at the middle-school level, the Ministry of Education has prepared separate sets of the "Study of Professions" textbooks for boys and girls. Sewing, nursing, and food preparation are emphasized in girls' texts, while boys learn about farming, civil engineering, and other such professions.

ROLE OF TEACHERS IN THE ISLAMIC REPUBLIC

Teachers are specifically instructed and assigned to become role models for the children, not only in their teaching but also in behavior and dress codes. A campaign (called *paksazi*) to clear the entire educational body of those persons whose attitudes, values, behavior, and appearance are viewed as being un-Islamic has had a dramatic effect. An estimated 30,000 teachers judged as nonconformist and uncommitted to official goals and dogma have been either purged or retired early from their positions.[3] It is not an exaggeration to suggest that never before in Iran has the teacher been as important a role model for students as in the Islamic Republic today.

Teacher-training institutes, under the authority of the Ministry of Education, consider teachers to be the direct molders of the revolution's future generation, and their primary mission in society is to guide children toward the path of God. As such, they are required to obtain spiritual and moral as well as academic skills before being eligible to lead others.

The government has established admissions criteria for teacher-training institutes so that only ideologically loyal individuals can enter. The teacher-training curriculum now requires ideological courses which reinforce Islamic morality and ethics. Reportedly, strict ideological and ethical screening of teacher candidates, combined with low salaries, has led to a serious scarcity of qualified teachers in Iran.

Beginning in the summer of 1980, gradual pressure was exerted on women to veil in public, and on July 5, 1980, the government issued an order that all female government employees had to wear a *hijab*. This affected half a million urban women who held jobs outside the home, 9 percent of the female population.[4] Later, in 1981, the parliament passed a law requiring all women to observe the Islamic dress code, with punishments of up to one year in prison for violations. Accordingly, all female students and teachers are required to wear specially designed Islamic uniforms in dark colors (gray, black, brown) and head scarves leaving only the hands and face exposed. Any student or teacher disobeying the order is suspended, dismissed, or punished.

METHODOLOGY

On the assumption that the written word is one of the most important means for instilling the values and change in attitudes about gender roles, rights, and responsibilities, textbooks of grades 6 through 12 were selected and their contents analyzed. To study the content of the textbooks and the message they convey regarding gender roles and position, a total of 10,922 relevant words were identified and classified. A quantitative and qualitative analysis of the topics and content description of the themes in the textbooks were carried out to identify the norms and values deemed desirable by the Islamic Republic.

Topics discussed in Iranian textbooks can be divided into two basic categories. The first and largest category consists of nongender, informative material, and the second category consists of gender-related topics. Given the purpose of this study, only the second category of topics is addressed here. A total of thirty-four books, containing 5,348 pages, were chosen and all the words and idioms pertaining to gender were identified and marked. The following categories were identified: (1) gender roles, (2) gender identity, (3) role functions, (4) role traits.[5]

Results were operationalized and analyzed both quantitatively and qualitatively.

I. GENDER ROLES

Data on the roles assigned to women and men are presented in Tables 1 and 2.

Table 1 illustrates the traditional gender roles assigned to females. Clearly the most frequent (72.9 percent) role assigned is "mother," with "girl" following in distant second place (12 percent). The girl, however, is often being groomed and trained for the role of mother. The working woman (1.3 percent) presented is usually a peasant woman who works on a farm. Farm women mostly work close to home and are clearly performing these jobs in addition to their housekeeping and mothering roles. Very few women are depicted as grandmothers (4.4 percent), and the term "old woman" is used in seven out of ten cases where such roles appear. No explanation can be found for this absence, despite the fact that in Iran today, just as before the revolution, grandmothers are still venerated by members of the family and often exercise great authority in the areas of child rearing and family decision-making.

Men are also depicted in the traditional roles of provider and protector

TABLE 1

Female Roles in Islamic Republic Textbooks

Role	Number	Percentage
Mother	164	72.9
Girl (little girl)	27	12
Wife	21	9.3
Old woman (grandmother)	10	4.4
Working woman	3	1.3
Total	225	99.9

TABLE 2

Male Roles in Islamic Republic Textbooks

Role	Number	Percentage
Father	144	12.9
Boy (little boy)	56	5
Husband	25	2.2
Old man (grandfather)	26	2.3
Working man	870	77.6
Total	1,121	100

of the family, as is illustrated in Table 2. The role of "working man" has the highest frequency (77.6 percent) while interestingly enough, the role of "husband" appears in only 2.2 percent as compared to "wife" (9.3 percent). The man's role as "father" also appears infrequently (12.9 percent) in spite of the importance given to fatherhood by the Islamic government and the society as a whole. One explanation may be that, in presenting a man as a "working man," his role as head of the family, i.e. father and husband, is assumed.

2. GENDER IDENTITY

Tables 3 and 4 illustrate gender identities for men and women as presented in the texts.

Thirty-two percent of women are identified by personal name. However, personal names are mentioned only in reference to leading women of the early Islamic era, e.g. Khadijah and Ayishah (the Prophet's wives), and most frequently Fatimah (the Prophet's daughter and Imam Ali's wife). These are given as role models and sources of inspiration for the contemporary women

TABLE 3

Female Identity in Islamic Republic Textbooks

Identity	Number	Percentage
Personal name	115	31.9
Position/identity	11	3
Daughter	19	5.3
Sister	17	4.7
Woman	199	55.1
Total	361	100

TABLE 4

Male Identity in Islamic Republic Textbooks

Identity	Number	Percentage
Personal name	4,120	84.8
Position/identity	541	11.1
Son	92	1.9
Brother	19	.4
Man	85	1.8
Total	4,857	100

of Iran. In every case, they are characterized as the pious Muslim, devout wife, self-sacrificing mother, and loving daughter. Most often, however, the simple term "woman" (55.1 percent) is used, while their physical attributes and age are totally absent. Table 3 indicates that women as wives or mothers do not necessarily need personal identity; they remain anonymous. References to position (3 percent) are also solely with regard to the women of the Prophet's family. Of the eleven references, two were to the Persian poet Parvin E'tesami, whose poetry was presented in Persian literature texts.

As illustrated in Table 4, the highest frequency of men's identity is their personal name (84.8 percent) and position or occupation (11.1 percent). Perhaps more important than the percentages are the total numbers in each category as compared with those of women. Of all the personal names used in all the texts (4,235), 4,120, more than 97 percent, are men's, and only 115, less than 3 percent, are women's.

3. ROLE FUNCTIONS

The data collected from textbooks on role functions of females and males are summarized in Tables 5 and 6.

TABLE 5

Female Functions in Islamic Republic Textbooks

Role Function	Number	Percentage
Guide/protector of child	46	30.3
Cook, housekeeper	5	3.3
Moral guide	101	66.4
Total	152	100

TABLE 6

Male Functions in Islamic Republic Textbooks

Role Function	Number	Percentage
Protector/defender	742	17.6
Moral guide	349	8.3
Leader/ruler	2,482	59
Learned scholar	633	15
Total	4,206	99.9

Data in Table 5 again reflect the traditional functions performed by fe-males in society. One surprising finding is that direct discussion of differences between men and women and their functions rarely appears in textbooks. Most subject matters are approached from a gender-neutral perspective, using such terms as "person," "human being," or "one." On rare occasions, veiling (hijab) is discussed as a moral and ethical responsibility, without specific ref-erence to women, although it is clearly addressed to them. Specific and direct reference to women's function appears in separate textbooks of the "Occu-pations and Professions" series, where sewing, nursing, food preparation, and nutrition are included for girls, and carpentry, engineering, and agriculture are presented as options for boys. One must also note that the remaining parts of these texts include the same material for both boys and girls on subjects such as gardening, emergency medicine, health, and architecture. The sepa-rate treatment of other functions, however, supports at least indirectly the general proposition that the Iranian/Muslim woman is primarily expected to be a devoted mother and kind, caring wife. She is present to feed, groom, and protect her children. Her education prepares her to be a capable child-rearer and to assist her children in understanding those different gender roles.

Raising children is the most important responsibility of the woman in the family. As a mother, she is the sole person responsible for disciplining and bolstering her children's physical and emotional well-being. Of all the refer-ences made to her, 96.7 percent were related to caring for children and ad-vising them on the acceptable social, moral, and familial values such as obe-dience, respect for elders, cleanliness and personal hygiene, hospitality to guests, and kindness and caring for siblings. Women who were identified as working outside the home were usually rural women assisting their husbands in farming, milking cows, or weaving carpets, and some small peasant girls who tend sheep.

It must be made clear that, as in the "personal name" and "identity" cate-gories, the "moral guide" category also makes reference mostly to the leading women of early Islam, particularly Fatimah, whose life and actions are de-picted as a model for all women. This category drops to a mere 8.3 percent for men, for whom the highest frequency (59 percent) is as leaders or rulers. Most of these references are also to leading Muslim/Shi'i personalities and Imams or rulers. The next highest frequency male function (17.6 percent) is as the protector of the family and defender of Muslim society and government.

One unexpected finding was the very low frequency of the woman as housekeeper and cook (3.3 percent). This image is presented through a very few illustrations where the mother is pictured as serving or preparing food or doing other household chores. When a young girl is presented in illustra-tions, she is eternally smiling, satisfied, never showing any signs of fatigue or frustration at her work. She does all the chores assigned to her by her mother, is always neat and clean, helps her mother prepare meals with interest, and never complains. Overall, however, few texts had illustrations of women.

4. ROLE TRAITS

Most frequent references to females in the texts are in the area of stereotyped female traits predominant in traditional-religious societies. Women are portrayed as the tender, loving, self-sacrificing mother, and as hardworking, undemanding, and neat.

By repeating the historical narrative of Fatimah and her daughter Zainab's life, the texts set the agenda for young girls. Fatimah is characterized as a martyr, who happily gives up her own interests and desires for the happiness and satisfaction of her children. She struggles for justice (Ali's right of succession to the Prophet) and cares lovingly for her father, the Prophet. The theme of a mother who patiently gives up her own self-satisfaction for her children is repeated throughout these and other stories.

The little girl is obedient, always demonstrating gratitude to her parents and other adults, wiser than her age in conversation with them, quiet, dependent, extremely kind, considerate, and polite with other children. Her playtime consists of visiting her girlfriends, playing with her doll, or doing her homework. Of course, she, like her mother, is always pictured wearing Islamic dress (hijab) even at home with her parents and siblings. The little girl does not venture out; she is always at home. She helps her mother around the house and takes care of her little sisters and brothers when her mother is busy.

In sharp contrast, the father is depicted in the traditional stereotypical role of the provider and protector of the family. He is a hardworking man, whose job is usually mentioned. He is a caring, kind, and wise person looked up to by other members of the family. He spends most of his time outdoors and on weekends takes his son(s) on hiking trips or other outdoor activities. He is never shown helping around the house or performing any of the "womanly" chores.

The little boy is shown as ambitious, curious, outgoing, polite, and adventurous. He accompanies his father or other boys and male relatives on outdoor trips and listens to their guidance and advice. He addresses questions to his father or other male relatives. He is also obedient, courteous, and kind to others.

DISCUSSION

From the above content analysis of Iranian textbooks, the following general comments may be offered. The predominant orientation of the content, as expected, is religious, with emphasis on Islamic history, particularly that of Shi'i Imams and their doctrines. Although the focus of this inquiry was limited to gender images, it is significant to note that the material in textbooks is more concerned with religious and political ideology than with gender issues. This clearly reflects the leadership's intention to create political loyalty among its citizens and its anxiety about the population's supposed indifference or antagonism toward the Islamic regime.

Based on this study, we may suggest that overt gender discrimination against women is almost absent from textbooks, since gender-neutral pronouns are utilized and few topics related to women are described. But it may also be argued that this absence itself is an important indication of the system's inclination to deemphasize the role and function of women overall. This position can be supported by the statistical data showing that references to females in the textbooks are a meager 6.8 percent of the total 10,922 references, as compared to 93.2 percent references to males. The author is led to observe that this implies children can learn little from women, their lives, and contributions. In some way, this finding poses a contradiction since the Islamic Republic's leadership continuously urges women to participate in religious and political functions and sponsors a number of national and international conferences to study the position and role of women in Islamic society.

It may be useful to point out that a majority of Iranian women support the Islamic system and many actively participate to promote the official regulations and rules regarding women. One may argue that this is so because the official ideology taught through the educational system is totally in accordance with the indigenous culture. As such, it has been able to penetrate the hearts and minds of a majority of the population, particularly women. It is clear that the aim of the textbooks is to create a new generation whose values and beliefs include piety, martyrdom, and practice of Islamic social codes. Students are presented with a sharply defined worldview in which men and women perform different functions and play different roles both in family and in society.

Muslim doctrine makes no distinction between the private and public areas of women's world. The private aspects of women's lives are considered a public matter and therefore subject to state control. The most vociferous calls for the observance and enforcement of the Islamic hijab for women come from the members and leaders of various women's organizations. These organizations deal with issues affecting women and actually prepare draft legislation for the government on subjects like birth control, government support for widows and divorced women, child care, marriage subsidies for young men and women to start a family, health and medical facilities for women, education of women, Islamic laws regarding marriage, divorce, and inheritance, and women's literacy campaigns.

Women members of the Iranian Parliament have presented draft legislation that stipulates that at the time of marriage, the parties to be married must sign an agreement that lists the conditions under which the woman's rights to property, divorce, and alimony are protected. In 1990, the bill had not yet become law. However, it is made available to all couples at the time of marriage for their voluntary signatures. One of the most striking provisions in the agreement is the subject of equal division of all marital property in cases of divorce. No member of parliament has yet argued that this bill is not in conformity with the Shari'a, or Islamic code.

Although at present there are only three women members of parliament, thousands are active in many women's organizations, are vocal in making their demands known to the government, and participate in large numbers in both local and national elections.

Today many Iranian women believe that women have gained rights denied them under the Pahlavi regime before the revolution. Strong elements among these women have emerged, advocating the application and strict enforcement of conservative interpretations of their traditional roles as mothers and wives. They promote the full participation of women, indeed their obligation to participate, in social and political activities such as elections, voting, public demonstrations, and debates of issues in public forums. At the same time, they emphasize women's primary responsibilities and traditional roles as mothers and wives, and advocate the observance and practice of Islamic codes of behavior and dress. They reject ideas of women's equality with men, their independence or assimilation with men, and condemn western concepts of gender equality. Textbooks reflect, confirm, and teach these positions.

Finally, it seems that the current socialization effort within the educational system is proving to be effective and will be even more so as time passes and a new generation appears. Success is found particularly among that segment of schoolchildren whose family environment is in harmony with the religious, cultural, and social ideology of the state. These children not only learn about veiling, motherhood, and different gender roles through schooling, but also personally observe, experience, and imitate their own parents and family members as role models. This reinforces what they are taught in school.

NOTES

1. I. Kallab, J. Abu Nasr, and I. Lorfing, "Sex Role Images in Lebanese Text Books," in Ira Gross, John Downing, and Adma d'Heurle, eds., *Sex Role Attitudes and Cultural Change* (Boston: D. Reidel Co., 1982), p. 132.

2. Golnar Mehran, *The Socialization of Schoolchildren in the Islamic Republic of Iran:*

A Study of the Revolution in Values in Iranian Education (Ed.D. dissertation, University of California, Los Angeles, 1990), pp. 425 – 426.

3. Ibid., p. 381.

4. Dilip Hiro, "Iran: The Revolution Within," *Conflict Resolution* 208 (1989): 18.

5. These categories were used in the study by Kallab, Nasr, and Lorfing, "Sex Role Images," pp. 131 – 138.

CHANGING PERCEPTIONS
OF IRANIAN IDENTITY
IN ELEMENTARY TEXTBOOKS

by Patricia J. Higgins and Pirouz Shoar-Ghaffari

Some exposure to formal schooling has been a common feature of children's lives in Iran for many years. The literacy rate, including schoolchildren, was just 62 percent in 1986, and only 70 percent of the school-age population was enrolled (Iran Statistical Center 1992). Yet, with the gradual expansion of modern education during the Pahlavi era, increasing numbers of children have spent at least a year or two of their lives in school, being instructed in the rudiments of reading, writing, arithmetic, and other elementary subjects.

For the Pahlavis, as for the leaders of other twentieth-century states, universal elementary education was desirable not only for the skills it could impart; it was also valued for the role it could play in the development of national unity and support for the political status quo. Reza Shah Pahlavi (1925 – 1941) subscribed quite overtly to this philosophy of education, as did his son Mohammad Reza Shah Pahlavi (1941 – 1979). New schools were built, first in urban, then in rural, areas, and a single standard curriculum was mandated. Teacher training institutions and certification procedures were established, and a system of national examinations was instituted (Arasteh 1969, Pahlavi 1967: 107 – 117, Szyliowicz 1973). By the mid-seventies, 8 million students were enrolled in some 50,000 schools dispersed throughout the country (Iran Ministry of Education 1977).

The state system of education developed under the Pahlavis undermined and largely supplanted a preexisting system of Quranic schooling and higher education controlled by religious authorities (Akhavi 1980: 32 – 37, 129; Fischer 1980: 58 – 60; Street 1975). But the Islamic Republican government which replaced the Pahlavis in 1979 did not dismantle this state system of education. On the contrary, they too recognized the schools as potentially powerful mechanisms of political socialization. Their educational program, therefore, consisted of modifying the existing state system of education to better serve their goals for Iran, and fostering its continued expansion (Matini 1989, Mehran 1990, Mohsenpour 1988). By 1990–1991 the number of students enrolled had increased to more than 15 million and the number of schools to more than 87,000 (Iran Statistical Center 1992).

Textbooks are a feature of education especially amenable to state control. This is particularly true in a country like Pahlavi Iran, in which education was highly centralized and a single set of textbooks was published by the government for use in all schools—to be read, ideally, by an entire cohort of the population. With the success of the 1977–1979 revolution and the appropriation of the Pahlavi system of education by the Islamic Republic, textbooks were understandably targeted for rapid revision. Within six months new materials had been introduced for the elementary period, and within two years the major changes had been completed (Echo of Islam 1986a: 18, Mehran 1989: 37).

In this essay, elementary school textbooks in use during the last decade of the Pahlavi era and those in use in 1986–1987—eight years after the establishment of the Islamic Republic—are compared with attention to their portrayal of Iranian identity. We begin with a discussion of the role of textbooks in Iranian education and a brief review of previous analyses of textbook content. This is followed by a comparison of the major features of Iranian identity promoted by the Pahlavi and Islamic Republican governments through public pronouncements and government policies. Quantitative content analysis of the Persian language textbooks, supplemented by a qualitative analysis of the textbooks in all elementary subjects, is then used to determine the extent to which the elementary textbooks express these changes in state-supported definitions of Iranian identity. Special attention is given here to the presentation of Islam, Persian and Arabic languages and literatures, pre-Islamic customs and heritage, western culture, sex-role ideologies, and alternative class orientations.

TEXTBOOKS IN IRANIAN EDUCATION

The educational system of Iran, like that of many other Third World countries, can be characterized as a "textbook culture" (Kumar 1988). In contrast to systems in which teachers make at least some choices concerning the resources and methods used to implement a curriculum, in Iran, as (for example) in India:

1. Teaching in all subjects is based on the textbook prescribed by state authorities.

2. The teacher has no freedom to choose what to teach. She must complete the prescribed syllabus with the help of the prescribed textbook.

3. Resources other than the textbook are not available in the majority of schools, and where they are available they are seldom used.

4. Assessment during each year and examinations are based on the textbook (Kumar 1988: 98).

In effect, the content of the textbooks *is* the curriculum and it constitutes the bulk of the knowledge consciously transmitted in the schools.

One of the effects of such a textbook culture is that textbooks are not only read by school children but also memorized. The American-inspired educational reforms of the fifties and sixties had sensitized Iranian educators to the desirability of developing the whole personality of the child rather than focusing on "bookish instruction" (Iran Ministry of Education 1968: 6–7, Hendershot 1975: 80–82), and rote learning was much decried in educational circles. Nevertheless, practices common in the seventies even in urban middle-class schools encouraged memorization. Information on the pedagogical practices is based on Higgins' eighteen months of field research (1969–1971) in the schools and homes of a lower-middle-class community of Tehran (Higgins 1976) and her additional research on the guidance cycle in Tehran schools in 1977–1978. A typical lesson consisted of one student after another reading a selection from the textbook while the rest followed in their books. Then students would copy the selection into their notebooks, and the homework assignment would be to copy the same selection several more times. Mastery of the material was tested with verbatim dictation from the text. Elementary classes often finished the textbooks a month before the end of the school year, and the remaining time was spent in review of these same textbooks.

This situation is due in part to inadequate alternative teaching resources. Even in urban Iran in the seventies only elite schools had libraries or laboratories, and the typical elementary classroom was furnished with no more than desks and a blackboard. The only other reading materials regularly observed in Tehran schools were the biweekly *Payk* (*Courier*) magazines, published in three elementary-level editions and sold through the schools at a few cents a copy. The articles were closely coordinated with the textbooks in both subject matter and vocabulary, and they were occasionally discussed in class. In rural areas, students were unlikely to have any contact with other reading material, in school or out, save perhaps the Quran (Street 1975: 301).

Primary institutional support for the textbook culture, however, came from the examination system. Advancement from grade to grade was regulated by trimester examinations administered by school authorities, and achievement of the elementary certificate was dependent on the results of a final exam administered by local educational authorities. At least for the elementary period, these exams were largely restricted to the content of the textbooks and were designed to be answered by direct recall rather than requiring any reworking of the materials. Failure was a real possibility; 20 percent of the candidates for the elementary certificate failed the final exams in 1970 (Iran Ministry of Education 1972), and most classrooms included at least a few students who were repeating a year.

While we have not carried out systematic observational studies of elementary classrooms in Islamic Republican Iran, we have no reason to think that the textbook has lost any of its prominence. One set continues to be published by the government for use in all schools, promotion from grade to grade continues to be based on trimester exams, and success on a final examination administered by provincial educational authorities is required for the primary certificate (Echo of Islam 1986: 37). A series of magazines called *Roshd* (*Growth*) published by the Ministry of Education has taken the place of the *Payk* magazines as supplementary reading material sold in the schools (Echo of Islam 1986a: 19).

In other respects as well, the continuity in the Iranian educational system is striking, despite the rhetoric of the Islamic Republican government and its critics. During the late sixties a "New System of Education" had been implemented which established a three-year "Guidance Cycle" for grades six, seven, and eight, designed to evaluate and prepare students for tracking into a wider variety of secondary educational programs. Science was established as an independent subject from the first grade, all elementary textbooks were revised, and an accompanying set of teachers' guides was prepared. These reforms were inspired by educational goals and practices current in the United States in the post–World War II era, designed under the guidance of American educational and cultural missions, and implemented largely by Iranians educated in the United States. (For firsthand accounts of American influence on Iranian education see Filstrup 1976 and Hendershot 1975.)

There was some initial enthusiasm after the revolution for eliminating the Guidance Cycle and returning the structure of education to the form it had had in the fifties. More realistic voices prevailed, however, and it was decided to retain the basic form of the system at least temporarily (Parsa 1979: 11). To date there has been no major structural change in precollege education in Iran (Echo of Islam 1986b). Similarly, the particular subjects studied each year at the elementary level have remained the same, and individual textbooks are provided for all of the same subjects.

While the textbook culture appears to continue in the Iranian educational system, the content of the culture transmitted through these textbooks has changed. Most analyses have focused on the use of the textbooks to reinforce an Islamic worldview. Shorish concludes that the elementary Persian language and religion textbooks, as well as more advanced textbooks on religion, all have "one single focus: the development of a thoroughly committed individual to one God" (Shorish 1988: 59). Mehran concludes from a study of the social-studies texts (for elementary, middle, and secondary schools) that schoolchildren "are presented with a sharply defined image of the world, divided into pious, brave, uncompromising, honorable, morally superior Muslims and secular, unjust, greedy, inhuman, oppressive Westerners" and "Westoxicated" intellectuals (Mehran 1989: 49). Touba found that the patriarchal orientation of the Islamic Republican regime had been incorporated into the elementary textbooks (Touba 1987: 153). In a previous article we have focused on sex roles and sexual segregation using a quantitative content analysis comparing the elementary Persian language textbooks of the late Pahlavi era with those of the Islamic Republic (Higgins and Shoar-Ghaffari 1991).

Each of these studies has been based on a slightly different combination of texts, usually selected to illustrate most vividly the new government's efforts to use the schools in support of ideological reform. While reference is made to dramatic changes, most analyses have looked only at the Islamic Republican texts in any depth. (For a brief comparative analysis see Mohsenpour 1988.) This absence of a comparative framework has been accompanied by dependence primarily on qualitative rather than quantitative analyses. In addition, correspondence between state goals and policy and the textbooks has been largely assumed rather than tested in previous studies. While it is logical to expect a close correspondence in a highly centralized system, this has not always been the case. (See Mbuyi's 1988 comparison of textbooks and avowed state policies in Kenya and Tanzania.) An exception is the more recent article by Nafisi (1992) which compares Persian language textbooks for grades 2 through 5 for the two eras, uses quantitative as well as qualitative content analysis, and examines the textbooks in the context of other expressions of state ideology. Nafisi finds that in education and in other ways, the Pahlavis emphasized the pre-Islamic Persian heritage to legitimize their rule. Similarly, Islamic Republican textbooks concur with other ideological statements in emphasizing the Islamic era of Iranian history, the pulpit, and the faith itself as sources of legitimacy.

Here we attempt to supplement previous studies by comparing the elementary textbooks of the two eras with each other and with overt policies of the two governments concerning the definition of Iranian identity. We focus on the elementary period because it is the elementary textbooks that are read by the largest number of Iranian children. These were the years of compulsory education under the Pahlavis (Parsa 1979: 8), and Ministry of Education statistics have always shown a sharp decline in the number of students continuing beyond the elementary period. We selected the Persian language textbooks for quantitative content analysis because a textbook for this subject has been used in each year of the elementary cycle in both eras. Separate math and science textbooks have also been used from the first grade in both eras, and math and science texts can also convey notions of national identity (Kwong 1988), but there have been many fewer changes in such texts since the revolution. Our quantitative analysis of the Persian language textbooks is supplemented by a comparative, qualitative analysis of the math and science textbooks, the religion textbooks (introduced at grade 3), and the art textbooks (introduced at grade 4). Examining all these textbooks provides a more rounded view of the printed materials to which elementary students in these two eras of Iranian history have been exposed.

CONTRASTING DEFINITIONS
OF IRANIAN IDENTITY

The Pahlavi and the Islamic Republican states have each sought to establish and/or reinforce an Iranian identity that can help to bind the populace to the state and that can form a common core of national culture. The most obvious difference between these state-supported definitions of Iranian identity is the emphasis given to Islam by the Islamic Republic. This can be contrasted with the emphasis on Persianness—as expressed in language, literature, and pre-Islamic customs and heritage, including the monarchical tradition—that was characteristic of the Pahlavi definition of Iranian identity (Cottam 1978: 328–329; Higgins 1984; Menashri 1982: 54, 59; Richard 1989: 30). Such an emphasis on Persianness fits well with the Pahlavis' more secular orientation and in particular with their desire to separate religion from politics (Akhavi 1980: 23, Fischer 1980: 9).

The difference, of course, is one of degree. The constitutions of both governments identify Shi'a Islam as the state religion, maintain that ultimate sovereignty rests with God, and establish similar formal positions for religious minorities (Algar 1980, Saleh 1966). Leading figures of both states have been portrayed or portray themselves as ruling in part by divine grace. Both states also recognize Persian (Farsi) as the official language, and both seek to spread more sophisticated urban versions of Persian literacy and literature as well as of Islamic values and theology.

The two governments differ concerning the nature of Iranian identity in the international context. The Pahlavis sought to define Iran as a modern country, well on its way to becoming fully industrialized, among the developed nations of the world. By and large they took the United States and other western countries as their models of development and encouraged considerable cultural (as well as economic) exchange with the West. Radio, television, and film gave positive portrayals of many aspects of modern, urbanized, secular Iranian culture and denigrated many features of traditional Iranian culture as manifestations of backwardness (Naficy 1981, Tehranian 1980). One of the explicit goals of education under the Pahlavis was that the next generation "would welcome the desirable ideas of the modern world" (Iran Ministry of Education 1968: 2).

In contrast, the Islamic Republic takes the Islamic world—and secondarily the colonized, oppressed, underdeveloped nations of the world—to be the relevant international cultural context. Rhetorically, at least, the Islamic Republic has embraced a supranational pan-Islamic ideology and deemphasized Iranian nationalism, and leaders have made special efforts to express their appreciation of the cultural ties between Iran and the Arab world (Menashri 1982: 82, Ramazani 1987: 11, Rafsanjani as quoted by Zonis 1985: 87). Islamic Republican leaders have also made special efforts to deemphasize the differences between Sunnis and Shias (Khomeini as quoted by Hussain 1985: 73, Najmabadi 1987: 208).

Accompanying this shift is a thorough devaluing of western culture, which is seen as an insidious force that must be cleansed from Iranian society (Rafsanjani as quoted in Zonis 1985: 87, Keddie 1985, Najmabadi 1987: 215). Development now is taken to mean not large-scale industrialization and high levels of consumption of luxury goods, but smaller-scale use of appropriate technology, technological and economic self-sufficiency, the achievement of a modestly comfortable standard of living for all, and the development of a nonmaterialist, spiritually sound society (Karimi 1986: 38). Like the Pahlavis, Islamic Republican leaders see Iran as a leading country, indeed as a leader of Islamic countries and the Third World, a leader capable of standing up to Euro-American economic, political, and cultural power.

One aspect of the Pahlavi modernization program that was particularly alarming to Islamic leaders was its support for a western-derived sex-role ideology that emphasized the need to integrate women into a wide range of public roles. Under the Pahlavis, education for women was encouraged, legal reforms gave women more rights in the family, some institutional and legal support was provided for the employment of women outside the home, and women were given the vote and allowed to hold public offices. The veiling of women was ultimately banned or discouraged throughout the Pahlavi era, and the public mingling of the sexes was treated as normal. Similarly, customs designed to maintain sex segregation were portrayed as ignorant and back-ward (Haeri 1980, Fischer 1978, Sanasarian 1982).

While the Islamic Republican government has not eliminated female edu-cation, rescinded the vote for women, or even effected a significant decline in female labor-force participation (Mehran 1988, Moghadam 1988), it has strongly encouraged concealing clothing for women and segregation of the sexes in schools, offices, and other public places (Nashat 1980, Sanasarian 1982). Official support has been given to an Islamic ideology that stresses the distinctiveness of male and female roles and that places special emphasis on motherhood and women's nurturing qualities and roles (Nashat 1983, Ferdows 1985). Men are expected to provide the primary economic support for their families, and women should work outside the home only when necessary.

Along with the shift from Persianness to Islam as the focal point of Iranian identity and from the West to the Islamic and Third worlds as the relevant in-ternational reference groups, there has also been a shift in the social classes most closely associated with the government. While the Pahlavis made some at-tempts to win the allegiance of the lower classes and the rural population, and although they eventually alienated large sectors of all social classes, they con-tinued to be seen as most closely allied with the westernized middle and upper classes. Under the Pahlavis, western-educated, professional, middle and upper classes were thought to embody the ideal of Iranian identity. The Islamic Re-publican regime, by contrast, takes the lower-middle classes (more specifically, the petite bourgeoisie comprising small merchants and craftsmen) as the classes whose values and behavior most closely embody the new Iranian identity (Ak-havi 1987, Najmabadi 1987: 181). It is from these classes that the government has drawn its strongest support. Government policies since the revolution have resulted in a shift in private consumption within both the rural household and the bottom 40 percent of urban households, while the top 20 percent of urban households have borne the brunt of the economic decline (Karimi 1986: 35). According to Keddie there has been a shift in class orientations in recent years "away from workers and peasants and toward the middle, landed, and profes-sional classes — including bazaaris, landlords, and wealthy peasants and profes-sionals and technocrats" (1985: 12), but this shift is probably too recent to be reflected in the textbooks of 1986 – 1987. (See also Behdad 1989: 353.)

COMPARATIVE CONTENT ANALYSIS OF ELEMENTARY TEXTBOOKS

Given these contrasting definitions of Iranian identity and given the recog-nition by both governments of the potential power of formal education to shape such identities, we expected to find corresponding contrasts between the textbooks in use in 1969–1970 and those in use in 1986–1987. To test our expectations we developed a more detailed list of ways in which the definitions of Iranian identity espoused by the two governments might be expressed in elementary school textbooks. From this we derived a coding system to be applied in our content analysis of the textbooks.

In our initial quantitative content analysis of the Persian language textbooks we used the lesson as the unit of analysis. Our statistical analysis ignored the introductory material (title page, table of contents, preface, etc.) and the exercise pages of the books, but included the pictures as well as the written text of each lesson. Ideally the coding would be done by more than one coder, each of whom was unaware of the nature of the hypothesis; for present purposes, however, the coding has been done by one of the authors (Shoar-Ghaffari) in consultation with the other author and with one other native speaker of Persian. The data were analyzed using the SPSS crosstabs program, with chi-square the measure of significance.

The results of the quantitative content analysis led us to return to the Persian language textbooks for a more detailed and qualitative comparison of selected lessons. We focused particularly on those Pahlavi-era lessons removed completely from the Islamic Republican textbooks and the completely new lessons which replaced them. In addition, we reviewed all other textbooks that would have been used by an elementary student in either of these two academic years for their potential contribution to a definition of Iranian identity.

The most obvious and striking changes in the textbooks are in pictures. Whereas coeducation and unveiled women were regularly portrayed in the textbooks of the late Pahlavi era, Islamic modesty in dress and segregation of the sexes are portrayed in the new textbooks. In addition, illustrations in the new textbooks appear oriented toward the lower and lower middle classes— in the dress, housing, tools, equipment, and life-styles pictured—in contrast to the professional, urban, middle-class focus of the textbooks of the Pahlavi era. Even a casual glance at the contents of the textbooks reveals other interesting contrasts, such as the replacement of lessons focused on the shah and his programs with lessons focused on the revolution and on Islamic Republican government, and the removal (without replacement) of the portraits of the royal family with which each textbook of the Pahlavi era began.

While our analysis was directed toward expected differences in the two sets of textbooks, it is important to note the many areas of similarity as well. In our quantitative analysis of the Persian language textbooks we found that 13 percent of the Islamic Republic Persian language lessons were completely unchanged and another 40 percent differed only in small ways from the matched lessons in the Pahlavi-era textbook. The largest number of these unchanged or revised lessons was found in the grade 1 texts, in which 75 percent of the seventy-six lessons read by first graders in 1986–1987 were identical or slightly revised versions of lessons read by first graders in 1969–1970. Nor is there any change apparent in the basic method of teaching reading and writing, and in grades 2 through 5 each lesson contains a reading selection, a list of new words, a series of questions, homework assignments, and one or more grammar exercises.

In other subject areas, we found that the science textbooks are virtually unchanged in content, concepts, methodology, and the written text. More changes are apparent in the mathematics textbooks, but the changes appear to reflect increasing sophistication in the methods of teaching mathematical concepts, with less emphasis on memorization and drill, rather than any change in government ideology. We have been told that the math textbooks were revised between the 1969–1970 academic year and the revolution of 1979, but we have not been able to confirm this, whether by examining the texts in use in 1978–1979 or through contact with education officials responsible for such revisions.

The social studies textbooks were subject to more thorough revision. In the Islamic Republic, third-grade students are introduced to Iranian society by means of one family's travels, as occasioned by father's new job assignment. In the Pahlavi era the third-grade social studies textbook had presented a more formal and academic introduction to the study of society, an approach postponed in the Islamic Republican textbooks until the fourth grade. In other respects the format of social studies textbooks in the two eras is similar.

The most radical changes were reserved for the religious studies textbooks. During the Pahlavi era religion was included in the elementary curriculum, but the religious studies textbooks were quite thin (in comparison to the textbooks for other subjects), and they included no pictures or exercises. The new religious studies textbooks are more similar to the Persian language and the social studies textbooks in style and format. They too have brightly colored pictures and questions and exercises, and the lessons stress the integration of religion into daily life. This theme is expressed as well in their new title, "Religious Studies and Islamic Culture," which focuses attention not just on religion but on Islam.

FOCUS ON ISLAM

Our quantitative analysis confirmed that religion is given a more prominent role in the curriculum of the Islamic Republic not just through the reli-

TABLE I
Selected Topics by Period

	Pahlavi Era		Islamic Republic Era	
Religion	9	(4%)	37	(17%)
Pre-Islamic Iran	25	(11%)	3	(1%)
Others	192	(85%)	174	(81%)
Total	226		214	

Chi-square = 34.92, df = 2, significance 0.001

gious studies textbooks but through the Persian language textbooks as well. Whereas religion was the topic of only nine (4 percent) of the Persian language lessons in the Pahlavi era, it is the topic of thirty-seven (17 percent) of the 1986–1987 Persian language lessons (Table 1). The proportion of lessons devoted to religious topics varies by grade level, but for every grade this figure is higher for the Islamic Republican era. At the third grade nearly one third of the lessons in the new Persian language textbook are focused on religious topics. Furthermore, in fifteen of the eighty-five revised lessons (grades 1 through 5) the revision included adding a religious reference. For example, the camel's unique physical features are attributed to the hand of God rather than to adaptation, and a lesson on the practical social benefits of taking turns ends with a saying of Imam Hassan.

A sense of the quality of the changes can be achieved by comparing the specifically religious lessons in the two sets of texts. First-grade Pahlavi-era students read one lesson on prayer, one on God, one on the Prophet, and one on the Quran. These four lessons are retained in the Islamic Republican texts with only minor modifications in wording. In addition, first-grade students in 1986–1987 also read a lesson on Aid'e Gorban and the pilgrimage to Mecca and a lesson on the teachings of Ali. In the second grade, Pahlavi-era students read no lessons on religious topics in their Persian language textbook, while students in the Islamic Republican era read a poem on the power of God as creator, a story on the Prophet Muhammad's call to prophecy, and a lesson on Imam Sadeq's teachings concerning workers' rights.

In grade 3 Pahlavi-era students began the year with a prayer for success. This prayer is retained unchanged in the Islamic Republican texts, and students read ten additional lessons on religious topics. These include two lessons on prayer, a two-part Quranic story, two lessons on the Prophet Muhammad's teachings (on the insignificance of ethnic differences in Islam and the evil of property expropriation), a lesson on Imam Hussain and his martyrdom and another on his example of generosity, and two lessons on Imam Kazem's teachings.

In grade 4 Pahlavi-era students again began the year with a lesson in praise of God, a lesson which is retained with only a minor revision in the Islamic Republican textbook. Students in the Islamic Republican era also read about the Prophet Muhammad's patience and perseverance in preaching Islam, Imam Ali's teachings concerning social and moral behavior, and the teachings of several additional Imams. Students in grade 5 in 1969–1970 began the year with a poem in praise of God and later read a two-part story about Moses' childhood. None of these lessons was retained in the Islamic Republican fifth-grade textbook. Here students read three lessons on Islamic history, two selections from the Quran, lessons on the teachings of the Prophet and Imam Ali, and a selection from a passion play.

Contrary to our expectation that the Islamic Republic's aspirations to leadership in the Islamic world would result in a deemphasis of specifically Shia topics, students now read much more about specifically Shia religious figures and events in their Persian language textbooks than did students of the Pahlavi era. In fact, none of the religious lessons of the earlier Persian language textbooks focus on exclusively Shia figures or events, while nearly one third of the lessons on religious topics in the Islamic Republican era are specifically Shia. Similarly, the issue of succession to leadership in the Islamic community and other topics that differentiate Shia from Sunni interpretations are introduced earlier in the religious studies textbooks of the new era, and they are given more attention in the new social studies textbooks as well. At the fourth-grade level, however, the religious studies textbook of the Islamic Republican era explains that there are many similarities between Shias and Sunnis and that the enemies of Islam have tried to capitalize on their differences. The day is near, students read, when Muslims will be united and Islam will be victorious.

Not only do the few Persian language lessons focused on religious topics in the Pahlavi era ignore specifically Shi'a topics, but also seven of the nine are not specifically Islamic. They concern themes and topics that Islam shares with Judaism and Christianity. This is also true of six lessons in the Islamic Republican Persian language textbooks, but here such lessons constitute only 17 percent of those on religion. In the Pahlavi era these nonsectarian religious lessons constitute 78 percent of all the lessons on religion in the Persian language textbooks. In our qualitative analysis of the religious studies textbooks we found that they too gave closer to equal treatment to all major religions in the Pahlavi era, while the superiority of Islam is stressed in the religious studies textbooks of the Islamic Republican era.

In the Persian language textbooks of the Islamic Republican era one also sees a greater emphasis on Islamic holidays. Some, such as Aid'e Gorban and Ashura, have a history of general recognition in twentieth-century Iran; others are new or are newly emphasized as holidays. The latter includes a coming-of-age (to pray) ceremony which is described as occurring in girls' schools once a year for the third-grade students.

In addition, the newer texts give secular Iranian holidays a more Islamic tone. This is especially true of New Year's Day (the first day of spring) and Sizda Bedar (the thirteenth day of the year, traditionally celebrated by picnicking). For example, the lesson on New Year's Day in the second-grade textbook includes a reading from the Quran at the time of the turning of the year, and visiting the families of martyrs and praying for victory for Muslims as the first events of the day (before visiting one's kin). (Such customs were not mentioned in the Pahlavi-era textbooks, although the Quran was included as an item to be ceremonially displayed.) In the newer second-grade Persian language textbooks the lesson on Sizda Bedar has been completely replaced by one on Islamic Republic Day—the twelfth day of the year. After a short history of the revolution and the referendum of 1979, children read that from then on "we have celebrated Islamic Republic Day and New Year's together," a theme which is continued in the grade-3 lesson on New Year's.

We also expected to find in the new textbooks another expression of the emphasis on Islam: increased attention to handwriting and calligraphy, a distinctively Islamic art form which has experienced a major revival outside the school system. We sought to measure such an emphasis in these early grades by the number of lessons printed wholly or partially in script as opposed to newspaper-style print and by the emphasis given to writing in script in the exercises accompanying the lessons. A slightly larger proportion of whole lessons are presented in script in the Islamic Republican textbooks (14 percent vs. 12 percent), but when lessons partially in script are counted as well one finds that the Pahlavi textbooks gave students greater exposure to script (21 percent vs. 17 percent). On the other hand, handwriting is given greater attention in the Islamic Republican Persian language textbooks, particularly in grade 2, in which sixty-four pages are devoted to writing exercises. The introduction of these exercises is the one departure in the design of the Persian language textbooks.

Looking beyond the Persian language textbooks, we found no reference to Islam or to religion in the science or the math textbooks of either era, save for the invocation of God's blessing with which each book begins. Nor was script or calligraphy used in the math or the science textbooks of either era. Calligraphy was included in the fourth-grade art textbook of both eras. The

Islamic Republican art textbook also makes use of several illustrations with Islamic themes, whereas that of the Pahlavi era used no pictures of mosques, shrines, prayer rugs, or Islamic inscriptions.

On the other hand, religion and Islam are given more attention in the social studies textbooks in the Islamic Republican era than they were in the Pahlavi era. The latter used an evolutionary orientation for the understanding of life-styles, the organization of society, and the means of production, and treated religion as a social institution which developed along with law and commerce. This evolutionary perspective has been removed from social studies textbooks in the Islamic Republican era. Students learn in the new social studies textbooks that the physical environment was created by God, and they read about the lives of the prophets as well as tyrant kings so that they can better know right from wrong. In the civics portion of their textbooks the focus is on Islamic institutions—the mosque, religious endowments, interest-free loans, etc.—and Islamic values such as faith in God, respect for others, and frugality are featured.

PERSIANNESS DEEMPHASIZED

As we anticipated, the increased attention paid to Islam in the Islamic Republican elementary textbooks has been accompanied by a decline in emphasis on Persianness. The number of lessons focused on pre-Islamic Iran in the Persian language textbooks declined from twenty-five (11 percent) to three (1 percent) (Table 1). Similarly, the number of lessons in which ancient household furnishings were portrayed declined from eleven (29 percent) in the Pahlavi era to four (11 percent) in the Islamic Republic era (Table 2), and those in which ancient dress was portrayed declined from twenty-two (20 percent) to seven (6 percent) (Table 3).

Among the lessons with pre-Islamic themes in the Pahlavi-era Persian language textbooks were seven devoted to New Year's Day and associated holidays, six on the ancient Iranian holidays of Mehregan and Sadeh, two lessons on pre-Islamic historical sites, and ten lessons drawing from Persian literature on pre-Islamic topics. Two additional lessons concerned early humans and the origins of fire. Most of these lessons were found in grades 2 and 3, where they made up over 20 percent of all lessons, but some occurred at each grade level. All that remain in the Islamic Republic's textbooks are three lessons on New Year's, one each in grades 1 through 3, modified to give greater emphasis to Islamic customs. Other lessons have also been modified to remove references to ancient Iranians—for example, when discussing oil and when describing early attempts to fly.

TABLE 2

Style of Furnishings by Period

	Pahlavi Era		Islamic Republic Era	
Traditional Iranian	3	(8%)	21	(58%)
Western	16	(42%)	3	(8%)
Ancient	11	(29%)	4	(11%)
Institutional	8	(21%)	8	(22%)
Total	38		36	

Chi-square = 25.63, df = 3, significance 0.0000

TABLE 3

Style of Dress by Period

	Pahlavi Era		Islamic Republic Era	
Islamic	5	(5%)	61	(55%)
Western	75	(69%)	6	(5%)
Working	7	(6%)	37	(33%)
Ancient	22	(20%)	7	(6%)
Total	109		111	

Chi-square = 134.5, df = 3, significance 0.0000

Pride in a distinctively Persian Iranian heritage may also be encouraged in the textbooks through the use of classical Persian literature. Both sets of textbooks draw upon such literature, so that students are exposed to at least a few lines from the poet Sa'di as early as the third grade. The number of lessons incorporating poetry has declined, however, from fifty-five (24 percent of Pahlavi-era Persian language lessons) to thirty-five (16 percent of Islamic Republican lessons). The number of lines of poetry used has also declined from 334 to 265 (Table 4). While the practical poems of Sa'di are given even more space in the Islamic Republic's Persian language textbooks than they were in the Pahlavi era, Ferdowsi's poetry, with its focus on pre-Islamic kings, has been almost completely removed. Elementary students in the Islamic Republican era are not introduced to Ferdowsi until grade 4, where they read only two lines, in contrast to Pahlavi-era students who read 23 lines from Ferdowsi in grade 3 and another 14 lines in grade 4. Islamic Republic students do read

TABLE 4

Lines of Classical Poetry by Poet and Period

	Pahlavi Era		Islamic Republic Era	
Ferdowsi	41	(12%)	9	(3%)
Sa'di	46	(14%)	69	(26%)
Nezami	44	(13%)	5	(2%)
Bahar	44	(13%)	19	(7%)
E'tesami	9	(3%)	19	(7%)
Others	150	(45%)	144	(54%)
Total	334		265	

Chi-square = 62.97, df = 5, significance 0.001

TABLE 5

Prominent Type of Personal Name by Period

	Pahlavi Era		Islamic Republic Era	
Persian	51	(41%)	8	(8%)
Arabic	28	(23%)	75	(79%)
Western	11	(9%)	5	(5%)
Mixed	33	(27%)	7	(7%)
Total	123		95	

Chi-square = 69.52, df = 3, significance 0.001

another 7 lines of Ferdowsi in grade 5, but in all they read less than a quarter of the poetry by Ferdowsi read by Pahlavi-era students.

Another measure of the expression of Persianness found in elementary textbooks is the selection of personal names. The predominance of Persian personal names in the Persian language lessons declined from fifty-one (or 41 percent of the Pahlavi-era lessons with personal names) to eight (8 percent of such lessons in the Islamic Republican era) (Table 5). While some distinctively Persian names are still used in the Islamic Republic's textbooks, they are not used for primary characters. This is in sharp contrast to the wide variety of Persian names used in the Pahlavi-era Persian language textbooks and the bestowal of such names on the main characters of the textbooks.

The deemphasis of Persianness appears to be carried even further in the social studies textbooks. In the Pahlavi era pre-Islamic history focused on the benevolence of the kings, their compassion for the defeated people, their promotion of liberty, and their respect for other religions. In the Islamic Republican social studies textbooks there is no glamor or glory in accounts of early Iranian states. What is stressed is the inequality in society and the tyranny of the kings. The new textbooks particularly emphasize injustice and inequality under the Sassanians, the last dynasty before the victory of Islamic forces.

ARABIC LANGUAGE AND LITERATURE

Our expectations of greater focus on Arabic language and literature in the elementary Persian language textbooks of the Islamic Republican era were largely confirmed. While over 75 percent of the lessons of both the Pahlavi and Islamic Republican eras derived from Iranian sources, there was a sharp increase in the use of Arab sources, from three (1 percent) to thirty (14 percent) in the later period (Table 6). Most lessons from Arabic sources, however, are religious lessons focused on early Islamic history. Lessons from secular Arab sources remained few in number, only three (1 percent) in both the Pahlavi and Islamic Republican eras. The subject matter of these shifted, however, from stories set in the period of classical Arab-Islamic civilization (all three stories in the Pahlavi era) to contemporary issues. Two of the three secular lessons from Arab sources included in the Islamic Republican Persian language textbooks focus on the Palestinians and their struggle against Israeli oppression.

The predominance of Arabic personal names in the Persian language textbooks also increased dramatically—from twenty-eight (or 23 percent of the lessons including personal names) to seventy-five (or 79 percent) (Table 5).

TABLE 6
Source by Period

	Pahlavi Era		Islamic Republic Era	
Iranian	186	(82%)	164	(77%)
Arab	3	(1%)	30	(14%)
Western	24	(11%)	11	(5%)
Other	13	(6%)	9	(4%)
Total	226		214	

Chi-square = 28.72, df = 3, significance 0.001

Part of this increase, like the increase in the number of lessons from Arabic sources, is directly related to the larger number of lessons on early religious figures in the Islamic Republican textbooks. If such religious lessons are excluded, there is still a dramatic increase in the number of lessons in which Arabic names predominate, from twenty-five (or 20 percent of all Pahlavi-era lessons with names) to fifty-three (or 56 percent of such Islamic Republican lessons). Furthermore, the primary characters in the Islamic Republican textbooks are all given Arabic names. Amin and Akram are the young siblings who are the primary characters in the first-grade Persian textbook, for example, replacing the more Persian Dara and Sara of the Pahlavi era, and their friends include Fatemeh, Javad, Jalal, Tahere, and Asghar instead of Parviz and Parvin, Bijan and Jaleh, Zari, Zivar, and Ziba.

A third measure of increased focus on Arabic culture could be the frequency of use of Arabic words in the textbooks. While we did not code for this variable, we note that students are introduced to Islamic phrases in Arabic at the third grade in their Persian language textbook in the Islamic Republican era. Here the opening "In the name of God" is included in both Arabic and Persian, a practice repeated in grade 4; the Arabic opening is used alone from the earliest years in the science, math, and art textbooks of the Islamic Republican era. In the Pahlavi-era textbooks the opening is in Persian in all the elementary textbooks. We should also note that third-grade students in the Islamic Republic begin to learn to read the Quran in their religious studies book, about 40 percent of which is devoted to this activity; this emphasis on reading the Quran continues in the fourth- and fifth-grade religious studies textbooks of the Islamic Republican era.

ORIENTATION TOWARD THE WEST

Our expectations concerning changes in orientation toward the West were also substantiated. The number of lessons in the Persian language textbooks based on western sources declined with the change in government from twenty-four (11 percent) to eleven (5 percent) (Table 6), and the number of lessons using western personal names declined from eleven (9 percent) to five (5 percent) (Table 5). Similarly, the number of lessons portraying western furnishings declined from sixteen (42 percent) to three (8 percent) (Table 2), and the number portraying western dress declined from seventy-five (69 percent) to six (5 percent) (Table 3).

The lessons in the Persian language textbooks using western personal names were in every case among those deriving from western sources. In the Pahlavi era these varied from discussions of the Wright brothers, Thomas

Edison, Alexander Graham Bell, and the origin of the Red Cross to stories for or about children in European society, such as the tale of the Dutch boy who saved his town by putting his finger in the dike and "The Buckwheat" by Hans Christian Andersen. It is primarily the historical lessons on great inventors that are retained in the Islamic Republican textbooks. Most children's stories have been omitted, although the Dutch boy's story is still read, as are several tales with European settings. Even so, names and incidents are sometimes removed to make the western origins of these stories less obvious.

The move away from western goods and sources is less visible in the science and math textbooks, but here too household items pictured have a less western look and pictures of certain western foods (such as doughnuts and ice cream bars) have been removed. In the fourth-grade art textbook of the Islamic Republic the move away from dependence on western manufactured goods is promoted by teaching children how to make their own paints, clay, and other art supplies, rather than showing them the commercial paints and felt pens that are available for drawing.

An antiwestern orientation is implicit in some lessons in the religious studies and the social studies textbooks of the Islamic Republican era. For example, third graders learn that the Quran carries a revolutionary message to stand up to oppressors, a message which is illustrated by a drawing of a teenage boy in khaki, a Palestinian scarf over his shoulders, holding a machine gun in one hand and a Quran in the other and wearing a head band reading, "God is great." Fifth graders read in their social studies textbook that the Safavid establishment of foreign relations with the West in the seventeenth century and their reliance on European military advisors opened the door to a relationship ultimately harmful to Iran.

SEX SEGREGATION

The most striking and pervasive change in the elementary textbooks is in dress and in the association of the sexes. Most pictures in the Pahlavi-era Persian language textbooks showed people, whether children or adults, males or females, in western-style dress, including knee-length skirts, bare heads, and short sleeves on females, and short sleeves and sometimes short pants on males. In the Islamic Republican era, virtually everyone in Persian language textbooks wears more concealing clothing, either explicitly Islamic in style or working class (Table 3). The arms, legs, and hair of women and girls are always covered, and short sleeves, even on boys, are rare. While we did not count pictures in textbooks for other subjects, the contrast is equally evident.

In addition, many pictures in the Pahlavi-era textbooks showed boys and girls together, at school, at play, and on the street, as well as at home. The Islamic Republican textbooks are almost always illustrated with sex-segregated pictures. This sex segregation, with males and females rarely mixing outside the family, extends to the printed text as well.

Our quantitative analysis of the Persian language textbooks showed that this increased emphasis on sex segregation has been accompanied by a decline in the visibility of females. Lessons included female characters 63 percent as often as they included males in the Pahlavi-era textbooks, but only 35 percent as often in the Islamic Republic's textbooks. This decline in the visibility of females is a function of their lessened visibility in public. In both eras females were included in lessons set in private slightly more often than were males. The effects of the decline in female characters may be somewhat lessened, however, by the existence of a large number of ungendered characters, a situation facilitated by the structure of the Persian language which does not distinguish between "he" and "she" (Table 7).

On the other hand, we found no significant difference with respect to women's occupations in the Persian language textbooks of the two eras (Table 8). Even in the Pahlavi era half of all women pictured working were engaged in housework, and in both eras almost all other work done by women was either teaching or agricultural. No lesson in either set of Persian language textbooks portrayed women in blue-collar, clerical, or sales or service occupations, although a few women were portrayed in production activities—carpet weaving and textile and clothing factory work—in the science and math textbooks of the Islamic Republican era.

Also contrary to our expectations, we found no statistically significant differences in the proportion of Persian language lessons portraying family relationships, in the balance between nuclear and extended family relationships, or in the number of children per family. In both eras nearly all the family relationships portrayed were those within the nuclear family. While we could find no case of a residential extended family in the Persian language textbooks from either era, the focal family in the third-grade social studies textbook of the Islamic Republic era does include the paternal grandmother. All of the focal families in the textbooks of both eras have two children, a boy and a girl, and the average number of children portrayed in each family was one and a half in both eras. Despite the ideological emphasis on motherhood in the Islamic Republic, large families are not projected as the norm or the ideal through the elementary textbooks.

In the social studies textbooks of the Islamic Republican era students are given more exposure to the family as a social institution. In the fourth grade they learn about the importance of the family in Islam and the ideal division

TABLE 7

Number of Characters by Gender, Age, and Period

	Pahlavi Era	Islamic Republic Era
Males ***		
Adults	136	110
Children	87*	79*
Total	223**	189**
Females ***		
Adults	57	33
Children	83*	33*
Total	140**	66**
Total gendered	363	255
Ungendered ***	282	317
Total	645	572

* Chi-square = 10.45, df = 1, significance 0.01
** Chi-square = 10.84, df = 1, significance 0.001
*** Chi-square = 27.16, df = 2, significance 0.001

TABLE 8

Occupation of Females by Period

	Pahlavi Era		Islamic Republic Era	
Intellectual	17	(33%)	11	(33%)
Agricultural	8	(16%)	4	(12%)
Housework	26	(51%)	18	(55%)
Total	51		33	

Chi-square = 0.2268, df = 2, significance 0.8928

of labor between father, who is responsible for food and clothing and other necessities, and mother, who manages the household. The text stresses that in Islamic societies everyone must work, but that work is a means simply to acquire the essentials. In particular, Islamic women work to help others and to meet the needs of society, not just to have more money, as is the case in some other countries.

LOWER-CLASS ORIENTATION

Our final set of hypotheses anticipated a shift in the social class given the most prominence in the textbooks. As with sex roles and sex segregation, such a shift is apparent in the textbook illustrations in all subjects. Men no longer wear suits and ties, families sit on the floor rather than at tables and chairs, and household furnishings are more modest. In the Persian language textbooks there was a clear increase in the portrayal of traditional furnishings, from three, or 8 percent, to twenty-one, or 58 percent, of the lessons including furnishings (Table 2), and in the portrayal of working-style clothing, from seven, or 6 percent, to thirty-seven, or 33 percent, of the lessons including dress (Table 3).

There was no statistically significant difference, however, in the proportion of rural Iranian to urban Iranian settings portrayed in the Persian language textbooks of the two eras (Table 9). In both eras about 30 percent of the lessons had a rural setting. On the other hand, many rural settings are included in the science and math textbooks of the Islamic Republic era, so that the overall impression one receives is of increased prominence not only of urban lower-class but also of rural life-styles.

Surprisingly, there was no significant difference in the occupations portrayed for men or women in the two sets of Persian language textbooks. Among males, intellectuals were the focus in 36–40 percent of the lessons portraying any occupation in both the Pahlavi and the Islamic Republican textbooks. Blue-collar workers dominated about 6 percent of such lessons, and agriculturalists about 27 percent (Table 10). As noted above, there was a similar lack of change in the occupations in which women were employed (Table 8). Here again, our conclusions are modified somewhat when we consider the other textbooks. The math textbooks of the Islamic Republic era, for example, use men at work, including shopkeepers, tailors, factory workers, and fishermen, as a focus for word problems.

While there is little difference in the number and range of the occupations portrayed in the Persian language textbooks of the two eras, the class background of families featured in the textbooks is quite different. In the Pahlavi era first graders read about an urban middle-class family. Father wears a suit and tie at home (although his occupation is unspecified) and mother wears western-style dress. The children go to a coeducational (and therefore private) elementary school. The family eats at a table, sits on chairs and couches, and cooks on a built-in four-burner stove, and sick children sleep in beds. In the Islamic Republican textbook father does not wear a jacket or tie, and he is identified as a mason. His friends include a carpenter and a painter, and his brother is a gardener. The children go to sex-segregated elementary schools,

TABLE 9
Setting by Period

	Pahlavi Era		Islamic Republic Era	
Rural	49	(28%)	48	(32%)
Urban	81	(47%)	53	(35%)
Ancient	28	(16%)	25	(17%)
Other	16	(9%)	25	(17%)
Total	174		151	

Chi-square = 6.41, df = 3, significance 0.09

TABLE 10
Occupation of Males by Period

	Pahlavi Era		Islamic Republic Era	
Intellectual	36	(40%)	33	(36%)
Blue collar	6	(7%)	5	(6%)
Agricultural	25	(27%)	24	(26%)
Armed forces	13	(14%)	8	(9%)
Traditional	11	(12%)	21	(23%)
Total	91		91	

Chi-square = 4.56, df = 4, significance 0.3358

and mother and daughter both wear the Islamically modest scarf, pants, and long-sleeved tunic. The family eats, drinks tea, and visits on the floor, where the children also do their homework, and the mother cooks on a one-burner Aladdin heater. A similar contrast is seen in the first-grade science textbook, in which the middle-class family of the Pahlavi era has been replaced by a small-town or rural family in the Islamic Republican era.

CONCLUSION

Based on our comparative analysis of the elementary texts in use in 1969–1970 and those in use in 1986–1987, we agree with previous studies that the most pervasive changes are in their Islamicization. Such Islamicization goes considerably beyond strengthening the content of the Islamic studies textbooks and changing the dress in the pictures. Our analysis has shown that a substantial proportion of the lessons in the Persian language textbooks of the Islamic Republican era are directly concerned with Islam, and that many of the minor revisions also involve religious concepts and values. In these and other Persian language lessons there is also more focus on Arabic language and literature in the Islamic Republican era than there was in the Pahlavi era.

At the same time, both pre-Islamic Iranian culture and heritage and those of the West receive less attention in the newer textbooks than they did during the Pahlavi era. Changes in the sex-role ideologies supported by the two governments and in their social-class orientations are also reflected in the textbooks through dress and furnishings and the life-styles of the primary characters, although there is no change in the frequency of portrayal of different occupations for males or females.

While most of our expectations concerning frequency of reference to these topics were upheld, the shifts we anticipated between positive and negative references were not. Islam was never referred to negatively in the Pahlavi-era Persian language textbooks; it was simply ignored. Similarly, pre-Islamic customs and even western culture are not referred to negatively in the elementary Persian language texts of the Islamic Republic; they too are either ignored or Islamicized. There are some negative references to western values and pre-Islamic institutions in the social studies textbooks, but negative treatment in the Persian language textbooks is reserved for the Pahlavis, and even then only in the higher elementary grades. This is in contrast to the highly negative characterization of the West and westernized Iranians reported for secondary social studies textbooks (Mehran 1989).

Our analysis has also shown that there are many continuities between the elementary textbooks of the Pahlavi era and those of the Islamic Republic, in subject matter, style, and teaching methods, as well as in specific content. Nor did either set of textbooks reflect all aspects of the respective state ideologies concerning Iranian identity. The Islamic Republican Persian language textbooks stress the distinctively Shi'a features of Islam, for example, in contrast to the pan-Islamic pronouncements of Islamic Republican leaders. The Pahlavi-era textbooks did not give equal space to females, and they portrayed women in a very narrow range of occupations outside the home, despite the Pahlavi government's stated support for gender equality. Similarly, the Islamic Republican textbooks do not portray many more working-class occupations than did the Pahlavi textbooks, although they do give more prominence to working-class families.

Returning to the child in the classroom, it seems clear from comparing the textbooks of the two eras that those of the Islamic Republic, with their focus on lower-middle-class life-styles and their portrayal of fewer and simpler material goods, are likely to strike a more responsive chord in a large proportion of Iranian children. This is especially true of those children who have access to few other reading materials, and therefore less opportunity to discover alternate models with which they might identify. On-site research with Iranian children will be necessary to determine whether they do experience a greater sense of familiarity and easier identification with the textbook characters and whether this carries over into a stronger allegiance to the symbols and substance of the Islamic Republican regime.

REFERENCES

Akhavi, Shahrough. 1980. *Religion and Politics in Contemporary Iran: Clergy State Relations in the Pahlavi Period*. Albany: State University of New York Press.

———. 1987. "Elite Factionalism in the Islamic Republic of Iran." *Middle East Journal* 41: 181–201.

Algar, Hamid, trans. 1980. *Constitution of the Islamic Republic of Iran*. Berkeley, Calif.: Mizan Press.

Arasteh, A. Reza. 1969. *Education and Social Awakening in Iran: 1850–1968*. Rev. ed. Leiden: E. J. Brill.

Behdad, Sohrab. 1989. "Winners and Losers of the Iranian Revolution: A Study in Income Distribution." *International Journal of Middle East Studies* 21(3): 327–358.

Cottam, Richard W. 1978. *Nationalism in Iran: Updated through 1978*. Pittsburgh: University of Pittsburgh Press.

Echo of Islam. 1986a. "Educational Reforms and Innovations." *Echo of Islam* 6(2): 18–20.

———. 1986b. "Educational System of the Islamic Republic of Iran." *Echo of Islam* 6(1): 34–38.

Ferdows, Adele. 1985. "The Status and Rights of Women in Ithna 'Ashari Shi'i Islam." In Asghar Fathi, ed., *Women and the Family in Iran* (Leiden: E. J. Brill), pp. 13–36.

Filstrup, J. M. 1976. "Franklin Book Program/Tehran." *International Library Review* 8: 431–450.

Fischer, Michael M. J. 1978. "On Changing the Concept and Position of Persian Women." In Lois Beck and Nikki Keddie, eds., *Women in Muslim Society* (Cambridge, Mass.: Harvard University Press), pp. 189–215.

———. 1980. *Iran: From Religious Dispute to Revolution*. Cambridge, Mass.: Harvard University Press.

Haeri, Shahla. 1980. "Women, Law, and Social Change in Iran." In Jane I. Smith, ed., *Women in Contemporary Muslim Societies* (Lewisburg, Pa.: Bucknell University Press), pp. 209–234.

Hendershot, Clarence. 1975. *Politics, Polemics, and Pedagogs*. New York: Vantage Press.

Higgins, Patricia J. 1976. "The Conflict of Acculturation and Enculturation in Suburban Elementary Schools of Tehran." *Journal of Research and Development in Education* 9(4): 102–112.

———. 1984. "Minority-State Relations in Contemporary Iran." *Iranian Studies* 17: 37–71.

Higgins, Patricia J., and Pirouz Shoar-Ghaffari. 1991. "Sex Role Socialization in Iranian Textbooks." *NWSA Journal* (forthcoming).

Hussain, Asaf. 1985. *Islamic Iran: Revolution and Counter-revolution.* New York: St. Martin's Press.

Iran Ministry of Education. 1968. "Educational Aims and the New System of Education in Iran." Publication 57 (mimeographed). Tehran: Department of Planning and Research.

———. 1972. "Educational Statistics in Iran." (In Persian.) Tehran.

———. 1977. "Summary of Educational Statistics for 1976–77." (In Persian.) Tehran.

Iran Statistical Center. 1992. *Iran Statistical Yearbook 1369* (March 1990–March 1991). Tehran.

Karimi, Setareh. 1986. "Economic Policies and Structural Changes since the Revolution." In Nikki R. Keddie and Eric Hooglund, eds., *The Iranian Revolution and the Islamic Republic* (Syracuse, N.Y.: Syracuse University Press), pp. 32–54.

Keddie, Nikki R. 1985. "Islamic Revivalism Past and Present, with Emphasis on Iran." In Barry M. Rosen, ed., *Iran since the Revolution: Internal Dynamics, Regional Conflict, and the Superpowers* (Boulder, Colo.: Social Science Monographs), pp. 3–19.

Kumar, Krishna. 1988. "The Origins of India's Textbook Culture." In Philip G. Altbach and Gail P. Kelly, eds., *Textbooks in the Third World: Policy, Content, and Context* (New York: Garland Publishing), pp. 97–112.

Kwong, Julia. 1988. "Curriculum in Action: Mathematics in China's Elementary Schools." In Philip G. Altbach and Gail P. Kelly, eds., *Textbooks in the Third World: Policy, Content, and Context* (New York: Garland Publishing), pp. 227–245.

Matini, Jalal. 1989. "The Impact of the Islamic Revolution on Education in Iran." In Adnan Badran, ed., *At the Crossroads: Education in the Middle East* (New York: Paragon House), pp. 43–55.

Mbuyi, Dennis. 1988. "Language and Texts in Africa." In Philip G. Altbach and Gail P. Kelly, eds., *Textbooks in the Third World: Policy, Content, and Context* (New York: Garland Publishing), pp. 167–201.

Mehran, Golnar. 1988. "The Creation of the New Muslim Woman: Female Education in the Islamic Republic of Iran." Paper presented at the Middle East Studies Association Annual Meeting, November.

———. 1989. "Socialization of Schoolchildren in the Islamic Republic of Iran." *Iranian Studies* 22(1): 35–50.

———. 1990. "Ideology and Education in the Islamic Republic of Iran." *Compare* 20(1): 53–65.

Menashri, David. 1982. "The Shah and Khomeini: Conflicting Nationalisms." *Crossroads* 8: 53–79.

Moghadam, Val. 1988. "Women, Work, and Ideology in the Islamic Republic." *International Journal of Middle East Studies* 20(2): 221–243.

Mohsenpour, Barham. 1988. "Philosophy of Education in Postrevolutionary Iran." *Comparative Education Review* 32: 76–86.

Naficy, Hamid. 1981. "Cinema as a Political Instrument." In Michael E. Bonine and Nikki Keddie, eds., *Continuity and Change in Modern Iran* (Albany: State University of New York Press), pp. 265–283.

Nafisi, Rasool. 1992. "Education and the Culture of Politics in the Islamic Republic of Iran." In Samih K. Farsoun and Mehrdad Mashayekh, eds., *Iran: Political Culture in the Islamic Republic* (London: Routledge), pp. 166–177.

Najmabadi, Afsaneh. 1987. "Iran's Turn to Islam: From Modernism to Moral Order." *Middle East Journal* 41: 202–217.

Nashat, Guity. 1980. "Women in the Islamic Republic of Iran." *Iranian Studies* 13(1–4).

———. 1983. "Women in the Ideology of the Islamic Republic." In Guity Nashat, ed., *Women and Revolution in Iran* (Boulder, Colo.: Westview Press), pp. 195–216.

Pahlavi, Mohammad Reza. 1967. *The White Revolution.* Tehran: Pahlavi Library.

Parsa, Mohammad. 1979. "A Qualitative Study of Public and Guidance Cycle Education in Iran." *International Education* 9: 7–11.

Ramazani, Rouhollah K. 1987. "Revolutionary Iran's Open-door Policy." *Harvard International Review* 9: 11–15.

Richard, Yann. 1989. "The Relevance of 'Nationalism' in Contemporary Iran." *Middle East Review* 21(4): 27–36.

Saleh, A. P., trans. 1966. "Constitution of Iran: The Constitutional Law of December 30, 1906." *Constitutions of Nations.* The Hague: Martinus Nijtoff.

Sanasarian, Eliz. 1982. *The Women's Rights Movement in Iran: Mutiny, Appeasement, and Repression.* New York: Praeger.

Shorish, M. Mobin. 1988. "The Islamic Revolution and Education in Iran." *Comparative Educational Review* 32: 58–75.

Street, Brian. 1975. "The Mullah, the Shahname, and the Madrasseh." *Asian Affairs* 62: 290–306.

Szyliowicz, Joseph S. 1973. *Education and Modernization in the Middle East.* Ithaca, N.Y.: Cornell University Press.

Tehranian, Majid. 1980. "Communication and Revolution in Iran: The Passing of a Paradigm." *Iranian Studies* 13(1–4): 5–30.

Touba, Jacquiline Rudolph. 1987. "Cultural Effects on Sex Role Images in Elementary School Books in Iran: A Content Analysis after the Revolution." *International Journal of Sociology of the Family* 17(1): 143–158.

Zonis, Marvin. 1985. "The Rule of the Clerics in the Islamic Republic of Iran." *Annals of the American Academy of Political and Social Science* 482: 85–108.

Palestinian orphans in summer camp, near Amman, Jordan
PHOTO BY HEATHER LOGAN TAYLOR

PART VI

CHILDREN, POLITICS, AND WAR

When you fell, you said, oh master,
oh pardon, oh lord, I am only a young boy.

EGYPTIAN LAMENT FOR A CHILD WHO HAS DIED

Islamic law provides that certain rights should be granted to children, such as food, clothing, and shelter, as well as the right to a guardian who will protect his or her property and other interests until the time of puberty. Maryam Elahi points out in "The Rights of the Child under Islamic Law: Prohibition of the Child Soldier" that children should be altogether under continuous supervision until the time of puberty and are prohibited from participating in war or conflict until they are at least fifteen. Yet the exigencies of everyday life make children part of public life, including hostilities, despite their subordinated condition. Children participated in protests and uprisings long before the end of colonial rule, in the early twentieth century, serving as message bearers, for example, from Turkey to Egypt to the Algerian revolution from 1955 to 1962. Direct documentation of more recent participation in Middle East conflicts is given by Kari Karamé in "Girls' Participation in Combat: A Case Study from Lebanon." Hoda al-Namani's poem pays tribute to the boys and girls who helped perpetrate and continue the Intifada, or uprising against Israeli governance, by Palestinians on the West Bank and in the Gaza Strip.

Evelyn Early describes the way the Syrian Baath political party has incorporated local cultural heritage into its political program for youth. And Farhad Khosrokhavar shows that the Iranian revolution of 1979 has had unexpected effects upon young people. His research among teenagers suggested that to young people the Iranian revolution represents not a return to tradition but a radically different Islamic modernity.

Today, more and more young Muslims throughout the Middle East are seeing the future in Islamic terms and establishing a new identity and purpose for themselves as part of that reinvigorated religious discourse.

Children taking part in election campaign, Amman, Jordan
PHOTO BY THOMAS HARTWELL

THE RIGHTS OF THE CHILD
UNDER ISLAMIC LAW:
PROHIBITION OF THE
CHILD SOLDIER

by Maryam Elahi

In recent years, the frequency of children's participation as combatants in armed conflicts has risen at an alarming rate. According to a 1988 UNICEF report, "[c]hildren are currently the victims of armed conflict in almost 50 countries of the world—and children and women typically comprise three quarters or more of the victims." Children are readily being used to supply the manpower for armies and insurgency movements around the world—in Iran, El Salvador, Vietnam, Mozambique, Nicaragua, Cambodia, Uganda, Guatemala, and other regions of violent confrontation. In 1988, the United Nations estimated that there were approximately 200,000 "child soldiers" in the world. With the massive induction of children into military activity there come large numbers of child casualties. The Islamic Republic of Iran alone has lost hundreds of thousands of child inductees to the eight-year-old Iran-Iraq War. These children were, for the most part, frontline combatants.

This essay examines the rights of children under Islamic law. It first reviews the protection prescribed for children in the classical sources of Islamic law, particularly with regard to their participation as combatants in war. It then discusses the recruitment of children for the Iranian Army with particular focus on the state structure enabling the Muslim jurists to defer Iran's obligations under international human rights law. In the final analysis, the chapter concludes that the use of children in armed conflict is in direct contravention of the fundamental sources of Islamic law.[1]

This is an abridged version of an article published in *Columbia Human Rights Law Review* 19, no. 2 (Spring 1988). For a more in-depth discussion and sources, please refer to the original.

CLASSICAL SOURCES OF ISLAMIC LAW

The two general sects within Islam are the Sunnis and the Shias. Sunni jurists consider the four primary sources of jurisprudence (*usul ul-fiqh*) to be the Quran (words of God as revealed to the Prophet Muhammad), the Sunna of the Prophet (Muhammad's words, deeds, and customs), ijma (consensus among Muslim jurists on a particular issue), and qiyas (reasoning by analogy). The Shia community, in general, holds the primary sources for the Shari'a to be the Quran, the Sunna of Muhammad, and the Sunna of the Imams, who the Shias believe were the divinely inspired descendants of Muhammad.

The Quran contains the scriptures of Islam. Muslims believe it to be the words of God as revealed to Muhammad and follow its tenets with absolute conviction. The 114 chapters (*suras*) within the Quran were delivered in a period of twenty-three years, from when Muhammad was called upon to lead the community in the path of God until Muhammad's death.

The Quran is not a legal treatise. It is primarily a declaration of social and economic values. In fact, only 190 verses (out of a total of 6,237) address any legal issues. Yet, Muslims believe that the governing rules for all social interactions are to be found within the Quran, and that law, politics, and religion are inseparable. Therefore, since the Quran supersedes all other sources of law, it is fundamental to the drafting of a constitution or legal code in a Muslim community to search within the Quran for provisions which can legitimize the establishment of social and legal obligations.

The second source of Islamic law, the Sunna, is a collection of narrative stories (*hadith*) discussing the customs and sayings of Muhammad. The Sunna derives its legitimacy as an irrefutable source of Islamic law from passages in the Quran that affirm Muhammad's authority as the messenger of God and a leader (in religious as well as in political terms) of the Muslim community.

The third source of Islamic law in Sunni jurisprudence is ijma, or consensus by learned Muslim jurists (*mujtahed* or *faqih*) on a particular issue of law. The authority of ijma as a source of law is derived specifically from a hadith that states that "my community will never agree in error." This hadith has been interpreted to imply that the opinion of mujtaheds should be sought and followed in order to resolve points of conflict or questions of law. According to one school of Muslim thought, ijma is the most significant tool for change within the fundamental sources of Islamic law since it allows the Shari'a to respond to the changing needs and demands of society while remaining within the framework of Islamic principles.

The fourth primary source of law for the Sunni community is qiyas. Qiyas is the use of analogy by jurists to resolve issues not addressed in the Quran and the Sunna. In order for the application of qiyas to be valid, it must be proven that its reasoning is derived from a Quranic verse or the Sunna.

The distinction between the legal structure of Sunni Islam and that of Shia Islam is rooted in their historical differences and methods of extrapolating laws from the original sources. A method of legal derivation which is generally used within the Shia communities as well as the Sunni is ijtihad. Ijtihad, or legal reasoning by a mujtahed, through the use of his own reasoning and based on the Quran or Sunna, is used to interpret the texts and decide on points of law. Ijtihad is distinct from qiyas in that no use of analogy is allowed in Shiism since it is believed that analogy could distort the meaning of the original texts.

In Shiism, the training and credentials of the faqihs are of utmost importance since they have the capacity for individually interpreting the Quran and drafting legislation in conformity with Islam. According to Shia doctrine, the faqihs who extrapolate laws from the primary sources are not infallible or divinely inspired; rather, they have acquired their status through rigorous years of learning such that they have an in-depth knowledge of the Quran and Sunna and are able to verify the authenticity of the hadith. The role of the faqih is to deliver legal opinions (*fatwahs*) based on the usul ul-fiqh with regard to specific factual cases or questions. Law as it develops through fatwahs never attains the unimpeachable status of the primary sources and may be revoked at a later point.

The variations in Islamic practice and legal systems are due to the influence of the cultural contexts in which Islam took shape. The clergy in Iran has traditionally played a significant role vis-à-vis the state in fostering the society's norms and values. The high-ranking mujtaheds are the "source for emulation" (*marjah taqlid*) for the entire Shia community and act as the vice-regent for the Twelfth Imam during this waiting period (called *intizar* or "complete occultation"). Therefore, distinctive to Shiism in Iran, the doctrine of the Imamate invalidates any secular leadership over the Muslim community, thereby *de facto* establishing the faqihs as the legitimate source of legal authority.

THE CONCEPT OF CHILDREN AND WAR UNDER THE CLASSICAL SOURCES OF THE SHARI'A

CHILDREN'S RIGHTS IN ISLAM

The concept of children's rights is based on provisions within the Quran and the Sunna and is therefore applicable to all sects within Islam. The importance of children as a class unto themselves is derived from Quranic provisions as well as the Muslim tradition of holding the family as the focal unit within the community. Although childhood is not explicitly defined, the predominant view is that social responsibilities attach to individuals upon puberty, which is often held to be the age of fifteen.[2] The protection due to children, therefore, should apply at least up to that age.

The primary sources of Islam have been interpreted to extend a diverse set of rights to children. For example, the infant is entitled to food, clothing, and shelter; and it is the duty of the father to provide the mother with the essential materials for the child's survival and development. If the infant's father is dead or incapable of providing for the child, and if the child has no inherited property, then it becomes the duty of the child's grandfather and other relatives to provide for him. During infancy, it is the duty of the mother to take care of the child. If the mother is incapable of doing so or if she is judged to be unfit to fulfill her duties, then it is the duty of the closest female relative, preferably on the mother's side, to take care of the child. Once the child is beyond infant years and physically less dependent on the parents, she or he must be guided by a spiritual guardian who is usually a relative on the father's side. In the case of the male child, if he manifests maturity upon puberty, the spiritual guardianship terminates. Otherwise, the guardianship is retained until a later time when it is noted that the child can act responsibly. In the case of the female child, the guardianship is retained until marriage and is generally resumed upon divorce.

In addition, the child has a right to a guardian who will protect his or her property interests. The guardian who undertakes the protection of the child's financial matters is normally his father or whoever the father appoints. The guardianship over the child's property terminates when the child reaches puberty, contingent upon the child's showing of maturity in dealing with financial matters.[3] The sanctity of this guardianship and the obligation of an adult to attend to a child's best interests are rooted in scripture. The Quran has express commandments regarding the obligation to protect the property of minors until they come of age. Moreover, the Quran explicitly discusses the inheritance rights of children.

The duties of a guardian extend to all commercial interests of the child. Under Islamic law, a minor does not have the capacity to make a contract, especially if the contract is "entirely to his own disadvantage." If there is doubt as to whether the contract is to the advantage or disadvantage of the child, then a guardian's approval is necessary prior to the conclusion of the contract. Finally, children are denied the Muslim rights of granting immunity from harm (*aman*) and pledging security to non-Muslims (*dhimmis*) within their community.[4] Under the laws of Islam, children are altogether under continuous supervision and are not allowed to make any serious decisions until it is evident that they are old enough to be cognizant of and responsible for the consequences of their acts.

Despite the aforementioned provisions in the primary sources of the Shari'a, the Islamic Republic of Iran has yet to define and enforce the rights of children.[5] The sole article of the Iranian Constitution which makes a marginal reference to children's rights is under the provisions for the protection of women: "The government . . . shall provide for . . . protection of mothers, especially during pregnancy and the childrearing period, as well as the protection of children without guardians . . . [and for the g]ranting of guardianship to fit mothers, to protect those children who have no legal guardian."[6] The Constitution also states that all subjects of the Islamic Republic of Iran shall enjoy "human, political, economic and cultural rights according to Islamic standards."[7] The fulfillment of this article would require, at the very least, the official recognition of the special status of children by implementing their rights in accordance with Islamic standards through legislation and policy.

REQUISITES FOR PARTICIPATION IN WAR

The concept of holy war (*jihad*) is central to Islamic political ideology for it is justified on the grounds of its necessity to sustain, defend, and expand the Muslim community. It is the duty of the leader of the Muslim community to declare jihad and call upon believers to fight in the path of Islam. The jihadist must be male, sane, mature, economically independent, and strong. Muhammad had excused children from participating until the age of fifteen. He also forbade the killing or molesting, *inter alia,* of women, infants, and minors. The Shafiite school of law holds that youngsters cannot participate in jihad unless they have their parents' permission. This opinion is based on a hadith which relates an incident where Muhammad sent a young jihadist back home from the warfront to attain his parents' approval. Another hadith tells of a time when Muhammad would not allow a young follower, Ibn-Umar, to fight in the Battle of Uhud at a time when he was fourteen, but in one year's time allowed him to participate in another jihad. Children were therefore categorically not permitted to participate in jihad.

These standards with regard to the age of the participants in jihad were adhered to during a period when Islam was in its most critical stages of development and Muhammad was in desperate need of a strong army to establish and ensure the stability of the Islamic state. Therefore, any contemporary Muslim nation, despite a state of emergency, internal strife, or war, is bound to follow these standards. The two most fundamental sources of the Shari'a recognize the especially vulnerable position of children and strictly forbid their participation in jihad even though it is generally considered to be a Muslim's religious obligation. An analysis of the Quran and the Sunna leads to the conclusion that the age requirement for participating in jihad is fifteen, contingent upon the further manifestation of maturity.

GOVERNANCE BY THE JURIST
IN A CONTEMPORARY SHIITE STATE

The 1979 revolution in Iran led to the adoption of a legal and sociopolitical framework based exclusively on the faqihs' understanding of Islam. A council of Muslim jurists, the Supreme Judicial Council, was set up to review and revise the prerevolutionary civil and criminal codes and to draft a Shia constitution. The new constitution was adopted in 1979 and the new codes were ratified by the National Assembly in 1982. Under the new constitution, the Shari'a prevails not only in all national realms but also in any international matter in which Iran is concerned.

Iran maintains that it will abide by international human rights treaties only in cases in which they are judged to be consistent in substance with Islamic law. In 1987, the Permanent Mission of the Islamic Republic of Iran presented its official position to the United Nations Commission on Human Rights by stating that the Islamic Republic of Iran was adhering to the articles within the two international covenants on human rights that were clearly consistent with Islamic principles until a future time when the Iranian Parliament would determine the compatibility of the covenants in their entirety.[8]

The Islamic Republic of Iran called the war with Iraq a jihad, and encouraged all Iranians to fight against the threat to Islam and welcome martyrdom. Although the official drafting age in the Islamic Republic of Iran was eighteen, younger boys were recruited and children as young as nine were used as cannon fodder and mine sweepers in the war with Iraq.[9] According to one account, more than 100,000 Iranian schoolchildren were sent off to the warfront in 1985.[10] A 1984 Anti-Slavery Society report based on International Red Cross estimates announced that more than 50,000 Iranian children had been killed in the war and approximately 2,000 were being held as prisoners of war in camps in Iraq. Several Iranian child POWs in Iraqi camps, when interviewed by a CBS news reporter, claimed that they had no idea what the war was about or where the gunfire was coming from.[11] Iranian officials captured by the Iraqis have stated that 90 percent of the Iranian child soldiers had been killed because they were purposely placed in highly vulnerable positions without any weapons or were forced to undertake suicide attacks.[12]

In 1983, the *International Children's Rights Monitor* reported that Iranian children are heavily indoctrinated into volunteering for the army, are misled with regard to their functions at the front, and, once there, are threatened with death if they refuse to charge into the mine fields.[13] According to a correspondent for the *New York Times,* the children are often bound together by rope to prevent any who faint or have a change of heart from leaving.[14] One Iranian newspaper, *Ettala'at,* reported that the children sometimes "wrapped themselves in blankets, rolling themselves across the mine field, so that the fragments of their bodies would not scatter."[15] Their objective is to become martyrs. The government's objective is to clear the fields for the tanks.

The concept of martyrdom is a hallmark of Shiism and the regime has nurtured this sentiment to such a degree that the calling for jihad has become tantamount to the calling for martyrdom. The children, having been given "keys to paradise," are promised that they will go directly to heaven if they become martyrs.[16] In October 1982, Khomeini declared a fatwah permitting child volunteers to enlist in the army without even notifying their parents.[17] This fatwah is in direct violation of the primary sources of the Shari'a which strictly forbid the participation of children in jihad.

CONCLUSION

Provisions within Islam have been construed to hold that children have the right to be under the protection of a guardian, to be financially provided for, and to be spiritually guided. They are forbidden from being a party to a contract, from giving pledges of safety to non-Muslims, and from managing their own financial matters, until the age of fifteen. At that time, they must manifest the required mental maturity to take control of their own resources. Children also are prohibited from participating in war until they are at least fifteen, provided further that they are capable of comprehending the severity of their commitment.

The phenomenon of the child jihadist in the Iranian Army is in direct violation of the Quran and the Sunna, the two most authoritative sources of Islamic law. A jurist is entitled to interpret the primary sources of Islam, not to alter them, and any opinion inconsistent with the Sunna and the Quran cannot become a part of the corpus of the Shari'a. Therefore, the recruitment and employment of children as combatants in the Iranian Army cannot be justified on the basis of Islamic law. Iran should acknowledge and implement the rights of children as expressed in these fundamental sources in order to conform to explicit commandments within Islamic jurisprudence.

NOTES

1. It is beyond the scope of this essay to assess whether Iran is indeed fighting a holy war (jihad), as is argued by the Islamic government of Iran. *Boston Globe,* February 11, 1987.

2. A minority of Islamic schools of thought maintain the age of majority to be twelve years for boys and nine for girls, if puberty is reached at that age.

3. In determining the "coming of age" of the child to handle his or her own financial matters, actual age is far less important than the child's manifestation of maturity. In Egypt, where family law is based on the Shari'a, it is only at the age of twenty-one that a youth is given control of his or her property and finances. Abu Zahra, "Family Law," in M. Khadduri and H. Liebesny, eds., *Law in the Middle East* (Washington, D.C.: Middle East Institute, 1955), p. 157.

4. M. Khadduri, *The Law of War and Peace in Islam* (Baltimore: Johns Hopkins Press, 1940), p. 70. It is evident that in Islam, children as a class are prohibited from making serious decisions. With the exclusion of children, all Muslims, regardless of sex, race, social, or political background, have the right to give aman to a dhimmi. Khadduri, *loc cit.*

5. In recent years, widespread violations of children's rights have been reported in *The Abuse of Human Rights in Iran* (London: House of Commons, Parliamentary Human Rights Group, 1986), pp. 41–45. See also "Unabated Gross Violations of Children's Rights in Iran," *International Children's Rights Monitor,* Spring 1983, p. 16; "Iran Chronology of Childhood Lost," *International Children's Rights Monitor,* Autumn 1983, p. 5.

6. Constitution of the Islamic Republic of Iran, article 21.

7. Ibid., article 20.

8. 44 United Nations ESCOR Annex 1, Agenda Item 12, p. 8, UN Doc. E/ CN.4/Sub.2/1987/35 (1987).

9. *Abuse of Human Rights in Iran,* p. 41.

10. "Iran's Spurious Holy War," *Washington Post,* October 5, 1986.

11. "A Decent Respect . . . ," *New York Times,* April 26, 1984.

12. "The Child Soldiers of the Ayatollahs," *Economist,* September 17, 1983, p. 34.

13. "Unabated Gross Violations."

14. *New York Times Magazine,* February 12, 1984, p. 21.

15. "West Threatens Child Convention," *Human Rights Internet Reporter* 12 (Winter 1988): 109.

16. *New York Times Magazine,* February 12, 1984, p. 21.

17. Irandokhte, "Children of War in Iran," in *Children and War* (Geneva: Geneva International Peace Research Institute, 1983), p. 97.

CHILDREN OF FIRE
(Ribat al-Fatah)

by Hoda al-Namani
Translated by Najib Mokhtari and
Christopher Middleton

A little girl of fire
Has come to the citadel
Which gave to the mountain its name;
She takes to the stone,
They name her rebel.

The children will not be famed.
They fight the ceiling of silk
Embroidered with wheels from Persia;
Theirs is their pride, their justice
To kindle the flame from ashes.

With water the ashes had been doused
Till like the sun their patience dwindled;
The thresher blades had been honed
To spare time's hands, like golden dishes
Never to be worn down.

All others dead and gone—
No more prophet's warriors.
Pistachio trees drip blood
From the fallen, from the mutilated
Who never gave up faith.
A dream had led them on,
They jumped on trotting horses,
Rode out to strike the foe.

This poem was read in Washington, D.C., in 1988.

375

Indomitable they fought,
Unfamed they fight
And are for us a bridge
Across the water we could drown in.

———————

As if from earth they came, remade,
A fresh circlet round a wrist,
The children of fire, myriads of them,
A bridge mirrored on the water
And us, from stone shall we be reborn?

A marble surface
Veined, like a breast or an arm,
Furrowed and dappled by time,
By thunder sculptured,
Bestowing milky pearls and jasmine
As gifts from death.

———————

Ah Jerusalem, above you
God's sublime countenance unfolds,
Life streams inside the rock
Bethlehem purifies the human faces
No wonder their faith is growing stronger,
For it is worship to enter the rock,
To enter the cave is to dance
And sing holy songs.

God who told us to stand up,
Poison him if you will, our house
Still stands, and pollution
Is the religion of desire, though
Frozen water shines pure,
Sparkles like the lightning Alborak!

For three days a guest is king,
But when the hand, when the host
That welcomed him
Is gone, what then? Bells in hand,
Through Sacred Night you run;
For all your fine words,
You inhabit the depths of hell.

———————

Torn from us the land, from the land
We have been torn. Yet even now,
Sculptured on our foreheads
The stone, like radiance
From the moon, means sweetness:
An avowal in that outline—
Arabs we are, we are Gabriel
With the book of the sun in his hand,
Jesus cries out, his cry spills honey
This is the promise,
And our disgrace will become
The world in madness,
If ever we mistreat them:

The fire—children
Like Ribat al-Fatah,
Who choose the stone,
Whose name is rebel,
Rebel, word of smoke,
But secret, like God,
Like God a wonder.

GIRLS' PARTICIPATION
IN COMBAT: A CASE STUDY
FROM LEBANON

by Kari H. Karamé

A number of young women and girls (around 300) have taken direct part in the combat in Lebanon, mainly on the Christian side, fighting either in one of three female units or in mixed troops. They come from different social backgrounds and different educational levels, but are united in a common cause: the defense of their country. The military engagement was a rupture with the traditional role of the Lebanese woman as subordinate and mainly restricted to the domestic area. This has influenced their relations with their parents, friends, the educational system, and with global society. In the female units one can isolate tendencies pointing toward general conclusions about female behavior in combat. However, their cause has remained national; they have not engaged themselves in women's rights or in politics on a broader level.

On April 13, 1975, the war in Lebanon broke out, and at the time of this writing, fourteen years later, it continues unabated. During these years the country has gone through profound transformations culturally, socially, and economically. It has been divided, and this has also been the fate of the capital, Beirut. A great number of its inhabitants have been forced to flee their homes and find themselves today refugees in their own country, and others have moved more or less temporarily away from the frontlines to relatively safer areas. At the same time there has been a clear tendency toward a reinforcement of some of the aspects of what we could call traditional folk culture, for instance, the place and influence of religion and the family in everyday life. Those aspects constitute some of the few stabilizing factors in a constantly moving and insecure world.

The majority of the population has tried heroically to adapt to the ever-changing situation, which has been marked by the violence of war and terror, and some longer periods of relative calm. Work should be attended to, the home and family kept together as much as possible, and the children helped through an often irregular education. A small but so important amount of recreation should also find its place within ever narrower geographical and economic limits.

Others have chosen a more active form of resistance and have joined one of the many militia groups. Already during the last years before the outbreak of the war, which often witnessed conflicts between different groups, many men and also many women and girls had learned to use weapons. Many also bought their own hand weapons with the aim of defending their lives and property. As time went on, these rather spontaneous groups changed into voluntary, organized forces, most of them composed of young men. But some young women also chose the same path and have actively taken part in combat instead of restricting themselves to the more traditional female activities in war: medical service, communication, etc. This phenomenon is, above all, known among the Christian militia, where one could count three female units during the first part of the war (1975–1976), two of which are still active as groups today, though under other auspices and with other aims, as will be shown in the following account. In all, around 3,000 young women have received extended military training during the war, and 250 to 300 of them have actively taken part in the fighting over a substantial period, most of them in one of the female units and some in mixed troops, side by side with fathers, uncles, brothers, cousins, and neighbors.

The purpose of this essay is to give a presentation of these girls, their reasons for choosing military participation as a means to defend their cause, and further, the implications of this choice for other aspects of their lives, like their relations with family, friends, and society as a whole. As their taking part in combat has been voluntary, and as most of them have joined female units, this has had a great influence on their behavior. It would therefore be interesting to see if it is possible to draw the outlines of female behavior in this connection. It is also necessary to ask whether their military engagement has resulted in political engagement on a broader level than simply patriotism.

Who then are these young women? They were born between 1950 and 1965, with a concentration in the years 1957 to 1962. The large majority were very young when the war started, and age is certainly a factor that influenced their choice, though there are examples of married women fighting shoulder by shoulder with their husbands. The youngest was eleven years old when she first received military training. She and her sister, who was then thirteen years old, were taken by their father to a training session. Certainly he did not realize that this was the beginning of an engagement that would last for so many years.

Most of the girls were born close to the demarcation line, on either side of the line, which stretches from downtown Beirut to Araya in the lower mountains east of the capital. Others come from other fronts, like Chekka and Batroun in the north, and Bickfaya and Zahle in the Beqa'a Valley to the south. This indicates that living near the areas of fighting constituted a decisive factor for these women, because they felt directly attacked. But others come from villages in areas far from the front and, until recently, considered safe; so proximity cannot be considered an exclusive reason for joining the fighting.

Concerning their social background (using the father's profession as a basis), there is striking variety. The fathers cover a range from physician and lawyer to peasant and daily worker. The majority of the mothers do not work outside the home. Social background does not seem to have been important in this connection. It should be noted, though, that a rather large number of the girls come from lower-middle- and middle-class levels of society.

Where did they get their sense of patriotic engagement? They could of course have been influenced by the political background of their parents or by their social surroundings. The fathers are often politically engaged, whether a member of a party or not. The mothers seldom show political interest, but are often open to patriotic engagement. Both parents will usually accept their sons' engagement, but are more reluctant concerning their daughters' doing the same. The girls have consequently received little support either for developing their political interests or for their military engagement. Some parents were so opposed to what their daughters were doing that the girls had to hide their military activities and pretend that they were attending to some "innocent" tasks far behind the lines. It was certainly easier for the girls whose parents were engaged in the same cause, but this again cannot be considered a decisive factor, because many girls obtained permission to participate in combat from parents who were engaged neither in a political nor a patriotic way, even if they were reluctant (for reasons I will come back to) to see their daughters join the armed forces. On the other hand, parents who were themselves involved sometimes refused the idea of having a daughter on the front line, and these girls would then be obliged to hide their activities.

The years before the war witnessed a growing political engagement among the Lebanese, especially among the younger generation. Some of the more grown-up girls included in this study had become members of one of the political parties, most frequently the Kataëb Party. Others joined the parties later on, but started their engagement as a purely patriotic one. All of them felt directly threatened and wanted to defend their civilization, their way of living, their country. This last term encompasses for them all of Lebanon, and they express a deep desire to return to the coexistence of the different religious communities that constitute the nation of Lebanon. A small Christian state is no solution for them; rather it must be a coexistence based on mutual respect for each community's particularities and freedom.

Why did they choose to take up weapons instead of the more traditional female occupations in war, as did so many of their sisters, cousins, and friends? To this question I have received many and very different answers. For many of them it came little by little. They started by preparing sandwiches or running errands for the combatants, who were, as we have seen, close neighbors or parents. When a girl brought food or other things to the barricades, which were never far from home during the first years of the war, she usually stayed a little and often helped the men with smaller tasks like cleaning the weapons, replacing them as guards, etc., while the men got a little rest. It followed that she had to learn to use the arms, and as soon as possible she would attend one of the training sessions—much more efficient than the rather hasty instruction given by the combatants. During these training sessions she would come in contact with the girls who had already joined one of the female troops, because they often served as instructors. Such encounters would encourage the girls to leave their close neighborhood for a more extended engagement. In addition, there was a significant number of sisters and cousins fighting together. It is possible to isolate several groups composed of four to five cousins inside each female unit. Close family bonds have clearly been of great importance for their choice of kind of engagement.

Others started directly by seeking military training, but for different reasons. The majority of these girls considered the training to be a logical consequence of patriotic engagement, which was often felt as a need to take direct part in the defense of their country when they believed it was threatened. These were usually girls who had been involved in politics, often in the students' organizations in schools and universities, and thus very much aware of the dangerous situation that was building up in the country. These girls were mentally prepared and physically trained to participate in combat from the first days of the war, and they often became central persons in the female troops.

Some of them declared that they liked the military, the discipline as well as the uniform. It was something new, a contrast to the ordinary way of living. They admitted that they liked to shock a little, but this was secondary, coming far behind the wish to do something for their country.

A few pointed out that they joined to overcome the fear that paralyzed them in the beginning of the war. To overcome this feeling they wanted to learn to use arms. During the training sessions they were integrated into one of the groups active on the terrain.

Many of the girls were guides, and a lot of them were engaged in the Lebanese Red Cross or other social and religious youth organizations. Most of them preferred sports to more sedentary activities like paying or receiving visits, so important among women in the Middle East. During periods of calm, they usually devoted their weekends to these activities. When the security situation changed, military life took over and became their main preoccupation. In spite of a difficult situation, they managed in this way to lead an active life, and in fact, this enormous energy seems to be the only thing they all have in common. Coming from different social backgrounds, from different schools, and from different parts of the country, they joined each other in the defense of a common cause.

Most of them were still in school when the war started in 1975, and many of them had already started some military training in 1973–1974, together with their brothers, cousins, parents, and other close relatives. If some political activity was accepted in certain (but far from all) schools, military training was totally excluded. In fact there were often tensions between the administration of the schools and the young members of the militias, both male and female. A few of the schools changed their attitude as the war went on, but they had to take into consideration that many of the students considered themselves neutral in the conflict. This attitude can be seen as a parallel to the lack of identification with the state expressed by so many Lebanese belonging to all communities. The state has never been able, and in fact has never tried, to impose itself on the mind of the people as a central and unifying power. The militants, male and female, felt this lack of support on the part of the schools and perceived the neutrality expressed by some of their fellow students as a rejection of their own engagement. For the girls, this led to a double perception, the rejection of the cause they were fighting for and a suspicion toward them as girls carrying weapons. This sometimes led to conflicts, but more generally to a mutual ignorance of each other. Still the situation was difficult for the girls to live with because they were so few in each school, often even alone, and for this reason they preferred not to talk about their military engagement at school. It was not because they were afraid or ashamed, but because they found it difficult to share this experience with someone who had not lived it. The same behavior has been observed among soldiers and members of the resistance in Europe after the two world wars. The girls taking part in combat developed a feeling of being something special and, above all, a strong sense of belonging.

The degree of participation by the girls in combat was highest at the beginning of the war (1975 to 1976), before the militias were organized into more regular forces. During these years there were two female units in Beirut and its suburbs, and one in Bickfaya. One of the troops in Beirut constituted itself directly for combat. The corps was made up of thirteen girls, most of whom were born and raised in downtown Beirut. All of them were politically engaged, if not members of a party. They took part in combat in the center of town, in the battle of Chekka and other fronts in the north, and in the mountains. The second troop was founded by one girl who had originally been fighting together with her older brother in one of the close suburbs southeast of Beirut, this being the condition imposed by her parents to let her remain away from home. When her brother was badly wounded, she found herself without the possibility of continuing the battle so important for both of them. Following the example of the girls from downtown, she made contact with other girls from her own area and organized them into a female troop. In this way she obtained once more her parents' permission to go out. The troop participated in the defense of their area, and was dissolved by the end of 1976, after which many of its members joined the troop in downtown Beirut. The troop of Bickfaya was composed of girls from this mountain town and of girls having family ties to it. They took part in the battles in the mountains east of the town and on other fronts of the North-Metn district. They still have a role in the defense of their part of the front, but act less as a group than the troop from Beirut. On the other hand, the group feeling is still strong; they help each other in difficult situations and share each other's pleasures.

The three troops had, and have kept, an independent status in their relationship to the command of the area, and later to the central command of the Lebanese Forces. This was made possible by the partisan character of the first years of the war, when all the groups were fighting with their own weapons. These were soon complemented by light and semiheavy automatic arms. The girls were, with a few exceptions, trained to use lighter weapons, and found this normal, even if it meant that they were restricted to dangerous close combat. The use of heavy weapons gave more prestige and was usually reserved for the male combatants. As the war went on, this created a difference in the kind of participation by male and female. This fact is not necessarily an expression only of current male-female differentiation but also of a generally shared feeling that the participation of girls in combat was temporary. Combat was never expected to become a way of life or, for instance, the beginning of a military career, as could be the case for the young men. These three factors—the independent status of the female units, the use of personal weapons, and the attitude that their military engagement was not for life but for "the time being"—had an important result in that the girls had great influence on their way of fighting and also on when, or rather in which battles, they would participate. Their engagement was national, and as a rule, they never took part in internal conflicts, for instance the ones preceding the centralization of the command of the Lebanese Forces in 1977 and the Intifada in 1985. They had, of course, their opinions about these important events and gave their political support to one or the other of the factions, but they refused to use weapons in conflicts opposing people normally fighting on the same side, often close relatives.

The voluntary and independent character of their participation also had a decisive influence on their way of fighting. But before developing this, it is necessary to show that these girls did in fact take part in real combat. I will take here the example of the troop from downtown Beirut. They were assigned to protect the headquarters of the Kataëb Party, specifically a barricade between the building and the Place des Martyrs, which was considered the center of the town, a melting pot before the war and from the beginning of the war recognized as the border between East and West Beirut. The girls soon noticed a building under construction on the other side of the Place. It was not permanently occupied, but attacks often came from it during the night. If this building was neutralized, the constant shelling of the headquarters would be eased. So they decided to occupy it. The commander of the area refused, but the troop decided to follow their own opinion and took the building the next night. They kept this post from autumn 1975 until the arrival of the Syrian Army in October 1976. Just before this, and after the arrival of the Syrian observers, they were exposed to a hard attack, which they repelled victoriously, in spite of the fact that the other barricades in the area had been evacuated and that they almost ran out of ammunition. One of the girls in fact had to run across the devastated Place to command headquarters to get ammunition and run back again carrying it on her back, in complete darkness and with only a hand grenade to protect herself. Some members of the troop also participated in the dramatic battles of Chekka, a small town built around some cement factories south of Tripoli, whose peaceful inhabitants were attacked several times during the summer of 1976. The situation was at its worst on September 24 when more than forty persons were killed. Christian combatants from all over the country rushed to the north to help the people of Chekka, and with them came fifteen girls from Beirut. They were at first assigned to the protection of a bridge far behind the front line, an assignment which they refused, arguing that they had not left Beirut and the tough situation there to go on a picnic, and threatened to return. Seeing their determination, the commander sent them to one of the most exposed posts, which had posed some problems because it was isolated from the others. The girls held it successfully the last three days of combat, without seeking contact with headquarters.

These first two years of the conflict are the most important in determining whether it is possible to talk about female behavior in war, because it was in this period that the girls were the most active in combat and also the most independent, and thus had the greatest influence on their own actions. It is striking that they brought with them to the front line all their female knowledge and behavior. They cleaned, cooked, took care of smaller wounds, and also tried to humanize their physical surroundings. All this contributed to making them independent and self-sufficient, well adapted to the rather unorganized situation of these first years and to any form of partisan war. The male combatants counted on the women behind the lines to feed them, clean them, and even comfort and entertain them. In the building in downtown Beirut, which was soon called the "girls' building," they arranged a corner for praying, with a statue of the Holy Virgin. As often as possible, they brought flowers to the statue. In another corner they put up a bookshelf, and those who had books at home put some of them there. To kill the time during the long hours of waiting (more frequent than the hours of fighting), they read together and even did their homework, which was given by the schools when they were closed. In this way the younger girls could learn from the older ones, and the less educated from the more educated. They had separate places for eating and sleeping, and even brought clean sheets for their beds. This behavior was at the same time a way of humanizing a difficult situation, and a way of occupying a territory, a clear way of telling their fellow combatants that they would not move around from one barricade to another, as was done by the men.

Their way of fighting was a defensive one; this was expressed both by their way of talking and their way of acting. In fact, the whole reason for their engagement—military, political, and patriotic—was, as we have seen, the defense of their country and their way of life. When they spoke, they never used the term "occupy" but always "defend" or "take back." They never tried to advance further than to an unoccupied building in a no-man's land, even if the building was close to, in fact touching, enemy land. Sometimes they made incursions there just to state their presence, but they never tried to move any further. This defensive manner was also expressed in the way they arranged their posts. When they had access to electricity, they installed big spotlights on all passages to the west. In addition they brought a lot of small stones and covered the same passages with them, so if somebody walked there, they would hear it immediately. They tried in fact to avoid open fighting as much as possible, first, of course, to spare their own lives, but all of them also expressed a rejection of the idea of killing somebody if it is not strictly necessary. They also refused to shoot at civilians, and put snipers lowest on a scale of action in war, at the same level as terrorist acts like car bombings.

When it comes to their skill with weapons, the experience from the mixed training camps shows that the girls can easily compete with the young men if they get the same training. Concerning cleaning weapons, they were quicker and did it better. Given the same possibilities, the girls showed themselves able to compete with the boys, but as the war went on and bigger arms were used, the gap widened because the girls were excluded from training with these arms. The girls had been able to enter a field until then considered exclusively male, but they soon realized that the subordination of women to men continued.

This research is far from complete, but it already shows some tendencies that allow us to draw the outlines of female behavior in combat, at least when the girls have some influence on forming it. First, they are not limited by any given image of a female combatant. They therefore bring with them their general female behavior and take care of a lot of things that would normally be attended to by others. They cook, clean, and care for the persons they are with and for their surroundings. This makes the female troops independent, which is both good and bad. It lowers the costs and lightens the burdens on the people behind the lines. At the same time it keeps the girls busy, taking their minds off bad memories and worries about what might happen. There is, for instance, no evidence that these girls have used drugs. But on the other hand, it may also lead to a rather marginal position in relation to the general militia command.

The most striking fact in this relation is their general attitude that war is defensive. There is no doubt that they like the military, the discipline, the hard work, and the excitement. They are proud and feel that they are doing something useful for their country. But this does not give them any prestige, as it gives the young men. They engage in fighting only when necessary and only to defend themselves and the area that they are responsible for, and go into enemy territory only to mark their presence, never to occupy new areas.

It is of great importance for them to be clean and neat, and also that their surroundings should be the same. They attach a lot of importance to their own behavior and, above all, to their way of talking. All swearing and the use of blasphemous expressions are forbidden, and they have noticed that the male combatants change their language in their presence. In fact, they very much want to be a humanizing factor in a tough world.

For the girls fighting in mixed troops, the situation is of course different, but in fields where it is possible they have the same behavior and attitudes as girls in the female troops. They rarely cook or clean, because they are too few compared to the group and also because nobody expects them to do so. But they have the same opinion of war as being defensive. This corresponds to the results published by Marie Maksoud in her thesis on Lebanese youth during the war, both Muslim and Christian. She states that boys as well as girls who have participated in combat often say, "We did not fight, rather we defended our country," or "We have been fighting for Lebanon" (Maksoud

1980: 154). In conclusion, at this stage of the research it is possible to draw the outlines of female behavior in combat, in terms of both actions and attitudes.

What have been the implications of military engagement on the relations between the girls and their family, friends, and society as a whole? From a modern, occidental perspective Lebanese society is still a traditional one, characterized by a division into a female domestic and a male public domain. Women gained the right to vote in 1954, but they still need the signature, thus the accord, of a male parent to get a passport or open a bank account. Women are totally absent from political life; there has only once been a female member of the National Assembly, and never a cabinet minister. Their power belongs to the domestic area, where it is strong, and may be extended to the public area as wife or mother of a political personality. Girls are encouraged to seek education, but have to give way to their brothers if the parents cannot afford to pay for an education for every child. Women are present in all professions, but only those who have a high-prestige occupation will identify themselves by their profession. They are first of all daughters, sisters, wives, and mothers and, of course, are brought up to be that. The large majority of married women, even those who have received higher education, have no job outside the home. Their occupations in public will above all be of a social and cultural character. Lebanese of all communities and classes value the mild, sweet, virtuous girl, growing up to be a perfect wife and housekeeper and mother, her main and often only model. There must be no doubt about her virtue and femininity. Except for her studies, the young girl is expected to stay at home with her mother. There is a saying: "The girl is for the mother," meaning that the daughter is expected to stay with the mother, to help her and, in that way, prepare herself for her future role. One expects from her obedience toward her parents and that she will bring a touch of sweetness to family life. This is just the opposite of what is usually encountered in military life.

It is easy to imagine the reaction of parents to their daughter's desire to join the combatants. In addition to the fear of her being wounded or even killed is the worry about how this act might be perceived by the rest of the society. Above all they fear that this would influence her possibilities of getting married. As we have seen, this attitude varies according to whether the parents were themselves engaged in a political party or in a patriotic activity. These parents would give their permission more readily than others. But even they would react in different ways to the military engagement of their son and of their daughter. The fear for the child's life would, of course, be the same, but although it was accepted as a duty for the boy, and he could even get some prestige from his participation in combat, it would be considered almost an anomaly if a girl did the same. The sincerity of their engagement is never questioned, but the path they choose is.

As an affair of the domestic area, the education of the children is almost exclusively the mother's responsibility. The girls would therefore have to convince their mothers first, who would then obtain the permission of their fathers. This was necessary, as the girl would leave the domestic area for a common life outside the control of her parents. If the mother accepted, it was generally rather easy to obtain the agreement of the father. This may be because he felt less responsible, but also because fathers were more often involved in patriotic engagement than mothers, and therefore understood more easily their daughters' choice. Some of the girls knew in advance that it would be impossible, for different reasons, to convince their parents, and they went to the front without their knowledge. This situation was experienced as a deep conflict between two duties, on the one hand the respect and the obedience they owed to their parents and, on the other, the cause they wanted to defend. It was perceived as a loneliness in the face of the dangers they confronted. One of them used to say, "Tell your mothers to pray for me, because mine does not know where I am." Many parents did not have a choice because the situation had developed little by little. They had allowed their daughters to go to training sessions and camps because so many girls did, in fact more than 3,000, and even to take part in the defense of their street or village because it was so close to home and they stayed there with parents or close neighbors. As the war went on and developed, the combatants, male and female, were called to fronts far from home, like Chekka in the north and the mountains, and even downtown Beirut, geographically close but completely out of the parents' control, and where the girls had to sleep. Sleeping outside of the house became for many the real obstacle; many parents just could not accept it. The girls who spent nights, sometime weeks, away from home were often victims of bad rumors.

The relations with their parents were, as we have seen, rather complicated, and the girls tried to find ways to make up for the fears and worries they had put their parents through. One way was to wipe out the military image as soon as they were back home. They put on a dress, made up their hair, and stayed at home with their parents and visited relatives and friends as much as possible. This often led to a double life, in which the military was excluded from the domestic.

An important number of them would seek education. First of all, they knew that for them the military life was only for the time being, as long as Lebanon was in danger, and that they would have to—and also wished to—leave it for a normal life. Education would help them in this passage, and was also a factor that underlined that they were just ordinary, good, young women when they took off the uniform. Education was useful for their re-integration into general society. But in this domain also they lived, as we have seen, in two separate worlds, the military on one side and the school or university on the other. At the same time, combat and military discipline had taught them to face difficult situations and to control their nerves. Above all, they had acquired a great deal of self-confidence, both from their military engagement and from the efforts they had been obliged to make to convince their parents and others that their military participation was the right thing for them. All this helped them both in their relations with the school and university administrations and in their studies in a situation where the educational institutions closed and opened in accordance with the security situation. More than half of the girls have either finished an education at the university level or are studying at a university, one third of them have completed secondary school, and about one sixth primary school. Their level of education is thus high, but this cannot be seen as a main determinant of their engagement, because they started their studies afterward, and the military life was led as a parallel to school life. This becomes even more evident when the girls' level of education is compared with that of their parents. One fifth of the fathers and one ninth of the mothers have a university education, almost half primary education, and the rest secondary education. The results were the same for both fathers and mothers. This difference between parents and children may be partly explained by the good economic situation for the middle class in Lebanon from the sixties until the beginning of the war, which allowed parents to give their children the education they wanted. Education has always been valued, above all by the Christians, and the education of one family member was considered to be a means of social progress for the whole family.

Concerning the professions chosen by the girls, it is again the variety that is striking, from medicine, architecture, law, teaching, journalism, photography, and dance, to officials and employees in the private and public sector, as well as sewing and knitting. However, only half of the girls are actually working. Some of them are still students; others are married and do not work outside the home. Several unmarried girls are without professions, even though they have an education. This indicates that it is not marriage as such that keeps the Lebanese woman away from working life, but rather the attitudes of the society and also the difficulties of finding an occupation economically interesting enough to leave the house.

In conclusion, it may be said that their participation in military action has not had a negative influence on the educational level of the girls. There are some exceptions, usually concerning a delay in the studies and an instability expressed by the fact that many of them have changed subjects several times.

On the other hand, it seems that the close contact with older and more educated girls may have stimulated the younger and less educated ones to continue their studies.

As for the girls' relations with close relatives, friends, and the global society, they follow the same pattern as their relations with parents and educational institutions, depending on their attitude toward the girls' military action. If their attitude was positive or they at least expressed respect for the girls' actions, the relations were generally without problems. Lebanese society is very family-oriented, with close relations within the extended family, so the opinions and reactions of uncles, aunts, and cousins are of great importance for the individual. However, if these girls met negative reactions from their close relations, they would give priority to their patriotic engagement. The same attitude was expressed toward friends and other persons with whom they were in regular contact. If they met a negative reaction, they would weigh this against the importance of, for instance, the friendship, and eventually establish a two-world set of relations, separating their social relations from the world of their military life. Still, it is obvious that most of their friends are militants, even if they do not participate in combat. The relations with other militants are easier because the girls do not have to explain or even defend their kind of engagement. Many of them have married combatants, even if the number of such marriages is too small to be significant. At the same time, most of the unmarried girls express the opinion that they would prefer to marry a man who shares their patriotic feelings and respects their military engagement. "If not, I would have to close the most important part of my heart," said one.

Finally, it would be interesting to see if this patriotic engagement has led to a political engagement on a broader national level or in the fields of women's rights.

Some of the girls were active in political parties before the war started, others became members later on, and still others never joined any political party. Their engagement has clearly been, above all, a patriotic one, not ideological. Many of the young men sought and got political power through their patriotic engagement, either on a local or on a national level. The most famous example here is the late president-elect of the republic, Sheik Beshir Gemayel, who was the commander-in-chief of the Lebanese Forces before he was elected president. It would therefore seem natural for these well-educated and courageous young women to try the same path. But the war put the national cause above any other. They felt that the nation was threatened and therefore devoted themselves to its defense. This is concordant with the conclusions of Margaret and Patrice Higonnet, who draw a common thread from the different essays in a book on women and the two world wars: "The dominant ideology of wartime for women remains nationalist" (Higonnet and Higonnet 1987: 39). They would even feel guilt if they deviated from the main cause. The Lebanese girls say that women's rights will have to wait; it is not yet time.

As for participation in politics on a national level, the question is much more complex. The seats in parliament are redistributed by the National Pact of 1943 among the different religious communities, as are the different departments in government and posts on all levels in the public administration. Within each community, political power is usually the domain of certain families, except for some cases in the main towns where political parties have some influence. Also, Lebanese women's life to a great extent is confined to the domestic area, and only one woman has been elected to parliament. Consequently a woman will meet many obstacles as she strives toward a place in political life and power, obstacles related to religion, family, and the gender system. In addition the girls in this study express a repulsion against the traditional political class and qualify politics as "dirty" and "immoral." They have no illusions about their ability to change this and prefer to work on another level. A great number of them work within social affairs, either as volunteers or as professionals. One of the female units, the one from downtown Beirut, since 1985 has distanced itself from military action, without denying its past, and on May 31, 1988, the members constituted themselves as a pacifist movement. Their cause is still the national Lebanese cause, although they no longer think weapons to be the proper way, but rather focus on the education of their fellow sisters about the Lebanese cause, the cohabitation of all the communities, civil education, and the question of how each one of them can contribute to the country's survival.

BIBLIOGRAPHY

Bethke Elshtain, Jean. *Women and War.* New York: Basic Books, 1987.
Higonnet, Margaret R., and Patrice Higonnet. *Behind the Lines: Gender and the Two World Wars.* New Haven and London: Yale University Press, 1987.
Accad-Sursock, Rosine. "La Femme Libanaise: De la tradition a la modernité." *Travaux et Jours* (Université Saint Joseph, Beirut) 52 (1974).
Lorfing, Irini. *Effect of the Fathers' Labor Migration on the Structure of the Family.* Beirut: American University, 1984.
Maksoud, Marie. *Les Adolescents Libanais et la guerre: Attitude et reactions des jeunes de classe terminale à Beyrouth et en Banlieue.* Université de Paris V, 1980.
Salloum, Souhaila Rizk. *Valeur et fonction du groupe politique à l'adolescence.* Beirut: Université Saint Joseph, 1983.

ATTITUDES OF TEENAGE GIRLS TO THE IRANIAN REVOLUTION

by Farhad Khosrokhavar

The work that follows attempts to show the evolution of "Islamic" ideas in the Iranian youth who took part in the revolution. A long interview made in November 1980 with two young sisters and their half-brother, who is a generation older, is partially translated and reproduced here. This is part of a series of interviews whose aim is to show the rupture between the mentality of the new Iranian revolutionary youth and that of the older generation.[1]

Two girls who still demonstrate numerous "traditional" characteristics were intentionally chosen to show that these characteristics suppose an imaginary representation of Islam which is clearly different from tradition.

As a consequence, the thesis according to which the Islamic revolution in Iran was a neotraditionalist revolution[2] needs to be reconsidered. In fact, it is not a return to tradition that is being claimed, but another type of modernity in which a totally different role is given to Islam. This does not entirely invalidate the thesis of neotraditionalism. The present work places limits on this latter thesis by displaying the new aspects of the mental structure of revolutionary youth. The main actors of the Islamic Revolution were the young people and they weren't neotraditional. The clergy that was involved in this movement had a neotraditional outlook but its role was subordinated to that of Khomeini, who was not considered primarily, by this youth, as a clergyman.

The interview took place in the town of Qom in September 1981. Those present were Mr. Jalil, a man of fifty (who appears as D in the text), and his half-sisters Moneer, sixteen, and Masume, fourteen at the time of the interview. They are all members of the lower middle class in Qom. Their father is a retired primary-school teacher who from time to time sells rugs in Qom. Jalil is his son by his first marriage. Several years after the death of his first wife from tuberculosis, he married in his sixties a woman thirty years younger. From this marriage he had five children; Moneer and Masume are two of them.

THE ABYSS BETWEEN THE GENERATIONS

ISLAM VERSUS THE NATION-STATE

One of the most striking characteristics of the interview is the gap which exists between Jalil and his two half-sisters Masume and Moneer. This is apparent in their interpretation of the major phenomenon—the revolution—on which this interview was focused. There is not a simple generation gap here, but an abyss. This essay will outline some of the features which separate them.

The first is their relationship with Islam. Jalil belongs to the nationalist middle class whose youth was marked by the Mossadegh movement of the fifties. The two girls belong to the generation which made the Islamic revolution. He believes in the nation-state, its relevance, its grandeur. The two sisters think in terms of the expansion of Islam. The nation is not as important for them. For Jalil, who saw the fall of Mossadegh through the efforts of the local populace and the CIA,[3] the "Great Powers" (the USA and the Soviet Union) are all-powerful and this means that no major event within the Iranian society can take place without their prior consent. Even the Islamic revolution was their doing. In contrast, for the two girls, revolution is possible, and the proof is the Islamic revolution which has come into being by the efforts of the Muslim people of Iran, of whom they are a part. Jalil thinks about the inner politics of dependent societies in terms of heteronomy (superpowers make the major political decisions about Iran); the two sisters think that a very large autonomous political scene exists in Iran. Jalil thinks that all is decided in advance by the superpowers; the two sisters are of the opinion that with the Islamic revolution people have put an end to superpower hegemony on the Iranian political scene.

ACTOR AND NONACTOR

The two sisters are much less alienated than their half-brother, who is a generation older. If the revolution has been made by young people like these two and not by their father's generation, it is precisely because, for people like Jalil, the revolution is simply impossible due to the mystic power he attributes to "hegemonic powers." For the young, no such power exists to create obstacles to their political action. To say that the Iranian youth of the seventies (those who took part in the revolution) were politicized means also that their memory was unencumbered by the failure and, ultimately, by the overthrow of the Mossadeghist movement in the fifties. This youth does not feel humiliated by western or any other hegemonic power.

TWO HETEROGENEOUS FACES OF ISLAM

ISLAMIC OR MUSLIM?

The two girls truculently insist that a great ayatollah (*ayatollah ol ozma*) is not necessarily an "Islamic man." In the western world we differentiate "the Islamist" from "the Islamic." The first applies to the new activists who are reclaiming Islam, while the second refers to Muslims who conform to tradition. One finds here, in the portrait depicted by Moneer and Masume, a dichotomy which is in accordance with this dual picture. Islamist (*eslamee, in* their word) is opposed to Muslim (*mosalman*). The second term is not explicitly formulated in the dialogue but is found in others, not reproduced here. The two sisters have a low esteem for the traditional Muslim and state that genuine Islam (*eslam rasteen*) is theirs, that is, political Islam of the youth.

What distinguishes this Islam from that of tradition?

First, the acceptance of Khomeini as the Guide (*rahbar*) of the revolution. This is not seen any longer as the same as the choice of the traditional source of imitation (*marjah taqlid*), which did not exclude respect for other sources of imitation. The two sisters go so far as to deny the quality of being Islamic, that is, of proceeding from "true Islam," to those who do not subscribe to Khomeini's leadership. Those who do not accept the Guide are not worthy of being treated as Muslims, even if they are great ayatollahs (sic). This is not only shocking but also simply heretical to traditional mentality. For it, all grand ayatollahs and more generally all religious dignitaries are to be respected, and no one has the right to state that a religious dignitary is non-Islamic.

Finally, even the idea of the Guide is an innovation of postrevolutionary youth.[4] The emergence of new social actors in society is the direct result of the intolerant modernization of the sixties and seventies in imperial Iran, where the closure of the political system prevented the emergence of democratic actors on the political scene.

Moneer and Masume come from a traditional milieu, from a city with a reputation even more traditional than their family. After all, Qom is the central holy city in Iran, equal to Meshed, and the site of the most important school for Shi'ite clergy. Still, Moneer and Masume show a new spirit.

Their belief in miracles proceeds from that same spirit. Traditional religion is often full of recourse to miracles or to what modern people call superstitions. The sisters quote several instances of the thaumaturgical qualities of Khomeini to explain his saintly nature: he ages less quickly than ordinary mortals; he is in touch with the Imam-of-the-Age (the Twelfth Imam, who is in occultation); he makes predictions which prove his gift of seeing; he was able to predict that Carter would lose the presidential election in the United States. But on looking more closely, one can perceive clearly what separates their belief from those of traditional Muslims: they insist particularly on the fact that Khomeini is the Guide because *they have chosen him*. This element of personal choice is decisive. The Guide is not a simple source of imitation (marjah taqlid); he is the political and religious director, not one whose directives one follows only in religious matters. The political function is essential, and all the statements of Moneer and of Masume show that it is not religious ritual but political options that the youth recognize, eager to see themselves as social actors in the full sense of the word.

The nontraditional side of their mentality comes to the fore once again in their perception of imperialism. For the two girls, the essential difference between the Islamist regime and that of the shah is that the latter was not independent; it was under the thumb of imperialism, subservient to America. If Moneer and Masume support the clergy and find it natural that the postrevolutionary state is dominated by it, it is because the clergy fought against the Pahlavi regime. It is not the traditional clergy which is privileged but those clergymen who are allied to the Guide and who waged the struggle against the Pahlavis. This fact is *political*. The clergy legitimized by the two girls is the clergy that is "following in the way of the Imam" (*khatté emam*) just as the two sisters are following in the way of the Imam. In this way, Islam is modernized and politicized.

ISLAM AND REVOLUTION

A second element involves the belief that the true Islam is one which advocates revolution. This also is very different from the traditional view. Traditional religion does not recognize the idea of revolution; it recognizes under certain circumstances the revolt against an unjust power.[5] The youth are involved not only in exalting the revolution but also in making their participation in it one of the essential ingredients of their Islam. As for the question of knowing who "made the revolution," the two sisters unanimously reply, "We made the revolution, people like us made the revolution." The expression "to make the revolution" (*enghelab kardan*) is difficult to translate because it involves much more than the idea of participating in the revolutionary movement; it implies having played the major role in it, having been its main proponent. The key to the understanding of this new revolutionary Islam is that it is not a religion of submission to power, even a just power,[6] but a religion which advocates revolution. In the second place, it is a religion which no longer has the group as a common reference but the politicized individual, man or woman alike. In this interview the sisters often refer to their participation in the revolution. They took part in revolutionary activities contrary to the urban tradition that women should stay within the household (*andarun*); the two sisters define themselves as *zoon politikon*. During the interview they dare to answer their half-brother back, although he is thirty years older (this would have been impossible in the past). They express themselves without the slightest modesty on questions related to politics, and above all, they describe everything related to their school with a political sense that sharply contrasts with the attitude of older generations. The positions of Moneer and of Masume are reminiscent of those of another revolutionary girl, Sakeene, who speaks about her "interior revolution." [7] Sakeene, a rural girl, challenges all the norms which are associated with traditional Islam regarding young women's relationship to the public sphere; she ignores the bans on women's public participation in protests, armed combat, and meetings. She asserts that her interior revolution has made her pure and, thus, authorizes her to get in touch with men, without fear of sullying her reputation.

The views of the two girls Moneer and Masume are similar to Sakeene's: they take part in stormy meetings in their school classes and help politicize their school. They do research on the poor of their city, take part in the wheat harvest organized by the Crusade for Reconstruction,[8] and identify with revolutionary ideas when traditional people, including the fathers of Sakeene and the two sisters, are casting a suspicious eye on women's participation in political meetings, believing that this participation would corrupt them.

Interpretations which attempt to see the conduct of revolutionary Iranian youth in a framework of neotraditionalism do not take into account the novelty of this behavior and the modernized yet intolerant aspirations and demands of the youth. These young people are using tradition to further new modern aspirations which no longer have anything to do with tradition itself. Youth, even in Qom, a city closer to tradition than many other Iranian cities, think and act on the basis of different norms from those associated with the past. The way Khomeini is promoted, the "Guide of the revolution" is at the same time intolerant. It shows that modernization has been antidemocratic during the reign of the shah. Revolutionary Islam is deeply influenced by this intolerant modernization.

FREEDOM, A NEW COGNITIVE CATEGORY OF YOUTH

Maheen, a girl of working-class background, said in an interview (winter 1980):

> At the beginning of the revolution [1979], no one was tortured, but dictatorship returned little by little. During the first year of the revolution we were free, but now, we aren't. Censorship and repression [*ekhtenagh*] are back. In the

beginning, newspapers and magazines with a variety of ideas circulated in our school, but now they are forbidden; we no longer have the right to do so. In class, the first year [of the revolution], everybody talked about freedom, but now, it's not possible.

The difference between Maheen and the two sisters of Qom is that she is in sympathy with extreme left Islamic groups, whereas Moneer and Masume belong to Hezbollah, the new repressive revolutionary group affiliated with Khomeini. Still, despite differences in their political position, one thing is shared by all three: the recourse to political categories as a key to express new ideas. Maheen refers explicitly to freedom, as do the two sisters. Each defines the boundaries of this liberty according to her own political ties. But on the desire to be free, there is no divergence. In other words, freedom has become the fundamental category of the new subjectivity, its desires and claims expressed in reference to that category. At the same time, each group is intolerant and disrespectful of the other. In a peculiar way, the desire for political freedom and political intolerance go hand in hand in the new Iranian youth. Maheen believes that one is not yet free enough. She wishes to extend freedom to all spheres of social life. The new Islamism, even when it is repressive, is related to freedom and not to community and tradition. Even in the repressive side of Islamism there are ingredients of modernity and not the reproduction of past conducts. In the case of Moneer and Masume, they declare their allegiance to the Islamist regime because it promises independence for their country from imperialism and, above all, the right to speak. On this last issue, their position is ambiguous in the sense that at the same time, they claim a more resolute repression of the opposition. However, they politicize the world; they define themselves on a political field where they see themselves as modern social actors and not members of the community, imbued with a traditional turn of mind. Their reference is no longer the traditional community but the "people" (*mardom*). If the shah was deposed, it is because people did not want him. People have chosen Khomeini; they are social actors, not the great Shia patriarchs, not the clergy.

THE SCHOOL, THE PLACE OF CONFRONTATION BETWEEN POLITICAL GROUPS

The importance of the secondary schools in the Iranian revolution is well known. After the revolution, the school became the site of new confrontations between various political parties. The account given by Moneer and Masume is close to that of Maheen, who describes the lively debates and intense antagonisms at her school:

QUESTION: How old is your principal?

MAHEEN: She's young, twenty-four, twenty-five years old; she has just finished her university degrees; she's a Hezbollah. During the morning physical exercises at school, the Modjahedin girls did their exercises apart from the Hezbollah. In contrast, the Fedai [a Marxist group] did their sports activities with the Hezbollah, for the sake of the [unity of the] people and [the support of] the war. But the Modjahedin refused to do sports with the Hezbollah. The other day somebody stuck up the Modjahedin newspaper on the school wall and spoke of the Saadati affair [a member of the Modjahedin who was jailed and shot later by the Islamist regime]. There was a fight. Another time somebody stuck up the Islamic Revolutionary newspaper of Banisadr, but our principal tore it down. She said no one had the right to bring this paper into the school. Only the Islamic Association of our school had that right, although ordinarily one ought to discuss it with the Pupils' Council. Yet they had not done it. The Islamic Association published a paper which contained only articles from the *Islamic Republic,* a Hezbollah paper. Still, despite everything they did to intimidate us, I am not afraid to say what I think; you know that if you are found with the newspaper *Kâr* [of the leftist Marxist group, the Fedai], you can be condemned to six months in jail. I still buy it, though, and read it; I have no problem, I'm not afraid!

During the first two years of the revolution, the politicization of the secondary schools was intense, at least in the large cities. Different political groups found the school a good place for recruiting new followers. The issues which mobilized the young people in these schools (boys and girls, rich and poor, pupils from residential and nonresidential areas, from important cities like Tehran or from less important cities like Qom) were freedom of speech, freedom of political affiliation, and, to a lesser degree, for the girls, the emancipation of women. This is what Maheen, the girl from a poor area of the Tehran suburbs, says:

In the school, tracts were distributed like little loaves of bread: *Kâr* [the Fedai paper], *Mardom* [the paper of Toudeh, the Iranian communist party]. All were distributed without constraint, but this year [the second year of the revolution] many [leftist] professors are fired. This year the professors no longer dare speak freely; they are afraid to be fired. At the beginning of the year, before classes began, we proposed a free discussion meeting [*bahse azad*] to one teacher. She replied, "Don't talk about religion and things like that!" She feared that such a discussion would cause her dismissal. We had a teacher of literature, a woman. In the course of a composition, one pupil said, "The Modjahedin sympathizers use an electric dryer for their hair. They pay five hundred tumans [around $70] for an electric dryer!" The professor replied, "The Modjahedin watch how they look; they wear a scarf [*rusaree*] that covers their hair; how can you see under the scarf that they use a dryer?" [Later] this professor was accused of communism [by the authorities].

In the school described by Maheen, one can see concretely the progressive disappearance of freedom and the shadow of a new repressive political order. In other words, the young pupils have a clear understanding of what real freedom means. More than that, they are acutely aware of its progressive disappearance with the consolidation of the new state. Still, some young people (like Sakeene, Moneer, and Masume) are in favor of the new political order, not for neotraditional reasons but because they want to preserve the revolution or they find it to their advantage.

QUESTION: What did His Eminence [*ichan,* Khomeini] say about the oppressed [*mostaz'af*], the underprivileged, the poor?

SAKEENE: His Eminence said that we must take care of the oppressed; he said that there is no reason for them to be poor, that all the people should be equal [*dar yek sath*]. Why should there be any oppressed people at all, since they are the ones who made the revolution and have led us to the new situation? What His Eminence said is true, that it is the oppressed who have saved Islam in all cities, villages.

The oppressed youth defend Khomeini because they think he will help overcome the bad lot of the poor and that he alone has the power to do so. For this reason they support Khomeini in the struggle against other political currents. It is not the religious factor in the traditional sense which is the main cause of their support for Khomeini, but the feeling that Khomeini's Islam advocates the well-being of the oppressed and, thus, assures their social and economic promotion.

FREEDOM FOR WOMEN

Moneer and Masume understand that they are reinstituting Islam in their country, but their Islam is not the one that encloses women in the shackles of tradition. Their Islam gives women the right to take part in the affairs of the city and in public life, almost in parity with men. Although the two sisters speak about all this in a somewhat muddled way (notably because their half-brother does not let them discuss their aspirations) they nevertheless do not fail to state their wish for action in the political arena. They think of themselves as having changed their country's destiny, of having taken part (and continuing to do so) in social and political action. Other girls of working-class origin formulate more explicitly their idea of an Islam that would fight the current inequality between men and women. Such is the case of Sakeene, a rural girl who takes pride in her "interior revolution," by which she rejects the attempts of her father to isolate her from public life according to his traditional, nonrevolutionary Islam.

QUESTION: What do you think of your father?

SAKEENE: My father hasn't one single revolutionary thought in his head. I call revolutionary he who has made a revolution in his being, an internal revolution. Someone said, "How good it would be to attend collective Friday prayers! If I didn't have something else to do, I would go like a shot." But a true revolutionary doesn't just talk like that, he goes. A revolutionary boy or girl runs away during the night from the paternal home if the father opposes his or her going to the battlefields [the war against Iraq]. The next day, the child writes to the father to tell him what's happened. Those who have made an internal revolution are not afraid to be taken to task by their fathers. My father pretends to be a revolutionary and he goes to the mosque every evening. I said to him, "How can you be so satisfied with yourself? How can you expect your daughter to respect you when you don't respect her? I have duties toward you but I'm not the only one to have them. You have some duties toward me as well." He only responds by saying that then the family's reputation or their interests will be endangered. He has me under his protection so that my name will not be endangered. He has me under his protection so that my name will not be spoken about badly, but he won't help me, he won't let me be free to become somebody, he won't allow me to go on the Crusade for Reconstruction [djahad sazandegi]. Why? Because people will say that the daughter of this family has dubious morals. He says to me, "You don't need to take the trouble to go on the Crusade because you shouldn't go alone and I should go with you." Well, that's no internal revolution! When one has gone through an internal revolution in all of its pure intent, one should be able to go [alone in the public place], and since I am his daughter and my intent is pure, he should allow me to go [on the Crusade]. Those who take part in the Crusade are not people of bad intent, and the times are different [from the shah's]. Those men are not the kind who want to take advantage of women. But when one has not made his internal revolution, one thinks like that. My father knows that I have no such silly thoughts in my head, that I am chaste and want to stay that way. He can see that a real revolution has taken place in my mind. But because he hasn't gone through the same experience, he won't allow me to go there; he criticizes and scolds me.

Sakeene rejects the traditional Islam of her father in order to take advantage of her own interior revolution and escape the shackles of family, traditional society, and communal Islam. For her father traditional Islam forbids the involvement of the *names* of the family (the honor which implies the protection of women outside family circles) in public life. Sakeene, on the contrary, wants to be active in the outside world, free from the constraints of the family. She wants to break with tradition which she rejects in the name of Islam, so as to become a public being, not just someone restricted to the limited world of her home. She wants to communicate with the outside world, not as a traditional woman but as a new individual who has undergone her own internal revolution. Because of that, she feels now able to work and talk like men.

QUESTION: Do you take part in the community prayers on Friday?

SAKEENE: Yes. When I go there, it is a lively world and you see each time new things. Since I like talking, I talk with all kinds of people. Last time, in a taxi, a woman asked me if, in this heat, I wasn't suffocating under my scarf and chador. I told her, "No, not at all, I'm used to it, and if you put it on, you'll get used to it too!" I got out of the taxi at Valye Asr Square and walked the rest of the way [to the Friday prayer]. I also talked to a girl who is a follower of Pichgam [a leftist political group]. She didn't know much about Islam, so I said, "How come you know so much about Pichgam but not about Islam?" She answered that people were making an idol of Khomeini and that this was unacceptable, that people might as well go back to the past regime that made an idol of the shah. I have a lot of discussions like this during the Friday prayer. . . . As for the Modjahedin, I've talked with them too; they are ignorant. . . . They don't know anything about Islam. In my village, my sister is in the ninth grade and her friend asked her to join the Modjahedin. Why? Because she speaks up in class every day, even though she doesn't know anything. These people are mostly like that, but I'm sure of what Islam is: it is not what the Modjahedin say! These people have no Islamic ideas, they are all Marxists!

In the course of her attendance at Friday prayers, Sakeene meets many people, middle-class women, girls of leftist leanings, but also young men, followers of the Modjahedin. Her Islam authorizes her to go into the mosque and to meet men, something that traditional Islam condemned as being immoral, as an assault on her *namus* (sexual honor).

Maheen, the working-class girl from the poor southern district of Tehran, is even more radical in her condemnation of the traditional Islam of her parents and of other adults:

For example, if a young girl speaks up in public, they feel obliged to punish her in the name of Islam. However, the Saint Zeynab [sister of the third Shi'ite Imam, Hosein] even fought in the war. If you tell them that, they say you are a liar. For them a girl should get married early, she shouldn't speak in public, she doesn't have the right to protest [against inequalities].

It is not out of the desire to return to the realm of tradition that youth (and especially girls) are embracing revolutionary Islam, but out of the desire to break with traditional religion that they denounce in the name of genuine Islam. If the revolution has gone badly, if the new state has imposed, in the name of Islam, an intolerant behavior pattern, this should not be understood as an attempt to return to tradition. On the contrary, modernization has so deeply estranged the youth from traditional patterns of political conduct that they radicalize their action in a way that is very untraditional.

The following is a partial text of the interview with Jalil, Moneer, and Masume:

QUESTION (Q): What do you think of the Islamic revolution?

JALIL: Me, I've seen the past of this country. I took part in political movements like that of Mossadegh [1951 – 1953] which was put down in the twenty-eighth Mordad coup [the military coup in 1953 which, with the help of the CIA, toppled the legal government of Mossadegh and restored the shah to the throne [9]]. In my experience, in Iran or in similar countries where eighty percent of the population is illiterate and without the least understanding, a popular revolution is impossible, unless the dominant power [the USA] finds it according to her wishes. It is only when she wishes to replace her puppets that she makes a revolution. She creates the discontent, she brings the crowds into the streets. And the people don't understand anything. I can prove to you that those who are making protest marches are people from the streets, ignorants! No intellectual, no educated intelligent man stands in the street to cry, "Long live this, death to that!" In my opinion [said with a mocking grin] this wasn't a revolution, it was unrest orchestrated for the change of pawns, of puppets! . . .

Q: In what sense do you think that the revolution was Islamic?

JALIL: It wasn't a question of Islam. They made the revolution to depose the shah, not for Islam. Haven't we always been Muslims? It wasn't a question of an Islamic revolution. It was a question of founding a republic, not a communist republic or a republic of mullahs [akhundee] . . . but a republic directed by a nationalist, an Iranian, a patriot. . . .

Q (to Masume and Moneer): For you, the revolution was Islamic?

MASUME: Yes, it certainly was. We made the revolution to free ourselves from the oppression of the shah. You know that it was in [the town] of Qom that the revolution began. Now, since we have made it, we accept privation and poverty.

Q: What Islam [do you have in mind]?

MASUME: The true Islam [*eslam rasteen*] that God proclaims in the Quran.

Q: What His Eminence [Khomeini] says, is the true Islam?

MASUME: Of course!

Q: Why? He is not the only great ayatollah [*ayatollah ol ozma*] in this country.

MASUME: Not all ayatollahs are Islamic men! People say that even the shah prayed too. He went to Meshed on pilgrimage!

Q: Why is His Excellence Khomeini superior to other great ayatollahs?

MASUME: Because, since the beginning [of the revolution], we have chosen him as our Guide. As soon as he declared his program, announced his predictions, everyone was on his side.

Q: What did he predict?

MONEER: Everything he predicted from the beginning, in Paris and afterwards. He predicted in Paris that the shah would fall. That happened later. His proposals, his declarations, when he asked people to storm into the streets, when he asked soldiers to desert. . . .

Q: Why was His Eminence right?

MASUME: Because we chose him from the beginning and everything he predicted came true; we believe in him.

JALIL: . . . [You say] everything [Khomeini] says is right? . . . Wasn't the revolution the work of the people in the street rather than Khomeini? They [the people] decided it!

MONEER: Who were those people? They were people like us; we marched in the street ourselves!

JALIL: You? You weren't even born when Khomeini was exiled [in 1963] from Qom!

MONEER: But our parents helped us understand and be aware of it.

JALIL: Khomeini carried no weight in this country; he was nothing.

MONEER: If he was nothing, why did they exile him, why did the shah fear him so much? . . .

Q: What do you want Khomeini to do? Certainly, his rule has marked a new era, and the situation in the rural areas has improved. What do you want him to do?

MASUME: If you want our opinion, the overall situation has not deteriorated. We haven't seen anything of that sort.

Q: And the people who complain?

MASUME: They've been complaining since the revolution began.

MONEER: They cannot get rich illegally [*bokhoran*] like they did before.

MASUME: Our society hasn't suffered at all. Think about the Algerian people who suffered a million deaths in the war [of independence]. A people like ours who haven't experienced want ask one day for freedom and the next day for food! And more than that—they then complain they have neither this nor that!

Q: You think there's plenty to eat?

MASUME: We have also the problem of the economic boycott [by the West].

JALIL (heatedly, angrily): Why break off our diplomatic relations with other countries when it is clear as day that we have nothing?

MONEER: If we don't do it, we can't rebuild the country.

Q (addressed to the two sisters): You took part in the Crusade for Reconstruction, didn't you?

MASUME: Yes, last summer. There was so much wheat to harvest that a large part was still there after we left.

MONEER: And women worked more than men!

MASUME: Even children worked. They loved it. At six o'clock in the morning we gathered in the mosque. We climbed into two or three trucks and took the road to Tehran. It was very hot. . . .

Q: What did you do during the revolution?

MONEER: We took part in demonstrations all the time. . . . Before the revolution we went to our cousin's for lectures on the Quran. One day they told us that he was no longer in Qom, that he was sent to Torbat-Djam and he could no longer receive us. He came back to Qom after the revolution. He took part in the anniversary of the death of Ayatollah Kachani in the great Mosque (of Qom). He is pro-clergy. You know what he said? That he would keep on backing the clergy even if they burned his house, his car, and everything he owned. The next day, somebody stole his car. That evening they told him that his house would have the same fate as his car. Who did that? Followers of Banisadr. . . .

Q: Is your school pro-clergy or pro-Banisadr?

MASUME: There are all kinds of sympathizers. They threw one of Banisadr's followers in prison, and all her colleagues stayed with her at prison.

Among them was one of my friends from school. When we took our exams she shouted, "Long live Banisadr!" . . .

Q: What is the relationship between Islam and the veil?

MASUME: Islam lets us go out without a veil?

JALIL: Islam leaves each one free to do as he wishes!

MASUME: It leaves us free not to wear the veil?

JALIL: Those who don't wish to wear it are free to do so, yes.

MASUME: No one is free to put the veil away.

JALIL: Wasn't the [revolution] started with the slogan "Liberty, Independence, Islamic Republic"? Recently your Khomeini said, "What do people want anymore? They wanted liberty and we gave it to them; independence they already had; as for the Islamic republic, it's there!" I should say, however, that in terms of independence, part of the country is occupied by Iraq. And as for liberty, may God bless its soul! We don't even have the liberty we had under the shah. All that's left is the Islamic Republic of Khomeini!

MONEER: How were we free under the shah?

JALIL: Wasn't life different for you under the shah?

MONEER: Every day, as if it were the anniversary of the birth of the shah, his majesty would appear in uniform; and let's not talk about TV and its programs!

JALIL: Now it's worse. Every day there are demonstrations or public meetings; it is awful. You turn on your TV or your radio, and from morning till night, it is Imam Khomeini. You open the newspaper, it is Imam Khomeini. I wish he'd go to hell!

MONEER: People didn't want the shah. When the shah spoke on TV, my father would say [to him], "Shut up!"

JALIL: Now I say the same thing to Khomeini; more people than I say it; everybody does it!

MONEER: Not everybody.

MASUME: The majority is with His Eminence [Khomeini].

MONEER: Perhaps not in Tehran.

MASUME: In Tehran, from what I've seen, some people are against the clergy, but that isn't to say that they are also against His Eminence.

JALIL: You made the revolution so that all the world would wear the veil?

MASUME: No, no one is forced to wear the veil!

JALIL: Well then, why did you make the revolution?

MASUME: We made it to be free.

JALIL: What freedom? Before, you weren't free and now you are?

MONEER: The freedom to wear the veil at school. If the inspector found you veiled, the principal would say, "Why are you dressed like that?" And she would remove the chador from your head.

JALIL: What other liberty do you have now that you didn't have then? For which freedom did you make the revolution?

MASUME: You are free to speak now. For example, the subject of compositions. I never praised the shah. But I wrote with fear and trembling. I couldn't say what I thought. Now I can.

JALIL: If one of the pupils is against the regime, she can say that?

MASUME: Yes, one girl who is pro-Fedai was in our class, and she did.

MONEER: These days one can criticize the whole world, the clergy, Banisadr.

MASUME: The pro-Fedai girl in our class didn't write directly against His Eminence Khomeini but she wrote things against the clergy, against censorship in the media, on radio and TV. Who stopped her? Nobody.

MONEER: Our teacher Mrs. Ashraf, when she wrote something during the time of the shah, they stopped her and threw her in jail.

Q: Something else. What is meant by *imperialism* these days?

MASUME: It means a relationship based on domination. It means taking over the whole country.

MONEER: For Lenin, imperialism developed with the dividing up of the world. In countries like Iran, America, or Russia, or even in other countries, the imperialists looked for a way to take over. We threw the imperialists out.

Q: Imperialism dominated you under the shah and now it no longer dominates you?

MASUME: The shah was under the yoke of America. Anything America asked him, he did. They threw people in jail by orders of the shah. And the shah took his orders from America. All the world was living under the illegitimate control and oppression [of the shah and America].

Q: After the revolution the clergy took over power. But some people weren't pleased with that.

MONEER: The mullahs had been in prison. Mr. Montazeri, Mr. Taleghani, and Mr. Khomeini—they had been in exile. . . . It is normal that they take power into their hands, that the clergy takes power in the name of the Imam [Khomeini]. We are happy with that!

Q: In your own city [Qom] what did people think about the political debates?

MASUME: People had different opinions. Some were one hundred percent for Banisadr. Others were for the clergy and against Banisadr. One of my friends learned to use weapons with the pasdars and brought a Colt [revolver] to school. In class, we discussed the Constitution. We read articles and spent maybe two hours in discussions. Banisadr supporters would argue with the pro-clergy and vice versa. We were very noisy. Our teacher didn't pay much attention to the veil. She was very kind. She never said anything against clergy, but her opposition to it was obvious, one way or another. The pro-clericals spoke to the school administration and demanded her dismissal. My friend [a girl], who had been trained by the pasdars, informed the Ministry of Education. She talked to the director of national education in Qom, who was a friend of Mr. Rejaee [minister of education at the time, later prime minister]. I asked my teacher if she would teach the next year. She said, "I think I shall be purged [*paksazi micham*]." In class it is always the same thing: fighting between [rival] groups. A week before *noruz,* the New Year, the administration forbade our teacher from discussing the [new Islamic] constitution. She was to read the articles one by one, comment briefly, and pass on to other things. I remained impartial in class. Banisadr supporters said things about the Islamic Republican Party. They stuck up a picture of Banisadr on the wall of the school; the others put up photos of clerics. . . .

JALIL: Since his return to Iran, Khomeini has opened a bank account, number 100, so that people can help the poor. One poor woman offered her only gold bracelet. There was another account, number 780 [for the same purpose]. From the beginning, they begged. Didn't they say that there was enough oil in the country, so that everyone would be rich? Didn't they promise to give each one a share in the oil company? Didn't they say, "We are going to lower the prices of water and electricity?" Now it is more expensive than before. . . . Why did these people promise what they couldn't afford?

MONEER: They wanted to give some freedom, but people misused it.

JALIL: No, they deceived everybody. They robbed everything, they took for themselves the riches of the country, they stole all the goods that were expropriated. People like Hamadanian, Ilghanian, and other millionaires had enormous wealth, innumerable properties. What happened to all that? With all that, they managed to build only two or three schools in Qom. That's all!

MASUME: They built according to need. In Qom, lots of people don't send their daughters to school.

JALIL: They don't send them because the mullahs say, "Why educate a girl?"

MASUME: Most of them get married early. Then they attend evening classes.

JALIL: Yes, they are given in marriage at fourteen, fifteen, sixteen. That is an old-fashioned idea, dating back to twenty-five hundred years ago. The Great Satan [the United States] is a pal of Khomeini himself, who let us fall into his arms. He has the cheek to call Carter the Great Satan! He himself deceived thirty-six million people in the country [the approximate population of Iran at the time of the revolution in 1979]. Is there anything more demonic than that?

Q: What about the hostages? Why were Americans taken hostage [at the American Embassy]?

MASUME: Do you think they shouldn't [be taken hostage]? Weren't [secret] documents found there [at the American Embassy]? They were spies. They were in Iran to spy on us. Didn't Carter himself try to free them? Remember the American attempt at Tabas [to free the hostages by a military operation].

JALIL: . . . The Americans wanted to send arms to the Afghan rebels through Iran. Several times the Russians warned them against that, but they didn't listen. This time, the Russians shot the American planes with their MiGs. Still, several Americans were there, with a helicopter in good condition. Under orders, Iranian planes bombed them and they killed all the Americans, every one, before the affair was disclosed. In the end, Banisadr said, "We will no longer allow the Russians to violate our air space." The head of the army in Tabas said, "It wasn't the storm that caused the airplane accident." This was also published in [the official Iranian newspaper] Ettala'at.

MASUME: Couldn't a miracle have done it? It is surely a miracle that the sand got into the airplane motors, the sand raised by the storm.

JALIL (laughing): You are joking!

MASUME: No, I'm not joking at all, I'm very serious!

Q: What do you mean by miracle?

MASUME: I mean that God threw sand into the motors of the American planes, so they would fall to the ground. There is a *sura* in the Quran about this [an allusion to the sura of the elephant: birds threw grains of hot sand on the elephants of a king who wanted to destroy the Ka'ba, the dwelling place of God].

JALIL: This imbecile eighty-year-old man with bushy eyebrows, have you looked at him closely recently? His eyebrows are still black, but his hair is white. Showering abuse on him is to do him too much honor!

MONEER: You will age more quickly; he [Khomeini] is the Guide of the revolution. He has in him something divine; his faith is from God. He rules because an invisible hand protects him in his room. He speaks to the Imam [the twelfth and last Imam]; his shoes step [automatically] aside before his footsteps!

NOTES

1. These interviews are reproduced in Farhad Khosrokhavar, *La Rupture de l'un-animisme dans la révolution iranienne* (Doctorat d'Etat, EHESS, 1992).

2. See S. A. Arjomand, *The Turban for the Crown* (New York: Oxford University Press, 1988).

3. See R. W. Cottam, *Nationalism in Iran* (Pittsburgh: University of Pittsburgh Press, 1964).

4. Paul Vieille and Farhad Khosrokhavar, *Le Discours populaire de la révolution Iranienne* (Paris: Contemporanéité, 1990). Farhad Khosrokhavar, *L'Utopie sacrifiée: Sociologie de la révolution iranienne* (Paris: Presses de la fondation nationale des sciences politiques, 1993).

5. Bernard Lewis, "Islamic Concepts of Revolution," in Vatikiotis, ed., *Revolution in the Middle East* (London: Allen & Unwin, 1979).

6. A. K. S. Lambton, "Quis custodiet custodes: Some Reflections on the Persian Theory of Government," *Studia Islamica* 5 (1956).

7. See Farhad Khosrokhavar (pen name A. Mahdjoube), "La Revolution interieure d'une militante Khomeiniste," *Zed* 1986, translated in *Women of the Mediterranean*, Monique Gadant, ed.

8. An organization, set up after the revolution, to promote rural development, at the same time preventing the rural youth from getting involved in "counterrevolutionary" activities.

9. Cottam, *Nationalism in Iran*.

POETRY AND PAGEANTS:
GROWING UP IN THE
SYRIAN VANGUARD

by Evelyn Early

Sing with children; play with them; learn from them, and teach them.

BANNER AT VANGUARD POPULAR CULTURE
FESTIVAL IN DEIR AZ-ZOR, APRIL 1982

The problem is that most children's plays are simply pieces borrowed from adult plays without any artistic planning to make them suitable for children.

DIRECTOR OF VANGUARD THEATER

In the Syria of the eighties, an important factor for social mobility was the Baathist Arab Socialist Party. Students who were members of the Baathist youth parties—Vanguard (at-Tala'i) for middle-school students and Youth of the Revolution (Shabibat al-Thawra) for high-school students—participated in sports, cultural, and other extracurricular activities and earned scholarships and special places in the university.

In Syria, the political party, along with the family and the school, plays an important role in the socialization of the youth. Youth party activities are shaped by Baathist social and cultural values. This chapter considers the Baathist view of popular culture and of children's socialization, as well as the performative discourse of the Vanguard Party. The core theme of the Baathist view of culture is authenticity. The theme is rendered "child appropriate" through the use of folkloric and children's game themes. Baathists feel that one should listen to children and keep things simple. The child's view of heritage molds Vanguard performative discourse.

The discussion is based on my interviews with Vanguard Party officials and on my observations of such Vanguard cultural events as photographic exhibits and plays, especially the weeklong 1982 Regional (Syrian) Seventh Vanguard Festival held in Deir az-Zor. As an official guest of the Vanguard theater director, I joined party leaders and journalists, and shared a classroom bedroom with several women youth leaders who donate their time to such Vanguard activities as festivals and summer camps. Adult-youth interaction at camp and at performances exhibited the quintessence of Baathist culture: a foundation of socialist nationalism with an overlay of Arab culture.

Baathist nationalism is based on a combined political agenda of Arabism, nationalism, and socialism, which informs the Vanguard performative discourse of children's plays. Indeed these performance situations serve as typical avenues for inculcating specific cultural values. The Vanguard has adopted traditional culture, formats such as ceremonial greetings, and the recitation of classical Arabic poetry for its Baathist youth party secular ritual and performance conventions.

POPULAR CULTURE: AUTHENTIC? DIVISIVE?

Authentic heritage is a critical component of Baathist Arab nationalism. "Pure traditions" (*turath shaabiya saliha*) are valorized through performances of folk dances and ideologically motivated plays and through exhibits of folk crafts and other handiwork. However there is disagreement among the Syrian Baathists concerning the threat of western (outside, nonauthentic) cultures, and on the role of ethnic, local (and potentially divisive) culture. Some oppose adopting western culture in any form, and criticize, for example, the National Theater in Damascus for presenting Shakespearean plays rather than exclusively Arab plays. Ironically, "Arab theater" started in Syria in 1847 with an adaptation of Molière's *The Miser* (McDonnell 1981).

The controversy over the role of folklore and popular culture in supporting the Baathist quest for authentic culture revolves around personal understandings of these concepts. The director of the Vanguard theater at the Deir az-Zor festival pointed this out and said that he himself felt that folklore was a way to present and preserve authentic tradition. He distinguished folklore from popular culture, which he defined as comprising various factors, but broadly "the popular characteristics which express the relations of the people to their life and . . . people's feelings about their life," not "just folkloric traditions." However, he continued:

> There are those who consider popular culture an obstacle in the path of Arab unity and who therefore oppose popular culture as a regionalistic divider. They

see, for instance, dialects as an obstacle to Arab unity. . . . Much of popular culture is oral, not written. Those who oppose the study of popular culture hate colloquial dialects. The Arab Writers' Union does not even recognize colloquial dialects; writers who write in the colloquial have been forced to write some of their works in classical Arabic so that they will be respected. . . . Some groups such as the progressives and nationalists consider popular culture a worthless topic, with no part being worth saving.

Other researchers have noted the vital link between folklore and authenticity. Layne analyzes an exhibit of everyday tribal objects in the Kreimah Community Center in the East Jordan Valley as an act of honor in which the Jordan Valley tribes "think of themselves as *asil* (genuine) and believe that *asil* tribes have honor and that non-*asil* tribes do not. Knowledge of one's own tribal history is of value in and of itself" (Layne 1987). Zubaida notes that a persistent theme in the ideological reconstruction of popular culture is "purification—popular culture must be rewritten to fit in with the general construction of an essential *national* history which establishes the identity of the modern national entity in time" (Zubaida 1987).

An authentic Arab, or a nationalist Baathist, is thus defined in opposition—both culturally and politically—to the West. While Baathists remain unsure of the balance between retrograde, local, popular culture and regional Arab nationalism, they are united on the need to speak of shared Arab traits such as bedouin hospitality.

The Vanguard Party links heritage with respect for environment. In the exhibits at Deir az-Zor, adult sponsors and their fledgling protégés alike repeated the theme enunciated to me by the director of the Vanguard artistic section. "We want the children to use their creative power, to discover the environment and that it should be preserved but that it can also be used creatively. We don't want them all to be Picassos but at least to be able to judge good and bad artistic quality."

As I admired pottery, embroidery, and other folkloric articles, eager children told me over and over how these pieces "preserved authentic tradition." A perverse anthropologist, I pressed them to define what was genuine about the displays. One youth pointed out an oil painting of a stick person composed of amuletic numbers and letters. The traditional element was obviously folk beliefs about curing; their presentation as a person, albeit a stick figure, presented a creative mix of tradition and the present. Another explained to me that an old-style pottery oil lamp festooned with a new knitted cover and a basket with colors matching those of dresses presented by the groom at a wedding were authentic because they presented an "old piece" with new covers and colors. I remained frustrated because I could not understand authenticity any better than I had when I started my tour of the exhibits. With time, I decided that I had learned a lesson similar to that of Layne's in Jordan: if everyday objects such as lamps or baskets are important folkloric pieces or— better yet—usable today with their new knitted covers or their well-chosen colors, then they are *asil,* genuine, and a material statement of honor—thus Baathist values. Baathist aesthetic discourse joins tradition with utility. Syrian Baathist youth are rewarded for the material salvaging of heritage. We turn now to consider Baathist views on socialization.

BAATHIST VANGUARD: ACTIVITIES FOR THE CHILDREN

When I interviewed the director of Vanguard education about party peda-gogy, he started with his own children, saying his first goal with them had been to be their friend; his own father had worked too hard and never seen his children. "You need to train children indirectly, to be polite and to co-operate." He explained that the Vanguard sees children as an important re-source, and values child-oriented expressive forms such as plays and exhibits. As we sat talking, he stood up several times to help move something or to talk with a child. He asked several passing children to introduce themselves to their American guest. Their response was always packaged in flawless classical Arabic: "I am comrade X from town X in the Syrian region of the Arab nation."

The education director remarked on the role of children's cultural events in inculcating Baathist, pan-Arab ideals of nationalism and socialism: "The plays at this cultural festival afford an opportunity for children to experience the principles which they have learned." The Vanguard Party offers a chance for children to be children, to perform at their own level. As the party slogan says, "Adults should learn from the children." What does this mean in prac-tice in an organization where leadership and planning is adult?

The deliberations of the committee for play awards at the Deir az-Zor festival provide a helpful insight. They criticized one play for being no more than a "bunch of movements" rather than choreography appropriate for chil-dren. The panel faulted another play (on the fall of the city of Aleppo) as too heavy and too full of historical detail to be appropriate for children. The following excerpt of the children's expressive culture committee's discussion crystallizes the Vanguard view: children's expressive culture should be true to history but not be too esoteric or abstract for children to understand. Follow-ing are excerpts of a discussion I attended in which invited nationally known artists ranked the festival plays for awards.

CRITIC ONE: The acting was bad; the children were not convincing performers.

CRITIC TWO: The performance showed no understanding of how to present an historical perspective artistically. The tragedy was complicated and not suitable for children. If the world falls apart, responsible adults should be the actors to present that, not children.

DIRECTOR OF VANGUARD THEATER: The problem is that most children's plays are simply pieces borrowed from adult plays without any artistic planning to make them suitable for children. In this play, there was no theme or scenario underlying the dancing. For example, the children's entrance dancing from the two aisles was simply the addition of elements which adults use. Children's plays require careful artistic guidance to avoid simply reproducing adult plays.

CRITIC ONE: The play had many unnecessary gestures.

CRITIC THREE: The performance was contradictory. For instance, the music was not appropriate for the mood of the play.

CRITIC FOUR: The performance forced adult music on the children. . . . The music should be the backbone of the text.

DIRECTOR: It seems that the composer does not know children. . . .

CRITIC THREE: For the child, everything is play. He could talk about conquering France and sing a ditty. After Islam, music changed from a formal structure to a popular trivialized one.

The Vanguard judges preferred expressive forms appropriate for children, songs at pitches children can sing, gestures which children can understand, and so on. Yet at the same time the critics felt that child-oriented culture should not distort history. Children should neither be patronized nor forced into adult expressive modes. In Vanguard performance, tradition is the "authentic goodness" of folk heritage; to be nationalistic is to preserve that heritage in public performances which use folklore to coalesce ethnically diverse groups.

Performance, for the Vanguard, should express the cultural understandings of nationalism, of corruption, of the polity and society in an arranged, scripted form. Performance is thus the representation of the shared understandings (culture, ideology) acted out within the framework of political/social realities to forge ethnic group identity, to critique government corruption, or to deliver other critical sociopolitical messages. Performance orchestrates a special meaning of the text—be it a folktale of martyrdom or a bedtime story of occupied cities.

Performances such as festivals or films are ritually set off from ordinary life at the same time that they crystallize cultural understandings of everyday life in a cultural map of that life. Syrian Vanguard cultural festivals with theater, poetry declamations, and folkloric dances and songs provide rich examples of mundane performance at the same time that they provide a window onto Syrian views of socialism and of performative discourse.

CHILDREN'S THEATER:
HEADY TOPICS MADE SIMPLE

Vanguard performative discourse is child-tailored. Puppet plays are an example of children's media. In 1981–1982, the puppet theater of Damascus presented *From the Nobles,* a play about aristocratic life and love, and *The Goose,* a fanciful "animal Disney World" play which encouraged the audience to participate in identifying the beasts of the wild. The children were instructed to call out every time the wolf appeared to threaten the goose; they predictably became carried away with other events and forgot to cry out. Then the goose was eaten up!

Children's plays at festivals such as the one at Deir az-Zor present contemporary themes (Palestine, Arab unity) and historic themes (oppression, feudalism, Arab glory). While the themes are serious, the plays are cast lightly in a child's everyday play world and often introduce colorful folk heroes.

One play staged at the festival was the story of Na'im, a ruler who allowed an Arab he was holding captive to go back to visit his family on condition that he return. The Arab, having given his word of honor, of course returned. Na'im, impressed by the power of the Arab word of honor, gave up his evil ways. The child actors set the scene for the Na'im play with girls prancing around on cardboard horses, shooting arrows at boys dressed in blue and red sultan costumes. This play was typical of Vanguard plays; it used an historical event to make a moral point and highlight an element (honor) of Arab identity. It mixed playful and historic scenes and used costumes and scenery which were colorful but not necessarily historically accurate.

In another Deir az-Zor play, a father told his children a bedtime story of a hero who spilled his blood for Palestine. His blood enriched the soil so much that trees (read, other patriotic fighters) rose to fight. When the father finished, the girls (in their nightgowns) joined peasant-dressed boys to mourn the martyr. The boys shook hands and embraced as the evening call to prayer sounded. Girls celebrated martyrdom's promise of a new life by dancing around a pole resembling a maypole. A similar admixture of the historical, the political, and the playful marked most of the festival's plays.

One play used simple lyrics suitable for children. The children tugged and chugged to push a train through many borders. When the train broke down, the children's chorus sang: "Go oh train, choo, choo, choo!" When officials requested passports, the children showed a blue and green map of the Levant and North Africa, and chanted in good Baathist fashion: "There are no borders and no need for identity cards; all Arabs are one." When a band of outlaws, presumably enemies of Arab nationalism, stopped the train, the children beat them off.

In another play, children's games predominated, such as tug of war, rope jumping, ball bouncing, and London Bridge. Boys came to "knock on the door of the antiquities," aptly symbolized by the moat crowns and mottle brick shawls worn by the girls. The queen of the antiquities lectured the children on the virtues of nationalism, self-sacrifice, and reverence for the antiquities they visited. The children then took photographs with their miniature cameras. The message, "respect your antiquities and heritage," rang clear.

Water figured prominently in another play. A child emerged from a brown cardboard well on the stage, and a fight over who had rights to the well water began. "Why don't we draw water from the well? Water to all!" Next came an interlude during which the children danced and engaged in a mock fight. Then a strolling water seller called out: "Prices are rising—in eggs, in chickens. . . . This is the beginning of exploitation. . . . Chickens now cost twice as much." The children joined in a chorus about water—asking whence it comes, how a community should give water to all, and who should drink first. Next, they demanded that the representative of the well owner bring down the price of the water. They chanted, "Bargaining accepted but decreased price forbidden. . . . The beginning of exploitation." The crowd threw stones at the representative of the well owner. Once again we have a clear Arab cultural theme—the sacredness of water and the right of access for everyone portrayed in the context of children's play around the well, plus the political theme of exploitation.

Exhibits and plays at Deir az-Zor were expressive activities of children, closely monitored by adults and carefully fashioned into cultural statements of the Baathist worldview.

THE POETRY MINBAR: THE PERFORMANCE THAT BINDS

Poetry readings were another important performative discourse at the 1982 festival. During the Deir az-Zor Festival, I attended a typical poetry *minbar* (reading) at Abu Kamal, a town almost on the Iraq border, about two hours from Deir az-Zor. Such readings are the local miniversion of the larger festival. While the party is centralized, it does not neglect the importance of local organizations sponsoring mini-events such as poetry readings. Local cultural events fete national guests and help bind the periphery to the center.

The Abu Kamal minbar consisted of a morning program of dance and poetry, a student art exhibition, and an elaborate tea party. The minbar ritual event began with our departure in a microbus from Deir az-Zor. A bunch of journalists, party leaders, and an anthropologist, we were in a party mood. We had no responsibility but to observe and enjoy (and for some, to report); we felt the euphoria of guests who did not fret about the quality of the tea, the caliber of the performers, or the weather. We paused at a coffeeshop to drink coffee and order take-away sandwiches. A few kilometers out of Abu Kamal we were met by the military commander of the town, representatives of the schoolteachers, and white-ribboned youth. The adults lined up on one side and the children on the other and we proceeded through the column to the accompaniment of special Vanguard handclaps—three sets of five quick claps followed by one set of three slow claps.

An official meeting us explained the town's features: "Abu Kamal has a paper factory, and rich soil which is not fully exploited because many of the youth are working in the Gulf. There are twenty-five thousand inhabitants or, if you include the suburbs, more than twenty-five thousand. A lemon orchard and an orange orchard were planted recently and the government has begun to pay more attention to this neglected area, though government funds are low because of the imperialist Iraqi harassment from across the border." (The Iraqi border is about five miles away.)

At the school two columns of children dressed in folkloric costumes clapped us in. One of them held a picture of President Asad, and two others held a banner announcing the festival and its patron, the president.

The walls were decorated with pictures of the president, party slogans, and welcome notices in addition to the student newspapers, which were large sheets of posters with party photos and the president's photos interspersed with snippets of information about the topic at hand—be it physics, sports, or the family. There were also party decorations—streamers of crepe paper and bows and flowers. On interior corridor walls other student work displayed included a physical-education digest, a map of Indonesia, and a student Vanguard newspaper.

We entered the school courtyard where dignitaries were seated by rank in the first few rows which, unfortunately, were smack in the sun. At such events representatives of the president or the local administration are seated in the front middle row, flanked by Vanguard officials, then press and teachers. After the first ten seats or so, there is little discrimination. Children sit anywhere they find a chair or a lap. Vanguard students, who are usually busy performing, stand anyplace they can find.

The minbar, like all other Vanguard events, opened with the party song and a round of welcoming speeches by local party officials. Then came a series of dances interspersed with poetry and music. A particularly memorable dance at Abu Kamal portrayed harvest and abundance, acted out with actual scythes wielded by young girls sweeping about in a circle. At the end of the performance everyone adjourned to admire the handicraft exhibit and corridor posters and newspapers.

The program at Abu Kamal resembled that of the Deir az-Zor festival. What was different about the minbar was the hospitality and ritual greeting by local residents during the event. After the performance we were invited to tea at a table groaning with mounds of stuffed grape leaves and platters of creme caramel. We remarked on the local specialties, such as the trufflelike sweet we discovered at Abu Kamal. After eating we were invited to discover the outlying provincial town's history on a visit to the archeological site of Mari. The Abu Kamal teacher led us carefully through all the period relics, and then invited us to a sumptuous lunch of kebab at a local restaurant.

A minbar such as Abu Kamal's promotes the local and the folkloric, in the service of the pan-Arab, modern socialist vision. The minbar ritual is as much a popular expressive discourse as the folkloric historical themes of children's plays; both use traditional forms (hospitality, heros) in a modern context to embellish the political ideology of Baathist socialist pan-Arabism. As the village is tied to the regional center of Deir az-Zor, so Deir az-Azor is tied to Damascus, which is in turn tied to other Arab cities outside the *qatar,* or region of Syria.

History defines polity. The definition of the heritage and the utilization of folklore are intimately connected to contemporary political discourse. When that discourse is one of and for children, the themes must be appropriately clear and light. The Vanguard aims to preserve what it perceives as authentic and true through folklore and art. The performative discourse of a children's dance in which they harvest a crop or invite villagers to a wedding is a combined statement of traditional Arab hospitality and of Arab nationalism. Performances appropriate for children present plays, stories, and dance to communicate ideological messages. In effect, Baathist socialization is a heavy dose of nationalism and socialism overlaid with Arab tradition in a flowery and compelling panoply of performance, sports, and academics. Adult attention to children and to heritage guarantees a distinctive, Baathist youth culture.

BIBLIOGRAPHY

Bourdieu, Pierre. 1977. *Outline of a Theory of Practice.* Cambridge: Cambridge University Press.

Layne, Linda. 1987. "Artifacts of Everyday Life: Inventing Culture and Tradition in the Jordan Valley." Presented at American Anthropology Association meetings, Chicago.

Manning, Frank. 1983. *The Celebration of Society: Perspectives on Contemporary Cultural Performance.* Bowling Green, Ohio: Bowling Green University Press.

McDonnell, Patricia. 1981. "Syrian Theater: Its Past, Present, Future." *Syrian Times,* June 4, 1981: 3.

Mitchell, Tim. 1989. "Culture Across Borders." *Middle East Report* 159 (July/August 1989): 4–6.

Turner, Victor. 1982. *Celebration: Studies in Festivity and Ritual.* Washington, D.C.: Smithsonian Institution Press.

Zubaida, Sami. 1987. *Mass Culture, Popular Culture and Social Life in the Middle East.* Boulder, Colo.: Westview Press.

Swimming in the sea, Casablanca, Morocco
PHOTO BY HEATHER LOGAN TAYLOR

PART VII

CHILDREN AND PLAY, CHILDREN AND THE ARTS

Sing with children; play with them;
learn from them, and teach them.

BANNER AT YOUTH FESTIVAL, SYRIA, 1982

Expressive arts in Middle Eastern society have always included children and continue to do so today. Traditional *hikayahs* ("true" stories) and *khurafahs* (fantasy stories) recited in families, coffeeshops, and neighborhood gatherings to groups of children and adults are still told, but sometimes in different settings and with new characters or adventures to reflect a different historical period. A few professional storytellers still hold forth in places such as the square of Djemaa el Fna in Marrakech, Morocco, but many of those storytellers now read or act out the old stories on radio and television. The animated version of "The Adventures of Sinbad the Sailor" from the collection *A Thousand and One Nights* is a popular children's feature on television all over the Arab world. The popular *garagoz* or puppeteers of Egypt are seldom seen tramping along the streets of villages and cities these days, ready to set up their portable stages, pull their puppets out of their pockets, and proceed to entertain children with the old story of the lady, the policeman, and the cruel husband. But many of those old puppet dramas, such as the tale of Imad-el-Din and his donkey, have been dressed up and transferred to the stages of theaters or made into films, where they reach millions of children.

Stories and songs once performed orally have been written down and are often found in school textbooks. The children's games and songs in this section are excerpted from a major volume collected and edited by the Egyptian folklorist Muhammad Amran. Ahmed Sweity, who translated them, remembered playing many of the same games as a child in Jordan. Children continue to contribute to musical traditions, as demonstrated by Veronica Doubleday and John Baily's essay "Patterns of Musical Development among Children in Afghanistan."

Children's written literature has become an important new middle-class

Boy playing and singing, near Herat, Afghanistan
PHOTO BY VERONICA DOUBLEDAY

genre in many countries, published in book form and also in special children's newspapers and magazines. Miftah Muhammad Dyab, of the Libyan University in Tripoli, sees this new children's journalism as playing a role in "developing children mentally, morally, socially and emotionally," expressing the same sentiments once attributed to traditional oral arts. Such children's publications date from 1887 in Egypt, with the appearance of *Rawdat al-Madaris,* published by Rifaah al-Tahtawi, a member of the first Egyptian delegation sent to Europe by Muhammad Ali to learn about the West. In the 1960s, children's magazines sprang up in Egypt, Libya, Morocco, Saudi Arabia, Jordan, Syria, Iraq, Kuwait, and Tunisia and continue to appear in the nineties.

Major literary figures have recently begun to write for children; an example is "The Small Lamp," by Ghassan Kanafani. And other new stories are being developed in response to a changing political landscape, as Taghreed Alqudsi-Ghabra shows in "Themes Reflected in Palestinian Children's Literature."

The oral arts live on, if passively, on television. A conservative estimate places television sets in over 60 percent of Middle Eastern homes. Children thus see many kinds of programs, American imports such as *Roots, Little House on the Prairie,* and westerns, as well as local productions ranging from dramatized traditional stories to modern soap operas. In 1979 Kuwait, hoping

Girl singing at cultural festival, Syria
PHOTO BY EVELYN EARLY

to improve educational programs for children, financed an Arab version of *Sesame Street* called *Iftah ya Simsin*. This series has been widely aired in the region, and the evaluation of the programs by Dr. Misbah al-Khayr and Dr. Hashim al-Samira'i of Baghdad University is one of many research projects dealing with increasing television watching by children. In this medium, children are exposed not only to traditional values and arts but also to values from all over the world. This is clearly a new phenomenon, and its long-term effects on children's attitudes toward themselves, their parents, and members of other societies are only now beginning to be a subject for study.

CHILDREN'S GAMES AND SONGS IN EGYPT

by Mohammed Omran
Translated by Ahmed Sweity

JUMPING ROPE

Jumping rope is widespread in Egypt, played by boys and girls from the age of six. Two players stand facing each other, and the distance between them is determined by the length of the rope, the ends of which are held by a player at each end. They spin the rope and a third player enters to jump over the rope whenever it approaches his feet. He bends over whenever the rope approaches him. This game is accompanied by a song, sung mainly by the girls, and particularly by the two girls spinning the rope:

> One two
> Uncle Husein
> Three four
> In the printing press
> Five six
> They opened the road
> Seven eight
> They cooked okra
> Nine ten
> They cut onions

These are from *Children's Games and Songs in Egypt* (Beirut: Dar al-Fata al-Arabi, 1983).

The singing continues and does not stop unless the rope is obstructed by the feet of the player who is jumping. Then another player jumps instead of the first player, and so on.

BALL GAMES

Playing ball is very common. It varies in its methods and differs from one region to another. It is often played by girls between five and thirteen years old.

Abaliy

This game is played by two girls. One stands near a wall, facing it. She throws a small ball against the wall, catches it, and then throws it back against the wall. Each time—after throwing the ball and before catching it—depending on her ability, she claps her hands once, twice, or three times before the ball bounces back from the wall.

The skill of the player and her superiority over her companion depend on her ability to keep the ball from falling to the ground for the longest possible period. Whichever player comes up with more moves (such as clapping in front and in back, or spinning around quickly) will be the most skillful. While playing, the player sings the following song:

> Abaliy Abalandi . . . hey kids.
> French bread . . . for money.
> The daughter of an Effendi
> Sleeps while I play.
> I feared she'd beat me
> I scored (one) against her.

If the player finishes the song while still keeping the ball in play, she scores one point against her companion. Then the song is repeated, to score another point. The player counts the number of points she obtains in the last phrase of the song. The first time—if the ball does not fall—she says, "I scored one against her." The second time—again, if the ball does not fall—she says, "I scored two against her," and so on.

One Two Three

This game is similar to Abaliy except that the ball is thrown to the ground and not against the wall. It is played by two girls. One of them bounces the ball on the ground, and whenever the ball bounces up from the ground, she repels it with the palm of her hand, while singing:

> One two three
> Uncle Husein shahata
> Seller of chocolate
> Peas O peas
> May Papa live and stay
> And may he plant the nab'a

If the ball falls, the player loses her right to play, and the competing player takes her place, singing.

In Minya County and the surrounding area, the following text is sung with the game:

> Hatta O duck
> O chin of the cat
> Sa'ida is coming
> from al-Gharbiyya
> And this is the jar
> And this is its lid
> And this is the Prophet
> Whom we are with

GAMES FOR SPECIAL OCCASIONS

SHAM IN-NASIM

On Sunday afternoon, the day before Sham in-Nasim day, boys carry life-sized cloth dolls on their shoulders along the street. Originally, the doll represented the British commander in Egypt, Lord Allenby, and has since then taken the form of various politicians and other figures. Today the doll is an effigy of any generally despised person and is ultimately burned. The boys wear feather belts and color their faces and shoulders with dyes, while performing a stereotypical "black African" dance and singing to the dolls:

> O Allenby
> O son of alambuha
> And your wife
> Became infamous

They continue:

> What is the matter with Allenby today
> He had a hair cut
> Death visited him
> Touched him and crushed him

At midnight they build a fire, throw the dolls in it, and sing while circling around the fire:

> O graveyard with two gates
> Where did you take Allenby?

Play and fun around the fire continue until dawn; then the boys go to the seashore to bathe and play other games with the coming of the new day.

ASHURA

In Siwa Oasis, on the night of Ashura, boys and girls celebrate this occasion by stripping leaf stalks from palm trees; they decorate them with henna and palm leaves. At their tops they fix a piece of cloth soaked with oil and they light the cloth.

Then they climb to the roofs of their houses and wave their palm-leaf stalks, while singing:

> My feast my feast
> O Hammudi
> O palm-leaf stalk
> O decorated
> Ashur walked away and left us
> If God wills, he will meet us next year
> Abu Mubarak O stangilah
> The palm trees have lots of dates.

RAMADAN

The month of Ramadan is one of the religious occasions that make children happy. During this time they play many games, especially games whose songs deal with the special meaning of this holy month.

O Breaker of Ramadan Fasting

In the early days of this month—before the time to break the fast—children (five years of age and above) show off to other children their ability to endure the hardships of fasting. Even boys and girls who are not fasting do not declare their breaking the fast, or else their peers will sing to them about their inability to fast:

> O breaker of Ramadan fasting
> O loser of your religion
> May the knife of the butcher
> Cut your intestines

This song became so widespread that children began to sing it while playing, not only to specific people who broke their fast. We observed that it is sung in most regions of Egypt by children moving in a circle with their hands joined, signaling their happiness and joy in this month.

Hallu O Hallu

After Ramadan breakfast, boys and girls go out carrying lanterns and walk around the quarter, singing:

> Hallu O Hallu
> Ramadan is kind O Hallu
> Open the sack, and give us a tip
> So that we go and not come back O Hallu

The Uncertain Ramadan

In the last day of Ramadan, boys, while playing, sing songs to say farewell to this month. In observance of the last day of the holy month—especially if the feast has not yet been announced—they sing the following song, while running and jumping about:

> O Ramadan O month of uncertain end
> Eat your predawn meal tonight
> O Ramadan O month of the copper basin
> O month present in all countries

And if the crescent moon is observed, and the following day is the first day of the feast, boys and girls rejoicing in the feast sing while running and turning in circles. The most widespread song for this occasion is the following:

Tomorrow is the feast and we shall celebrate
And shall slaughter a sheep
And shall put it in a pot
Come over and eat with us.

The Feast: My Rope Is Long

One of the favorite games for children is the game of clapping hands. During the feast, children and especially girls take care to keep their new clothes clean, so they avoid playing games that cause their clothes to get dirty. Two girls stand facing each other and clap their hands together, the right hand of the first player with the right hand of the second player, and the left hand with the left hand, while singing:

My rope is long O mama
It fell in the well O mama
I descended down to get it O mama
The Bey met me O mama
He gave me a pound O mama
What shall I buy with it O mama?
I shall buy a duck with it O mama
And the duck is *shouting* O mama
And it says: O my thighs O mama
O thighs of bad omen O mama
Abd al-Qayyum O mama
Grows lemons—O mama
His lemons are sour O mama
The sound of guns O mama
On the day of the feast O mama
The candles are lighted O mama
And I played then, O mama!

PATTERNS OF MUSICAL DEVELOPMENT AMONG CHILDREN IN AFGHANISTAN

by *Veronica Doubleday and John Baily*

The purpose of this essay is to describe musical performance among Afghan children and, more specifically, to examine the way in which children acquire their musical skills. Our data were collected during the seventies in the city and environs of Herat, the third-largest city in Afghanistan. Situated close to the Iranian border, Herat has strong historical links with Persian culture. In the past, poor communications kept Herat culturally distant from the capital, Kabul. Since the thirties the central government has exerted increasing influence on Herat and other provincial centers.

While our specific data derive from Herat, our general analysis applies to Afghanistan as a whole. However, we would point out that since the Soviet invasion of 1979 there have been radical changes in Afghan society. Civil war has made it impossible to carry out detailed research within Afghanistan, but we know that there has been considerable disruption in all aspects of Afghan life, including the musical activities of adults and children. Much of western Afghanistan has been devastated by war. Parts of Herat city have been destroyed; numerous inhabitants have been killed, and many have become refugees. We would expect patterns of musical development among social groups to change very little, but clearly some forms of musical expression will have been adapted and transformed.

Children do not learn music in isolation; their development is very much a response to stimulation and encouragement—or censure and discouragement. Our account of musical learning focuses on the social environment of

This is an expanded version of a paper originally presented by John Baily
at a conference on music and child development, under the title
"Children's Music in Afghanistan."

the Afghan child and its crucial impact on musical performance. In this essay we describe the general social context of music in Herat and then examine musical differences between the children of professional and amateur musicians and between boys and girls. This examination demonstrates distinct patterns of social and musical enculturation. Respectively, boys and girls from professional and amateur backgrounds developed very different levels of musical competence according to the richness of their musical environment and the expectations with which they grew up.

Music has been recognized as a sensitive indicator of cultural values. In Herat the traditional Muslim separation of the sexes affected all aspects of social life, including the performance of music. Another important factor was the orthodox religious prejudice against instrumental music, which meant that hereditary professional musicians were stigmatized for their work. The significance of gender and professionalism was clearly reflected in the musical achievements of Afghan children.

Beyond the intrinsic anthropological interest of these findings, the study of musical enculturation helps us to understand musical systems as cognitive phenomena. We can analyze how cognitive schemata are built up and from this we can extrapolate the information necessary for understanding their development. This in turn illuminates the nature of musicality and allows us to differentiate between innate biological components and those that are socially generated.

THE PLACE OF CHILDREN IN HERATI SOCIETY

Afghan society was—and is—firmly based upon the home and family. There was no government provision for health care or care of the aged, and members of the extended family supported one another in many ways. People were highly aware of kinship relationships and obligations and usually lived in extended-family households. Child care was the exclusive domain of women and girls. Women bore many children and the ideal was to have a large family. The infant mortality rate was high, which meant that children were greatly valued. Babies were treated with the utmost care.

Children grew up in a secure and physically intimate environment. As babies they were swaddled for several months, slept next to their mothers, and were regularly sung lullabies and rocked to sleep. They were not left to cry, but always picked up and comforted, and they were usually breast-fed for two years. Toilet training was a relaxed process. Generally speaking, children were treated with considerable affection.

In Herat there was strict segregation of men and women. Only a very small group of educated women lived unsecluded lives, moving openly in the public world of men. The vast majority of women wore a veil in public and worked and socialized within the domestic sphere. Men spent most of the day outside the house. The separation of gender roles began at an early age. Girls were expected to run errands for their mothers and help with housework. Boys helped with certain chores and later often became apprenticed in a trade or joined in agricultural work. Although male and female children played together, many of their games were gender-linked. Both boys and girls could attend mosque schools for a period of religious education. The general level of education was rather restricted, but girls' attendance at secular school was far lower than boys'.

THE PLACE OF MUSIC IN HERATI SOCIETY

The eminent ethnomusicologist John Blacking made a useful distinction between music as a cultural system, defined as something "which members of different societies categorize as special symbol systems and kinds of social action," and music as a human capacity, "an innate, species-specific set of cognitive and sensory capabilities which human beings are predisposed to use for communication and for making sense of their environment" (Blacking 1990: 71). In looking at children's musical development, we examine music as a human capacity, but we also include everything in the Herati children's environment that relates to melody, rhythm, and dance.

It is important to realize that the Afghan definition of "music" differed in certain ways from European or American concepts of music. The Afghan view of music was narrow: music (musiqi) was produced by musical instruments, especially melodic instruments. Thus many activities which are intrinsically musical, according to a scientific view of music as a human capacity, fell outside the Afghan definition. Singing was not musiqi, so religious singing, such as the call to prayer, women's singing, even when accompanied by the frame drum (daireh), and children's singing and drumming were not thought of as music. (See Sakata 1983, Ch. 4, for further discussion of the Afghan concept of music.) Instruments played by women and children were not considered real instruments (Sakata 1987: 86).

The seclusion of women had important consequences for musical performance. All social occasions, apart from intimate family gatherings, were segregated. Outside the theater, with its courtesan singers, it was rare for boys and girls or men and women to make music together. At weddings—the prime occasion for singing, dancing, and playing musical instruments—men and women gathered separately, often in neighboring houses. There were important differences between men's and women's musical styles, instruments, repertoires, and knowledge of music theory. These were gradually inherited by children.

Music occupied an ambiguous place within the Herati value system. Although it was conceded that music played an appropriate role in rituals and celebrations, it was generally disapproved of by religious authority. Orthodox mullahs (Hanafi Sunni) preached that the playing of musical instruments was a worthless and even sinful activity. The profession of musician occupied a low status. Although musicians were sometimes admired for their skill and artistry, they were also despised and stereotyped as bad Muslims. However, the orthodox puritanical disapproval of music was counterbalanced by popular and Sufi traditions which emphasized its positive spiritual values and considered music to be food for the soul. In certain contexts music was even used for devotional purposes.

The low status of the music profession resulted in an important social distinction between male amateur players and professional players (see Baily 1979). In Herat city, music at public or semipublic gatherings such as wedding parties and concerts was performed by hereditary professional musicians called *sazandeh*. Male amateurs were known as *shauqi* (literally "enthusiast"). They played for themselves and for friends, and strove to disassociate themselves from the derogatory sazandeh label. They emphasized that they played music for its own sake, not in order to earn money. They also stressed that their sons would not become musicians and this was not their inherited profession. (See Slobin 1976: 23–24 for further discussion of the term *shauqi*.)

Among women there was an obvious and clear-cut distinction between professional musicians (also known as sazandeh) and ordinary women who played music at home. Female sazandeh had an unambiguously low status because they played for strangers and received payment. They wore veils in public, but in their work they were unable to observe the proper rules of modesty. They were stigmatized as "easy women," if not prostitutes. (The courtesan girls who sang and acted at the theater did not come from the Herati sazandeh kinship group and are not considered in this study.)

Religious attitudes had other restrictive effects upon the status of music. In prewar Afghanistan instrumental music played no part in either the traditional or secular school curriculum. The mullahs who imparted basic literacy and religious education to young boys and girls at the mosque schools were strictly opposed to instrumental music. Nor was music taught as a subject in government schools. The singing of *tarana*, rousing group songs, did take place in schools, but never accompanied by musical instruments. Nursery education was in a fledgling stage: a few schools had opened in Kabul under the aegis of foreign advisors, and music was exploited as a useful tool for learning through songs and action games. This use of music in education was still unknown in Herat. After the communist government came to power in 1977, music education may seem to have been incorporated more into the school curriculum.

A formal theory of music known as the science of music existed in Afghanistan, but was jealously guarded by the male sazandeh. It included the Indian *sargam* system of oral and written notation (comparable in many ways to tonic sol-fa). The only children who had direct access to this formal knowledge were the male offspring of male sazandeh. In certain cases, ordinary parents took the unusual step of arranging instrumental tuition for their children by a sazandeh, but this was very rare.

THE PERFORMANCE OF MUSIC

A full description of the variety of musical styles played respectively by men, women, and children in Afghanistan is given by Baily (1988). The music played by male sazandeh was technically the most complex. They played instruments which required specialized techniques and exact tuning, such as the *rubab* (a short-necked lute) and *tabla* (a drum pair imported from India). While part of their repertoire duplicated what male amateurs, women, and children played, they alone played *kelasik,* the technically sophisticated classical art music.

In Afghanistan most musical instruments were gender-typed. In Herat only women played the women's frame drum called *daireh.* (The jew's harp, *chang,* was also played by women in some other regions.) Female sazandeh also used two other instruments of Indian origin which had been adopted by male professionals during the past fifty years: the harmonium and tabla. (In India the tabla is viewed as a male instrument.) Other specifically Afghan instruments such as wind instruments or lutes were viewed as exclusively male. (For a discussion of gender-typing and music, see Koskoff 1987: 1 – 23.) From the outset, children adopted their respective musical gender roles. Small boys participated in domestic music-making sessions but shunned the daireh as a girl's instrument. Girls never showed any interest in playing male instruments.

Unlike children in some other societies, Herati children did not have a distinct music culture of their own. Among the Venda of South Africa, for instance, John Blacking (1967) found that all children learned special children's songs and that children composed new songs themselves. In Herat there was little in the way of a specific children's musical repertory. Children did not compose new songs, although they did sometimes adapt the texts of adult songs. A variety of children's games have been documented in Afghanistan (van Oudenhoven 1980), but these did not appear to have a strong musical element. Some did have texts which were chanted rhythmically but not sung.

By contrast, children's musical performance centered around the imitation of adult models. They played songs heard from adults and copied the singing and dancing they saw at weddings. The fact that children tended to act out wedding rituals in their play demonstrates that wedding celebrations—with their high emotional charge and continuous music-making—were experienced by children as powerful and dramatic social occasions. In structural terms the music children played was no different from what we may call women's domestic music, and very often children played music with older girls or women.

It is also significant that there was no large body of songs for adults to sing to children. The lullaby, which was sung by women as they vigorously rocked babies or young children to sleep, was the only manifestation of this sort. At its most basic, the singing consisted of an extended repetition of the phrase "Allah Hu," but very often women sang a long selection of verses which were religious and often plaintive in nature. Closely associated with the rhythm of the rocking cradle and the trancelike state before sleep, the lullaby was undoubtedly an important early musical experience common to virtually all Herati children.

We will now examine the process of learning music by looking at four distinct categories of children, distinguishing between girls and boys and between children from ordinary (nonsazandeh) families and those from hereditary musician families. It is necessary to point out that the number of sazandeh in a city like Herat was very small, about thirty females and twenty males in this case.

GIRLS FROM NONSAZANDEH FAMILIES

Herati girls in nonsazandeh families learned to perform and participate in women's domestic music. This consisted of singing, either solo or in a group, usually accompanied by the daireh. This drum was also used to play the rhythms of a number of distinct dances. Women performed this kind of music on happy occasions connected with weddings or the birth of a new baby. Girls usually joined in eagerly with music-making, clapping in time with the daireh and joining in the choruses and refrains of songs. Such occasions afforded ideal circumstances for girls to listen, learn, and actively participate in music-making with gifted and motivated adult performers.

Children, particularly little girls, played this kind of music as a game, on their own or under the supervision of older females. If the family did not possess a daireh, girls would use a metal tray. They might even imitate the tabla drums with an upside-down washing bowl and bucket. Improvised instruments like these were characteristic of children's music-making because children did not normally possess instruments of their own.

Drumming and clapping played an integral role in these singing and dancing sessions, and rhythms were learned at an early age. Little girls were encouraged to dance almost as soon as they could walk, and they were sometimes called on to display their precocious talents in front of guests. The daireh clearly required some performance skill, but women didn't consider this something to be deliberately learned: it was a skill that was taken for granted. Girls learned to execute the various daireh rhythms by watching others.

Before reaching puberty, girls had a good deal of time for playing music and often developed a passion for this pastime. As they grew older, playing music was gradually discouraged. While music was seen as harmless for children, it was seen to be unseemly for older girls to express themselves in this way. There were other general restrictions: when the men were at home, for instance, girls would quiet down. If there had been a death in the neighborhood, loud domestic music-making was avoided out of sympathy for those in mourning.

As girls approached puberty, they played much less music, except when there was a valid cause for celebration. They realized that music was seen as flippant and childish and that they had to grow out of it. They strove to become more responsible, modest, and hardworking. They knew they would soon be married and that older women were already judging them as prospective daughters-in-law. A strong interest in musical performance could be interpreted as a sign of flightiness and reluctance to work hard. The desire to play music had to be curbed and therefore girls' musical talents had little chance to progress. Given the very low status of female sazandeh musicians and the fact that girls could not take paid lessons from men, ordinary girls never received formal training in music.

BOYS FROM NONSAZANDEH FAMILIES

Boys from nonsazandeh families were also exposed to women's domestic music and participated in it to some extent. They sang, clapped, or took part in the dancing, but did not play the daireh. In the villages there was a tradition of solo singing while at work in the fields, where boys could sing as loudly as they liked, exercising their voices and building up a repertoire of sung poetry. A seasonal occasion for boys' group singing occurred during the evenings of Ramadan (the month of the fast), when boys went from house to house singing special verses and begging for treats. This singing was fun and rowdy.

Just as girls improvised drums from common domestic objects, boys made their own toy instruments. In Herat the chief instrument of male amateurs was the *dutar* (a local type of long-necked lute), which could be imitated with a wooden spoon fitted with strings or rubber bands. Drums could be made from tin cans. Few boys had access to real musical instruments because they were expensive, delicate, and even slightly shameful—therefore kept well out of the hands of children.

Research on the way adult dutar players acquired their instrumental skills (Baily 1976) showed that they usually claimed to be self-taught, and were proud of the fact. They normally began playing the dutar at the age of about twelve, and learned by copying another performer (generally a relative or friend) without revealing what they were doing. They would listen, watch, and then practice in private. They often borrowed an instrument surreptitiously when the owner was out of the house. Acquiring a dutar of one's own, usually an old instrument bought from the dutar maker, was an important step. Boys were often discouraged by their relatives from learning music, being told it was sinful. They had to overcome many obstacles to learn to play the dutar.

As they grew older, boys had more freedom than girls to extend their musical knowledge. Groups of friends would get together to play music, a new type of learning situation which involved participation. The coordination of various melodic and rhythmic instruments was a more complex process than anything encountered in women's domestic music-making. A group of young amateurs might play dutar and drums together; the harmonium could be added and more rarely the rubab. A few amateur musicians took formal paid lessons, usually from hereditary musicians, to learn particular compositions and to find out something about music theory.

GIRLS FROM FEMALE SAZANDEH FAMILIES

While in some sazandeh families both men and women worked as musicians, in others only the men followed this profession and their women were kept in strict purdah. Those whose fathers but not mothers were sazandeh received no special encouragement to develop musical skills. On the contrary, the men of the family were at pains to distinguish their women from the low-status female sazandeh.

Here we examine girls whose mothers were professional musicians, although their fathers often followed another profession. These girls grew up in a world which was dominated by the performance of music. They all came from the same kinship group and lived in one particular area of the city, which reinforced the richness of their musical life. All the girls who worked in these professional bands were recruited through kinship or marriage, and they all acquired an acceptable level of competence in daireh-playing and singing. No girl from that kinship group was barred from playing in a band on the grounds of being unmusical.

A woman's band usually had four or five members, playing harmonium, tabla, and one or more dairehs. They performed dance music and popular and traditional songs to entertain women at weddings and engagement parties. These celebrations lasted for several hours or overnight, so women musicians took their daughters, babies, and young children with them. Family life went on: mothers could breast-feed their babies and older girls minded the small children. It was also a convenient way for these girls to learn about their prospective profession.

In the music profession, apprenticeship followed a pattern similar to other professions. Normally children of about nine or ten performed menial tasks in the workplace for a year or two, at the same time absorbing much important information about the skills they were to learn. For instance, weavers said that boys who constantly saw adults at the loom had no difficulty in learning to weave: they already understood the process. In the same way sazandeh girls, minding their younger siblings at weddings, watched and listened to the music and dancing.

At about ten or eleven, sazandeh girls began performing solo song-and-dance acts at weddings and would be rewarded by their patrons with small gifts of money. Far from being discouraged from music-making like other girls of their age, sazandeh girls were actually rewarded for being outgoing and confident performers. They competed for attention and were increasingly given opportunities to play the daireh and sing with the band, which was organized flexibly so that any member could drop out to rest or feed a baby when necessary.

The next task was to master the tabla. The female sazandeh played these drums with their own rather crude technique. They were ignorant of the correct Indian style and used simple flat-handed strokes. Their drums were of poor quality, and they made no attempt to tune them. Thus, although it was musically effective, in many ways the women's tabla playing fell short of the men's in quality. Some girls never became good enough to play tabla in the band, remaining in the subordinate role of singer and daireh player.

A few girls progressed from tabla to harmonium. They taught themselves, picking out familiar tunes with the right hand and pumping the instrument with the left. In the early stages the novice harmonium player might play only dance pieces; later she learned to use the harmonium to accompany her singing. A talented girl could lead a band, select songs, and structure a half-hour program of music by the age of about fourteen, and by sixteen or seventeen she could be an accomplished musician and independent band leader.

In contrast to the male sazandeh, the female sazandeh did not place great emphasis on technical finesse as instrumentalists. There was no tuition, apart from the correction of faults. Women encouraged and praised learners, but ultimately motivation was left to the individual, who learned through imitation. While female sazandeh expected any girl to be able to join in the singing and play the daireh, they recognized that the tabla and harmonium were instruments that had to be learned through the musician's own efforts. (For a more detailed account of the lives of women musicians in Herat, see Doubleday 1988.)

BOYS FROM MALE SAZANDEH FAMILIES

Boys raised in musician families grew up in a musically more complex world. While male sazandeh played the popular music repertory performed by women, they also performed various genres of art music closely related to the classical music of India and Pakistan which female sazandeh did not know. One of the distinguishing features of the male sazandeh's repertory was music theory, essentially a variant of Hindustani music theory with its *rag*s and *tal*s (melodic modes and metric cycles). Male sazandeh believed that music should be learned through the medium of notation and emphasized the importance of the master-student relationship through which musical knowledge should be transmitted. However, despite these ideals, it seems that boys learned music in much the same way as sazandeh girls: by ear, through exposure to the sounds of music, imitation of musical performance, and individual trial and error in a social environment in which they were encouraged by family members. There was no formal music training, no exercises of the type used to learn Hindustani music, and little notion of sitting down for a practice session.

Male musicians had some interesting ideas about musicality and its development. They recognized that some individuals were naturally musical and thought this had to be nurtured, like blowing on smoldering embers to make them burst into flame. They believed that early exposure to the sounds of music was especially important in the development of musical ability, and brought their small sons to sit with them on the bandstand. Even if the child slept, they said the sounds of music were still absorbed. If at the age of five or six a boy showed a lively interest in a particular instrument, he would be allowed to experiment with it. Of course, parents supervised this process—the instruments were too valuable to be left with small children. Parents would encourage what they saw as correct, but tended to avoid pointing out faults. This was a psychologically sound strategy, reinforcing the child's interest and motivation. Boys from those families in which the women were also musicians had the additional experience of going with their mothers to wedding engagements when young. They even occasionally played tabla in the women's bands.

By the age of about twelve, when amateur boys were starting to learn an instrument, the young male sazandeh was ready to begin his professional career as a member of a band. As soon as he went out regularly in a band he had an opportunity to develop more advanced skills through playing with others. A young singer–harmonium player of twelve might be able to lead a band for a set of songs and by the age of about sixteen could be a full-time bandleader. Although musicians were normally identified as players of a particular instrument, they often played other instruments—though not usually in public—and this was taken as a sign of musical maturity.

Within male sazandeh families, some boys did not become musicians. This was not because they were unmusical, but because they chose or were encouraged to go into some other profession. Sazandeh bands tended to be organized as family businesses and there was work for only a rather small number of full-time professional musicians. (For a fuller account of the lives of male musicians in Herat, see Baily 1988.)

DISCUSSION

We have demonstrated that there was a striking contrast in musical competence between children of sazandeh and ordinary families. Sazandeh children developed more advanced musical abilities in terms of cognitive and motor skills and knowledge of repertory. This difference did not arise from a distinction between what one might term formal and informal modes of music learning. One could not really talk about music education or musical training in this context, for these terms imply a "directed learning process" (Merriam 1964: 146)—the deliberate intent to create a learning situation—which was hardly the case among Herati sazandeh. Whether from an amateur or professional background, Herati children learned music in much the same way, through imitation and participation, in what one might describe as a course of self-paced instruction. The difference in the musical abilities of the two groups of children must have been caused by their exposure to different social environments. The learning situations and the learning processes were inherent in their respective family lives.

Imitation has not received the attention it deserves as a method for learning music. Merriam was surely wrong to see the role of imitation as simply a "first step," to say that "special skill requires special training," or that "formal training is required to become a real musician" (Merriam 1964: 147, 150). In Herat, imitation seems to have been central to the learning process. Imitation implies learning in a situation in which the child attempts to reproduce the thing itself. Acquisition has not been separated as a course of instruction, systematized for pedagogic purposes. Visual information is very important; it is often necessary to see how things are done in order to understand how to do them. Imitation requires the child to work things out for himself or herself; there are no systematic explanations. The difference in terms of ability between sazandeh children and other children lay in the musical resources available to be imitated and the way that imitation was encouraged.

A number of factors enriched the musical environment of the sazandeh child.

1. There was frequent exposure to the sounds of music from the earliest age.

2. There was strong encouragement to engage in musical play activities, with access to musical instruments.

3. There were models for emulation, frequent opportunities to watch and question adults and other siblings playing musical instruments, and to observe closely their instrumental skills.

4. There were regular opportunities to participate actively in the performance of music by skilled adults.

5. Sazandeh children grew up in a social world in which playing music seemed to be what life was all about, not a matter for inhibition.

These differences in musical environment are sufficient to explain the apparent differences in the musicality of sazandeh and ordinary children. There is no need to look for explanations couched, for example, in terms of genetic factors.

Learning by imitation has important consequences; inevitably the child reproduces what is going on around him or her. This is an example of culture as "a setup for learning behavior of very complex and specific types" (Gillin, cited by Merriam 1964: 162). This principle is clearly shown by a second contrast in the data: the variation between boys and girls.

Gender relations in Herat were clearly manifest in musical terms. Girls' and women's access to material goods and information was considerably restricted. Women played virtually only one instrument, the daireh, and they did not play the genres of art music. Differences in knowledge between sazandeh men and women were marked. Although they were professional performers, the women knew virtually nothing about formal music theory or specialized techniques such as tuning instruments. They did not play chordophones and did not know how to tune their tabla drums. In terms of melody and rhythm, the music they played was structurally simpler than that played by male sazandeh.

These gender differences in access to musical knowledge were counterbalanced by the fact that all children were exposed, to a greater or lesser extent, to women's domestic music. This was the simplest of the adult styles we have examined, and also the most widespread; there were far more female than male amateur performers in Herat. We see women's domestic music as the main enculturating experience for Herati children, the basic reservoir of music. From this children learned Herati rhythms, dances, and the basic popular and traditional song repertory.

The close relationship between women and children was reflected in their music-making. In structural terms there was little to distinguish women's domestic music from what children played. Women also provided children with the single most important early musical experience in the form of the lullaby. Rhythmical rocking, singing, drumming, and clapping constituted basic models for musical learning, all experienced within the home and maintained by constant contact between women and children. Moreover, this was a type of music-making sanctioned by religion, and therefore suitable for children. The separate worlds of men and women, of amateur and professional, were anticipated in the musical life of the child at home. From an early age the child learned to conform to the role that awaited him or her in adult life.

ACKNOWLEDGMENTS

John Baily's research was supported by a postdoctoral research grant from the Social Science Research Council while he was a research fellow in the Department of Social Anthropology, The Queen's University of Belfast, 1973 – 1978. During that period Veronica Doubleday collected the data relating to women's music in Herat.

REFERENCES

Baily, John. 1976. "Recent Changes in the *dutar* of Herat." *Asian Music* 8(1): 29–64.

———. 1979. "Professional and Amateur Musicians in Afghanistan." *World of Music* 21(2): 46–64.

———. 1988. *Music of Afghanistan: Professional Musicians in the City of Herat.* With accompanying audio cassette. Cambridge Studies in Ethnomusicology. Cambridge: Cambridge University Press.

Blacking, John. 1967. *Venda Children's Songs.* Johannesburg: University of Witwatersrand Press.

———. 1990. "Music in Children's Cognitive and Affective Development: Problems Posed by Ethnomusicological Research." In Frank R. Wilson and Franz L. Roehmann, eds., *Music and Child Development* (St. Louis, Mo.: MMB).

Doubleday, Veronica. 1988. *Three Women of Herat.* London: Jonathan Cape.

Koskoff, Ellen. 1987. "An Introduction to Women, Music and Culture." In Koskoff, ed., *Women and Music in Cross-Cultural Perspective* (New York: Greenwood Press).

Merriam, Alan P. 1964. *The Anthropology of Music.* Evanston, Ill.: Northwestern University Press.

Sakata, Hiromi Lorraine. 1983. *Music in the Mind: The Concept of Music and Musician in Afghanistan.* With two accompanying audio cassettes. Kent, Ohio: Kent State University Press.

———. 1987. "Hazara Women in Afghanistan: Innovators and Preservers of a Musical Tradition." In Ellen Koskoff, ed., *Women and Music in Cross-Cultural Perspective* (New York: Greenwood Press).

Slobin, Mark. 1976. *Music in the Culture of Northern Afghanistan.* Viking Fund Publications in Anthropology, No. 54. Tucson: University of Arizona Press.

Van Oudenhoven, Nico. 1980. "Common Afghan 'Street' Games and Child Development." *Afghanistan Journal* 7 (4): 126–138.

THE SMALL LAMP

by Ghassan Kanafani
Translated by Tura Campanella Cook

Sad news awakened the kingdom that morning. The kind old king, loved by all for his fairness, was dead. What was even sadder was that he left only a small daughter who was unable to rule.

In the king's will he said to his daughter, "To become queen, you must bring the sun to the palace. And if you can't do this, you must spend the rest of your days locked in a wooden box as punishment." The young princess summoned the old wise man of the palace and told him about the difficult mission her father had left her. She announced that she did not want to be queen.

The old wise man said, "The laws of the kingdom, written long ago, forbid a prince or princess from refusing to rule. You are daughter of a king and you cannot help but be a princess. Our kingdom has lived in happiness because everyone knows his duty and does not run away from it. Your father the king was wise indeed when he said that you must bring the sun to the palace or live in a box."

The next morning she decided to climb the high mountain from which the sun rose each morning. She asked the wise man what he thought of the plan and he replied, "My dear little princess, you have to fetch the sun without anyone's help." And so the princess set out to climb the mountain. But when she arrived at the summit, she discovered that the sun was still far away. It was impossible for anyone to grab hold of the sun. She returned sadly to the palace, locked herself in her room, and began to cry.

After two days the unhappy princess noticed a tiny slip of paper under her door. She rushed to it and picked it up. On it was written: "You will never find the sun in a locked room." The princess did not recognize the handwriting. But she decided to continue her quest for the sun, even if she had to climb the mountain every day.

That day the princess hung a notice on the outside wall of the palace. She proclaimed that anyone who was able to assist her in bringing the sun to the palace would receive a reward of jewels. Word spread throughout the kingdom that the little princess wanted to bring the sun to the palace. But no one was able to help her. Some people believed the princess was mad because she wished for something impossible. Others believed she was wise because she wanted to achieve the impossible. Yet no one was able to help her.

The old wise man told the princess that her time was about to expire. "Before his death," he said, "your father the king requested that I light a candle upon the moment of his death. If the candle burned down before you found a way to bring the sun to the palace, you would have to be punished." Then the wise man left the room. The princess sank into a deep depression. She felt she could never become a queen. She daydreamed about the royal robes which she would never be able to wear.

While she was absorbed in her sad thoughts, a very old man was trying to enter the palace. The guards tried to drive him away, but the old man was insistent. As the princess watched from her window, the old man cried out to the guard, "I want to help the princess!" "What can you do, old man?" shouted the guard. "I can be of much use to her," cried the old man. "Tell her that if an old person like me can't get into her palace, how can she expect the sun to come in?"

The princess tried to call to the old man but he had disappeared into a nearby alley. By the time she asked the guards to look for him, the old man could not be found. The princess returned to her room in the depths of despair. She started thinking about what the old man had said to the guards, but she did not understand what he meant.

She decided to summon the head guard, a trustworthy man who had served the palace for many years. The head guard told her that the old man came every night, but the guards would not let him in because they thought he was crazy. "He is only a poor man who carries a small lamp with him at all times," said the guard.

The princess said, "When the old man comes tomorrow, let him come in." But the old man did not return and the princess sank into grief and despair. While she was crying, she noticed another tiny slip of paper under the door. She rushed over, unfolded it, and read: "Time is running out. The big candle is about to burn out. Your tears and sadness don't solve any problems."

The little princess sprang up. If she didn't act she would truly spend the rest of her life in a locked box. She called the head guard and ordered him to bring to the palace every man in the kingdom carrying a small lamp. "All because of that crazy old man?" asked the surprised guard. The princess insisted. "I must test him. Perhaps the old man will be the solution."

The guards were sent to every corner of the kingdom with orders to wait until dark and then seize all men carrying small lamps and bring them immediately to the palace. That evening as the princess sat at her window watching the street, an amazing sight appeared. On the far dark horizon a thousand men carrying lamps were approaching the palace. The crowd grew with each passing minute, but the men were unable to enter. Then the princess ordered that the high walls be knocked down and the doors opened so everyone could enter the palace.

The princess came down to the palace hall, with the head guard at her side. In the hall, the brilliant light from the many lamps shone like the sun. The head guard exclaimed, "O princess, I cannot recognize the old man because all the faces here are alike!" The princess shielded her eyes from the great light and said to the guard, "I did not believe that so many lamps could be found in my kingdom."

"They're afraid of robbers," snuffed the guard. But the old wise man disagreed. "When darkness falls, every man carries his lamp in order to know his way."

The old wise man said to the princess, "Can you carry all these lamps at the same time?" "No, of course not," said the princess. "Thus it is with the sun," continued the wise man. "It is more light than one person can hold."

"Oh," cried the princess, "I finally understand everything now! The many small lamps all together became the sun my father spoke of!"

"Yes," said the wise man and pointed to where the sun was beginning to rise. Its glorious rays entered the palace.

"What a marvelous thing!" cried the princess. "It's happening for the first time."

"Yes, for the first time." The wise man smiled. "Why? Because you tore down the walls and doors. Have you forgotten? The walls hid the rays of the sun and kept the men with the lamps out of the palace." And the wise man placed on the head of the little princess the royal crown encircled with jewels. "You are the queen," he said, "because you fulfilled the will of your father. You brought sun into the palace."

CHILDREN'S GAMES AND SONGS FROM TUNISIA

Collected and translated by Sabra Webber

The children's nursery rhymes and lullabies included here were collected from all around Tunisia in the late sixties. They are a very small sample of what is to be found. Both lullabies and nursery rhymes differ from town to town and each town has many. Sometimes the same lullabies have different melodies in different towns. I have seen similar lullabies from other parts of the Arab world represented as poems. These Tunisian examples, however, are sung or chanted (like a religious chant) and most are meant to lull babies to sleep.

OLD MOTHER TAMBO (A GAME)

Some Tunisians say that this game is derived from a Phoenician sacrifice to the goddess Tanit. Phoenicians of the region are thought to have sacrificed a woman to Tanit in times of drought to make the rains come. In the modern game, two sticks are dressed to resemble a doll (Mother Tambo) and the children carry this doll from house to house singing the following song. The women in the houses which are serenaded throw a bucket of water on Mother Tambo (Tanit) and, consequently, on the children. The children must not flinch from the water or the game loses its power to bring the rain.

> Your old Mother Tambo, my children,
> Asked God to give her flowers
> Your old Mother Tambo, my little ones,
> Washed her djebba in the river
> Your old Mother Tambo, my children

Asked God to sustain her
By bringing the rain.
Dear God, dear God
If it is your will,
Make the rain fall;
Give us beans in the dewy morning;
God, give us pepper in the hot morning,
And corn too, for a full stomach.

BLIND CHICKEN
(A GAME LIKE BLINDMAN'S BLUFF)

What are you looking for?
My daughter's earring.
What's its color like?
A prickly pear ripening.
What's it wrapped in?
A red handkerchief!
Here! I've got it, my friend!
Here! I've got it, my friend!

BUTTERFLY

Butterfly, oh butterfly.
I didn't know where to put it
So I put it in a flower,
And ten little butterflies
Flew out to me.

THE TODDLER (A SONG TO SING WHILE A CHILD IS LEARNING TO WALK)

Toddler, toddler,
Oh my son! Look how he's growing;
He brought a basket of apricots;
He gave them all to his mother;
And none to us.

TRAVELER'S SONG

Rainbow in the evening
Catch your camel and ride away.
Rainbow in the morning
Get off your camel, rest, stay.

DEM-A-REENA-DAY-DAY

Dem-a-reena-day-day
The meat is tender day-day
Oh my friend Bou Deleaf,
Dance for me awhile and then . . .
A little money I'll send you
To buy some cigarettes, I say,
Dem-a-reena-day-day.

SERVANT'S SONG

He who would buy me,
You see, I'm for sale!
Feed me and fill me,
I'll work, I'll fly!
An hour for work;
An hour for sleep.
Try to wake me—
I don't want to wake
Go! Leave me!

LULLABY

Now he is coming from Manouba
Oh drummer, give him music!
Oh revelers, make him welcome as he comes
With his mule and his saddle
And his servant with him.

CHOCOLATE BAR

A bar of chocolate went along to Mecca
After warning her children,
"Watch the house while I'm gone."
If there should come a robber,
Give him two quick slaps,
If there should come a beggar,
Give him money just as fast.

LULLABY

As he had one son, he will have many
And gather them together around me
Fill up the garden and orchard with little ones
And give to those who have nothing.
The women see my son
And pray for a child so fine
The virgins see my child
And crowd around my door.
One said, "I'll marry him."
One said, "I'll take him and run."
One said, "As Allah knows,
I dreamed of him
While he was yet in his mother's womb."

TEETA, TEETA, TEETA

Teeta is a game like patty-cake with a grown-up helping a child make the hand motions.

Teeta, Teeta, Teeta
Papa brought a little fish,
We're going to eat it in olive oil.
My frying pan is sputtering.
The cat's already nibbling the bones,
Papa washed his hands, but found
The Asaida prayer was finished.

So he clapped his hands to his face.
Teeta, oh Aneba
What did Papa bring us?
He brought us lots of henna
So I'm going to put on henna
And give the rest to Shoosbena.

THE CAT

My cat sent me a letter from Sousse
And gave me seven kittens;
Three of them ran away
And one is shy
Oh teacher, my cat reads and writes.
I swear on the head of my big brother,
I don't lie.
Oh Papa, my cat scratched me on the leg.
My cat stole my bread from my hand
Oh, my sorrow, the neighbors took my cat from me.

HEAVEN HELP ME!

Heaven help me! Heaven save me!
I refuse to marry a bedouin's son
I want a ministry secretary
For in an airplane he'll take me
And in Paris he'll promenade with me.

Heaven help me! Heaven save me!
I won't marry the partying one
The one who eats
Prickly pears with melon.

Heaven help me! Heaven save me!
I won't take a man who's always praying
I'll take the one who can drum and sing,
One who makes the music ring.

THEMES REFLECTED IN PALESTINIAN CHILDREN'S LITERATURE

by Taghreed Alqudsi-Ghabra

The Arab world today is a clear example of Third Worldism. Its aspirations and dreams for economic, social, and political relief continue. At the beginning of the twentieth century, with the collapse of the Ottoman Empire, the British and French colonized the area. The end of the colonization period marked a stage of independence for many Arab countries, and a new era of nation building began.

In this new era, people's struggle for social and political as well as economic equity is the major concern. Economic development is still insufficient, even with the oil revenues of oil-rich Arab countries. The population of Egypt, whose 50 million people constitute one third of the Arabs, suffers from extreme poverty. The gap between the haves and the have-nots is increasing.

Modern schooling and education have contributed a great deal to fast social development. Yet problems and conflicts between modernity and tradition are visible. Conflicting images appear everywhere to reflect this condition, whether among different classes, social strata, or between men and women. Political equity is another major concern. Problems of different Arab states in this regard vary in intensity depending on the kind of regime in power.

With other Arab states gaining independence following the end of British and French colonization in the area, the Palestinians faced another era of foreign rule. The introduction of the Zionist project has brought thousands of Jewish immigrants from all over the world with the intention of making a Jewish majority and therefore a Jewish state in Palestine. The 1948 war ended with the declaration of the state of Israel and with the transformation of Palestinian society into a population of refugees.

Palestinians presently number 4.9 million. Around 2 million live inside

Israel and in the occupied West Bank and Gaza Strip. The remainder of the Palestinian population is scattered around the world, with major concentrations in Jordan (1 million), Kuwait (350,000), Lebanon (300,000), and Syria (250,000).

Since 1948 different forms of Palestinian art have reflected the Palestinian tragedy and quest for nationhood. Children's literature also reflects this quality. Children's literature plays a major role in the lives of Palestinian children. Its role is not relegated to mere entertainment. Education and the reproduction of a value system that represents adults' viewpoints are a function not only of Palestinian children's literature but also of any kind of children's literature.

This essay examines several children's books published by Dar al-Fata al-'Arabi Publishing House. Dar al-Fata was started in 1974 and marked a new trend in publications for children and young adults. It is the first Arabic publishing house in the region dedicated to publications directed at children and young adults as its audience. The authors and illustrators who work with Dar al-Fata are Arabs. Therefore it is directed at an Arab readership and produced by Arab minds. This makes the productions of this publishing house true and native expressions of native attitudes, beliefs, aspirations, and frustrations.

An investigation of all of Dar al-Fata's stories would clearly show that its authors and illustrators are representative not only of the entire Arab world but also of its interests. Here I will concentrate on Palestinian stories and how they reflect specific themes of Palestinian life. The principal themes found in the stories include:

1. A work ethic among Palestinians.

2. A history of Palestine and the lessons it provides.

3. A love of the land, which is the basis for a strong national feeling.

My translations of the five stories and poems are appended to the end of this essay.

IMPORTANCE OF WORK

Before the 1948 war and the dispersal of the Palestinians, Palestinian society was predominantly a peasant society. Men and women worked together on the land. Tilling the land and taking care of the crops and harvests were major activities for the villagers of Palestine, so work was a major part of their day.

After 1948, just to survive, people had to work very hard. Since the war, Palestinian hard work and education have been their only means of survival.

Continuous economic and political crises in the Middle East affect Palestinians and result in a lack of choices for them. Wherever they live, they must abide by that country's rules and laws. For the Palestinian, survival means working very hard to prove that he or she is invaluable.

The Guardian of the Spring (Appendix 1) is a story about a disabled little girl named Samaa' (sky). To feel productive Samaa' insists on guarding the village spring while the villagers work in the fields. She is to pull a rope and ring a bell if she witnesses any suspicious movement. But Samaa' gets tired, sleepy, and her chair slips away from her while she is on guard. At the approach of danger, after several attempts to reach the rope, she finally manages to stand up and pull on it, saving the villagers.

When the villagers come to check on her, she has disappeared. The villagers get together and sew a flag that reminds them of her. This becomes the village flag, and its colors are

> Red for Samaa's rosy cheeks,
> Green for her green eyes,
> White for her clean heart and
> Black for her beautiful hair.

This story begins with a detailed description of Samaa's insistence on work, on doing something for her people and feeling productive as a result.

HISTORY AND ITS LESSONS

This story deals not only with work but also with history. In this story, the spring had been attacked before. Throughout its history Palestine also has witnessed and withstood one invasion after another. Palestinians are taught this at a very young age. It is significant for it provides the Palestinians the hope that this era will have an end as previous ones had. In the psychology of the Palestinians this has worked two ways. On the one hand, it has provided them with the ability to continue on and see an end, even though real circumstances might have indicated otherwise. On the other hand, continuous invasions have created a Palestinian character that is skeptical and suspicious. As a result there is a feeling that conspiracy is everywhere.

This suspicion as a result of a history of invasion is clearly demonstrated in *A Story of Colonization* (Appendix 2). Despite the book's short length, its pictures tell a great deal about the dispossession of the Palestinians, about their becoming refugees in tents, depending on the help of the United Nations Relief and Works Administration. In this picture book, although the Palestinians have welcomed the strangers and foreigners, they are nevertheless betrayed. This reflects the reality of a history in which Arabs fought with the allies against the Ottomans, yet Britain granted the Balfour Declaration to the Zionists.

LOVE OF THE LAND

In many stories love emerges as a source of power. In *The Guardian of the Spring* the village people's love provided Samaa' with the strength to fight her weakness and stand on her feet and pull the rope, to announce to the villagers that strangers were coming toward the village. Another sentiment often expressed in Palestinian literature is the love for the land. Not only do the people of Palestine love the land, but the land itself loves its children. In fact its love is what is going to bring the Palestinian people back again to the land. This notion is clear in the *White Pigeon* story (Appendix 5).

On another level of analysis, these stories represent ideological points of view central to the Palestinian situation. Palestine should be the Palestinians' center of attention, in other words, the center of their struggle. The complexities of Palestinian conflicts and arguments about prioritizing the major conflict over the secondary ones emerge as lessons taught to Palestinian children at an early age. Their situation among the Arabs and the role they play in an independent movement, which is nevertheless part of the Arab system, is indicated in these stories. It is clear in *The Guardian of the Spring* that Samaa' stands on her own two feet. Samaa's action signifies the Palestinian resistance that started independently of Arab policies. The villagers' flag signifies Palestinian identity and independence. An important message is conveyed here. Even though Samaa' disappears physically, her spirit remains. The flag is a continuous reminder of this spirit; the colors of Samaa's flag are the colors of the Palestinian flag. This flag, like Samaa's, is a national symbol that should be loved, admired, and remembered.

In Palestinian literature and poetry, Palestine is always portrayed as a woman, generally as a mother and her children, giving and loving, with the characteristics of a loving and caring mother. This is illustrated in the poem *She* (Appendix 3).

Looking again at *The Guardian of the Spring,* we note that Samaa' is a young woman. Her youth signifies the relatively young age of the revolution. For Palestinians who are assisted in all aspects of life by the PLO (in education, health, and employment), this revolution is a source of giving. For others who are well-to-do and who themselves contribute to the Palestinian movement, it is a source of pride restored to them that had been lost in the pre-revolution era between 1948 and 1965.

The importance of the Palestinian movement to its people is symbolized by the good luck the village people attributed to Samaa's birth. For the Palestinians, the revolution marked a happy beginning after the loss that marked their lives in the 1948 war. Palestinian literature of that era reflects this loss clearly.

The fact that Palestinians attribute all their problems to the loss of their homeland adds to the importance of the resistance for them. The reality of the quality of life people had lived in Palestine becomes insignificant compared to the problems resulting from losing Palestine. For these people true happiness is to go back and live in their homeland. In *The Homeless Little Nightingale* (Appendix 4) a bird is kicked out of his orchard by crows, becomes sad, and stops singing. When asked to sing, he answers, "I only sing in my own garden! I only sing for my own garden."

All of these lessons and sentiments, directed to small children, represent a culture and express a point of view that is often repeated to ensure its reproduction. The propagation of these ideas provides Palestinian children with a sense of identity, and with the ability to counteract what the "other side," the "enemy," says about them. Palestinian stories thus help to guarantee the continuity of the community and of its attitudes and beliefs.

APPENDIX 1

The Guardian of the Spring

STORY BY ZAYN AL-'ABDEEN AL-HUSAYNI

A happy farmer lived with his wife in a small village. The couple used to help everybody. Everybody in the village loved them in return and wished God would send them a child to fill their life with happiness.

This wish was granted and the couple had a baby girl [detailed description of her green eyes, red cheeks, black hair]. Her birth coincided with a good harvest. The village people decided to name her Samaa' [sky].

A year passed and Samaa's legs did not grow. Her mother and everybody were sad that Samaa' couldn't walk. Samaa' grew to be eight years old [detailed description of her beauty and comparison to nature]. The children of the village used to go and keep her company, tell her stories, and teach her to read and write.

She could not dance and sing with the others at the end of the harvest time and this made her very sad, but the spring water told her that she could guard the spring instead of sitting under the olive tree. The village people used to take turns guarding the spring. In fact, thieves had tried to take it over several times and divert the water to their fields. The village people hung a bell on the branch of a tree and rang it whenever there was any danger.

Samaa' decided to ask whether the village people would allow her to take on the job of guarding the spring. She was very happy when they agreed to let her do it once every two weeks.

The day she was to start her work, her parents helped her to the spring, gave her food for the day, and told her what to do if she saw a stranger. Samaa' sat there for a while. It was noon and she felt tired and started feeling sleepy, but the waves of the spring water woke her to warn her that her people were about to lose the holy spring. While she was asleep, her chair had slipped so she could not reach the rope to ring the bell. After several desperate attempts, Samaa' managed to reach it [extensive details], especially when she remembered the people's love of her.

Samaa' saved the village people. But when they went to see her, she was gone. But they were sure that she would be back.

So the villagers decided to make something that would remind them of her. Every family bought some silk and each made a flag of four colors to hang over their houses.

> Red for Samaa's rosy cheeks,
> Green for her green eyes,
> White for her clean heart, and
> Black for her beautiful hair.

This is how Samaa's colors became the colors of the village people's flag. They were sure that Samaa' would come back again to ring the bell when the thieves tried again.

APPENDIX 2

A Story of Colonization

IDEA BY BASIM SIRHAN

This is a picture book with only two small pages of text as follows:

The strangers came from behind the sea. The people (our people) were hospitable and kind. They welcomed them. Suddenly the strangers' true ugly face appeared and their bad intentions became clear. The people had to fight the invaders.

The pictures appear as follows:

A picture of a calm, green village.

Some guests come (wearing western clothes and hats) and the natives welcome them.

Suddenly an armed man appears, to the astonishment of the natives.

More and more of these people come.

A native is killed.

At the same time, trees are cut and homes are built.

A native comes with a gun.

The gun cannot withstand the more complicated weapons of the invaders, who bring more and more.

Houses are built and people settle in them, and the natives look from a distance at what used to be their olive grove.

The natives are put in tents and given sacks of flour by the same strangers.

A picture of a gun and a hand stretched to grasp it.

A picture of an armed native going toward the newly built houses.

APPENDIX 3

She

BY HILMI AL-TUNI

She is as proud as the mountain.
She is as deep as the ocean.
She is as vigilant as the moon.
She is as warm as the sun.
She is as generous as the clouds.
She is as fertile as the land.
She loves all that grows.
And I am a tender plant.
She is my mother.
She is my Homeland.
 Palestine

APPENDIX 4

The Homeless Little Nightingale

BY HASSIB KAYALI

Wafa is a pretty little nightingale with light brown feathers. Wafa learned to sing from his parents, both of whom were well-known musicians whose fame and songs had spread both inside the country and abroad.

Wafa, like his parents and grandparents, had been born in a beautiful orchard by the seacoast. Everyone, even those in faraway countries, knew that it was the most beautiful orchard in the world. Its soil was so fertile that there were many orange, lemon, and tangerine trees, also olive and pomegranate trees; they were all crowded together and intertwined, like the trees of a dense forest.

So beautiful was that orchard that its whole fence was made of crimson roses, anemones, jasmine, and lilies.

Wafa had a very great love for his garden and would awake each day with the first streaks of dawn light. A rose that grew near his house would call out to him, "Wafa!" and Wafa would answer, "What is it, dear neighbor?"

And the rose would say, "First of all let me wish you a good morning."

"And a rosy morning to you," Wafa would say.

The two of them would laugh and the rose say, "Wafa, sing us a song."

"Certainly, fragrant neighbor," the nightingale would say, and Wafa's voice would flow out into the quietness of dawn, as delicate as the day, as tender as a mother's heart, as sweet as spring water drunk by a thirsty man.

Most of the songs told of the beauty of his homeland, of its trees and flowers, and of Wafa's love for it. Once he sang this song:

> O most beautiful of homelands.
> O sweet orchard mine.
> What do I love about you
> More than anything else?
> Is it your lovely hedge?
> Your flowers of pomegranate?
> The blueness of the boughs
> of your olive trees?
> The lemon blossom?
> Or your lovely perfume?
> I love all of you—my homeland.

The crows were envious of the nightingales in the orchard, so black flocks of them attacked it and chased the nightingales from their homes. Among them were Wafa and his family. Some of the nightingales were pecked on the head by the crows and died in the orchard, while others suffered serious wounds. The rest managed to escape and wandered about as homeless refugees.

Wafa and his family took shelter in a nearby orchard where some relatives of the family lived. The relatives gave them a very good welcome and made room for them, inviting them to live with them. But they remained sad, for they were far from their orchard and their home.

One of the roses in the new orchard learned of the arrival of Wafa and his family to their orchard, so he whispered in the ear of a neighbor, "Do you know who has settled in our orchard?"

The other rose looked at the apricot tree on the branch of which Wafa stood, and asked, "Isn't he the one who's standing on the branch of this apricot tree, right close by?"

"Yes, he's the one," said the first rose.

"But he seems so sad," said the second rose.

"How can he not be sad," said the first rose, "when the crows have chased him and his family and all the inhabitants of their orchard from their homes!"

"Come along and let's ask him for a song. Perhaps that will console him and we ourselves will be made happy."

"Wafa!" the first rose called out.

"What do you want, neighbor?" answered Wafa in a sad voice.

"Sing us a song," requested the first rose.

Wafa gave a deep sigh. There were tears in his voice as he said, "I only sing in my own garden! I only sing for my own garden!"

APPENDIX 5

The White Pigeon

STORY BY ZAKARIYA TAMER

The pigeon flew down and landed on a river bank where she sat crying. A fish looked up at her from the river and said, "Why are you crying? Aren't you feeling well?"

The pigeon said, "I'm crying because when I returned to my nest I didn't find my daughter there. She must be lost."

"You are right to cry," said the fish, "for I too am a mother like you and I well know how mothers feel when any harm comes to their children."

"And what makes it even more painful for me," said the pigeon, "is that my daughter is still young and hasn't learned how to defend herself."

"I shall help you," said the fish, "by looking everywhere in the river for your daughter."

"There's no point in your looking for my poor daughter," said the pigeon, "because you won't find her in the river. Someone with wings doesn't live in the water."

"Then you'd better carry on your search for her yourself," said the fish, "because crying is no use and won't bring back your daughter."

The pigeon flew off and went on searching for her little daughter who was lost, but after a short time she became tired and landed in a green field. She imagined to herself her daughter, a little pigeon with weak wings, confused and terrified, calling out to her mother to come and save her. When the mother pigeon broke out crying, a rabbit asked her, "Why are you crying? If you're crying because you're hungry, I shall show you the way to a garden full of the best kinds of carrots."

"It isn't hunger that's making me cry," said the pigeon. "I'm crying because I've lost my little daughter. I've looked for her everywhere but haven't been able to find her."

"I am able to run quickly," said the rabbit, "and I'll help you in your search."

The pigeon thanked the rabbit for his wanting to help her, but said to him, "Young pigeons all look the same, and if you saw my daughter you wouldn't know she was mine. No one except me, her mother, is able to recognize her."

Once again the pigeon flew off to continue to search for her lost daughter. Then the pigeon saw a donkey busy eating a mound of grass. "Have you seen a small white pigeon?" she asked of him.

In surprise the donkey said, "What a strange and extraordinary question to ask! Has anyone ever seen a donkey staring up at the sky? Donkeys look down at the ground to see where their hooves are stepping in case they fall into a hole."

At that moment a black cat came up to the donkey and the pigeon. "What are you talking about?" he asked curiously.

"Have you seen a small white pigeon?" said the pigeon to the cat.

"I wish I had," said the cat. "If I'd seen it, it would by now be lodged in my stomach."

"What a badly behaved cat you are!" said the pigeon. "Is that the way to talk to a mother who is suffering?"

"Let me eat you," said the cat, "and then all your sufferings and sorrows will be over."

The donkey became angry and said to the cat, "If you don't go away at once I'll give you such a kick you'll find yourself in the middle of a hundred dogs."

So the cat took to its heels, while the pigeon said, "What shall I do? The sun will shortly set and night is about to fall."

"Off with you," said the donkey. "Off with you and continue to search for your daughter instead of wasting time talking to a donkey."

So the pigeon flew off and went on searching for her daughter, while darkness gradually descended. When the fields had become dark, the pigeon returned, weeping sadly, to her nest. On arriving back at the nest she was surprised to find the little pigeon already there.

"Is it you?" she exclaimed joyfully. "Where were you? Were you lost?"

"I fled from the nest," said the little pigeon.

"What are you saying?" said the mother. "Do you flee from your mother who loves you so much?"

"I fled away," said the little pigeon, "to have a look at the world outside the nest; then I got lost."

"And how did you get back?" asked the mother.

"I don't know," said the little pigeon.

Then the mother remembered how, one day when she was young, she had lost her way and was guided back to the nest by her love for the place in which she was born. Then she said to her little daughter, "All those who are lost and far away from their homes will be guided back to them by their love for their homes."

IFTAH YA SIMSIM (OPEN SESAME) AND CHILDREN IN BAGHDAD

by Misbah al-Khayr and Hashim al-Samira'i
Translated by Ahmed Sweity

For many years, the Gulf Cooperation Council (GCC) for the Arab Gulf countries considered producing a children's program along the same lines of Sesame Street. Consultations were held among GCC countries to discuss how to go about producing a program as good as Sesame Street, while meeting GCC's objectives of serving Gulf and Arab and Islamic children.

GCC countries, therefore, decided to establish the Joint Program Production Institution (JPPI) to take up, in cooperation with the Children's Television Workshop in New York, the production of Part 1 of Open Sesame. The budget was allocated for this and other programs to be produced by these countries to enhance and to develop the Arab heritage, traditions, and customs of the region, while reviving its history and folklore, with particular attention to desert and sea life.

Upon its establishment, JPPI formed a special team to visit the Children's Television Workshop in New York and to negotiate joint production terms for completing Open Sesame. The committee set up the objectives of the new program based on recommendations made by the JPPI's board of directors, who are the undersecretaries in the ministries of information of the GCC. A contract was, therefore, concluded for the production of 130 programs, each thirty minutes long, to serve the preschool and primary children.

The committee organized by the JPPI was primarily concerned with setting up programs related to the Gulf, Arab, and Islamic environment. Goals included teaching the children about Islamic principles, positive social behavior, personal manners, and the importance of such traits as honesty, respect for parents, loyalty, and social interaction. Other purposes were to illustrate, with audiovisual methods, characteristics of the Arabic language and its alphabet. For example, programs were designed around the letter F, Fataha (to open); the letter K, Kho'urouj (going out); the letter D, Dou'khoul (coming in), and so forth.

464

Live action, puppets, and cartoons were used. The use of puppets of course draws on Arabic cultural traditions, from the shadow puppets of Syria to the puppeteers of Egypt.

After Part 1 of Open Sesame *was completed, it was broadcast in all Arabic-speaking Gulf, Arab, and Islamic countries. The outcome was very positive and agreeable to the viewers, particularly the children, who were the primary target of this production.*

Two years later, JPPI invited a number of children to Kuwait from other Gulf, Arab, and Islamic countries to assess their assimilation of the program. Educational, media information, and social specialists evaluated children's attitudes toward the program. The general result was that children aged 5 to 7 years had acquired an impressive quantity and quality of information from watching the program, as the following article demonstrates.

The Ministry of Education, in turn, initiated its own scheme for televising the series at the preschool level, to be watched by those children who had not had the chance to see it earlier.

JPPI received a great number of letters of appreciation and was commended for its efforts in this area. Parents have stated that the effect of the program on their children's learning was reflected in the children's own imitations of the sounds and movements made by characters on the program. These sounds, said the parents, helped the children to produce a proper alphabet and to express themselves further.

Following the great success of Open Sesame, *JPPI has decided to proceed with the production of Parts 2 and 3 to continue with the education and entertaining of children.* Open Sesame *has helped children of preschool and kindergarten age to accumulate sufficient information and to prepare to absorb the knowledge and training of later years. The children, the target of* Open Sesame, *have also given their enthusiastic approval to the project.*

Iftah ya Simsim (Open Sesame) has stimulated the imagination of Arab children through the television screen since 1979. Since then the flood of studies evaluating this creative program has not stopped regardless of whether these studies are scientific research or doctoral or master's theses submitted to Arab, European, or American universities. The most recent evaluation of this program appeared in *Al-Buhuth* No. 21, a magazine published by the Union of Arab States Radio Stations and the Arab Center for Research in Baghdad. This research was conducted by Dr. Misbah al-Khayr and Dr. Hashim al-Samira'i from Baghdad University.

This new research aims to evaluate the influence of *Iftah ya Simsim* on the information and knowledge of Baghdad children in language, general information, mathematical and social information, and in the areas of the sciences and moral principles. The study was confined to investigating the validity of the central hypothesis of the research, which proposes the existence of abstract differences between the information and knowledge level of children before watching the *Iftah ya Simsim* program and after doing so.

The experimental method was relied on in this study. Two samples of Baghdadi children were chosen, a control sample and an experimental sample. Each sample consisted of forty children. Each group was subjected to two experiments, a pretest and a posttest. A random set of ten episodes was video-taped. The children watched the episodes daily in a carefully controlled environment.

The two axes around which the segments of the two experiments revolve are general information (language, math, history, geography, and science) and moral and educational principles. The results were statistically analyzed.

The results showed that *Iftah ya Simsim* generally had a tremendous effect on all levels of knowledge and comprehension which the experiment investigated. The following is a summary of the results.

Language ability

The results showed an increase in the level of children's knowledge of language. The linguistic goals of *Iftah ya Simsim* emphasize growth in children's language acquisition and an increase in their repertoire of vocabulary items, as well as developing their expressive abilities and reading skills. The results of this study also have shown a tremendous increase in the abilities of children for reading and writing the Arabic letters and in using them to write familiar words in their daily life.

Mathematical knowledge and reasoning

The program presents a mutual relationship between knowledge and perception by means of adding new and tangible experiences that enrich the child's knowledge and improve his reasoning and rational discrimination. The study showed that the program is successful in doing this through teaching children arithmetic, the correspondence between numbers and figures, numerical configuration, addition and subtraction, recognition of some geometric shapes, and the distinction between one shape and another. The program is also successful in teaching rational perception (reasoning) by means of recognizing differences and similarities between objects and sets of items, or through comparing the elements constituting each, regardless of whether this is done by means of tactile, visual, or auditory perception, or by all these means.

The natural environment

The results of the experiment showed an improvement in the level of the children's knowledge about the natural environment after watching the series of *Iftah ya Simsim* episodes. The program has as one of its goals the development of children's knowledge about the natural environment, that is, of the phenomena surrounding man, and the organic connectedness between it and the resources of human life such as food, drink, clothing, fruits, and animals, and knowledge of such things as that eggplant is a vegetable, that fish live in water, and that the chicken is an egg-laying animal that reproduces through its eggs.

General knowledge

The program has also achieved its goal of developing in children an understanding of the effects of technology on society, whether represented by tangible aspects such as means of communication (telephone and wireless) or means of transportation (airplane, car, boat), or by intangible aspects such as the relationship of man with time and his relationship with the components of the external environment. Also, the children's social awareness increased, as did their comprehension of social roles and the functions of social groups.

Geography

Results showed tangible improvement in the children's knowledge of the geography of the Arab world, their knowledge of the various countries in the Arab world, and their capitals and cities. This achieves an important aim of the program: developing the children's feeling of belonging to the Arab nation, and taking pride in that feeling.

Arab history

The children's knowledge of some of the bright pages of the history of the Arab nation increased. This was achieved by introducing them to some castles and fortresses that witnessed historical battles, and to events that have left their imprint on contemporary reality.

The sciences

The program paid attention to scientific thinking in children and the effects of technology on society. This was accompanied by concern about the natural environment and the influence of the sciences on children's knowledge. The children were taught such things as how sugar is extracted from cane, and the difference between materials such as sugar and salt. The results of the study showed, for example, an increase in the number of answers children could give about plants. This shows that the children comprehended the scientific information presented in the program.

Moral principles

The study also showed that a principal aim of the program is reinforcing the values and ethics that are derived from the teachings of orthodox Islam and inspired by the Arab nation, in order to help children develop a sound moral vision on the basis of which they will build their family relationships, and which will reinforce the values of cooperation, love, and justice.

Finally, the research undertook to investigate the extent of the children's interaction with the series in respect to their admiration of the presented segments, or their attachment to specific characters. The purpose was to ascertain the degree to which the children followed the series because of the effect this may have on the influence that the program exerts on the children's behavior.

It became clear to the researcher that a large percentage of children, about 85 percent of the sample, watched all or most of the series. This indicates that the program has established an intimate relationship with its audience of children. The most attractive segments for children are cartoons, followed by songs, then puppets, then numbers, and finally letters. Children most love the characters of Niman, Anis, Karkur, Abdulah, and Hisham, in that order. Therefore, the importance of *Iftah ya Simsim* becomes evident especially in the Iraqi environment, as is testified by the children of Baghdad.

CONCLUSION

The children now coming of age are the first generation to be born and to grow up since independence from colonial rule, and therefore the first generation to perceive themselves as members of nation-states. This is the first generation to take for granted and expect free secular education; the first to grow up with raised expectations for the future; the first to grow up with television and its widespread representation of other places, life-styles, and consumer products; the first to grow up in a vastly changed class system, as the old aristocracy has declined and a middle class emerged; and the first to grow up under world capitalism in conditions very different from those of their parents.

However, the family remains a central concern, the cultural ideals about it well in place. But it is changing, adapting to new needs in order to survive, and helping its members survive in a difficult economic time, as the gap between rich and poor widens. Though the larger kin group may be more or less dispersed, some of the signs of unity remain. The rituals of childhood continue—naming, circumcision, graduation from school, marriage—but in somewhat different form. Naming ceremonies are still widespread among all economic groups, but boys' circumcision ceremonies are becoming less frequent in some areas as this operation becomes a routine part of hospital deliveries. Circumcision of girls is declining even in rural areas.[1]

Family ceremonies now respond to events set not only by the family unit but also by the requirements of the larger social world. Graduation from Quranic school, though still an important rite of passage in some families, has been superseded by graduation from secondary school. When the student who has successfully passed his or her baccalaureate exam, the key to further achievement in the society, finds his or her name published in the national newspapers, the entire family honors the new graduate with a feast reminiscent of older celebrations. In all Middle Eastern countries, a farmer or working-class young man's rite of passage to adulthood is two years' compulsory military service, usually in an area of the country far from home. Once he has completed his military service, he is free to marry and start a career. In Turkey, the entire village or neighborhood turns out to see the boy off on his bus journey into adulthood. Puberty no longer marks the end of childhood and the beginning of adulthood; an intervening stage, the construct known in the West as adolescence, is beginning to be documented.[2] Marriage, the final ritual which marks the beginning of adulthood, is occurring later. Engagements are lasting longer, and the choice of marriage partner is becoming a matter of negotiation between children and parents, rather than between parents alone.

In this urbanizing-industrial society class is becoming increasingly important as the gaps between the rich, the new middle class, and the poor widen, and the old signs of social status—birth and religious affiliation—are being replaced by educational achievement and the accumulation of wealth.[3] The lives of children reflect this: those whose parents have some means are able to take advantage of the new educational and health opportunities, to move into newer jobs and become part of the middle and upper-middle class system, often referred to as the western modern sector of the economy. Other children, whose parents are struggling with crushing economic problems, must help to maximize, often by wage labor, the minimal source of income at their disposal. While the cooperative values of such families are admired, their material conditions are deplored by governmental pronouncement and frequent media attention.

Today, children and teenagers may also be seen as exerting political force, not only in the West Bank and Lebanon but also throughout the area. Growing up to expect that a better life is their right, reading newspapers, exposed to international media on a regular basis, they put pressure on national leaders to achieve stated goals. Most Moroccans would agree with the government official who stated that "children and their problems and aspirations are the nightmare of the King."[4] Here in the United States, as our population ages, it is difficult to conceive of the explosive possibilities of such a new youth-centered society, its aspirations often thwarted, its expectations unfulfilled.

The family of tomorrow in the Arab world may be smaller and less male-dominated, its child-rearing practices more varied, according to new class divisions and income differences, but the child is still perceived as the crucial link between the present and the future, crucial to the future not only of the family but also of the entire nation-state. In her recent monumental, three-volume "Les Représentations de l'enfant dans la société marocaine," Dr. Aisha Belarbi found that parents and teachers continued to characterize children as "creatures lacking 'aql or reason and needing discipline." Children in the same study, asked to characterize themselves, said, "I'm just a person aged so-and-so. I'm a person." [5] These persons constitute the overwhelming majority of today's population in the Middle East.

NOTES

1. Unpublished papers presented at "Changing Status of Sudanese Women" conference at Ahfad University, Omdurmam, Sudan, 1979; see also proceedings of "Bodily Mutilation of Young Females" seminar in Cairo, Egypt, Cairo Family Planning Association, 1979.

2. Susan Schaefer Davis and Douglas A. Davis, *Adolescence in a Moroccan Town* (New Brunswick, N.J.: Rutgers University Press, 1989).

3. John Kenneth Galbraith, *The Nature of Mass Poverty* (Cambridge, Mass.: Harvard University Press, 1979); Malcolm Kerr and Sayed al-Yasin, eds., *Rich and Poor States in the Middle East: The New Arab Social Order* (Boulder: Westview Press, 1982); Hind Abou-Seoud Khattab and Greisa el-Daeif, "Impact of Male Labour Migration on the Structure of the Family and the Roles of Women," Report 2 (Egypt: The Population Council [West Asia and North Africa Region], 1982).

4. Muhammad Abdelkebir Alaoui M'Daghri, "The Code of Children's Rights in Islam," *Matin du Sahara* (Rabat, Morocco), April 26, 1988.

5. Aicha Belarbi, *Les Représentations d'enfant dans la société marocaine* (Thèse pour le Doctorat d'Etat Université, Paris V René Descartes; Sciences Humaines, Sorbonne, 1988).

CONTRIBUTORS

DAISY AL-AMIR is one of the outstanding writers in the Arab world today. An Iraqi citizen, she has lived in Lebanon for over twenty-five years, and is a former director of the Iraqi Cultural Center in Beirut. Her collection of short stories, *The Waiting List,* has just been translated into English and published in America.

AICHA BELARBI, a Moroccan sociologist, is a member of the Faculté des Sciences de l'Education in Rabat. She holds a Ph.D. from the Sorbonne, Paris V Henri Descartes, where she wrote her dissertation (recently published) on "Representations of the Child in Moroccan Society." She has been a visiting scholar at the Center for Middle Eastern Studies, Harvard University.

JERINE B. BIRD lived in Saudi Arabia for ten years between 1962 and 1982, and in other Middle Eastern countries for an additional ten years. She was a teacher of English in Jiddah and a sewing instructor for village women in the Eastern Province. The wife of an American diplomat, she had extensive contacts with government leaders and has written articles about her work.

JUDY H. BRINK is an associate professor of anthropology at Lock Haven University of Pennsylvania. She has conducted research in rural Egypt on the effects of education, employment, and religious fundamentalism on Egyptian women. She has a Ph.D. in anthropology from the University of Pittsburgh.

DOUGLAS A. DAVIS is a professor of psychology at Haverford College, where he teaches courses in personality and culture. He received his Ph.D. in psychology from the University of Michigan. With Susan Davis, he is author of *Adolescence in a Moroccan Town* (1989).

SUSAN SCHAEFER DAVIS earned her Ph.D. in anthropology at the University of Michigan, Ann Arbor, and works as an independent scholar and as a consultant on economic development. She has written books on adolescence and on women in Morocco, and articles on those topics and on water and development.

SUSAN DORSKY works for Six County Inc., a community mental health agency in southeast Ohio. She remains interested in the welfare of children, doing individual, group, and family counseling, and participating in Family and Children First, a State of Ohio initiative designed to help children by strengthening their families. A licensed social worker, she has a B.A. in psychology, an M.A., and a Ph.D. in anthropology, all from Case Western Reserve University.

VERONICA DOUBLEDAY and JOHN BAILY did field work in Afghanistan during the 1970's before the 1979 Soviet invasion. John Baily was at that time a research fellow in the Department of Social Anthropology, the Queen's University of Belfast. During their stay in Herat, Veronica Doubleday collected data relating to women's music. She is the author of *Three Women of Herat*. John Baily is an ethno-musicologist teaching in Britain whose most recent published work (1988) is *Music of Afghanistan: Professional Musicians in the City of Herat* (with accompanying cassette).

EVELYN EARLY is an anthropologist who has written on popular Islam and, with Donna Lee Bowen, coedited *Everyday Life in the Muslim Middle East*. She is also the author of *Baladi Women of Cairo: Playing with an Egg and a Stone*. She has taught anthropology at the University of New Mexico, Notre Dame, and the University of Houston. She has a B.A. from Macalester College, an M.A. from the American University of Beirut, and a Ph.D. from the University of Chicago. At present she is a member of the U.S. foreign service.

HASSAN AL-EBRAHEEM is chairman of the board for the Kuwait Society for the Advancement of Arab Children, a position he has held since 1980. A former Minister of Education for Kuwait, he is a founding member of the Arab Human Rights Organization and a member of the International Advisory Council of the American University of Beirut. He has a Ph.D. in political science from Indiana University. He has published several books and articles.

MARYAM ELAHI is the program officer for Middle East, North Africa, and Europe at the Washington Office of Amnesty International. She is vice-chair of the board of directors of Defense for Children International USA. She has a B.A. in biology from Williams College, an M.A. from the Fletcher School of Law and Diplomacy, and a J.D. from Boston College School of Law.

EFTETAN O. FARRAG received a B.A. in psychology and an M.A. in sociology-anthropology from the American University in Cairo. She is the mother of three sons and lives in Cairo.

ADELE K. FERDOWS is a professor in the Political Science Department of the University of Louisville. She is the author of numerous articles dealing with women and Islam. She received a B.A. from the University of Tehran and a second B.A. from Southwest Texas State University. She has an M.A. and a Ph.D. from Indiana University.

FARHA GHANNAM is a Ph.D. candidate in the Department of Anthro-pology at the University of Texas at Austin. She has a B.A. in communica-tions and an M.A. in social anthropology from Yarmouk University in Jordan.

AKILÉ GÜRSOY is an associate professor at Marmara University, De-partment of International Relations. She has a B.A. from Durham University, England, and a Ph.D. from Hacettepe University, Ankara. She was a Rocke-feller fellow at the University of Texas at Austin, where she also served as visiting associate professor of sociology. She writes and lectures frequently on issues relating to the family in Turkey.

JAMAL ZAKI AD-DIN AL-HAJJAJI is a folklorist and lexicographer who lives in Luxor, Egypt. He is currently working on a dictionary of collo-quial Sa'adi Arabic.

BARTON R. HERRSCHER is an associate professor in the Depart-ment of Educational Leadership and Cultural Studies at the University of Houston. He is a graduate of the public schools and colleges of St. Louis, Missouri (A.A., B.A.), Southern Methodist University (M.Ed), and UCLA (Ed.D.). He is a former college president and holds the Distinguished Alum-nus Award from his undergraduate alma mater, Harris-Stowe State College in St. Louis.

PATRICIA J. HIGGINS is a professor of anthropology at the State University of New York, College at Plattsburgh. She has carried out research in schools and homes of a lower middle class district of Tehran (1969–1971) and undertaken follow-up research as a Fulbright lecturer at Tehran University (1977–1978). More recently she has been studying education and ethnicity among Iranian immigrants to California.

HOMA HOODFAR is a British-trained anthropologist teaching at the Department of Sociology and Anthropology, Concordia University, Montreal. She has carried out extensive fieldwork in Cairo, Montreal, and Tehran on the impact of social and economic change in the lives of Muslim women.

STAFFAN JANSON is a doctor in the Department of Pediatrics, Uppsala University, Sweden. During 1986–1989, he was responsible for the development of a Swedish-Jordanian project, the Institute of Child Health and Development, in Sweilah, a suburb of Amman. His research has been published in Uppsala.

GHASSAN KANAFANI, a distinguished Palestinian writer, teacher, and journalist, was born in Acre in 1936 and was killed in Beirut in 1972. His best-known works include *Men in the Sun, Return to Haifa,* and *All That's Left to You.*

KARI H. KARAMÉ, currently a sociologist at Oslo Institute of International Affairs, has lived, taught, and done research in Lebanon. The essay included in this book is part of a larger study of the Lebanese Civil War.

FARHAD KHOSROKHAVAR is an Iranian sociologist who collaborated with Paul Vieille on a project to explore people's attitudes toward the 1979 Iranian Revolution. Their joint publication, "Le Discours populaire de la révolution iranienne," appeared in *Contemporanéité* (Paris, 1990). Dr. Khosrokhavar's most recent book, *L'Utopie sacrifiée: Sociologie de la révolution iranienne,* was published in Paris in 1993.

ABDALLA AL-KURD was born in Jerusalem and educated in the public schools there during his father's tenure as technical director of education in the West Bank. He holds a B.A. in economics from Helwan University in Cairo, Egypt, an M.A. in political science, and an Ed.D. in educational leadership from the University of Houston. He is active in the Arab-American community in the United States.

HODA AL-NAMANI is a celebrated poet with five books to her credit. Her most recent translated work in English is *I Dreamed I Was a Point, I Was a Circle*. She is also a well-known painter. Born in Damascus, she now lives in Beirut.

MOHAMMED OMRAN is the leading folklore scholar in Egypt today. He writes and teaches in his own country and lectures frequently abroad. His book *Children's Games and Songs in Egypt* is a classic in the field.

SUZANNE QUALLS is a poet and monologuist who has performed in New York City and San Francisco. She has published poems and performance pieces in *Agni, Verse, The Threepenny Review,* and *Women and Performance*.

TAGHREED AL-QUDSI-GHABRA is a faculty member at Kuwait University. She has been coordinator and editor of the "Monthly Book Project," a program initiated by the Kuwait Society for the Advancement of Arab Children to publish Arabic children's books, since 1989. She serves as a consultant to the Public School Library Affairs at the Ministry of Education. She has a B.A. from Purdue University and an M.A. and a Ph.D. in Library and Information Sciences from the University of Texas at Austin.

ANDREA RUGH is an independent consultant working in the field of education in the subcontinent (Saudi and Pakistan) and the Arab world. She has written several books and monographs on social life in the Middle East. She has a B.A. from Oberlin and a Ph.D. in social anthropology from American University in Washington.

SETENEY SHAMI is chair of the department of anthropology at Yarmouk University, Irbid, Jordan. She received a Ph.D. from the University of California at Berkeley and most recently has been a visiting scholar at the University of Chicago. She has edited a book on migration within the Arab world and lectures frequently abroad.

TEIRAB ASHSHAREEF is an associate professor of Arabic at the University of Minnesota. A former Rockefeller fellow and a native of the Sudan, he received a Ph.D. from the University of Khartoum, based on his research in folklore and oral poetry among the Bani Halba of the Southern Sudan.

PIROUZ SHOAR-GHAFFARI, a former reporter and editor in Tehran, Iran, is an assistant professor of communications at Denison University. He holds a Ph.D. in mass communication from Syracuse University and has served on the executive board of the Center for Iranian Research and Analysis. His publications and research interests include studies of international news flow, press and foreign policy, and sex-role and political socialization in the Iranian educational system.

SUSAN SLYOMOVICS teaches in the Department of Comparative Literature at Brown University. She has written widely on folklore and folk art both in the Middle East and in the United States. Her Ph.D. is from the University of California at Berkeley, and her first book was *The Merchant of Art: An Egyptian Hilali Oral Epic Poet in Performance.*

AMIRA AL-AZHARY SONBOL is an associate professor of history at Georgetown University. She has an M.A. from the American University in Cairo and a Ph.D. from Georgetown. Her first book was *The Creation of a Medical Profession in Egypt, 1800–1922,* and she has just edited a collection of scholarly essays, *Women, Family, and Divorce Laws in Islamic History.*

THOMAS B. STEVENSON teaches anthropology in Ohio University's regional campus system. He has a B.A. in economics from Denison University, an M.A. in sociology and anthropology from Kent State University, and a Ph.D. in anthropology from Wayne State University.

HELMI R. TADROS, an Egyptian sociologist and demographer, has been for many years a senior researcher at the Social Research Center of the American University of Cairo. He publishes frequently in the *Cairo Papers in Social Science.*

LUCINE TAMINIAN, a native of Jordan, studied at Yarmouk University in Irbid and is currently working on her Ph.D. at the University of Michigan, Ann Arbor.

SABRA WEBBER is associate professor and chair in the Department of Comparative Studies at Ohio State University. Her book *Romancing the Real* is based on her research in Tunisia. She received her B.A. from Occidental College, her M.A. from the University of California, Berkeley, and her Ph.D. from the University of Texas at Austin.

JENNY B. WHITE is an assistant professor of anthropology at the University of Nebraska at Omaha. She received her Ph.D. from the University of Texas at Austin. Her first book, *Money Makes Us Relatives,* is a study of women and work in Turkey.